£137-50.

THE SALIENCE OF MARKETING STIMULI
An Incongruity-Salience Hypothesis
on Consumer Awareness

THE SALIENCE OF MARKETING STIMULI
An Incongruity-Salience Hypothesis
on Consumer Awareness

by

GIANLUIGI GUIDO, Ph.D.
(University of Cambridge, England)
University of Lecce, Italy
and University of Padua, Italy

Kluwer Academic Publishers
Boston/Dordrecht/London

Distributors for North, Central and South America:
Kluwer Academic Publishers
101 Philip Drive
Assinippi Park
Norwell, Massachusetts 02061 USA
Telephone (781) 871-6600
Fax (781) 871-6528
E-Mail < kluwer@wkap.com >

Distributors for all other countries:
Kluwer Academic Publishers Group
Distribution Centre
Post Office Box 322
3300 AH Dordrecht, THE NETHERLANDS
Telephone 31 78 6392 392
Fax 31 78 6546 474
E-Mail < orderdept@wkap.nl >

 Electronic Services < http://www.wkap.nl >

Library of Congress Cataloging-in-Publication Data

A C.I.P. Catalogue record for this book is available from the Library of Congress.

Printed on acid-free paper.

Printed in the United States of America

Contents

List of Figures

List of Tables

Preface

The *Incongruity-salience model* presented here thoroughly for the first time is part of a wider *Dichotic theory of salience*, implemented in marketing settings, according to which the *salience* of marketing stimuli (e.g., advertisements, products, brands) is due either to a contextual incongruity with perceivers' schemata or to a contextual congruity with their personal goals.

The research work produced for this book focuses on the salience triggered by external physical stimuli - like all marketing stimuli are, before being internalized by consumers - to explain and predict the conditions under which a marketing stimulus is able to achieve its communication outcomes in terms of processing and memory.

When considering the cluttered environment in which consumers live and the expensive budgets of advertising campaigns, it becomes apparent how the problem of obtaining *and* maintaining consumers' attention is not merely academic, but rather requires a complete understanding by marketers and advertisers of the theoretical antecedents and moderators of the consumers' information processing.

The *Dichotic theory of salience*, in general, and the *Incongruity-salience hypothesis*, in particular, are metaphors to approximate and interpret the cognitive processes of individuals: By putting together two streams of research, regarding salience and incongruity, they allow us to explore in greater depth the nature of consumer perceptions and the processing of complex marketing communications.

This book provides, together with an articulated theoretical discussion of the model, its implementation in an advertising setting to show operatively how it works. Moreover, a selected bibliography based on a rich review of more than 1,200 studies dealing - both directly and indirectly - with the concept of salience, can advise the reader where to turn if deciding to go deep into the topic.

Although this work, with its possible omissions and mistakes, is attributable solely to myself, its writing has benefited from the advice and suggestions of many distinguished persons that I wish to thank.

First of all, I would like to express my gratitude to Professor Nicholas O'Shaughnessy of the Judge Institute of Management Studies (JIMS) at the University of Cambridge, England, where I started my studies on salience while working on my Ph.D. dissertation. He was very supportive in encouraging me to pursue consumer research, thus allowing me to be the first *Doctor of Philosophy* to graduate with a marketing major in such a historical Institution.

I also would like to thank Prof. John O'Shaughnessy, Emeritus Professor at the Graduate School of Business of Columbia University, now in Cambridge, for the invaluable comments he generously offered to me in an epistolary exchange which had a tremendous impact on the initial stage of my research process, and Professor John Child, former Director of Research at the JIMS, for his helpful comments concerning earlier versions of the project.

I am also primarily indebted to Professor Gian Vittorio Caprara of the Department of Psychology at the University of Rome, "La Sapienza," Italy, where I carried out the experimental studies reported in this book. Since I was a student of his, ten years ago, at the University of California - Los Angeles, he has brought to my attention some crucial problems in social cognitive psychology which were fundamental in the development of my following research addressing both the field of marketing and the field of consumer psychology. His insights into various conceptual issues of the present research were indispensable, and our common studies in the field of brand personality provided me with the backbone for the experiments presented in this book.

Furthermore, I wish to thank Prof. Claudio Barbaranelli of the Department of Psychology at the University of Rome, "La Sapienza," Italy, who is to me a "cornerstone" in the field of research methodologies. His mathematical and statistical expertise was extremely important in helping me with a number of issues in the data analysis reported in Chapter Four of this research.

During the last few years, I have had the opportunity to carry out brief, but fruitful periods of research in many prestigious universities. Apart from the expertise I gained from both a teaching and a research perspective, I had stimulating conversations with Professors Joan Meyers-Levy and Jacob Hornik at the Graduate School of Business of the University of Chicago, and - when the model of in-salience was only an idea - with Professors Lydia Price and Niraj Dawar at INSEAD, in Fontainebleau, France. In Italy, I received continuous support to my research from Professor Riccardo Varaldo at the Scuola Superiore Sant'Anna in Pisa, Professor Franco Fontana at LUISS University in Rome, and Professor Luciano Pilotti of the University of Padua. The clues that their intelligent talks transfused were hopefully captured and included in this work.

The last version of this book was completed when I was *visiting researcher* at the Marketing Department of the University of Florida at Gainesville. There I had the chance to meet personally those who are to me the most exceptional personalities in consumer research today. Among these marvelous academicians, I wish to thank Professor Richard Lutz, for his encouragement and friendly support for this research; Professor Joe Alba for his bibliographic references kindly shared with me; and, last but not least, Professor Chris Janiszewski for his acute suggestions on the potential applications of my theory.

Furthermore, I owe very special thanks to Dr Maria Grazia Guido, who happens to be my sister, for the long discussions aimed at clarifying or challenging many points in the various versions of this text. The differentiation between the *force* and the *effect* of salience (cf. Chapter Three, Axiom Three) comes directly from her. She also assisted me in many capacities, including serving as a pre-tester, a coder, and a proofreader.

From an operative and editorial perspective - equally important for the success of this project - an essential support was provided by Ms. Ann Reater of the British Library in London in the finding of the review material, and by the whole personnel of the Experimental Psychology Library at the University of Cambridge. The same support I found at Kluwer Academic Publishers in Mr. Allard Winterink, senior publishing editor, whose continuous assistance was instrumental in helping me complete the writing of the manuscript and, at the University of Lecce, in Ms. Susan Perry for her careful work of proofreading.

This research was partially funded by a grant of the British Council (Ref. ROM/2280/2(93/94)) and the experiments reported in *Part One*, Chapter Four, were conducted with the material contribution of the McCann Erickson Company, Italy. I wish to acknowledge their help.

To all these gracious people, to my family, and to my students, whose efforts were "salient" to me, this book is dedicated.

Gianluigi Guido, M.I.B.A., Ph.D.
Associate Professor of Int.l Marketing
University of Lecce, Italy

Chapter 1

INTRODUCTION TO THE CONCEPT OF SALIENCE

Historically, the notion of *salience* has proven utterly refractory to definitional efforts. These difficulties arise from a lack of agreement on the conceptual nature of the construct and on its causes. In both consumer and social psychology, salience has been treated as an umbrella concept covering a variety of constructs (e.g., from accessibility to activation in memory, from availability to importance). The proliferation of definitions adopted so far - together with their theoretical vagueness (which, in turn, has resulted in recurrently wrong manipulations of the salient stimuli) - has impaired the development of a literature which was homogenous in its assumptions and, therefore, able to compare findings achieved in different areas of social sciences.

To address the fundamental issue raised here, the present research will attempt to accomplish four purposes: (1) To provide an overview of the salience concept; (2) To review the relevant literature in the social sciences regarding salient physical stimuli; (3) To produce the theoretical bases for a general model of incongruity-salience - according to our *Dichotic theory of salience*; and (4) To propose and test a set of research propositions relevant to the study of salience in an advertising setting.

1. PROBLEM DEFINITION

Salience has been generally referred to as an attribute of a particular stimulus that makes it stand out and be noticed (e.g., Sears, Peplau, and Taylor 1991). This definition, however, leaves unsolved many issues about: (1) What salience actually is - Is it a stimulus *quality*? Is it an *absolute property*? Is it an *effect*? - and (2) What its causes are - Are they *cognitive* and/or *motivational*? Are they associated with physical or figural factors? Are they traceable back to a common origin? -. To answer these questions, it seems reasonable to ask if salience is only a matter of *attention* or, also, of *interpretation* of the sensed stimuli. In the latter case, indeed, salience would display its effects also on a further stage of perception, thus affecting *memory* for those stimuli.

This interest in the definition of salience is not merely academic.[1] For many firms, getting attention is not a separate problem from making their products memorable. An important challenge in creating effective advertising is to secure that the advertisement not only attracts the target consumer's attention, but also generates interest and educates the consumer about product benefits and positioning (Aaker, Batra and Myers 1992; Menon and Soman 1999). A catalog retailer, for example, not only wants to encourage the consumer to view merchandise, but also to remember the merchandise that is being offered.[2] In spite of the tremendous amount of money spent on buying consumer attention, today's advertisers seem to use the rules developed 50 years ago (*Make it bigger, make it brighter, make is easier!*). Little to no research has been done on this topic: Partly because of the fragility of advertising's effects and the complexity of getting bias-free estimates, few studies have addressed issues about advertising effectiveness, such as how the effects vary by creative content, form, or medium (cf. Chung and Szymanski 1997; Tellis, Chandy, and Thaivanich 2000). Marketers have treated attention as a managed process, not recognizing that consumer attention - and what comes from it - is a *competitive* process that can only be achieved at the expense of others (cf. Janiszewski and Bickart 1994). From this applied perspective, research on salience allows marketers to gain a better understanding of the antecedents of consumers' mental processing affecting communication outcomes. It should be recognized that, due to the wealth of information available in the marketplace and to consumers' limited information-processing capacity, salient - though trivial - stimuli exert a strong influence upon attentional focus, and this impact may be reflected in preferential registration, encoding, and memory of salient stimuli.

1.1   Calls for Consumer Research on Salience

In consumer research, Krugman (1965) was the first to notice this capacity of salient stimuli to overcome potential barriers and reach the consumer audience. He argued (pp. 350-351, as reported in Hawkins and Hoch 1992, p. 212) that:

> "[S]o much of TV advertising content is trivial and sometimes even silly. Nevertheless, trivia have their own special qualities and some of these may be important to our understanding of the commercial or the non-commercial use and impact of mass media [...]. Much of advertising content is learned as meaningless non-sense material [...] nonsensical *à la* Ebbinghaus and unimportant *à la* Hovland alike."

Since then, many authors in consumer behavior have called for further research on salience. These calls can be largely classified into three types of issues raised for future studies. One issue is the definition of salience, its complementary constructs and moderating variables. Mowen (1983) was among the early authors to mention this need in a special session on this topic at the Association for Consumer Research (ACR) Conference. Although confusing salience with vividness - a complementary construct which does not require a competitive environment to display its attention-getting features (cf., e.g., Nisbett and Ross 1980; Taylor and Thompson 1982) -, he clearly expressed his vows for getting answers to certain basic questions (Mowen 1983, p. 57):

> "Just how do you define salience or vividness? Is salience a property of the stimulus, the person, or the person interacting with the environment[?] Is salience related to involvement? Is a high involvement product salient?"

Mowen (1993) emended his error in his later works, still stressing a lack of research in this area (pp. 100-101):

> "Finally, market research needs to be performed in order to investigate factors that influence the levels of exposure, attention, and comprehension shown by consumers to marketing communications."

His requests were supported by Alba, Hutchinson, and Lynch (1991), who specifically addressed the importance of including in a future model of salience influences on attention and on interpretation as well (p. 20):

> "Although the effects of salience have been described primarily in terms of recall, it is important to note that salient concepts can also affect the interpretation of stimulus information, particularly if the stimulus is ambiguous. [...] The importance of these interpretive effects, combined with the scarcity of relevant empirical research, makes this an important area for future research."

As maintained by Burton and Blair (1988, p. 33), salience remains "a somewhat imprecise term". Ten years later, Arnold (1998) recognized, in her dissertation about the influence of linguistic information on the salience of a referent and choices in reference form, that:

> "even though the concept of salience has repeatedly been invoked in the literature, it lacks a substantive definition. Things can be salient for many reasons. For example, people may tend to notice perceptually salient objects (such as a bright light), socially relevant actions (such as their boss entering the room), and the referent of linguistic pointers (such as the exclamation *Look at that!*)."

So that the demand for a general framework combining different instances of the construct constitutes the second issue raised in literature. Initially, it was in the field of social cognition that this common ground was implicitly addressed and requested as a merge of two areas of study, namely salience and incongruity. Hastie, Park, and Weber (1984) called it an "imperative" for future research:

> "From a review of research on memory for consistent, inconsistent, and irrelevant information, our major conclusion was that it is time to produce a general theoretical analysis to account for results from recall and recognition tasks as well as results from studies on memory for inconsistent information and irrelevant information. We believe that the ingredients for such an integration are available in the literature and that what is needed are experiments and theoretical developments to connect the two relatively independent areas of work." (p. 201).

Before them, Taylor and Crocker (1981, p. 111) had sustained that:

> "Although we have stated that expectations function as a basis for evaluating experience, nothing has been said about how this process occurs, save vague reference to a matching process. A more fine-grained analysis of this problem is needed [...]."

These demands were then reflected in consumer literature, where Heckler and Childers (1992), for example, noted that (p. 491, emphasis added):

> "[A]dvertisers often use information they consider to be incongruent as a ploy to grab the readers' or viewers' attention. [...] On the basis of the research presented [...], consumers' processing efforts appear to benefit most from incongruencies created with *unexpected* but *relevant* information. Therefore, it is very important for researchers and practitioners to identify the nature of the incongruency they are studying and creating because different hypotheses may arise regarding its effects."

Finally, the third issue stemming from consumer literature regards the critical role that salience may take in attitude formation and choices. As for the former consequence of the consumer information processing triggered by salient stimuli, Gardner (1983, p. 317) conclusively stated:

> "More research is needed to explore the nature of attitude formation and the important role of prominence in attribute use."

Similar opinions were expressed in a seminal paper by Lynch and Srull (1982, p. 33) on the role of salience in consumer choices:

> "[I]f consumers making memory-based choices recall only the evaluative extreme aspects of choice alternatives [... t]he decision process followed in this type of situation is an issue of considerable theoretical and practical significance, and deserves careful consideration in future research."

Such conclusions were renewed by Schindler and Berbaum (1983), who argued (p. 418):

> "An important goal of future research on salience and choice would be to determine the range of choice situations in which the salience of an alternative plays a significant role. In addition to affecting those choices where consumers perceive few meaningful differences between the alternatives, salience may also influence decisions in which the alternatives are highly differentiated, since salience may influence the selection of the alternatives themselves (Soelberg 1967). [...] Future research could explore the possibility of a common mechanism behind the effects of salience on choice and the effects of availability on the internal choice of which pieces of information to use in arriving at a judgment."

Consequently, they concluded (p. 418):

> "Thus, while it is clear that a great deal of research on salience and choice remains to be done, the rewards of such work could be rich, having the potential to increase our understanding of many aspects of consumer decision making."

Till now, these calls for further research have remained unanswered (cf. Pham 1997). There is neither a shared definition of salience, nor a general model to explain the different cases of salient stimuli illustrated in literature. In such conditions, the effects of salience on both consumer processing and choice can be adequately studied and compared, thus leaving a number of important issues unsolved.

1.2   Problem Areas

The lack of a general theory of salience - and of a common hypothesis on its origins - poses a number of related problem issues. Four main questions, in particular, are of special interest to the present research - as they are directly linked to the effect of salience on awareness. The first question regards the definition of salience in relation to physical, external stimuli. It should be determined which elements (e.g., context, perceiver's schemata, etc.) and which conditions (e.g., schema activation, accessibility, availability, perceptual resistance, normalization, etc.) are necessary to make a stimulus salient so as to generate a greater level of awareness in perceivers.

The second question regards how individuals process salient information. The vast majority of research studying the effects of salience on information processing has considered, as instances of salience, cases of mere attention-getting capacity of the stimulus. Apart from the evident truism (see, *below*, Chapter Three, *Axiom Three*), it must be recognized that salience cannot be simply hypothesized as descending from the Gestalt principles of figurality or dominance of the sensory field. To catch focused attention any stimulus requires a further processing stage indeed, namely an interpretation stage, that can either bring or not to the prominence of that stimulus in memory (see, *below*, Chapter Three, *Proposition Two*). As will be shown in the following pages, whether this further stage is able (or not) to bring to such a prominence will depend on a mis/matching of the information perceived in that context with a perceiver's schema (see, *below*, Chapter Three, *Proposition One*).[3]

The third question regards how salient information is compared with schemata in memory. Past literature has dealt with numerous definition of salience, most of the times considering salience as equal to either accessibility, or availability, or activation in memory, etc. (see, *below*, Chapter Three, *Proposition Three*). Salience, however, must be considered as something different from these constructs (as they rather refer to the schema instantiated by the salient stimulus). In other words, it must be recognized that accessibility, availability, and activation are constructs related to schemata which, in turn, act as moderators of salience occurrences. For instance, whenever an appropriate schema is primed, activation should facilitate the perception of a salient stimulus.

Finally, the fourth question regards how the relevance of information moderates the occurrences of salience. Relevance here refers either to the extent an individual perceives a stimulus to be self-related (i.e., *personal relevance*) or to the weight of certain elements within a schema (i.e., *attribute relevance*) (see, *below*, Chapter Three, *Proposition Four*). The issue of relevance is strictly connected with the crucial moderating variable of any information processing which is *involvement*. Past literature has shown that involvement can have different levels (see, e.g., Greenwald and Leavitt 1984). Now, it should be acknowledged that such levels, in turn, determine the impact of the salience occurrence. As it will be illustrated in the following pages, the more relevant a stimulus is, the more salient its impact is.

2.   A NEW MODEL OF SALIENCE

The aforementioned gaps in the salience literature - i.e., the nature of salience, the role of schemata, and the moderating function of relevance -

suggest that a great deal of research still needs to be done to know more about the information characteristics influencing the allocation of attention and memory. To be successful in this endeavor, researchers must pursue the development of a general framework of reference to set salience instances against a common background.

The incongruity-salience model presented here offers this opportunity by introducing a promising approach that addresses these gaps in an extension of a current view on schematic processes in human memory. According to this approach, which we briefly call the *In-salience hypothesis*, a stimulus is said to be (in-)salient when it is incongruent, in a certain context, with a perceiver's schema.

The in-salience hypothesis is part of a new *Dichotic theory of salience* (Guido 1998), whose development is under way. It considers this construct either as a contextual incongruity between a stimulus and a perceiver's schema, the so-called *in-salience* (as stated above), or as a contextual congruity between a stimulus and a perceiver's goal, the so-called *re-salience* (from relevance-salience - see, *below*, Chapter Three, *Proposition Four*). The present work will focus on the former part of the salience model (i.e., in-salience), without omitting references - where necessary - to its latter part (i.e., re-salience). By demonstrating the communalities between two streams of research - that is, *incongruity* and *salience* - the in-salience model will propose a common source for the different occurrences of in-salient stimuli, in order to more thoroughly explore, conceptually and empirically, the nature of consumer perceptions and the processing of complex marketing communications.

2.1 Purpose and Scope

The in-salience hypothesis is based on the view that the primary goal of marketing and advertising cannot be achieved if consumers are not at least *aware* of the marketing stimulus; this means that the stimulus must attract consumers' attention and must be interpreted - hopefully - in the way the marketer intended. In advancing a general definition of the construct, the model assumes that salience can neither be defined independently from the perceiver of the stimulus, nor from the context of perception, nor can it be explained circularly by its effect on attention.

In addressing the four broad problem areas mentioned above (Paragraph 1.2), we focused on as many research objectives fleshing these axioms out: (1) Ascertaining that memory of in-salient information is better than that of other stimuli, leading to greater awareness to subjects for in-salient information; (2) Demonstrating that in-salience affects both the attention *and* the interpretation stage of an information processing model; (3) Explaining the role of activation of schemata in the occurrence of the in-salience phenomenon; (4) Determining the role of relevance of certain schema elements (i.e., attributes) on the perceived impact of in-salient stimuli. Thus, the major implication of the proposed propositions is that in-salience generates *awareness*, a necessary step in any consumer choice (see, *below*, Chapter Three, Paragraph 2.5 on *Implications*).

To test these basic propositions of the in-salience model in a marketing setting, an experiment - containing these four levels of inquiry - was conducted assessing the differential effects on awareness of both in-salient and non-in-salient messages in print advertisements (see, *below*, Chapter Four).

2.2   Potential Contributions

The in-salience hypothesis is a *theory* in the widest sense of the term. It provides a systematic approach of the thought related to the topic of salience. It views this topic as something coherent and unified, but divisible into parts. Differently from previous treatments of the construct, the in-salience hypothesis considers the various occurrences of salience as traceable back to a common origin, namely a contextual incongruity between a stimulus and a perceiver's schema. Thus, in its widest sense of theory, it offers a system of thought - a method of analysis and synthesis - where to place different observations, phenomena, and activities that have been studied and documented in literature.

The study of in-salience in consumer information processing has potential benefits for both researchers and practitioners. From a theoretical perspective, positive results will extend both psychological and marketing fields' knowledge beyond its current state by increasing the understanding of how individuals process the information that they encounter in the marketing environment. In this sense, the in-salience model is not strictly a "consumer" model. It applies to the general cognitive activity of individuals and - together with re-salience, inside the Dichotic salience framework - it can be used as a key to understand and explain the process of human perception.

From an applied standpoint, strategic insight into the use of in-salient information in advertisements will help marketers to develop ad campaigns that maximize consumer awareness and knowledge for their products and advertisements. In addition, other elements of the promotional mix, such as point of purchase displays, web pages, personal selling, packaging, brand name, sales promotions, and public relations, may bear the fruits of a communication program that contains in-salient information.

2.3   Research Report Format

The rest of this book is structured in the following fashion. Chapter Two provides the review of perception-based definitions of salience. Chapter Three contains the theory regarding the incongruity-salience model. Chapter Four presents an experimental application of the model to test consumer awareness in print advertisements.[4]

More specifically, the text is organized as reported in the following paragraphs.

2.3.1   Content of Chapter Two

In Chapter Two, the research literature on the salience of physical stimuli is examined and reviewed, with a particular emphasis on salience effects on memory inducing consumer awareness.

This chapter begins by presenting a model of perception and information processing broken down into stages (i.e., sensation, attention, interpretation, and memory). It is argued that salience, which acts as an antecedent of any consumer processing, *does* influence all these stages - and not only attention, as often maintained in the past. Past definitions of salience, however, share a common ground on which it is possible to build a general theory of salience. This core significance of any salience construct is its nature of *prominence*. In light of recent evidence, the chapter considers Heider's (1944) suggestion that there are parallels between person and object perception, as perceivers selectively attend to prominent stimuli in both realms. Having the concept of salience traditionally be employed in the field of social psychology, it is found useful - under this analogy - to employ a well-known classification of the causes of salience in social perception - namely, Fiske and Taylor's (1991) framework - to review marketing and consumer literature.

Drawing on the aforementioned classification, we considered three major contexts in which all the different forms of salience occur and were studied in literature: *An immediate context*; *a larger context*; and *motivational forms of salience*. First, in *an immediate context*, salience is explained by the *principle of figure-ground*, according to which people direct their attention to those aspects of the perceptual field that stand out on a background. In such a context, we considered and reviewed research regarding three cases of salience: (1) Figurality, (2) Physical factors dominating the sensory field; and (3) Contextual novelty. Figurality concerns, specifically, bright, moving, and complex marketing stimuli; whereas dominating factors, such as intensity, position, and frequency, alter the weight of a stimulus in an environment. Finally, contextual incongruity contemplates those marketing stimuli that appear in isolation (a particular emphasis is placed in our review on the so-called *von Restorff effect*, the learning of an item isolated against a crowded or homogeneous background).

Second, in a *larger context*, salience is explained by the *principle of unusuality*, according to which a stimulus is attended when it violates a perceiver's prior knowledge and expectations. In such a context, we examined past research addressing the following cases: (1) Statistical novelty, (2) Unexpectancy, (3) Out-of-role behaviors, (4) Negativity, and (5) Extremity. Specifically, statistical novelty regards unique and unfamiliar marketing stimuli. Unexpectancy, on the other hand, includes *incongruent* stimuli - those stimuli which fail to confirm established expectations - which are crucial to the extent of our theory. They are discussed together with the effects of expectations (including, the process of causal attribution triggered by salience, so-called *top-of-the-head phenomenon*) and the techniques used to improve unexpectancy. Furthermore, research is reviewed on out-of-role behaviors - i.e., a particular class of social stimuli which derive from a mismatching of a person's social role, position, or identity - together with negative and extreme stimuli resulting, respectively, from the evaluative valence or extremity of information.

Finally, as for the *motivational forms of salience* - which are the remaining occurrences of the construct -, salience is explained by the *principle of involvement* and it regards two cases: (1) Instructions to attend to a stimulus, and (3) Personal goal relevance. Due to the scope of our review, these two factors are only mentioned here as they act on a motivational variable which is taken, in our dichotic theory, as an alternative cause of salience (namely, re-salience; see, *below*, Table 3). Nonetheless, particular attention is posed on an important *inhibition effect* on memory, which has been studied under instruction conditions. The section, then, concludes with a detailed summary of the chapter.

2.3.2   Content of Chapter Three

Chapter Three introduces the model of incongruity-salience (briefly, the *In-salience hypothesis*) which attempts to explain the conditions under which different marketing stimuli are able to produce consumer awareness. The model is part of a wider theory - the *Dichotic theory of salience* - that poses salience as the sole antecedent of any consumer information processing able to display communication outcomes (Guido 1998). Two are the forms of salience regarded in this theory: *In-salience* (the topic of our discussion), and *re-salience* (which is strictly motivational).

The *In-salience hypothesis* is built on *three axioms* and *four propositions* which have, as a major implication, the creation of consumer awareness towards in-salient marketing stimuli. The model's *Axiom One* states that salience cannot be defined in terms of its effects: Any definition which explains salience as the capacity to attract attention is a truism disguised as an empirical proposition. *Axiom Two* states that salience depends on the context in which the stimulus occurs: Salience is not an objective quality of the stimulus, but rather it depends on the situation in which the stimulus occurs. Finally, *Axiom Three* states that salience depends also on the perceivers of the stimulus: Thus, it is prior knowledge and expectations (i.e., schemata) possessed by each individual perceiver which determine the existence of salience.

Based on the foregoing assumptions, the model proposes four propositions which address as many research objectives (see, *above*, Paragraph 2.1): *Proposition One* is the original definition of in-salience. It states that a stimulus is in-salient when in a certain context it is incongruent to a perceiver's schema. Three elements are essential to this occurrence: Stimulus, context, and schemata. Their simultaneous presence is necessary for salience occurrence, but it is neither sufficient (in case of *cue normalizing* or *cue resisting*), nor predictive of the same positive results (as this will depend on the coincidence of *stimulus cue* and *information cue* and on the existence of a *moderate incongruity*). In order to set the bounds of the essential elements in the in-salience definition, *context* and *schemata* are then discussed. As for the former element, a definition is given both in a strict and in a larger sense; as for the latter element, a complete examination of characteristics, modality, and types of schemata is provided - together with a discussion of the process of instantiation, information congruity theory, spreading activation, and application in attitude research.

Proposition Two maintains that in-salience has to do with attention *and* interpretation. In-salience is not merely an attentional phenomenon, that is, the result of a figure-ground principle, but it implies a further stage, that of interpretation, in which the incongruity detected in a certain context is compared with a schema possessed by a perceiver. Thus, the figure-ground explanation of salience is undermined by the evidence that perception of salience is not innate, but rather it requires - for the maintaining of attention - involvement as a necessary moderator. The in-salience hypothesis is then supported, by showing the roles of context and schemata in the process of perception of in-salient stimuli.

Proposition Three states that in-salience is a different construct from *activation, accessibility,* and *availability* (as well as *importance*, which implies an evaluation of the object to which it is referred). In the past, salience has been also explained using these constructs, but there are specific differences that make them unsuitable as explanations of in-salience. *Activation* in memory is a process triggered by any external activity which consciously (*set*) or unconsciously (*priming*) initiate a cognitive elaboration process. *Accessibility* relates to available knowledge stored in memory that finds free access for elaboration because of the natural predisposition of the individual (i.e., perceptual readiness in regards of those stimuli) without any external manipulation. *Availability* regards the differences in knowledge structures (i.e., schemata) possessed by *expert* versus *novice* consumers. It will be show that, although these constructs are clearly unsatisfactory in explaining the intrinsic nature of in-salient stimuli, they do act as moderating variables of schemata in perceivers' salient information processing.

Finally, *Proposition Four* recognizes that personal relevance is a crucial moderating variable of in-salience. It acts as a moderator between the two types of salience - i.e., in-salience and re-salience. The latter one is defined as a contextual congruity between a stimulus and a perceiver's motive; therefore, whereas for in-salience the basic causal factor is "incongruity", for re-salience it is "personal relevance" (i.e., involvement). This should imply, for example, for high-involved consumers, the use of *important* product attributes - rather than simply *relevant* attributes - in situations of choice. This complementarity between in-salience and re-salience allows developing a dichotic model of salience based on different types of attention (involuntary or passive attention vs. voluntary or planned attention, respectively), different modes of processing (bottom-up vs. top-down), and different communication theories (complexity vs. consistency).

The *major implication* resulting from the previous propositions is that, once an in-salient stimulus has caught consumers' attention and has been perceptually encoded, it generates awareness. *Awareness* here is defined as a low-level form of memory impact and the minimum goal of any marketing campaign - as theoretically maintained by any hierarchy-of-effects model. It is argued that perceived in-salience is a form of retrieval bias that favors in memory in-salient stimuli over non-in-salient ones. Superior retrieval in memory can be assessed by recall and recognition measures, which have a long and detailed history of use in marketing as indicators of consumer awareness. An empirical test of the model in the following chapter provides an example of their use in an advertising setting.

2.3.3   Content of Chapter Four

Chapter Four contains an experimental application of the in-salience hypothesis in a marketing environment. It is designed to test the effects of in-salient print advertisements on consumer processing and memory. Specifically, consumer awareness of the ads is measured in terms of top-of-mind and free recall of in-salient ad messages over non-in-salient ad messages.

Research objectives generated from a review of salience and incongruity literature, transfused into the theoretical proposition of our models, are taken as bases of experimental inquiry. Thus, four hypotheses are constructed and tested in as many experimental levels of inquiry. In *Experimental Level One*, the memory effect of in-salience - defined as a contextual incongruity between a stimulus and a perceiver's schema - is examined to check the possible advantage of in-salient ad messages over the others. In *Experimental Level*

Two, special attention is directed towards the relationship between stimulus in-salience and ad exposure time to determine whether viewership length (i.e., length of time spent viewing) can be considered as a possible moderating variable. Moreover, in an unlimited exposure-time condition, time is tested as a moderator of memory strength for in-salient and non-in-salient information. In *Experimental Level Three*, research attention is focused on other constructs similar to salience, namely activation (or accessibility) and availability, in order to demonstrate that, when a particular schema has common elements available to all perceivers, the activation of such a schema can improve the memory effects of in-salient stimuli based on those common elements. Finally, in *Experimental Level Four*, having defined attribute relevance as the weight of each attribute within a product schema, it is tested as a moderating variable of the effects of in-salience on memory for those common elements in perceivers' schemata on which in-salient stimuli are created.

This study is implemented in two main stages. In *Part One*, following the associative network model (e.g., Wickelgren 1981), brand schemata are assessed in terms of brand images within the construct definition of brand personality (Reynolds and Gutman 1984). A list of attributes defining brand images of three different products is administered to both users and non-users of those products. In *Part Two*, some of the attributes shared equally by both users and non-users are selected to be employed in manipulations of in-salient ad claims. The executional strategy chosen for the creation of these in-salient stimuli is *resonance* (McQuarrie and Mick 1992), which consists in the development of alternative combinations of wordplay with relevant pictures that create incongruity. After two pretests used to prepare the experimental material, five independent variables (*message in-salience, ad exposure time, schema activation, time of measurement*, and *relevance levels*) and two dependent variable (*top-of-mind recall*, and *free recall*) are set and tested on a sample of two hundred and forty subjects.

A manipulation check (i.e., t-test of means) on ad message in-salience scores is successfully conducted to test proper manipulation of the construct. Statistical analysis (i.e., repeated measures ANOVA, interactions and simple effects) of results of the two measures of recall for the four experimental levels provides extremely significant findings. Hypotheses are supported and results show that factors such as ad viewing time, memory decay, and relevance play a major role in the occurrence of in-salience. Implications, limitations, and future research are presented and discussed. It is hoped that this study will stimulate further research to corroborate the model's potential for improvements - both in theoretical and applied research - in an area thought to be essential within and outside the field of consumer and economic behavior.

NOTES

[1] "This issue is gaining greater importance for several reasons. First, media advertising continues to draw a major proportion of the promotion budget, totaling $67 billion in 1996 (Endicott 1997). Second, because of the immediate and pronounced effects of sales promotions, advertising agencies are under increasing pressure to show the specific effects of advertising on sales. Third, the growth of electronic commerce and measurement has increased the availability of fairly precise records of advertising and sales. Fourth, despite four decades of work, few field studies answer the critical questions: Which ad works, when, where, and for how long?" (Tellis, Chandy, and Thaivanich 2000, p. 32).

[2] According to Chung and Szymanski (1997, p. 288): "Companies allocate an increasing amount of money each year to expose consumers to their brand names, and make substantial expenditures placing their products and brand names in movies, television shows, sport arenas, and outdoor billboards (Pracejus 1995). A few studies have examined the effectiveness of brand name exposure on brand name recall [...] and recognition [...]. However, the ultimate effectiveness of this strategy should be gauged by whether the exposure increases the likelihood that these brands are chosen in subsequent purchase occasions."

[3] A schema here is defined as a knowledge structure in memory that provide guidance for consumer processing (see, *below*, Chapter Three, Paragraphs 2.1.4-2.1.6).

[4] Throughout the following report, we have chosen to use - when necessary - only the masculine gender of the third person singular of a pronoun. This politically incorrect choice was dictated by the necessity to have short and simple sentences, rather than by an attitude that has been often stereotypically attributed to Italians.

Chapter 2

REVIEW OF PERCEPTION-BASED DEFINITIONS OF SALIENCE

Traditionally, the concept of *salience* has been mainly employed in the field of social psychology, that branch of psychology that concentrates on the aspects of human behavior which involve individuals and their relationships to other individuals, groups, social institutions and to society as a whole. In this literature, the origin of the term (*saliency*) dates back to Krech and Crutchfield (1948),[1] although similar concepts had been developed since the end of the 19th century under different names (see, e.g., Calkins 1894, 1896; von Restorff 1933). Only recently, however, has this concept found its current form with the studies of Taylor and Fiske in the field of person perception (Taylor and Fiske 1975, 1978; Fiske and Taylor 1984, 1991). While they referred to social stimuli (persons and their attributes), in past research the stimulus has been variously represented, from concrete objects to abstract entities (such as attitudes, values, interests, behaviors).

In this chapter, we shall focus only on *physical stimuli* - i.e., any unit of input from the outside environment to any of the senses.[2] In a marketing context, they embrace an enormous number of variables affecting consumer's perception, including "the product, its physical attributes, the package design, the brand name, the advertisements and commercials (including copy claims, choice and sex of model, positioning of model, size of ad, and typography), the position of the ad or time of the commercial, and the editorial environment." (Schiffman and Kanuk 1991, p. 158). Salience, as it will be defined here (in terms of *prominence*), allows these stimuli to differentiate from the infinite number of other stimuli that constantly bombard consumers every day. By discussing, in the present review, those studies in marketing and consumer behavior which have dealt - directly or indirectly - with salience occurrences and analyzed their effects on memory and consumer awareness, we shall provide the theoretical foundations for the incongruity-salience model presented in Chapter Three. *Whereas past literature has explained salience by reference to different principles (such as figure-ground, unusuality, etc.), we shall propose a common definition of salience - valid for the generality of salience occurrences and partially based on incongruity theory.*

The approach followed in our review will be based on the classification of the causes of salience originally developed by Fiske and Taylor (1984, 1991) in the field of social psychology. We shall start, in the first section, by discussing the nature of consumer perception and information processing which has its antecedent in the occurrence of salience. In the second section, we shall introduce Fiske and Taylor's definition of salience, which is intrinsically related to the notion of prominence. In the following three sections, we shall analyze this definition in consumer literature by considering three different forms of salience occurrences. Specifically, in the third section, we shall consider salience *in an immediate context*, which has been explained by the principle of figure-ground and includes stimuli that are figural (i.e., bright, complex, moving), dominating the sensory field (due to their intensity, position, frequency, etc.), or contextually novel (i.e., distinctive). In the fourth section, we shall consider salience *in a larger context*, which has been explained by the principle of unusuality and includes stimuli that are statistically novel, unexpected, out-of-role, negative, or extreme. In the fifth section, we shall consider *motivational forms of salience*, which have been explained by the principle of involvement and include stimuli that perceivers are instructed to attend to, and goal-relevant stimuli. Finally, in the last section, we shall provide a summary of the major points originating from the review that will be considered in the following model of in-salience.

1. THE NATURE OF CONSUMER PERCEPTION

A key question in consumer perception is the degree to which individuals can discriminate between marketing stimuli. Marketers, on the one side, try to create such discrimination by informing consumers about the differences between their brands and competitors' brands. Consumers, on the other side, differing in their ability to perceive marketing stimuli, tend to generalize among similar stimuli. A correct hypothesis on salience, therefore, must recognize these differences in perceivers, as well as those in the context within which stimuli occur.

In order to accomplish any of their effects, marketing stimuli must, first, attract consumers' attention; otherwise, it is unlikely they can achieve any other goal. Second, they must be interpreted in the way the marketer intended; otherwise, it is unlikely they can lead to the kind of result the marketer seeks. Each of these steps represents, in some sense, a perceptual barrier through which marketing stimuli must pass. Howard and Sheth (1969) pointed out that consumers can only select products from those of which they are aware of. They called *awareness set* those brands within a market that consumers are aware of; and *evoked set*, a sub-set of it, those brands about which consumers have positive feelings, such that among which they make the final choice.[3] One might say that consumer's attention is not a sufficient condition for positioning products in the evoked set; yet, it is a necessary condition for placing products in the awareness set. Every day, consumers are confronted with a mass of stimuli, which it is beyond their individual capabilities and interests to attend to. Moreover, with the growth in electronic media, the amount of information in our society has increased tremendously (Dholakia, Mundorf, and Dholakia 1991; Pool 1983; Rogers 1986). Not only do electronics make it possible to deliver huge quantities of information to the desktop phone or screen, much of the information is textual or print-like, a form that people of the video generation find hard to process.[4] What can be done to increase attention and comprehension in such situations?

The message for marketers is that understanding *what* attracts and maintains people's attention and recognizing *how* this happens allows them to manipulate those variables that yield to "break through" to achieve consumers' perception and increase the probability of their choice. Because salience in a marketing context has to do with attracting consumers' attention *and* influencing their interpretation, it has to do with perception. We shall maintain that, by acting on perception, salient stimuli will have important consequences to the outcomes on consumer information processing.

1.1   Perception and Consumer Information Processing

Perception is the critical activity that links the individual consumer to group, situation, and marketer influences. In a broad sense, perception is concerned with the translation from the external, physical world to the internal, mental world that each individual actually experiences. Although we don't often think about it, we are able to experience only a limited degree of the whole physical world, and our mental experiences are themselves usually biased to a greater or lesser extent. Since choosing, buying, and using activities all require interactions with the external world, the topic of perception is crucial to the understanding of consumer behavior. Since the salience of a stimulus is an antecedent of any consumer information processing, it is clear that, from a marketer's point of view, a comprehension of perceptual processes is important. The final customers' decision to purchase a product will be influenced to a large extent by the way consumers perceive the marketing stimuli that constitute and surround the product. Their perception will be affected not only by the qualities of the product itself, but also by the attributes which the successful marketing manager is able to lend to the product through advertising, packaging, and other promotional activities.

Perception is the term used to cover those processes that give coherence, unity and meaning to a person's sensory input. Perception, as a matter of fact, has been defined as "the process by which an individual maintains contact with his environment" (Gibson 1959) and, elsewhere, as "the process whereby an individual receives stimuli through the various senses and interpret them"

(Kollat, Blackwell, and Engel 1970).[5] The process of perception is the *initial part* of a more general process by which consumers acquire stimulus inputs, manipulate these inputs to derive meaning from them, and use this information to think about products and services. This more general process is usually referred as *consumer information processing*. Information processing is a series of activities by which stimulus inputs are transformed into information and stored in memory for later retrieval. An appreciation of information-processing principles and findings provides some important lessons for the practice of marketing. Although advertising is the best beneficiary of what we know about the way in which consumers process information, these lessons can be applied to many other areas of communication, including selling, packaging, branding, training of salespeople, and so on.

1.1.1   Breaking Down the Process of Perception

Perception has been usually modeled in consumer literature as a process segmented in discrete stages. Table 1 recognizes how this process has been divided according to some well-known textbooks on consumer behavior, among those that clearly distinguish perception from information processing.[6]

Table 1. Stages of Perception in Consumer Behavior

N.	Author (Year)	Perception Stages
1.	Williams (1986)	Selection + Organization
2.	Wilkie (1994)	Sensation + Selection & Attention + Interpretation
3.	Schiffman and Kanuk (1991)	Selection + Organization + Interpretation
4.	Assael (1992)	Selection + Organization + Interpretation*
5.	Hawkins, Best, and Coney (1992)	Exposure + Attention + Interpretation
6.	Engel, Blackwell, and Miniard (1997)	Exposure + Attention + Comprehension**
7.	Mowen (1993)	Exposure + Attention + Comprehension
8.	Peter and Olson (1998)	Exposure + Interpretation[†]

Note. *Interpretation = Categorization + Inference Making; **Comprehension = Categorization + Elaboration + Organization; [†]Interpretation = Attention + Comprehension.

To its followers, this stage approach has the major advantage of illustrating in an easily understandable way a process that is difficult to study - and, therefore, subject to different interpretations (cf. Foxall 1990; Foxall, Brown, and Goldsmith 1998; O'Shaughnessy 1992) - for the incredible speed with which it is accomplished and, most importantly, because it is largely hidden to external examination. As a matter of fact, a vast majority of information-processing activities are internal to the individual and, therefore, unobservable.[7] This derives from the fact that individuals are not merely passive receptors of stimuli, but active processors and organizers of the received information. The mental processes that enable individuals to give meaning to their environment and experiences during perception and learning[8] are grouped under the name of *cognition*. Perception and cognition roughly correspond to the two extremes of Baron's (1980) continuum of (social) knowing: One can come to know the world through direct perception or through reflective cognitive activity (Ostrom 1984). Salience, in this sense, could be referred to either as the prominence of an external stimuli or as their reflection - in terms of relevance - in memory.

1.1.2   A Model of Information Processing

In Figure 1, we present a simplified model of consumer information processing. This model diagram views information processing as having four major steps (or stages): Sensation, attention, interpretation, and memory. Usually, the first three of these form the general area of study called *perception*.

Figure 1. A Model of Perception and Consumer Information Processing

Sensation
↓
Attention
↓
Interpretation
↓
Memory

Source: Adapted from MacInnis and Jaworski (1989).

Sensation occurs when the person is exposed to a stimulus and the stimulus is detected by his senses; *attention* occurs when the person allocates processing capacity to the stimulus; *interpretation* occurs when the person assigns a meaning to the received sensations; and *memory* is the short-term use of that meaning for immediate action or its long-term retention.[9]

Salience, in the past, has been basically linked to the first stage of this model, namely sensation, claiming that the principle on which it mainly relies, the figure-ground principle (which will be discussed, *below*, in 3.1), produces its effects on the second stage of the model, namely attention. We shall argue, instead, that a further stage is also required to generate salience effects, namely the interpretation stage, in which detected contextual incongruities are compared with the schemata possessed by the perceiver (see, *below*, Chapter Three, *Proposition Two*). In order to explain our hypothesis on the necessity of this further stage, we shall consider in particular, starting from the next section, how salience of physical stimuli has been treated and defined in past literature.

1.2   Social vs. Non-Social Stimuli

Before reviewing such definitions, however, we must make a preliminary distinction. We have mentioned at the beginning of this chapter that most of the literature on the salience of physical stimuli has been originally developed in the field of social perception, where stimuli are constituted by persons. Therefore, before applying these concepts to consumer research, it seems necessary to check if it is possible to use these findings regarding social stimuli, which are mainly *person-related*, in relation to marketing stimuli, which are mainly *object-related*.

Cognitively oriented social psychologists have chronically been concerned with the differences between social and nonsocial knowledge. Since the first comprehensive integration of cognitive research on social behavior (Krech and Crutchfield 1948) to most of the current papers (e.g., Brewer 1988; Feldman 1988; Schneider 1991), a section contrasting "social" with "nonsocial" cognition has always been present.[10] The possible links between the two types of knowledge have always intrigued psychologists. Heider (1958), for example, based his theory of causal attribution upon an analogy with Brunswick's (1952) *Theory of object perception*.[11] Although no comprehensive review is yet available of research on the differences between social and nonsocial cognitive processes,[12] many social psychologists have speculated about the possible differences. Ostrom (1984) summarized their considerations into three main points of view.[13] However, despite the fairly large number of differences between social and nonsocial knowledge proposed over the years, no fully cogent classification system has gained acceptance, so most discussions of the topic take the form of lists of differences.[14]

In general, the categorization models developed in social cognition appear applicable to the product context. Essentially, product schemata are like person schemata in that they contain well-organized beliefs that guide the interpretation of new information. Product schemata may differ from person schemata in that the latter may be associated with higher levels of affect (Sujan and Bettman 1989). The main differences can be traced in that product categories are less variable in their structure; they are more hierarchical in their nature; they rest more on perceptual attributes rather than inferred abstract attributes; they are less rich of attributes, less complex, and less dynamic. In conclusion, though there may be important differences between person and object perception (Lingle, Altom, and Medin 1984), there is empirical evidence of the soundness of the applicability to the product context of structures and processes developed in the social field (Heckler and Childers 1992; Kardes 1986; Sujan 1985; Sujan and Bettman 1989). These opinions, moreover, have always been implicitly acknowledged by advertisers when trying to make their ads physically salient (e.g., Brandt 1942; Krugman 1988).

2. PROMINENCE

2.1 Salience as Prominence

Across several studies in various fields of social sciences, the notion of salience has been interpreted and proposed in different ways: As level of activation of a stimulus in memory, as accessibility of available knowledge, as synonym of attention, importance, preeminence, and so on. It is possible, however, to derive a common denominator from these different conceptualizations. This core significance, common to all the diverse manipulations of the salience construct, is *prominence*. A stimulus is said to be salient when it is prominent, that is, when it has - under different aspects a superior impact than that of other perceived stimuli. The term "prominence" correctly suggests the essence of the salience construct, that is, a relationship between the salient stimulus and "something else" - i.e., between the salient stimulus and other non-salient stimuli (a *context*); and, more generally, between the salient stimulus and some pre-existing cognitive structures (prior knowledge and expectations; i.e., *schemata*) possessed by the individual perceiver.

This definition of salience as prominence provides two evident advantages. First, it allows the original etymological connotation of the word "salience" to be embraced into its meaning. As we learn, for example, from an old edition of the Oxford Dictionary, salience is the quality of leaping, springing up, or projecting beyond the general outline or surface: E.g., salient are those animals who jump, or the water which jets forth or leaps upwards. Salient are material things (prominent among a number of objects) and immaterial (standing out from the rest, conspicuous). Furthermore, salience means the first beginning of life or motion (i.e., *salient point*, in old medical use, was the heart as it first appears in a embryo) and, in general, the starting-point of anything. We do believe that salience is indeed at the beginning of any process of conscious perception: By studying the conditions under which a stimulus engenders perceivers' awareness, it is possible to gain a better idea of modalities and outcomes of a perceiver's information processing.

Defining salience as prominence enables us, secondly, to recognize the selectivity of the process of perception (cf. Kahneman 1973). When people encode external stimuli, they do not pay the same attention to all aspects of the environment: Because attention is an integral part of encoding,[15] salience determines the extent to which a stimulus is perceived (that is, noticed and interpreted). We shall enunciate, in Chapter Three (*below*), the assumptions and the propositions that regulate a model for studying salience occurrences that originate from contextually perceived incongruities. Such occurrences share a common ground that is retrievable in each of the different instances of salience provided by the literature.

Whereas consumer researchers have never built on such a common ground (with rare exceptions - which appear as attempts - e.g., Gardner 1983), a fundamental contribution for the classification of all the different forms of salience has been provided in social cognition by the work of Shelley E. Taylor and Susan T. Fiske. In the following sections, we shall employ their classification to review the work on salience in the marketing and consumer literature, which will be subsequently used in the discussion of our in-salience hypothesis.

2.2   Taylor and Fiske's Definition of Salience

The concept of salience is an umbrella-concept. It has been used to explain different constructs, grouped under a single conceptualization without any adequate cognizance and analysis of the existing diversities. In the field of social cognition, where the notion of salience has been frequently evoked, Fiske and Taylor (1984, 1991; Taylor and Fiske 1978) have provided a fundamental work in reviewing most of the published material and presenting a general definition of the construct.

Fiske and Taylor (1991) classified the causes of social salience according to the context in which the stimulus occurs, thus distinguishing three cases. Following their categorization, a stimulus can be salient to a perceiver: (a) *In an immediate context*, by being: (1) *Figural* - e.g., bright, complex, or moving (McArthur and Ginsberg 1981; McArthur and Post 1977, Experiments 1, 2, and 3); or (2) *Novel*, either *contextually* - e.g., solo status (Crocker and McGraw 1984; Heilman 1980; Higgins and King 1981, Experiment 1; Kanter 1977; McArthur and Post 1977, Experiments 4 and 5; Nesdale and Dharmalingam 1986; Nesdale, Dharmalingam, and Kerr 1987; Oakes and Turner 1986; Spangler, Gordon, and Pipkin 1978; Taylor et al. 1977, Experiments 1 and 2;

Wolman and Frank 1975), or *statistically* - e.g., visual rarity (Langer et al. 1976; Taylor and Langer 1977);[16] (b) *In a larger context*, by being: (3) *Unusual* in reference to prior knowledge or expectations - e.g., unexpected, out-of-role, negative, or extreme (Fiske 1980; Jones and McGillis 1976; Langer et al. 1976); and (c) *In relation to other attentional tasks*, by being: (4) *Dominating* the sensory field - e.g., for its intensity, position, frequency, etc. (Eisen and McArthur 1979; Fiske and Taylor 1975, Experiment 1; Iyengar and Kinder 1987); (5) *Attended under external manipulation* - e.g., under direct instructions (Cupchik and Leventhal 1974; Regan and Totten 1975; Taylor and Fiske 1975, Experiment 2); or (6) *Goal relevant* - e.g., involving (Berscheid et al. 1976; Erber and Fiske 1984; Neuberg and Fiske 1987; Ruscher and Fiske 1990; Taylor 1975).

Drawing on their classification, we reviewed more than 1,200 studies in social and consumer psychology dealing with salient marketing stimuli, including products, brand names, ads, commercials, and so on (Guido 1996b, recently updated). Addressing the search for common origins among the different instances of salient stimuli, we suggest slightly modifing Fiske and Taylor's (1991) classification, by considering: (1) Among the cases occurring *in an immediate context*, also those factors dominating the sensory field; and (2) Among the cases occurring *in a larger context*, also statistically novel stimuli. Using their rationale, indeed, these stimuli can be explained, respectively, by the principle of figure-ground and by the principle of unusuality. This leaves space for a third, non-residual category of salience occurrences, i.e. those explained by the personal involvement of the perceiver.

Table 2 summarizes these cases schematically.

Table 2. Categories of Salient Stimuli

A stimulus can be salient to a perceiver:

a) In an immediate context (according to the *principle of figure-ground*):
    1. By being figural (bright, moving, complex);
    2. By dominating the sensory field (for intensity, position, frequency, etc.);
    3. By being contextually novel.

b) In a larger context (according to the *principle of unusuality*):
    1. By being statistically novel;
    2. By being unusual in reference to prior knowledge (unexpected, out-of-role, negative, or extreme).

c) Due to perceiver's motivations (according to the *principle of involvement*):
    1. By being observed under external instructions;
    2. By being relevant for personal goals.

Source: Adapted from Taylor and Fiske (1978) and Fiske and Taylor (1991, p. 248).

The above-mentioned categories are considered the antecedents of salience, which is defined as "the *extent* to which particular stimuli stand out relative to others in their environment" (Fiske and Taylor 1991, p. 246, emphasis added). This definition of salience was chronologically the last among those provided by Fiske and Taylor and, to our knowledge, the best. It stresses, indeed, the *prominence* of salient stimuli in reference to other non-salient stimuli (the environment, or - as we shall say - the "context"). This definition seems more correct than a previous one provided in the glossary of a book in which Taylor was a co-author, where salience was defined as "the *quality* that makes a particular stimulus stand out and be noticed" (Sears, Peplau, and Taylor 1991, p. 557, emphasis added). Salience, indeed, is not "a quality" of a stimulus because, as we shall argue in the next chapter, it depends on the perceiver and does not exist in absolute. Bright, noisy, colorful, and novel stimuli, which are usually taken as instances of salient stimuli, are not salient in any case, because it is not possible to determine *ex ante* if they are perceived as such. Nevertheless, a deep-rooted conviction about the use of the term always makes people consider these stimuli as though salience was a quality that belongs objectively to these stimuli. This conviction - only moderated by the use of the word "extent" (rather than "quality") in the definition of the construct - descends in our opinion from the general reference to the figure-ground principle as an exhaustive explanation of the salience phenomenon.

3.   SALIENCE IN AN IMMEDIATE CONTEXT

3.1   The Principle of Figure-Ground

Much research on salience has been grounded on references to a major principle in perception, the *figure-ground principle*. According to this, "people direct their attention to those aspects of the perceptual field that stand out - the figure - rather than to the background of the setting - the ground." (Sears, Peplau, and Taylor 1991, p. 45). The figure-ground segregation is one of the fundamental organizing concepts in visual perception (see, e.g., for brief reviews, Shank and Walker 1989; Hoffman and Singh 1997). If at a sensory level a figure could not be separated from the ground, we would see nothing. Arnheim (1974) argued that figure-ground at the basis of perceptual processes is more elementary than even detection of shape. Shape, after all, cannot be detected if no difference between figure and ground is discerned.[17]

The characteristics of the figure-ground organization, analyzed in detail by Rubin (1921) and by the Gestalt psychologists, are currently used in social perception to explain the phenomenon of salience in *an immediate context* (cf. Fiske and Taylor 1991, pp. 248-249), in relation to those cases in which the stimulus is: (1) Figural (i.e., bright, complex, moving); (2) Dominating the sensory field (for its intensity, position, frequency, etc.); or (3) Contextually novel (i.e., distinctive - solo status).

3.2   Figurality and Salience

Examples of the first type of stimuli are provided by most research on salience in consumer behavior. All these studies have usually stressed the salience effect on memory. According to Gardner (1982, p. 179), "[s]alience is strongly affected by external stimuli. Things which stand out in an environment may receive more attention and so, be more easily recalled (e.g., Taylor and Fiske 1978). Advertisers can use attention-getting devices such as color, letter size, and typeset to make a particular attribute stand out in an ad. Under such circumstances, the prominent attribute is more likely to be recalled than when it is merely mentioned in the body copy. In addition, when one attribute is prominent, other attributes are less mentioned in the body copy. Making one attribute prominent seems to direct attention to it and away from all others (Gardner 1981). Calkins (1894) reported similar findings using color to manipulate the prominence of numerals in a list. (For discussion of the underlying process, see [Feigenbaum and Simon[18]] 1962)."

In general, *brightness, movement,* and *complexity* have been named as the factors able to attract attention - with bright colors, moving items, and complex formats appearing the most noticeable. *Brightness* refers to the perceived magnitude of a stimulus.[19] Together with hue and saturation (which is defined as the absence of whiteness), it describes perception of chromatic colors.[20] Bright, saturated colors tend to capture people's attention because they are easier to identify than dull, diluted ones.[21] That is why, for example, stores often use bright colors to differentiate among their different shopping areas.[22] Research on the impact of color in newspaper advertising concluded that color attracted 53 percent more readers than black-and-white ads (Auchincloss 1978), while "median sales gains (on reduced-price items) of approximately 41 percent [... were] generated by the addition of one color to black-and-white in retail newspaper advertising" (Sparkman and Austin 1980, p. 42). The influence of color in cuing consumers' perceptions was demonstrated by Tom et al. (1987) with a study in which a vanilla pudding, colored to look like chocolate pudding, was perceived by consumers as tasting like chocolate.[23] Color may also serve such functions as assisting the interpretation of product attributes, emphasizing a distinctive trademark or symbol, and influencing mood and emotional behavior (Sandage, Fryburger, and Rotzoll 1979). Indeed, apart from its impact in perceptual terms, color may have a psychological effect upon - and a symbolic meaning to - each audience member (cf., Britt 1978, pp. 150-152).[24] While it is evident the importance of a correct use of colors to attract attention, which would otherwise be lost, empirical research has shown that "advertisers are [still] not using color to improve advertising response among target customers." (Lee and Barnes 1989/1990, p. 29; see, also, Childers and Jass 1995).[25]

Movement is another device that stimulates the sensory receptors and sparks them to send impulses. Moving signs and store displays, for example, are employed to help a stimulus stand out, while much of the great success of TV commercials is due to their ability to portray movement to our eyes (Wilkie 1994). However, when we consider these stimulus factors as salient cues, we must acknowledge that *the impact of contrast can reverse their effects*. That is, bright colors or movement by themselves cannot grant attracting attention, but rather it is the change in the individual sensory system that activates sensory receptors and stimulates attentional processes. This change can be explained in terms of contrast with the context (the latter being one of the three elements at the basis of our in-salience hypothesis). That is why, for example, "if all the ads in a magazine are in color, a black-and-white ad may attract substantial attention." (Hawkins, Best, and Coney 1992, p. 226; and also Schindler 1986).[26] Similarly, as referred by Crane (1972), "[s]ince most elements in a landscape are static, a car moving along a lonely highway attracts attention. However, in a stream of traffic, it may be the stalled car that is seen first just as it is the unmoving rock in a brook that draws the eye. Thus, flashing lights and signs that revolve invite us to stop and buy and stop-motion photography at the movies emphasizes a director's message." (p. 210).[27] Zaltman and Wallendorf (1983) stressed the importance of context in the perception of motion, by stating: "Not everything that appears to move is actually in movement. Movement can be induced by changing the surroundings without moving the object. Factors such as the time interval between two stimuli, space between the stimulus, the intensity of the stimulus, and the observer's past experiences influence movement perception." (p. 586).

Stimulus *complexity* - in reference, for example, to a product or to a message - is another element that stresses the importance of the relationship between stimulus, context, and perceivers to release any processing effect. Complexity depends, first of all, on contextual factors (Britt 1978; Hansen 1972): Namely, the number of distinguishable stimuli in the context,[28] and the perceived dissimilarities among such stimuli.[29] Secondly, complexity - like novelty - depends on learning. What is perceived as complex is what the individual finds unfamiliar (see Alba and Hutchinson 1987, on novices vs. experts). Therefore, format complexity strongly interacts with individual characteristics: What some individuals find to be complex, others may find interesting.[30] Britt (1978, p. 64) postulated that "[a] more complex message will not have as high a level of attending as a simple one, unless it is novel or is of high interest to the audience." This should explain why past investigations found different results on the attentional potentialities of simple and complex stimuli. On the one hand, research has maintained that simple, straightforward marketing stimuli receive more attention than complex ones. For example, advertisements "that lack a clear visual point of reference or have inappropriate movement (too fast, slow, or "jumpy") increase the processing effort and decrease attention." (Hawkins, Best, and Coney 1992, p. 227). Likewise, audio messages that are difficult to understand due to foreign accents, inadequate volume, deliberate distortions (computer voices), loud background noises, and so forth also reduce attention. In a program of work that has investigated complexity's effects on attention and memory, Schleuder, Thorson and Reeves found that simple product commercials elicit more attention than complex ones (Thorson, Reeves and Schleuder 1985, 1987; Schleuder, Thorson and Reeves 1987, 1988; Schleuder and Gaiser 1989). Although their findings were rigorous with product commercials, they were only partially confirmed with political ads as both simple and complex political ads were found to elicit attention (Schleuder 1990).[31] In general, various studies provided substantial support to the idea that elements in a message that increase the effort required to process it tend to decrease attention (e.g., Walker and van Goten 1989). It has been argued that individuals have a maximum capacity for processing perceptual information - that is, a limited span of attention.[32] Therefore, the more easily the information is organized into distinguishable features, the more successfully and completely it will be attended (Miller 1956). On the other hand, a preference for more complex as opposed to simpler stimuli was found in another stream of research. Classic work by Berlyne (1958, 1966, 1970) found that subjects spend more time looking at the more complex than at the less complex member of a pair of stimuli (also, Mackworth and Morandi 1967; Lowrey 1998). Berlyne (1973) made the distinction between interestingness and pleasantness in terms of stimulus complexity, with the former increasing with complexity and the latter reaching the peak at intermediate levels of complexity.[33] The question for advertising researchers has been whether visual complexity makes ads easier to remember or more difficult to remember (Lang and Lanfear 1990). There is good evidence to support the hypothesis that elements of visual and audio structural complexity can make a stimulus figural. Visual features like cuts, edits, onsets, and unusual cinematography increase attention, in the involved viewer, to a television commercial by eliciting a reflexive attentive response called the *orienting response* (Alsop 1988; Lang 1988; Reeves et al. 1985),[34] as well as audio structural features, like changes in voice, sudden silence, music, and loud noises, attract the attention of the inattentive viewer (Anderson and Levin 1976; Kohan 1968; Thorson and Zhao 1988). Thus, to some extent, a stimulus can be figural by having in itself these elements of visual and audio structural complexity. Not any stimulus complexity, however, seems to be profitable to advertisers. Very high degrees of complexity, which results in high levels of attention, may turn in low levels of memory for the content of the ad (Berry 1983; Gunter 1987; Lang and Lanfear 1990; Lang and Thorson 1989; Thorson and Lang 1988).[35] Some researchers have argued that elements of complexity - like novelty, change, surprise, and incongruity - increase the amount of arousal stimulated by the environment, the so-called *environmental arousal potential* (Berlyne 1960; Hansen 1972; Hebb 1966; and Rosenzweig 1966). Moderate stimuli would generate a proportionate amount of salience (or activation), but an extremely complex environment would cause a steep drop in arousal.[36] This phenomenon is known as *perceptual blocking*. Consumers protect themselves from being bombarded with complex stimuli by simply "tuning out" such stimuli from conscious awareness. Research shows that consumers mentally screen out enormous amounts of advertising; and this may be more common for television than for print (Schiffman and Kanuk 1991, p. 163). Such a phenomenon is much similar to "perceptual defense" which especially occurs with novel stimuli (see, *below*, Paragraph 4.6).

3.3   Factors Dominating the Sensory Field and Salience

Also physical factors associated with the stimulus - such as intensity, position, and frequency - can generate salience, as they *dominate* the sensory field (visual, auditory, etc.). The presence of these factors can give the stimulus a figural value - like in the cases discussed in the section above - and, in addition, a prominence on every other stimulus present in that physical context.

Intensity is one of the factors that determines if a stimulus is detected once a perceiver is exposed to information, and whether or not the perceiver goes beyond mere exposure to actively attend to and focus on it. Intensity, however, is not the same as loudness or brightness, although they are often confused.[37] As also noticed (Note 19, *above*), whereas loudness or brightness are perceived magnitudes, intensity is a physical value. As the intensity of a stimulus increases, the probability that it will be sensed becomes higher, yet its loudness or brightness will always depend on the environment in which the stimulus occurs. For example, a common complaint by consumers is that television advertisements are louder than the programs that they accompany. However, the maximum intensity of sound coming from a commercial is no greater than that coming from a program, it is their loudness that gives the sensation that it is greater. Advertisers are skilful at creating the impression of loudness through their expert use of different techniques (cf. Koten 1984). These include (Mowen 1993, p. 79): Much less variation in intensity of sound level during a commercial than regular programming (i.e., sound levels in commercials tend to stay at or near peak levels); filtering of any noise that may drown out the primary message (because low-frequency sound can mask higher-frequency sounds); varying electronically voice sounds so that they stay within two to six kilohertz (because the human voice has more auditory impact in the middle of frequency ranges); writing scripts that use lots of consonants (because people are more aware of consonants than vowel sounds); beginning commercials with sounds that are highly different from those of the programming within which the commercial is buried (because people become adapted to the type of sounds coming from programming, so that a dramatic change in sound quality can draw viewer attention).[38]

In general, audience members will more likely attend to an intense message than a message that lacks intensity, that is, lacks strength and emphasis (Britt 1978). This applies to both visual and auditory stimuli. As for the former type of stimuli, Berlyne (1960, p. 38) concluded from a series of tests that more intense stimuli (i.e., lights) would be attended more rapidly than less intense stimuli; but further, he noted that size may be regarded as an equivalent to intensity because it is the quantity of light falling on the retina that apparently determines perceived intensity. A similar relationship appears to apply as well to hearing (see, e.g., Robinson and McArthur 1982). It has been proposed that the apparent duration of a brief interval is influenced by the intensity of the stimuli that delimit it.[39] Analogously, research in person perception provided evidence that behaviors that are intense and/or novel have more influence upon social perceptions than those that are less attention-drawing - although it couldn't be ascertained whether these results were due to the greater intensity or to the greater novelty of the stimuli (McArthur 1981; by the same token, also, Popper and Murray 1989). *Clarity*, like intensity, can have a major role in allowing visibility and further consequences. Zuckerman, Mann, and Bernieri (1982, Experiments 2 and 3), for example, showing a videotape in which only a subject or only an experimenter was clearly visible, found that the observers were more likely to generalize from the behavior of a visibly salient subject to other subjects' behavior than to generalize from the behavior of a subject that was not salient.

The *size* (or *magnitude*) of a stimulus operates in much the same manner as intensity: Larger ads and larger signs are likely to receive more attention, in part because a consumer is simply more likely to see them. Thus, for example, all else equal, a full-page advertisement is more likely to be noticed than a half-page advertisement relative to smaller advertisements placed near them (Lucas 1942, p. 247). Moreover, ads with longer copy have been found to be more effective in attracting the attention of industrial buyers than ads with shorter copy (cf. Hawkins, Best, and Coney 1992, p. 226). Although recognition measures like the ones used in these studies could be considered poor surrogates for attention (MacKenzie 1986), they are adequate for suggesting those physical properties of ads that may be related to attention. A substantial amount of advertising research goes, indeed, to this direction. Ad size, size of illustration, area of copy, type sizes, number of illustration units, and number of copy units have all been found to be positively related to recognition (e.g., Diamond 1968; Finn 1988; Hanssens and Weitz 1980; Holbrook and Lehmann 1980).[40]

Although the use of the largest possible space can be effective in making a stimulus salient, it is the impact of contrast which has been proposed as the key to using size to its greatest advantage (Britt 1978). For example, "Lucient Picard's Swiss wrist-watch's illustration was about one-sixteenth of a dark and somber page, with copy a minuscule one-quarter-inch high. Because this small-sized object appeared amidst large advertisements, it was attended to by more readers than otherwise." (Britt 1978, pp. 65-66).[41] Contrast basically regards prior knowledge. Popper and Murray (1989), for example, by manipulating two layout components of an in-ad health warning (the size of the type used and the background color), demonstrated that - rather than the physical qualities of the stimulus (the size and the color) - it was the novelty and the unusuality of the manipulated elements which produced the effects on attention. The ad message, in other words, was not attended because of its size or its color, but because it was different from consumers' expectations. Also, results in Barlow and Wogalter's (1993) study on alcoholic beverage warnings can be interpreted in terms of the context (i.e., the medium and the background noise) and of the contrast (i.e., the novelty of warnings in the high conspicuous condition) which were found necessary to have an impact on incidental attention and memory.

Position is another physical factor that has been usually evoked to explain salience. It refers to the placement of an object in a person's visual field. Position works because there is a higher probability that a consumer's sensory system will encounter the stimulus. For example, targets placed near the center of the visual field are more likely to be noticed than those near the edge of the field (see, e.g., Nazir, Heller, and Sussmann 1992). This is a primary reason why consumer good manufacturers compete fiercely for eye-level shelves in grocery stores and for a maximum amount of shelf space (Curhan 1973). And, whenever possible, point-of-purchase displays are used and are often extremely effective (Chavalier 1975; Schindler, Berbaum, and Weinzimer 1986).[42] Consumer research in supermarkets and discount stores, using sophisticated cameras to track the movement of consumers' eyes during shopping, has found that consumers' eyes travel along certain paths, so that products on an upper shelf receive 35 percent greater attention than those on a lower shelf (cf. Wilkie 1990, p. 242). Likewise, advertisements on the right-hand page receive more attention than those on the left (see Wilkie 1990, note 15, p. 242): In cultures that read from left to right, consumers' eyes have been trained to proceed in a systematic manner across a page; in turn, this training carries over into their casual scanning as well. For example, consumers' eyes are most likely to drift to the top left as they turn a magazine page. Therefore, an ad tends to receive greater attention when placed on the upper half of a page than on the lower half or, also, on the left-hand side than on the right. In addition, organization of elements inside print ads (i.e., design and layout) has been shown to influence attitude formation. The evaluation of a brand name, for example, has been proved to depend on its placement relative to the ad's focal information

(Janiszewski 1988, 1990; see, also, Fink et al. 1999; Shapiro 1999; Shapiro, MacInnis, and Heckler 1997).

On the one hand, advertisements that lack a clear visual point of reference generally tend to cause perceptual blocking which decreases attention. On the other hand, isolation (e.g., the use of "white space," such as placing a brief message in the center of an otherwise blank or white advertisement) and format (i.e., the manner in which the message is presented) can supply easy points of reference where to focus attention (see next paragraph).[43] Furthermore - what is relevant to our in-salience model - position of incongruent cues has been found to affect the detection of cue incongruity (Meyers-Levy 1988a).[44] This hypothesis concerning cue positioning is based on the results of studies that have examined the "spacing effect," which have consistently found that memory for a repeated item is enhanced when repetitions are discretely spaced rather than massed (Hintzman 1974).

Although there has been much discussion on whether advertising position in print media can increase the probability of exposure, no superiority has been yet definitely established, the value of a specific position being dependent upon the amount of audience traffic flowing past it (Britt 1978, p. 78). Covers, both inside and outside, are sufficiently preferred by magazine advertiser that will pay more for them than for other pages. It might be assumed that for some magazines of general interest, advertising in the first part of the issue are attended to more often because of incomplete reading; or, also, that advertisers try to exploit "order effects." Order effects (also called, serial-position effects) refer to the high recall probability observed for either the initial items (i.e., primacy effect) or the last items (i.e., recency effect) of a serial presentation (i.e., a sequence of pieces of information during learning).[45] Perception is affected by the order in which different items are presented: Asch (1946) determined that the first few terms of a series establish a context in which later terms are evaluated.

Analogously, vast audience differences occur between different positions - times and adjacent programs - in broadcast media. Television preference viewing, for example, can vary greatly according to the pod position (i.e., the commercial position in a sequence of commercials) and viewers' involvement (Murry, Lastovicka, and Singh 1992), as well as to life styles, demographics, and shopping orientation of the audience (Lumpkin and Darden 1982). Media decisions, traditionally based largely on "ratings" (that is, quantitative descriptions of size and composition of the audience), has been increasingly directed towards a closer control of the environment in which the advertisement appears, typically the television programming (Hoffman and Batra 1991).[46] Recent research indicated that television programming surrounding commercials is, indeed, an important determinant of advertising effectiveness (see, e.g., Schumann and Thorson 1990). Specifically, both program elicited feeling states (Goldberg and Gorn 1987; Kamins, Marks, and Skinner 1991) and liking for the program (Schumann 1986) have been found to influence commercial evaluation.

Finally, a particular case of position is constituted by individuals' *spatial perspective* at the occurrence of perception, when individuals attend to a particular stimulus by virtue of their own physical vantagepoint. The increased tendency for movie theaters to show commercials prior to the beginning of a show is an evident illustration of how it is possible to gain consumers' attention by advertising in circumstances in which people have little choice but to attend to the information presented. Although the cost per thousand viewers is higher than that of television advertising, theater advertising is claimed to be recalled three times better (cf. Mowen 1993, p. 88).[47] A similar case has been examined in social perception by Taylor and Fiske (1975, Experiment 1), where point of view was manipulated by restricting subjects' visual focus to permit a view of only one participant to a conversation, rather than others. By means of chair placement, some subjects could see both conversationalists equally well, whereas others could see only one of the conversationalists. It was hypothesized - as argued by Norman (1969) in his summary of the literature on attention and memory - that people remember what they attend to.[48] Taylor and Fiske (1975) found that a person who is visually salient during a conversation is later judged as having been more causally relevant in determining the nature of the conversation (so-called *Top-of-the-head phenomenon* - see, *below*, Paragraph 4.3.1). However, no evidence was found for differential recall of verbal or visual information relevant to the character that was visually salient. In general, research has demonstrated that, not only the visual perspective, but also the emotional and cognitive point of view from which the individual experiences a social stimulus (e.g., being the actor or the observer) influences the way that information is encoded and retained (see, *below*, Paragraph 5.3).[49]

Frequency is another physical factor named among the causes of salience. It refers to the repeated exposure to the stimulus. For example, insertion frequency (e.g., the number of times the same ad appears in the same issue of a magazine) has an effect similar to ad size: Three insertions generate more than twice the impact of one insertion (cf. Hawkins, Best, and Coney 1992, p. 226). In broadcasting, *duration* of the stimulus (e.g., the amount of time a person is on camera) has similar effects (cf. Eisen and McArthur 1979). For example, this sheer visual exposure effect holds for political issues: The amount of time an issue is aired on the evening news affects how much weight people give it in subsequent decisions (Iyengar and Kinder 1987).

Like order effects mentioned for position, there is also a "frequency effect" for certain items which acts as a *prime*, thus influencing perception and recall (see also, *below*, Chapter Three, Paragraph 2.3.1 on *The role of activation*). The frequency effect is mainly related to repetition. It has been often maintained that repeated presentations of a stimulus may enhance its salience which, in turn, increase its recall (Brosius 1989; Crowder 1976; Sawyer 1973).[50] Therefore, heavy advertising should heighten recall of both brand names and their associated attributes, although it could also produce important unintended effects (see Alba, Hutchinson, and Lynch 1991; Malaviya and Sternthal 1997; Pieters, Rosbergen, and Wedel 1999).[51] In marketing, the strengthening of the signal can be obtained in different ways. For consumer packaged goods, this may mean using frequent advertising, achieving concentrated distribution, and securing a substantial number of shelf facings in retail outlets. For industrial goods, signal strength can be accomplished by increasing the number of salesperson contacts with customers and using heavy repetition advertising schedules (cf. Sternthal and Craig 1982, p. 93).

Through the use of repetition as a tool, frequency creates familiarity with a stimulus, acting in a similar - yet, opposite - sense of statistical novelty in the generation of salience (see, *below*, Paragraph 4.2). The former increases the *relevance* (i.e., the weight) of, say, a product attribute, whereas the latter emphasizes the relative novelty of the *content* of that attribute (see also, *below*, Chapter Three, Paragraph 2.1.9). However, in the intentions of marketers, both frequency and statistical novelty try to create - or to capitalize on - a difference relative to concurrent stimuli. In both cases, as an effect of salience, recall should be heightened: In the case of repeated stimuli, because their frequent activation should increase their availability in memory (cf. Higgins and King 1981, pp. 79-80);[52] in the case of novel (less frequent) stimuli, because they should induce extensive processing aimed at distinctively encoding their content information, thus, resulting in strong memory (Eysenck 1979). Results of two studies by Meyers-Levy (1989ac) on memory for brand names - composed of high vs. low frequency words - suggested that the discriminating factor is the number of the associations related to them: Brand names composed of words encountered frequently in the language are better recalled when association sets are small, whereas brand names composed of low frequency words are insensitive to the size of association sets.[53]

It has been argued that not only does the frequency of activation of the stimulus increase its accessibility in memory (cf. Higgins and King 1981), but it does this even *regardless* of the content of the stimulus. For example, Bond et al. (1987) supported the notion that if the perceived salience of vocal nonverbal characteristics - i.e., frequency - is raised above that of the message content, then the extent to which the listener uses the non-verbally encoded information may increase, independently of what the speaker is saying. Such *frequency heuristics* has been studied also in consumer research: In general, it has been shown that frequency knowledge - i.e., a tally of the number of positive and negative attributes associated with a brand, irrespective of their meaning or importance - can influence judgments and choice, particularly when other types of information have been poorly encoded, poorly remembered, or poorly understood (Alba and Marmorstein 1987). For example, knowledge of the mere number of attributes of a brand (i.e., feature frequency) can significantly affect preference for that brand, regardless of the importance of those attributes (Alba and Marmorstein 1987) and over time (Alba, Marmorstein, and Chattopadhyay 1992).[54] Similarly, in some instances, the number of message arguments favoring a position has been shown to exert a powerful influence on persuasion (Petty and Cacioppo 1984). In promotional activities, the perception of deal frequency for a specific brand has been shown to influence preferences and choices (Krishna, Currim, and Shoemaker 1991), whereas in moderately incongruent brand extensions, ad repetition favored positive judgments (Lane 2000).

3.4   Contextual Novelty and Salience

Contextual novelty pertains to another class of stimuli, whose salience has also been explained with the Gestalt principle of figure-ground. In its different operationalizations, contextual novelty involves the "isolation" of the stimulus to which it is referred (e.g., an object) from other stimuli (e.g., other objects). There are three major ways isolation has been manipulated (Wallace 1965). A first way involves performing an additional operation on an item within a group of similar alternatives (e.g., printing it in red when the remaining list items are printed in black). A typical example is provided by the studies of Schindler and his associates (Schindler and Berbaum 1983; Schindler, Berbaum, and Weinzimer 1986) on the effects of salience on choice. In their experiments, they used a lottery game where the choice involved selecting one out of a group of numbers printed on a page, in which one of the numerals was randomly printed either much darker or much lighter than the others to make the salient alternative. They found that subjects chose an average of once every ten choices the alternative which stood out perceptually from the others, even though the payoffs in the game were determined by chance (Schindler, Berbaum, and Weinzimer 1986).[55] Their results support the view that perceptual salience may be a common mechanism behind a wide variety of marketing and merchandising techniques, especially for products and services for which consumers perceive much similarity among the many alternatives and where they have a little basis for making a quick choice.[56] For example, many consumer packaged goods (e.g., soap pads or paper towels on a supermarket shelf) can be so low involving that consumers are not motivated to become aware of the features that differentiate the various brands (Olshavsky and Granbois 1979). If consumers see few meaningful differences between those different alternatives, it is plausible they could make the easier choice and select the first alternative that they notice. According to Schindler, Berbaum, and Weinzimer (1986), this effect is mediated by two factors: (1) The situational meaning that is mistakenly ascribed to a salient alternative;[57] and (2) The consumer's information processing limitations which induce to place the salient alternative into the evoked set.[58]

A second way isolation has been created is through direct manipulation of the items, that is, inserting a different type of item within a group of similar items. Broadbent (1958), Berlyne (1958), Koffka (1935), and others demonstrated that the focus of attention is attracted by this kind of stimulus novelty. Involuntary attention can occur when a distinctive item is presented without warning (Kahneman 1973).[59] A distinctive advertisement, for example, is one that is different from the other ads, so that it stands out from a clutter of commercials (Eastman 1998). The work of Koffka (1935) is particularly relevant in that it discussed the relationship between the focus of attention and the stimulus novelty in a situation containing two or more groups of objects that do not change over time. He indicated that, given two groups of objects, attention will tend to focus on the quantitatively smaller of the two groups because that group is quantitatively more scarce - i.e., more novel (distinctive) - than the larger group of objects. Thus, for example, in a text, people tend to focus more attention on italicized words because they are fewer in number and thus more novel than the larger group of non-italicized words. In synthesis, "[p]eople *selectively* attend to distinctive stimuli" (Zaltman and Wallendorf 1983, p. 330, emphasis added). Examples of this type of salience are profusely offered in person perception literature, in relation with the case of the "solo," a person who is situationally at the center of attention due to his attributes of sex, race, and other visual characteristics, which are different from the rest of the people. In advertising, the use of "white space" - that is, placing a brief message in the center of an otherwise blank or white ad - is also based on this principle (Hawkins, Best, and Coney 1992, p. 242). Brandt's (1942) classic study, which attempted to measure the attentional value of pictorial copy when varying the amount of isolation, found that 25 percent white space increases the attention-time above than that of no isolation, and that isolation exceeding 50 percent of the total area demands less attention-time than when the space is filled.[60] Such an effect was also found at an aural level with *silence*, increasing attention and recall, both for radio (Olsen 1997) and television commercials (Ang, Leong, and Yeo 1999).

A third way isolation has been manipulated is through the structural organization within a group, a method which was originally developed to minimize intraserial interference differences between massed and isolated items in a list (Siegel 1943).[61] Whereas the first two methods of manipulating isolation involve differences in absolute numbers between massed and isolated terms, the third one makes use of two element types and the same number of items from each type. In its rigorous application, this method has more relevant methodological implications than marketing potentialities. In consumer literature, an interesting exemplification is offered by order effects in the presentation of advertisements, which provide more attentional value to those ads which are at the beginning or at the end of a string, or in a position of relatively low generalizability to the rest of a series (see Webb and Ray 1979; and, *above*, Paragraph 3.3). Similarly, in reference to a recognized effect of salience (see, *below*, Paragraph 5.2.1: *The inhibition effect on memory*), it has been reported that highly salient brands may produce order effects on questionnaires. For example, making particular brands (or attributes) salient at an early stage when responding to surveys has been shown to inhibit recall of other brands (Alba and Chattopadhyay 1986, p. 368).

3.4.1   The von Restorff Effect

Contextual novelty, which derives from the isolation of a stimulus, has an important consequence that has been the subject of deep inquiry and that has came to be known as the *von Restorff effect*, from the name of the author who first contributed to these studies (von Restorff 1933). The results of von Restorff's research may be summarized in the following statement: Isolating an item against a crowded or homogeneous background facilitates the *learning* of that isolated item.[62] Usually, this effect is reported as if isolated items had a facilitating effect on memory rather than learning (see, e.g., Mowen 1993, p. 122),[63] but this is not perfectly true. Since the first two decades of experiments immediately following von Restorff's studies, it was apparent that learning (operationalized as immediate recall) was on average improved, whereas retention (as delayed recall) did not always show better differences (cf. Green 1956; Saul and Osgood 1950; and, for a detailed review on the effect, Wallace 1965). These inconsistencies in experimental findings could be attributed to the figure-ground explanation of the isolation phenomenon adopted in its original presentation, which gave impetus to further exploration of the effect along these lines. Von Restorff, indeed, incorporated her results into a Gestalt theoretical framework (Koffka 1935), by demonstrating that an item which stands out against a homogeneous background, irrespective of its class, is learned more easily. She suggested that the differences between isolated and massed items were attributable to the tendency for similar massed items to "agglutinate" (that is, assimilate with one another), thus destroying their distinctive characters.[64]

Alternatively, our model hypothesizes a different origin of this effect - i.e., the incongruity between the stimulus in a context and a perceiver's schema - which would account for past experimental findings. This explanation, moreover, traces back in a sketched form to the pioneering work of Green (1956, 1958ab) on the value of "surprise" in the von Restorff effect. This idea is further supported by the fact that the distinctive stimulus' uniqueness is crucial for producing isolation effects (Webster 1997).[65] Unfortunately, as mentioned by Wallace (1965, p. 422), the proponents of such a position did not elaborate on why such factors, as attention and organization, "would lead to more rapid learning. Consequently, the theories remained at a descriptive level."

4. SALIENCE IN A LARGER CONTEXT

4.1 The Principle of Unusuality

Apart from figure-ground, a second principle has been evoked in social cognition to explain salience in *a larger context*. In analogy to the "immediate context," which is a physical ground where a figural stimulus stands out (see, *above*, Section Three), Fiske and Taylor (1991, p. 249) refer to a "larger context" in relation to a customary situation - or one perceived as such - in reference to which an unusual stimulus stands out.[66] *Unusuality*, in this broader case, is the cause that make stimuli salient and *prior knowledge* - that is, information stored in memory - is the crucial element for their perception. Much empirical evidence supports the view that prior knowledge affects information processing activities (see, for reviews, Bettman 1986; Cohen and Chakravarti 1990; Tybout and Artz 1994; Jacoby, Johar, and Morrin 1998). In consumer behavior research, several studies have explored the effects of variables related to prior knowledge (e.g., familiarity, expertise, past experience) on various information processing activities (e.g., Alba 1983; Bettman and Park 1980; Johnson and Katrichis 1988; Johnson and Russo 1984; Srull 1983). Typically, these variables have been used interchangeably (Rao and Monroe 1988).[67] However, Alba and Hutchinson (1987) have proposed that consumer knowledge has two major components: Familiarity, and expertise.[68] These components are at the basis of organized knowledge structures, such as schemata, scripts, or categories, whose major role in perception has been widely recognized.[69] In a larger context, therefore, a stimulus is said to be salient when it is unusual to a perceiver, that is, when it violates a perceiver's prior knowledge and expectations he can derive from that knowledge. Fiske and Taylor (1991, p. 248), in these cases, refer to stimuli which are: (1) Unexpected; (2) Out-of-role; (3) Negative; or (4) Extreme. Also (5) Statistically novel stimuli belong to this context, because this form of novelty can be seen as a deviation from expectations. We shall review each of these cases, starting from statistical novelty.

4.2 Statistical Novelty and Salience

Statistical novelty regards stimuli that are rare from a statistical point of view or, in a word, unique. For example, innovations that define new categories or revolutionize existing ones generate so-called *really new products* (Cooper 2000; Lehmann 1994; Ziamou and Gregan-Paxton 1999), such as cellular telephones, electric cars, digital cameras, Internet-TVs, digital video discs (among those recently introduced to consumer markets). The extent to which a stimulus is novel to an individual depends on learning (Hansen 1972, p. 50).

Because frequency (repetition) and recency are important factors in learning, novelty can appear in two forms. A stimulus can be: (1) *Absolutely novel*, if consumers have never before been exposed to it; (2) *Relatively novel*, if consumers are exposed to a familiar stimulus not observed in the recent past. In his seminal work, Berlyne (1960, 1967) suggested that at the beginning all stimuli have the same ability to "create interest," but as a result of habituation, some of them lose part of their ability. He developed a set of variables representing the amount of new information in a stimulus (the so-called *collative properties*, which include novelty, change, complexity, conflict, surprisingness, and uncertainty) and found a consistent relationship between these variables and the amount of attention paid to a stimulus.[70] This relationship has generally assumed the form of an inverted U, with maximum attention paid to stimuli at intermediate values of these variables (Olney, Holbrook, and Batra 1991).

Applying an information-processing approach, novel information seems to be processed more extensively and, subsequently, may be more likely to be recalled than information that is redundant or expected to appear in a given context (Lynch and Srull 1982).[71] In advertising, available evidence suggests that: "The greater the use of novel executional cues, the greater consumers' motivation to attend the ad." (MacInnis, Moorman, and Jaworski 1991, p. 35). An advertising technique that resorts to novelty to improve attention and memory is *content variation*. An examination of past literature makes it apparent that there are different strategies for varying ads (Motes, Hilton, and Fielden 1992): They can be varied by changing either the message itself or less substantial factors, such as the format, the illustrations, or the print font.[72] Burnkrant and Unnava (1987) found greater brand recall when consumers are exposed to three variations of the same ad versus the same ad three times; yet, this novelty is usually short-lived, as commercial repetition and "me-too" advertising reduce the perception of novelty (Rethans, Swasy, and Marks 1986).[73] Elsewhere, it has been shown that novel and more salient conditioned stimuli promote greater amounts of conditioning and more rapid effects. Shimp, Stuart, and Engle (1991) varied conditioned stimuli novelty via brand familiarity and found that greater attitudinal conditioning resulted when novel unknown brands served as conditioned stimuli compared to when moderately known and well-known brands were used. Generally speaking, novelty may command attention, but will not, *per se*, command choice (Woods 1981, p. 280). Individuals may pay attention to novel stimuli for information purposes, as a result of their need to know (what Berlyne called "uncertainty"), in order to determine the utility or threat afforded; however, paying attention to and identifying a novel stimulus are not the same as using it.[74]

From a Berlynian point of view, in assessing the novelty of a marketing stimulus, two perspectives are relevant. From one perspective, which has been called *uniqueness*, novelty represents the degree to which a particular stimulus differs from other exemplars.[75] This perspective is similar to that of Mandler

(1982, see *below*), whose work suggested to Olney, Holbrook, and Batra (1991) that the novelty of a television commercial can be seen as an incongruity between a viewer's existing schema for television commercials and the nature of the commercial in question.[76] In this paradigm, consumers process marketing communications by matching visual and contextual cues from an advertisement (and possibly the media vehicle where it appears) to their prior knowledge of similar stimuli (i.e., memory of prototypical ads) stored in the appropriate schema (Goodstein 1993; McDaniel 1999). This view is confirmed by the use of different commercial formats (such as 8- vs. 30-second commercials and comparative ads) which might be very attention getting.[77] Advertising schemata, moreover, are argued to operate at a number of levels (i.e., general/abstract schemata; media-based ad schemata; ad genre schemata; product category ad schemata; brand ad schemata; specific schemata), such that incongruities can regard different types of expectations (Stoltman 1990). In many categories, there are several competing marketing products that have much the same characteristics and that deliver relatively similar benefits to consumers. In such situations, the essence of advertising becomes to make the product seem different from those of the competitor, setting the brand apart from others in its product category (Weilbacher 1984, p. 181). A means of achieving differentiation, in order to build involvement, is to make an attribute salient; thus, the prominent characteristic becomes a statistically novel variable. The product is no longer considered on the basis of its individuality, but the most salient part of it will determine the nature of many consumer interactions.[78] Novelty conveys this distinctiveness to products in the form of prototypicality. Research has shown that consumers appear initially to organize product knowledge around prototypical examples, using them as cognitive referents (e.g., Sujan 1985). Therefore, the pioneer has a unique distinctiveness which derives from its being representative of the category. Being perceptually distinct, the pioneer overshadows brands positioned nearby, especially "me-too" brands that frequently rely on the pioneer to establish their identity. In turn, differences in distinctiveness translate directly into market share differences (Carpenter and Nakamoto 1989). For usually expensive, higher involvement products that are perceived as means of self-expression (such as clothing and automobiles), consumers may value uniqueness in itself. Snyder and Fromkin's (1979) *Uniqueness theory* asserts that people have a basic need to feel moderately dissimilar to others, such that they price rare and unusual products, ideas, and experiences. This also suggests that when consumers buy products important to their self-concept, they may value atypicality *per se* (Ward and Loken 1988).[79] In the case of the so-called *positional goods* (e.g., goods requiring conspicuous spending), products are bought, rather than *in spite* of their high price, *because* of their price, for the social status they can grant to their owners (Hirsch 1976).[80] However, the preference for products that allow individual expression can go beyond the possessiveness component of materialism (Belk 1988; Wallendorf and Arnould 1988). In this case, uniqueness may derive from the individual attachment to "favorite objects," which are "singularized" through the mutual transfer of meaning and emotion between the objects and the individuals (McCracken 1986). Such singularization deactivates objects as commodities and turns them into priceless and seemingly unique icons for individual self-expression (Kopytoff 1986). Novelty, however, in the sense that Berlyne has discussed it, is more a perceptual rather than an affective or hedonic variable (Woods 1981, p. 480).

From another perspective, which has been called *familiarity*, novelty represents the degree of an individual's (lack of) prior experience with a given stimulus (cf. Baker et al. 1986). Novelty, in this sense, derives from the availability of prior knowledge which is representative of the stimulus. It is well established that prior knowledge moderates selective exposure, attention and interpretation (Brucks 1985; Johnson and Russo 1984; Simonson, Huber, and Payne 1988; Srull 1983). It is the availability of prior experience with the marketing stimulus that distinguishes novices from experts (Alba and Hutchinson 1987; see, also, *below*, Chapter Three, Paragraph 2.3.3 on *The role of availability*). The familiarity dimension of novelty could be manipulated through the use of *primes* (see, *below*, Chapter Three, Paragraph 2.3.1 on *The role of activation*), which could change the recency of an experience (e.g., free samples enclosed in a magazine), or the frequency of a stimulus (e.g., low frequency words as brand names).[81] It has been shown that the features of a product brand name (namely, its association set size and the distinctiveness of its processing) can influence perceived familiarity and, in turn, consumer attention (Meyers-Levy 1989a). Indeed, like other novel concepts, rare, infrequently encountered words receive greater attention (Warmer and McGray 1969) as individuals engage in a longer, distinctive processing to specify the meaning of, make sense of, and encode them (Eysenck 1979; Forster and Chambers 1973).

Consumers quite often seek *un*familiar stimuli in the form of new brands or products. At the basis of this activity, which has been called *variety seeking*, there is one of the most fundamental and primitive forms of attentive behavior, vigilance. Vigilance is an inherited or basic need which is "satisfied" through experiencing - and, in experiencing, curiosity is a key factor.[82] Humans are genetically programmed to be vigilant and, at the same time, to avoid boredom and seek novel stimuli which can provide an adequate level of arousal (Deci 1975).[83] Consumers' tastes, attitudes, and values do change and such changes generate the need for variety (cf. Markin 1974, p. 57). Furthermore, research has proposed that there are limits on the desired degree of arousal (not too much, not too little); thus, there appears to be an *optimal stimulation level* for the individual (Hirschman 1980). In the field of consumer behavior, this optimal stimulation level has been related to personality, demographics, and exploratory tendencies (Raju 1980; see, also, Goodwin 1980; Raju and Venkatesan 1980); and, also, to innovative shopping behavior (Mittelstaedt et al. 1976). When stimulation is below the optimal level, this theory proposes that the individual will experience a need and become motivated to pursue greater arousal (for example, by trying new products). The novel stimuli that humans will ordinarily pay attention to are visual. In contrast, consumers will be hesitant or reluctant to "inspect," say, novel foods (Woods 1981); although such foods could be inspected visually or by means of smell, they will be initially tasted in only very small amounts.[84]

On the other hand, when stimulation is too great, an individual could either attempt to reduce the excess trying to master the stimulus by understanding its complexity or he could cease (consciously or unconsciously) to explore the source of such an excess. According to Schiffman and Kanuk (1991, p. 163), *perceptual defense* implies that "[c]onsumers subconsciously screen out stimuli that are important for them *not* to see, even though exposure has already taken place. Thus, threatening or otherwise damaging stimuli are less likely to be perceived than are neutral stimuli at the same level of exposure. Furthermore, individuals may distort information that is not consistent with their needs, values, and beliefs." As a consequence, completely new stimuli, which tend to elicit uncertainty or surprise, are generally avoided or distorted (Biederman, Mezzanotte, and Rabinowitz 1982).[85] In reference to brands, perceptual defense will be the greatest when consumers have strong beliefs and attitudes about it; when they have consistent experiences with it; when anxiety is produced; or when the level of post-purchase dissonance is high (Assael 1992, p. 142). Such a phenomenon is similar to "perceptual blocking," which occurs with complex stimuli (see, *above,* Paragraph 3.2).

While the bulk of results reviewed in this paragraph provides substantial evidence that in a free situation of choice subjects will prefer a novel stimulus to a familiar one, there are empirical findings and theoretical formulations which appear to be in conflict with this. Research by Zajonc (1968, 1980) and his colleagues on the *mere exposure effect* indicates that familiar stimuli tend to be better liked than unfamiliar ones, even in the absence of recognition.[86] The results of Zajonc, which have been extended in consumer research by Janiszewski (1990; recently, Janiszewski and Meyvis 2000; and also Chung and Szymanski 1997), suggested that familiarity leads to greater liking, even without the mediation of awareness.[87] Since its first appearance, Zajonc's arguments have been the subject of debate (e.g., Jakobovits 1968; Maddi 1968). It has been suggested that other variables caused these differing results, like stimulus complexity (Berlyne 1971). However, if such favorable attitude toward the stimulus object is a symptom of greater attention, the wealth of data on variety seeking and orienting behavior stands in clear contradiction to this. To overcome such difficulties, we shall argue in our hypothesis that, on equal levels of perceiver's involvement, it is always the incongruity between the stimulus and the context - as perceived through individual schemata - which creates salience. Therefore, all other conditions being equal, a novel stimulus would be salient in a familiar context, whereas most probably a familiar stimulus (such as a recurring one) would be salient in a novel context (where other contextual stimuli are new to the perceiver). In this sense, our hypothesis draws on the same elements indicated by Maddi (1968) as the three possible limiting factors to mere exposure effect: (1) The meaning of the stimulus; (2) Monotony (which sets the context); and, (3) Individual difference characteristics (i.e., perceiver's schemata).

4.3   Unexpectancy and Salience

On the one hand, unusuality comes from the existence of individuals' organized representations of prior knowledge; on the other hand, *unexpectancy* - one of its major instances - comes from the existence of what has been viewed as a *by-product* of prior knowledge, that is *expectations.*[88] A great variety of definitions have been proposed for the concept of expectations (cf. Oliver 1993, 1997; Oliver and Burke 1999; Oliver and Winer 1987).[89] From a marketing perspective, consumer product expectations have been defined as pre-purchase beliefs or evaluative beliefs about the product (Oliver 1980; Olson and Dover 1979), predictions of affect regarding the product (Oliver and Linda 1981), user anticipation of product performance (Swan and Martin 1981), and expected degree of satisfaction (Trawick and Swan 1980). This proliferation of definitions has created the impression that it is the research study that determines the definition to be used (Barbeau and Qualls 1984). Generally, however, conceptual definitions of expectation have in common three fundamental dimensions: (1) The arousal dimension (bounded by an active versus a passive expectations processing state);[90] (2) The temporal dimension of the knowledge generating expectations (i.e., immediacy or anticipatory knowledge);[91] and (3) The uncertainty dimension (i.e., either risk or ambiguity).[92]

The sources of expectations can be generally traced in memories of past experiences, information from others, and inferences drawn from related experiences. Also imagery processing affects consumer expectations by interacting with consumer experience. Specifically, imagery processing leads to systematic biases in expectations (MacInnis and Price 1987, 1990). However, novice consumers (who have a relatively modest store of information in memory to build scenarios of purchase outcomes) are more likely to focus on positive outcomes in their imagining, whereas experienced consumers (who have a richer knowledge base) may imagine the anticipated event as unfolding in many ways; and, even if they too are likely to favor positive outcomes in their imagining, their past experiences may prompt them to consider negative outcomes as well.[93]

Katona (1975), who studied aggregate consumer expectations, focused on the three major sources (past experiences and inferences, on the one side, and external information, on the other side), by distinguishing two forms of learning (pp. 147-149): Learning by problem solving and understanding, and learning by memorizing (repetition). He maintained that, while some expectations derive from personal experience and insights about the relationships between the crucial factors in a problem-solving situation, other expectations are learned by repetition and reinforcement, and are extrapolated from the past or from mass media messages. In attitude research, Fishbein and Ajzen (1975) distinguished three types of beliefs (and, therefore, expectations) consumers develop by being exposed to these sources (see, also, *below*, Chapter Three, Paragraph 2.1.10): (1) Descriptive, (2) Informational, and (3) Inferential beliefs. *Descriptive beliefs* result from direct experience with the object (e.g., a product). They are usually held with much certainty. Consumers having experience with a product form stimulus-response bonds that allow them to know what to expect of it.[94] Such bonds are at the base of expectancy-value models (subjective expected utility and attitude models). *Informational beliefs* result from accepting the information provided by outside sources (e.g., the mass media). The degree of certainty with which such beliefs are held depends on source characteristics, such as the reliability, expertise, power of the information source;[95] and modalities of presentation, such as the format or framing of the message, or the salience of communicators (Chaiken and Eagly 1983; Kahneman and Tversky 1979). *Inferential beliefs* result from some logical reasoning, such as processes of causal attribution, cue utilization, and heuristics. For example, consumers may expect a high quality product or have different perceptions, knowing the high price or the brand name of the product (Allison and Uhl 1964; Bettman, John, and Scott 1986; Nevid 1981).[96] Under these processes of reasoning, the role of salience is twofold: Not only does it generally reflect the extent to which a stimulus is unexpected, but also it has been assumed to be at the origin of a causal, or at least a correlational, relationship with the expected event (*top-of-the-head phenomenon*).

The formation of expectations is mainly due to the above-mentioned reasoning processes: Cue utilization, heuristics, and causal attribution (van Raaij 1991). *Cue utilization* (weighing or combination) allows making inferences about a stimulus based on some items of information. Expectations can be formed with a considerable accuracy on the basis of weighted combinations of cues (e.g., multiple regression models). In consumer behavior, for example, Olson and Jacoby (1972) and Schellinck (1983) have studied this process. Cue utilization is also an aspect of *heuristics*, a simple and often biased way to collect information and form expectations. Under this form of reasoning, cues are superficial aspects of a stimulus used by less than perfect processors (i.e., human beings), instead of objective facts, to reach quick conclusions.[97] Four classes of heuristics are usually distinguished: Representativeness, availability, simulation, and anchoring (Kahneman and Tversky 1982a; Tversky and Kahneman 1974, 1981). When making inferences: (1) The *representativeness heuristic* matches information in the environment against existing knowledge structures (schemas) to determine the likelihood that the match is appropriate; (2) The *availability heuristic* pertains to the amount of information that is easy to bring to mind as a guide; (3) The *simulation heuristic* consists in imagining hypothetical alternatives to judge by the ease of particular endings; (4) The *anchoring* (and *adjustment*) *heuristic* allows us to estimate an incoming stimulus by referring to some existing similar value and then adjusting it to the new instance.[98] As far as our review is concerned, however, the most significant route to the formation of expectations is *causal attribution*. In an attribution process individuals put together information to make inferences about the causes of an event or of a stimulus occurrence: Classes of causes are internal (the person or the agent), external (the object or target), or circumstantial (the situation or contingency). Two sets of principles have evolved to deal with causal attribution (Kelley 1973): A covariation principle, which allows the individual to attribute an effect to the one of its possible causes with which, over time, it covaries; and a configuration principle, which allows the individual to discount the role of a given cause in producing a given effect if other plausible causes are also present.[99] Whenever an expectation about a stimulus - which has been formed through any of these three reasoning processes - is not matched, that stimulus becomes salient to its perceiver. Before discussing the nature and the effects of this incongruity, we shall examine a particular topic that has been widely studied in literature, that is, attributing causality to salient stimuli.

4.3.1   Top-of-the-head Phenomenon

The process of causality has been mainly explained according to two major points of view. In Kelley's (1972) original version, the process outlined is very complex: The principles guiding perceivers in inferring the most likely cause are supported by criteria like distinctiveness, consistency, and consensus. That is, in attempting to reach an explanation for an outcome, a person must assess, respectively, if the effect occurs only with one particular target and not with other targets; if the same effect is repeated over time; and if the same causal attribution is made by other observers. Taylor and Fiske (1975, 1978)[100] proposed, instead, that salience frequently influences perception of causality; that is, perceivers seek a single, sufficient, and salient explanation for a stimulus occurrence, often the first that comes along. Because this response to a stimulus in the environment the perceiver adopts may depend largely on what is salient, regardless of whether or not that explanation is accurate, they call this phenomenon *top of the head*. It implies that "the respondent has spent little time on the matter, gathered little or no data beyond that of the immediate situation, and responded with an opinion nonetheless." (Taylor and Fiske 1978, p. 252). Such an attribution process is low in consensus - as people, instead of employing information logically, are often more influenced by a single, colorful piece of case history evidence (e.g., Kahneman and Tversky 1973;

Nisbett et al. 1976) - and shows relatively little cross-situational consistency - as attributions are often shaped by usually trivial but highly salient information (e.g., Tversky and Kahneman 1974; Schuman and Johnson 1976; Wicker 1969).

It seems interesting to notice that, in social perception literature, this illusory causation effect was not demonstrated strictly with unexpected stimuli, but rather with figural stimuli (by virtue of movement, bright lightning, bold patterning), statistically novel stimuli, and stimuli perceivers were induced to observe by virtue of experimenters' instructions or by virtue of perceivers' physical vantage point (e.g., McArthur and Post 1977; McArthur and Solomon 1978; Taylor and Fiske 1975; see also, *below*, Paragraph 5.3).[101] This phenomenon has been considered so intrinsically linked to salience that the same salience construct has been defined against this effect. Taylor and Thompson (1982), contrasting vividness to salience effect, clearly stated: "*Salience* refers to the phenomenon that when one's attention is differentially directed to one portion of the environment rather than to others, the information contained in that portion will receive disproportionate weighing in subsequent judgments." (p. 175). Salience tends to draw the attentional focus of perceivers, and this attentional focus, in turn, has important consequences for various judgments made by perceivers. Paradoxically, however, McArthur and Ginsberg (1981) found that the fixation of the stimulus is positively related to salience but it is negatively related to causal attribution. Thus, salient stimuli are perceived as more causal *despite*, not because of, greater fixation of them, and a cogent explanation for the impact of salience on attributions remains to be found.

Together with illusory causation, also illusory correlation (or covariation) was observed both in person and in object perception (for consumer covariation judgments, see, in particular, Pechmann and Ratneshwar 1992). Whereas illusory causation is the tendency to attribute causal efficacy to salient stimuli, illusory correlation is the tendency to perceive salient pairs of events as correlated.[102] Such inferential perception is important in helping to explain prior events, control current outcomes, and predict future contingencies. McArthur (1980) proposed that the perception of salient stimuli as *causal* may reflect the way in which the perceiver picks up information about the environment, whereas the perception of salient stimuli as *correlated* may reflect the perceiver's attunement to particular environmental invariants.

Still the question remains as to why the top-of-the-head phenomenon occurs. Two explanations were suggested (McArthur and Ginsberg 1981). The first is that perceivers recall more about salience stimuli. However, the existing research evidence failed to support recall as a (Taylor et al. 1979; Fiske Kenny, and Taylor 1982). Fiske et al. (1982), in particular, considered as mediators both enhanced visual recall and exaggerated schema-relevant recall of salient stimuli.[103] The second explanation is that information about salient stimuli is more "available" in memory (Taylor and Fiske 1978; McArthur 1981).[104]

According to this hypothesis, it is the ease with which information is brought to mind, rather than whether or not it can be recalled, that mediates the effects of salient stimuli. More specifically, Taylor and Fiske (1978) pointed out that, given manipulations of visual attention, visual images of the salient stimuli are more available in memory than visual images of the nonsalient stimuli.[105]

To explain the tendency to attribute causality to *visually* salient stimuli, McArthur (1980) advanced two alternative hypotheses, one suggesting that causal attribution to salient stimuli requires visual scanning activity that registers an interchange in units that begin with the visually salient stimulus and end with the less salient one (i.e., the *Perceptual organization hypothesis*); and the other suggesting that causal attribution to visually salient persons requires direct competition for the perceivers' attention by salient and non-salient stimuli (i.e., the *Preferential processing hypothesis*). Robinson and McArthur (1982) sorted out these two possibilities by manipulating *vocal*, rather than visual, salient stimuli. Although their findings were able to rule out the latter hypothesis, a definitive explanation for the effect remained to be found.[106]

In order to examine the generalizability of this perceptual salience effect, Borgida and Howard-Pitney (1983) conducted two experiments on personal involvement as a delimiting condition. Other tasks and motivational variables had been shown in the past to delimit the robustness of various inferential tendencies, such as base rate fallacy (Borgida and Brekke 1981), covariation estimation (Crocker 1981), and overconfidence in judgment (Fischhoff 1982). It was expected that perceivers who were personally involved in an issue would be more motivated than less-involved perceivers to shift attention from salient cues to attitudinally congruent but non-salient message cues. Their results suggested that personal involvement indeed constitutes a boundary condition for salience effects: Ratings of highly-involved perceivers reflected more systematic processing of message arguments - regardless of which discussant was visually salient - whereas ratings of less-involved perceivers reflected top-of-the-head processing. Other studies have found that causal attributions are not automatically made during the acquisition of the information but in relation to the subject's goal (Bassili and Smith 1986; Lichtenstein and Srull 1985; Sherman et al. 1983; Smith and Miller 1979) as well his available attentional resources (Bargh and Thein 1985).

Finally, a further model has been proposed to overcome the basic epistemological problem of causal attributions, that of being huge - if not infinite - the set of possible causes for any event (see Hesslow 1988). According to the *Abnormal conditions model* (Hilton and Slugoski 1986), attributions are made to those conditions that stand out. A major advantage of this model is that it requires perceivers to coordinate each source of information with one and only one type of attribution; it does not require the more complex pattern matching in Kelley's original version. Nor does this model restrict attributions to the usual agent-object-situation classes of causes, since it assumes attributors to have many complex attribution possibilities at their disposal (given by the combinations of those classes). Another potential advantage of the abnormal conditions model, which makes it similar to our salience hypothesis is its explicit recognition that attributional processing is not "context free." The perception of abnormality is a matter not only of information presented but also of prior knowledge possessed by perceivers and brought to the task. In particular, for highly schematic activities (those which follow a script), high consensus and low distinctiveness information is already assumed. People seek consensus information only when it cannot be presupposed from their store of cultural knowledge (cf. Hilton, Smith, and Alicke 1988).

4.3.2   Incongruity

The perceptual events which occur when expectancies established through learning fail to be confirmed are the cause of incongruity: "An unexpected concatenation of events, a conspicuous mismatching, an unlikely pairing of cause and effect - all of these have in common a violation of normal expectancy." (Bruner and Postman 1949, p. 206). Several different terms have been used in consumer literature to indicate an *incongruent* stimulus (e.g., unexpected, discrepant, inconsistent, uncorrelated, uncoordinated). In recent years, the ACR Conferences have always included special sessions devoted to incongruity, both in US (Brown and Chernev 1997; Malaviya and Meyers-Levy 1998; Braig 1999) and in Europe (Pracejus 1999). Unfortunately, researchers conducting these studies have only vaguely articulated the theoretical foundations of these terms (Heckler and Childers 1992), without considering the systematic coincidence between incongruity and salience constructs for physical stimuli (what will be the subject of our hypothesis; see, *below*, Chapter Three, *Proposition One*). [107]

As a matter of fact, if it is maintained that "[c]ongruent stimuli are those believed to 'belong together,' and incongruent stimuli are those which violate some previously held belief" (Hansen 1972, p. 51), under the term "incongruity" many aspects of a stimulus can be disguised. An important distinction is between items that are incongruent with prior expectations and items that are descriptively inconsistent with the other items presented together (e.g., in a list). The former imply a sort of temporal novelty (to which we deserve, in this review, the term "incongruity"); whereas the latter imply a spatial novelty, which we discussed under "contextual novelty" (see, *above*, Paragraph 3.4). We shall argue, however, in our *In-salience hypothesis*, that - if we look closely - also contextual novelty (as any other instance of salience discussed here) can be explained by a mismatch (that is, an incongruity) between a stimulus and a contextually activated schema (see, *below*, Chapter Three, *Proposition One*). Indeed, the attention and memory deserved to "incongruent" (e.g., contextually novel) aspects of a stimulus can be explained by the perceiver's situationally activated schema (or *chart*, *à la* Sokolov [1969]), rather than by the size of the opposite aspects of the stimulus. Support for this argument is provided, for example, by Srull (1981) who examined situations in which items incongruent with a prior expectancy had a set size that is less than, equal to, or greater than that for congruent items. It was found that, contrary to the typical set-size effect reported in literature (see, *above*, Paragraph 3.4), even in the latter case, recall was greater for incongruent items (see, also, Hastie 1980).

Such an effect on recall is not found when the stimulus is *ambiguous*, rather than when it is simply incongruent. We call *ambiguous* a stimulus that cannot be matched with one specific schema. Ha and Hoch (1989, p. 354) define ambiguity as "the potential for multiple interpretations."[108] For example, Berlyne (1958) provided pictures of bizarre animals possessing incompatible attributes of two species (e.g., half dog and half elephant), thus leading to conceptual conflict between expectations aroused by each part of the animal: One feature of the bizarre animal gave little hint of what the rest would have been like. In instances like these, a subject may fail to achieve a perceptual organization at the level of coherence normally attained at a given exposure level. Recognition may not occur and, thus, what results may be best described as perceptual disruption (cf. Bruner and Postman 1949; Yi and Gray 1996).

Incongruity is normally interconnected with other variables that relate to situational settings in general (i.e., Berlyne's collative properties; see Note 70, *above*). In a sense, they all reflect the same underlying dimension, rather than being separate factors; they all have to do with the amount of information in the situation - particularly the amount of information that is new to the individual - and it makes sense to talk of them as one single variable (Hansen 1972). Walker (1964) and Hebb (1966), who talked of the total amount of "environmental stimulation", e.g., propose such a view.

In more recent years, a stream of research within consumer literature has examined the effects of incongruity on the perception of products, salespeople, and the processing of print advertisements. A fundamental result, common throughout these studies - and relevant to our hypothesis -, is: When individuals have expectations - either created within research procedures or schema-based - and receive information which is somewhat incongruent with their expectations, they engage in a more elaborative form of information processing than when information meeting their expectations is encountered (see Stangor and McMillan 1992, for a review of empirical studies). To illustrate this finding, hereafter we present some fundamental articles on the role of incongruity in the processing of marketing communications.

In relation to products, Meyers-Levy and Tybout (1989) considered the effects of congruent versus incongruent information on the development of attitudes towards products. They adapted Rosch's (1978) *Hierarchical categorization model* to products, and operationalized incongruity levels (extreme, moderate, and none) by describing products upon attributes. An incongruity was hypothesized to occur when the total configuration of a product's attributes is not represented in the activated schema. They found that a moderate level of incongruity led subjects to attempt to resolve the incongruity through a cognitive elaboration process and, in turn, to more favorable evaluations (see also, *below*, Chapter Three, Paragraph 2.1.3).[109]

In a study related to encounters with salespeople, Sujan, Bettman, and Sujan (1986) also examined what they termed "schema-incongruent effects." They suggested that, in a selling situation, information is processed differently if the salesperson is incongruent - rather than congruent - with a consumer's expectation of the typical salesperson in the category. In particular, they found that subjects engaged in more systematic or analytical processing when the salesperson encountered was incongruent with the salesperson schema in memory, and that they engaged in simpler or heuristic processing when the salesperson matched the salesperson schema in memory. Moreover, results were found to be independent from subjects' involvement.

In the field of print advertising, Houston, Childers, and Heckler (1987) examined the memory for ad messages when the pictorial material in the ad was either congruent or incongruent with the verbal information. Following the *Expectation-disconfirmation model* (Hastie 1980), they argued that pictures in ads establish expectations for the verbal information and predicted that ads would be remembered better if the copy was discrepant rather than consistent with the picture. Superior memory for the discrepant condition was found in memory for brand names and product classes, whereas both unaided recall and recognition measures were better for the consistent copy condition. More recently, drawing on social cognition research, Heckler and Childers (1992) presented an incongruity framework unrelated to schema theory, using the concept of *theme* - which originated in the study of verbal discourse - to explain the processing of complex information.[110] Under this approach, key dimensions of incongruity were considered the concepts of relevancy and expectancy. They posed *relevancy* as the degree to which a target stimulus directly pertains to the meaning of the theme communicated through a message (e.g., an ad); and *expectancy* as the degree to which a stimulus information fits into some predetermined pattern or structure evoked by the theme (e.g., in relation with the other components of an ad). Thus, congruent stimuli were identified as both relevant and expected; incongruent stimuli as both relevant and unexpected; irrelevant as uninformative. In their empirical analysis, Heckler and Childers (1992) found that unexpected, yet relevant information prompts elaborative processing of ad pictorial elements that result in greater recognition memory.[111]

The important point to be gleaned from this research is that pictures serve as theme-setting advance organizers that create an expectation for the remaining contents of the ad. This allows us to interpret results of the numerous studies that have been published for years on verbal and pictorial combinations in ads (amongst the most important, e.g., Childers and Houston 1984; Childers and Jass 1995; Edell and Staelin 1983; Hollander and Jacoby 1973; Lee and Mason 1999; Lutz and Lutz 1977; Miniard et al. 1991; Peltier 1989; Schmitt, Tavassoli, and Millard 1993; Stafford, Walker, and Blasko 1996; Unnava and Burnkrant 1991a).

Taken together, studies on incongruity suggest that, when information that is somewhat incongruent with prior expectations or schemata is presented, individuals engage in more effortful or elaborative processing. However, the studies by Meyers-Levy and Tybout (1986), Sujan, Bettman and Sujan (1986), and also O'Brien and Myers (1985) on comprehension difficulties that improve memory, suggest that the deviation from expectations need not to be extreme to have this effect.[112] Apparently, a *moderate incongruity* of the information is sufficient to prompt elaboration and it needs not be in direct conflict with expectations. We shall discuss this point under our hypothesis, in the following chapter (see Chapter Three, Paragraph 2.1.3).

4.3.3   Effects of Expectations

Expectations affect not only memory, but also perception of product attributes and their evaluations. A number of researchers believe that generalized expectations regarding the existence of relationships are a major cause of inaccurate, inflated perceptions (see, for review, Johnson and Katrichis 1988). According to this view, the knowledge schemata that facilitate perception and information processing also contain expectations that systematically bias and distort perceptions of attributes. For example, just knowing a brand name leads to different perceptions of the product. In a classic study, Allison and Uhl (1964) found that consumers, knowing the brand name of a beer, had different perceptions of the taste than consumers tasting unbranded beers.

The underlying factor is constituted by the individuals' *past experiences*, which are determined by cultural differences and one's training during life. Cultural and learned perceptions result in expectations that are crucial in product perception. Product attributes or physical characteristics may be divided into two groups based on when they are perceived: Anticipatory attributes (those that are expected or learned and that the consumer thinks a product must have) and actual attributes (those that are perceived when the product is seen). In some circumstances people may rely more on anticipatory attributes, and in others people may rely more on the actual attributes.[113]

There is also very interesting evidence that prior knowledge can affect the basic type of evaluative processing carried out. Fiske (1982) has proposed that individuals may evaluate stimuli in two basic modes. In *piecemeal processing*, the evaluation of a stimulus is the combination of the evaluations of the individual elements or attributes of that stimulus. In *category-based processing*, if a stimulus is successfully categorized in an existing category, the evaluation associated with that category is associated with the stimulus. Fiske and Pavelchak (1984) hypothesized a two-stage process: If the first categorization stage succeeds, then category-based evaluation processing ensues; if categorization fails, piecemeal processing is invoked. Sujan (1985) has examined this categorization approach in a consumer setting. He showed that when the information in a print advertisement matches expectations, there is evidence of category-based processing - faster impression times, more category verbalizations, and fewer attribute verbalizations. When the information does not match expectations, there is evidence for piecemeal processing. Moreover, these effects were found more pronounced for experts than for novices in the product category used.

Prechoice expectations also influence consumers' postpurchase satisfaction, providing an anchor for consumers' assessments of product performances (see, for reviews, Oliver and Winer 1987; Oliver and DeSarbo 1988). Expectations are retrieved as an input for the processes of (dis)confirmation and (dis)satisfaction (van Raaij 1991). If an advertiser emphasizes that his product will outperform all competitors - for example, will get your clothes whiter than any other detergent - then the consumer may have high expectancies for the product and be motivated to buy it.[114] A problem arises, however, if initially high expectations are not met: Not only is the consumer disappointed, but his expectations, the next time he sees the product advertised, will be a lot lower.

4.3.4 Techniques to Improve Unexpectancy

Advertisers have used a variety of executional strategies to improve the unusuality of ad cues and attract attention (see, for reviews, MacInnis, Moorman, and Jaworski 1991; Percy and Rossiter 1992). The common ground of the developed ad design techniques can be traced in the distortion of familiar stimuli to make them prominent and, thus, catch viewers' attention. Such distortions serve to provide memorable tokens to remind consumers of an opportunity which they did not necessarily have in mind when making a choice. Farb (1978, p. 326) noted that "[t]he full recollection of an experience can be triggered [...] by evoking the symbol for it" (see, also, Mick 1986). Then, he concluded that associations facilitates memory, and that they can be achieved only - by definitions - with an unusual, rather than everyday, phenomenon or object.[115]

This semiological conclusion seems to have been implicitly reached also by advertisers who use different devices to improve the level of unexpectancy of their ads. One of the best methods they have discovered for provoking a drift against consumers' expectancies is the use of "surrealistic" techniques, such as the use of chance effects, unexpected juxtapositions, and unorderly connections. By creating unique, unexpected, and dreamlike images in their ads, advertisers try to gain the attention of consumers, to fuel their fantasies and to induce them to view a product in a new light. As a result, surrealistic ads have been used to promote a variety of products (Homer and Kahle 1986). Surrealism, together with anthropomorphism, allegory, and hyperbole, has been classified as a form of *absurdity*, frequently used in advertising (Arias-Bolzmann, Chakraborty, and Mowen 2000), together with other types of rethorical figures (e.g., McQuarry and Mick 1996, 1999; see also Chapter Four, Note 23, *below*).

Distortions of everyday objects have been also achieved by the use of camera angles (Crane 1972, p. 198a). Only few researchers have examined this issue empirically and explored how the camera angle from which an object is viewed in a film or photograph can affect viewers' judgments of that object (Meyers-Levy and Peracchio 1992). These researchers found that when the item (e.g., a person or a box) was photographed from a low camera angle such that the viewer would seem to be looking up at it, the object was judged more positively than when a high camera angle was employed whereby the viewer would seem to be looking down on the object. When the object appeared to be at eye level, viewers' judgments were between the two extremes. Meyers-Levy and Peracchio (1992) contributed to this issue by suggesting not only how certain camera angles commonly used in photographing products for advertising can affect people's product evaluations, but also how readers' involvement acts as a moderator.[116]

The same effect of distortions obtained through a camera angle resulted by the use of cartoons in advertising. The distortion involved in over-large heads helps attract attention, and, by emphasizing man's most expressive feature, it allows more meaning to be packed into a small space. The faces arouse curiosity which is only partially satisfied by reading the one-line captions under them, such that full satisfaction requires one to read the copy block itself. Cartoons, in this context, serve two functions: They are relatively rare in advertising so that they can provide attention-getting contrast, and they promise the rewards of humor. They could be used, for example, in those ads that appeal to fear - so that they might scare readers away. Reducing such fears to the status of nuisances could avoid dangers inherent in those appeals (Crane 1972, p. 198c).

Humor is another popular means to stimulate attention and memory (see, for reviews, Alden, Hoyer, and Lee 1993; Goldsten, Suls, and Anthony 1972). Two general theories of humor that have both conceptual appeal and empirical support have emerged (Kuhlman 1985): *Motivational theories*, which emphasize thematic properties of jokes, cartoons, and the like; and *incongruity theories*, which emphasize, rather than the content, the process variables that pose some incongruity, puzzle, or cognitive dissonance to the individual. Whereas the humor explained by the former theories stems from gratifying a drive that otherwise would have remained pent up (e.g., sexual, aggressive humor); humor explained by the latter theories stems from the physiological arousal changes experienced as an amused sense of pleasure deriving from solving the modest amount of incongruity in the pun. Hence, the importance of timing in delivering jokes and the preference for moderate incongruity. For example, ads employing a contrast between everyday life and the unexpected are generally perceived as more humorous than those employing a contrast between everyday life and the impossible (Alden and Hoyer 1993). According to Speck (1991), incongruity occurs whenever: (1) Two or more elements in a stimulus field cannot be assimilated using a single processing schema; or (2) When the entire stimulus event does not comport with one's expectations regarding that event. A consumer's prior evaluation of an advertised brand, however, has been shown to moderate the effectiveness of humor in advertising (Chattopadhyay and Basu 1990), as well as the weakness/strength of arguments (Cline and Kellaris 1999).

The differentiation between motivational and incongruity theories of humor reflects, in a way, the basic determinants of, respectively, re-salient and in-salient stimuli (see, *below*, Chapter Three, Table 3). In synthesis, whereas taboo content violates the principles of conduct (behavior), incongruity structures violate the principles of logic (thought). Alford (1982) drew a similar analogy by describing taboo humor as a violation of "idealized expectations" and incongruity humor as a violation of "phenomenal expectations." It is not a case that research on humor and salience in the past was carried out as one (see, e.g., Goldstein, Suls, and Anthony 1972; Kuhlman 1985).

4.4 Out-of-Role Behaviors and Salience

A particular class of salient stimuli - linked to unusuality - is peculiar to the *social* context. It refers to people who are salient when they behave in ways that do not fit other people's prior knowledge about them as individuals, as members of a particular social category, or as people in general (Jones and McGillis 1976). As maintained by Fiske and Taylor (1991, p. 249): "[P]eople attend to schema-inconsistent information, across several types of schemas. The behavior of an introvert who suddenly runs for public office, an executive who defers to subordinates, or a person who chew his toenails will all attract attention because the behavior is unexpected for that individual, that role, or people in general. Physically disabled people attract attention in part because they are novel compared to people in general (Langer et al. 1976). All these types of salience depend on violating expectations by being out of character, out of roles, or out of the ordinary."[117]

Social information processing is often very top-down in nature (Srull 1981). One usually has some generalized expectancy of the type of behavior a person will show. These expectations can be developed in a myriad of ways, based, for example, on descriptions of the target from other people, familiarity with their past accomplishments, knowledge of occupation or social roles, or even manner of dress (see, e.g., Schneider, Hastorf, and Ellsworth 1979). Salience may occur because the perceiver's beliefs and, thus, expectations about how a person ought to behave in a certain situation do not match that person's behavior.

Expectations regard a person's social *role, position,* or *identity* (Levine, Resnick, and Higgins 1993). *Social roles* are comprised of the privileges, duties, and obligations of any occupant of a social position (Sarbin and Allen 1968). These expected behaviors are always interdependent with the behaviors of those occupying the other positions in the social structure. For example, in a marketplace, not only do the providers of a service - e.g., bank tellers - adopt a relatively standardized set of behaviors (i.e., read from a common script) when they work, but also this implicit structure is common to the totality of complementary roles - e.g., customers, co-workers, head teller, and branch manager.[118] When a person adopts a role, his behavior is appropriate to the positions he occupies in society and constrained by the expectations associated with the role.

One important result of proper role socialization is the acquired ability to predict the behavior of other role players. When someone is labeled nurse, clerk, or cab driver, one is able to generate a profile of this person based on the characteristics that are thought to covary with this title. The pervasive tendency to "fill out" one's knowledge of a person, given observation of religious, political, or occupational characteristics, is well documented in the literature on person perception and stereotypes.[119] Research in personal selling has found that the salesperson whose behavior is contingent upon the behavior of the customer is more effective than one who does not adjust behavior to meet the customer's specific needs (Weitz 1981).[120] Salesperson and consumer characteristics as well as perceptions about the encounter, such as the demands of the specific environment and other situational cues (Lutz and Kakkar 1976), dictate which behaviors comprise a satisfactory interaction and the particular script which is read within a set of learned behaviors (that is, a repertoire of roles). The customer role in an elegant restaurant, for example, involves very different actions than an appropriate role in a fast-food setting.

We have already mentioned, in the previous review on incongruity (see, *above*, Paragraph 4.3), that consumers' prior knowledge about salespeople has an effect on the type of processing independent of interest or involvement in the product category. Thus, Sujan, Bettman, and Sujan (1986) demonstrated that when a salesperson is consistent with a consumer's perception of the typical salesperson in the category, information is processed differently than when the salesperson is perceived to be inconsistent with the typical salesperson. Furthermore, when searching the most plausible cause for a salesperson's out-of-role behavior, consumers refer to intentional and contingent expectations (van Raaij 1987). Jones and Davis (1965) distinguished internal versus external attributions. With an internal attribution one infers a volitional disposition or attitude of the person - in this case, a salesperson - to tell his real opinion, such that the person can then be trusted. With an external attribution to the situation or convention the person will tell what is expected of him in that situation, and cannot be trusted to tell the truth. However, if a salesperson gives negative information about the company's products, this cannot be attributed to convention or role, and, therefore, it must be attributed to his intention. Jones and Davis (1965) call this a *non-common effect*. Consumer usually look for non-common effects, that is, cues to test the trustworthiness of salespeople.

Social positions imply expectations, too. They are defined as socially recognized categories of actors. When a positional category is assigned to a person, the individual is expected to possess particular attributes and is responded to on the assumption that he has these attributes (Stryker and Statham 1985). Yet, if on the one hand some social positions are social roles, which involve normative expectations regarding appropriate behavior, on the other hand other social positions simply involve probabilistic expectancies about how a person "will" (as opposed to "should") behave. Also this latter type of social position, like the former type discussed above, can cause salience. Assigning a person to a social position causes others to have certain cognitions about the person; therefore, when the person does not fulfill these expectations, the lack of the assumed characteristics makes him salient to the others.

Furthermore, in marketing communications, the vividness of the modality of presentation (audio/video vs. written communications) has been shown to enhance the impact of the information transmitted by the communicator. Chaiken and Eagly (1983) have argued that, when messages are transmitted in videotaped or audiotaped rather than written form, nonverbal cues (e.g., the communicator's physical appearance and/or voice) may draw message recipients' attention to the communicator, increasing the salience of his personal characteristics and, therefore, exert a disproportionate impact on persuasion.[121] Specifically, for positive cues conveying that a communicator is likable or expert, increased salience should enhance persuasiveness; whereas for negative cues conveying that a communicator is unlikable or inexpert, increased salience should decrease persuasiveness. This idea is consistent, moreover, with research on the salience of persons, which indicates that salient individuals are remembered better, viewed as more causally prominent, and have their personal attributes rated more extremely (McArthur 1981; Taylor and Fiske 1978; Taylor and Thompson 1982), and with our hypothesis on the coincidence of stimulus and information cues (see, *below*, Chapter Three, Paragraph 2.1.1).

Social identities, finally, relate to people that, when assigned to social positions by others, internalize these positional designations and come to view themselves as the others view them (Stryker and Statham 1985),[122] thus influencing their self-image (e.g. Graeff 1996).[123] Also activation of a social identity can cause salience and influence perception and judgment.[124] For example, socially categorizing another person as an ingroup versus an outgroup member can substantially affect how this person is perceived and treated (see, e.g., Messick and Mackie 1989; Wilder 1986). Such easily discriminated features as a person's sex, age, or race are particularly likely to be salient in a social situation, especially when those features are in the contextual minority (see, for a review, Higgins and Bargh 1987). McArthur and Friedman (1980), for example, varied the sex, age, and race composition of groups of stimulus persons and found that subjects' stereotypic beliefs influence the overall positivity of their trait ratings for a group member only when that target person was in the contextual minority.

Sex roles, in particular, can provide explanatory power to salience in the mismatching of assumed gender differences, although consumer behavior researchers have met with only limited success in relating sex roles to product perceptions (cf. Meyers-Levy 1988b; Stanaland 2000; and, for a review, Gould 1996). In addition to well-established gender-product and gender-brand interactions (cf. Cohen and Chakravarti 1990), gender preferences for achievement themes (males) and empathy/intimacy themes (females) in advertising have been advanced. Prakash (1992, pp. 49-50) maintained that appeals for males should "tend to portray a sense of mastery, self-assertion, confidence, and comradery, thus appealing to the achievement-oriented roles of the males"; whereas, appeals for females "should portray women socializing in competitive circumstances, but preferably in non-sports activities such as scientific research, journalism, space exploration, or business management. Women could also be shown in noncompetitive situations working by themselves or in some intimate settings with other females or males." The relationship, however, is likely to be far more complex. When sex roles were made salient in two very different ways (Meyers-Levy 1988b), males responded more favorably to self-oriented information whereas females responded more favorably to self-oriented and other-oriented cues (e.g., information on others' judgments and feelings).[125] Sex role activation (by priming introduced after the information but prior to judgment or by strong cues) was found critical in order to produce a gender-based effect. Across three experiments (Schmitt, LeClerc, and Dubé-Rioux 1988), gender schematic subjects (i.e., for whom sex is a particularly salient perceptual cue and organizing heuristic) did not differ from gender aschematic subjects.

4.5   Negativity and Salience

The principle of salience based on expectations has been extended to consider unusuality that derives from negative stimuli. Research in the social psychology field is extremely consistent in indicating that negative stimuli in general are more salient than positive ones and have a stronger effect on a variety of decision outcomes (see, for a review, Kanouse 1984).

The literature on negativity effects can be largely classified into three types of studies (Price 1993). The first consists of experiments that primarily document the existence of the effect (see Taylor 1991, for a review). A second type of study regards attempts to find variables - such as information source, information format, and product category - that moderate the intensity of the negativity effect (see Weinberger, Allen, and Dillon 1981, for a review). Finally, a third type of studies concerns proposals of possible causal explanations for the negativity effect (see Skowronski and Carlston 1989, for a review). Although several hypotheses have emerged, the most prominent is that "negative information is disproportionately weighted during integration processes in which diverse information cues are weighted and then combined, perhaps in accordance with an adding or averaging rule, to form unitary impressions." (Price 1993, p. 2).

Specifically, for the occurrence of salience from negative stimuli, the explanation that has been provided is that most people expect mildly positive stimuli in general. Most people are optimistic about the outcomes they expect from others and from life in general (Parducci 1968). As for social stimuli, for example, people usually tend to rate other individuals positively (cf. Fiske and Taylor 1991, p. 249). Hence, given this optimistic view, negative stimuli are relatively unexpected and, thus, salient. Fiske (1980) has argued that perceivers put both weight and attention into a person's most informative attributes. Considered that the evaluative scale value of an attribute can be broken down into valence (sign or direction) and extremity (polarization or intensity), she maintained that - apart from the influence of context - informativeness is the result of the properties of an attribute, such as its evaluative valence (positive or negative) and its evaluative extremity (distance from the scale midpoint). Considerable evidence has confirmed that negatively valenced attributes (but this principle further applies to extreme attributes - see, *below*, Paragraph 4.6) are informative: They attract selective attention at input, and also receive more weight than positive attributes (see Fiske 1980, for a review).[126]

Given the power of negative information, negative publicity is a primary concern for marketers especially today, as the ability to disseminate such information to large and geographically dispersed consumers is rapidly increasing (Klein and Shiv 1996). The use of "attack" ads by marketers, very popular both in political and in consumer product contexts, as well as the uncontrollable information spread through the Internet web pages and discussion groups, makes the use of negative publicity very dangerous for companies, due to its disproportionate effects. Two implications of negative information in advertising policy and consumer interactions are particularly relevant in our discussion on salience: Namely, the effects on messages framing and on categorization. Negatively framed promotional messages are those messages which focus on the adverse consequences or benefits lost from not using a product. Although most of the earlier studies have focused on messages that are positively framed (i.e., present benefits gained from product use, which are designed to generate positive emotions, affect, and cognitions), for a variety of circumstances - e.g., deodorant and health-related appeals - negatively framed messages have become an accepted and important strategic approach (Homer and Yoon 1992). Although their attentional value has been recognized, their effects on persuasion have produced mixed results (e.g., Levin and Gaeth 1988; Meyerowitz and Chaiken 1987; Shiv, Edell, and Payne 1997). Though conventional wisdom suggests that appeals identifying negative aspects or consequences of an issue can be highly persuasive if individuals are offered clear and effective solutions to the issue (Sternthal and Craig 1974), recent research has found that effectiveness of negatively framed appeals is a function of product risk, personal relevance, and involvement (Donovan and Jalleh 1999; Meyers-Levy and Maheswaran 1990; Maheswaran and Meyers-Levy 1990). This conclusion holds that negatively framed messages are more effective when individuals are sufficiently involved with the issue to process it in a predominantly detailed manner. Indeed, when issue involvement is low and the message is heuristically processed, messages that frame the appeal in terms of its benefits (positive framing) seem likely to be more effective.[127]

As for the effects of negative information on categorization, according to the *Accessibility-diagnosticity model* (Feldman and Lynch 1988; Lynch, Marmorstein, and Weigold 1988), consumers use a potential input for judgment and choice if it is accessible in memory and if they perceive it as more diagnostic than other accessible inputs.[128] The model emphasizes that, due to consumers' "cognitive misery" (Taylor 1981), easy accessibility and perceived (as opposed to objective) diagnosticity determine the likelihood of information utilization. In this perspective, not only is extremely negative attribute information salient (e.g., Fiske 1980), but also it is diagnostic because it suggests one categorization (i.e., low quality) over other possibilities. Further research on the negativity effect in impression formation has demonstrated that extremely negative attributes generally have strong implications for products' category membership, whereas less negative features are commonly owned by high-, average-, and low-quality products (Skowronski and Carlston 1987, 1989). For example, poor handling (an extremely negative attribute) is perceived as peculiar of only low-quality automobiles, whereas average handling (a neutral feature) can be found in many high-, average-, and low-quality automobiles. Hence, extremely negative information is useful for categorizing a product as low in quality, whereas less negative information is less useful. Even the impact of vivid and accessible word-of-mouth information is reduced when this extremely negative, more diagnostic information is available (Herr, Kardes, and Kim 1991). In general, extremely negative cues are less ambiguous than positive or neutral cues (for exceptions, see Skowronski and Carlston 1987, 1989), and this is especially apparent in product judgment contexts (see, e.g., Mizerski 1982; Wright 1974).

4.6 Extremity and Salience

The same principle evoked for negative stimuli has been used to explain salience generated by extreme stimuli (Fiske 1980). Based on the moderate positivity bias well-established in person perception research (see, *above*, Paragraph 4.5), it was demonstrated that perceivers give relatively high attention and weight to cues that deviate from the modal position (extreme cues) as well as to cues whose evaluations fall below the psychological midpoint (negative cues).

Extremity is defined as a deviation from the central tendency - so it can constitute either more or less of an attribute than usual. Models of categorization, such as the *Accessibility-diagnosticity model* (Feldman and Lynch 1988), formally support the relationship of extremity to informativeness: A certain amount of variation between stimuli serves to distinguish them, and one would expect higher weights to be placed on the cues taken as the bases for categorization in that setting. This result has been obtained in social perception (see, for a review, Fiske 1980): Modal attributes, or familiar ones, have been found to have less impact - since they do not differentiate stimuli - than non-modal information, whether their valence is positive or negative. "For example, people stare at extreme positive social stimuli, such as celebrities, and at extremely negative stimuli, such as car accidents. Since both positive and negative extremes are more unusual than moderate stimuli, extreme stimuli are salient." (Fiske and Taylor 1991, p. 249).

In the advertising literature, extremity regards either the nature of products, or the copy claims, or the pictorial part of the ads. It is rare that it is the nature itself of goods to generate salience. Nevertheless, in recent years, some controversial products - such as alcohol, tobacco, and condoms - have been banned, if not from magazines, at least from television in many countries, so that their appearance in media would cause salience at least for their rarity (cf. Wells, Burnett, and Moriarty 1992, pp 46-48; also, Fox et al. 1998).

A leisure danger theme may allow ads to make a contribution to consumers in a specific target market by elaborating on their cultural conflicts: As it is generally for *paired oppositions* (i.e., conflicting and competing categories that people use in thinking about certain phenomena), the extremes of fear and daring are not culturally neutral (Curlo and Lerman 1999).[129] When extremity is searched, rather than avoided, advertisers use it to position their products by giving them the lure of originality and uniqueness (cf. Mowen 1993, pp. 122-123). This conventional tendency of advertisers to use some degree of claim exaggeration (Wyckham 1985), although it may enhance attention, could have opposite effects on advertising effectiveness. Specifically, research in social psychology suggests that the optimal level of advertising claim extremity may depend on the level of source credibility, such as the advertiser reputation (cf. Goldberg and Hartwick 1990). According to Lutz

(1985), advertiser credibility and advertising claim extremity combine to affect ad credibility, the extent to which a consumer perceives claims made about a given brand to be truthful. In turn, ad credibility, together with other perceptions of the ad, is said to influence individual attitudes, toward both the advertisement itself and the brand being advertised.[130]

If a significant degree of exaggeration is used, when presenting advertising in advance of a consumer trial, such as sampling, the advertiser runs the risk that exaggeration will be inversely related to advertising benefits, in addition to the obvious possibility of legal problems for puffed or deceptive ads. In this case, consumers' expectations - as pretrial beliefs about the product (Olson and Dover 1979) - may be set at such a high level that when the product is sampled its performance is rated lower than it would have been in the absence of advertising (Marks and Kamins 1988). This contrast effect in perceptual judgments has been previously demonstrated for social stimuli (Hovland, Harvey, and Sherif 1957). It was suggested that reversal of expected results is a product of the extremity of the subject's initial position on an issue. Thus, stimuli that appear close to the initial position will tend to be judged closer than they actually are, while stimuli that deviate too far from the initial position will be judged to be farther away than they actually are. For example, in an exploratory study on sex roles in advertising, Kilbourne (1984) found that if subjects tend to view the individuals in the advertisements as similar to themselves or their roles, then results pursued by advertisers deriving from comparative appraisal should ensue. If, on the other hand, the roles depicted in the advertisements are seen as highly discrepant from their own, a boomerang effect might result as subject's attitudes would shift to an opposite direction. Whichever effect occurs it would depend upon the degree to which subjects' anchors differ from the roles portrayed in the ads.

In general, extremity has been used in advertising to do something more than to simply "promote" the product. It has been used to make an ad "great" in the context of social discourse, that is, to make an ad so unique that it becomes a topic of conversation.[131] Advertisements that "get talked about" have a common denominator, "that of being different from the mainstream, from the status quo. In the process, they surprise. They may even shock." (Marra 1990, as reported in Alperstein 1990, p. 16). However, since disgusting or horror scenes are usually discharged from ads as they can generate negative attitudes or perceptual defense, advertisers have turned to two main classes of extreme stimuli to achieve these results, namely, celebrity endorsement and sexual content.

Although the use of celebrity endorsement has become commonplace in advertising, certain characteristics of celebrity sources can stand out prominent in an ad (MacInnis, Moorman, and Jaworski 1991; Kirmani and Shiv 1998). However, as in all the ads that employ extreme cues, while the potential benefits of using celebrity spokespersons are significant (e.g., better ad and product recall, higher interest, potential better credibility and affect that could be generalized to the brand), so are the risks (cf. Lynch and Schuler; McDaniel 1999; Misra and Beatty 1990).

Analogously, although sexual content has become relatively usual in the mainstream media, it seems quite likely that explicit sexual stimuli in an ad will elicit attention to it. At the very least, blatant sexual content should elicit an orienting response - i.e., a short-term increase in attention (Baron 1982).[132] Attention has been shown to be correlated with physiological arousal (Appel, Weinstein, and Weinstein 1979).[133] Research examining the use of sex in advertising has defined sex according to two constructs: Nudity, and suggestiveness (cf. Belch et al. 1982).[134] It has been found that the use of both nudity and suggestiveness in advertisements elicit physiological and cognitive reactions from viewers, with women reacting much more to suggestive ads than do men. Moreover, both opposite sex and same sex nude ads elicit strong physiological reactions, with appealing and offensive cognitive reactions respectively (Belch et al. 1982). The implications for advertisers are apparent: Sex elicits more attention but, at the same time, there could be detrimental effects. First of all, reactions may not always be favorable; rather the arousal could be a result of offensiveness and/or dislike of the advertisement. There is also evidence that the desirable effects on attitudes and memorability of erotically based appeals are weakened or turn negative as the levels of nudity increase (see LaTour, Pitts, and Snook-Luther 1990, for a review). Second, sexual material may affect advertising impact by altering information processing strategies and attentional capacity. This argument assumes that sexual material may absorb attentional capacity, making the ad message a lower priority input than the sexual material and, thus, acting as a distractor drawing attention from the message of the ad (cf. Petty and Cacioppo 1986).[135] However, whereas it is often claimed that sexual content has a distracting effect, Severn, Belch, and Belch (1990) showed that, regardless of a verbal copy manipulation, an explicit sexual illustration (i.e., a nude depiction of a man and a woman in a suggestive pose), in a real magazine ad for a new brand of shoes, generated equal brand recall and significantly stronger brand purchase intention. Such results imply that sexual appeals in ads work for products for which implied sensory gratification or social approval for using the brand are among the possible purchase motives.

Furthermore, specific research was conducted on controversial sexual content (cf. Percy and Rossiter 1992). Bello, Pitts and Etzel (1983) demonstrated that controversial sexual content in television commercials fails to improve affect toward the product or purchase intent, but it does make the commercial more interesting. On the other hand, positive persuasion results were obtained for sexual appeals in magazine ads where there is an appropriate "match-up" (Baker and Churchill 1977; Kahle and Homer 1985; Kamins 1990; Stanaland 2000) or motivational rationale (Rossiter and Percy 1987) for using a sexual appeal in association with the product type.[136] Finally, while the above studies employed explicit sexual content, other research investigated the other extreme: The use of a subliminal sexual appeal. Caccavale, Wanty, and Edell (1982) examined the well-known speculations that sexual implants in brand advertisements increase the viewer's attitudes and purchase intentions.[137] They included in the experiment two types of copy: One having sexual connotations, and another much plainer. The sexual copy was based on theories presented by Key (1972) concerning verbal pronunciation and letter arrangement.[138] Results by Caccavale, Wanty, and Edell (1982), however, did not support these hypotheses. Ruth, Mosatch, and Kramer (1989), who based their study on the Freudian theory of symbolism obtained different results. By employing real magazine ads for liquor expertly coded for presence or absence of Freudian symbolism for intercourse, they demonstrated a significant effect of the intercourse-symbolic ads on purchase intention, which could be only weakened by some other possible confounding difference between the two types of ads, such as attitude towards the ad, which was not measured.

5. MOTIVATIONAL FORMS OF SALIENCE

5.1   The Principle of Involvement

Apart from the principle of figure-ground, which has been evoked to explain salience in an immediate context (see Section Three, *above*), and the principle of unusuality, which has been used to explain salience in a larger context (see Section Four, *above*), the remaining forms of salience can be explained by the principle of involvement, due to internal and (also) external factors to the individual. Specifically, Fiske and Taylor (1991, pp. 249-250) recognize two cases: (1) Instructions to attend to a stimulus (i.e., external manipulations); and (2) Personal relevance to perceivers' goals.

Deliberate interventions into the subjects' will are due to external causes, whereas personal relevance is due to internal drives. According to Menon and Soman (1999, p. 8), "[...] goal-oriented processing is likely to facilitate the learning of goal-relevant information in the message. Evidence suggests that recall and comprehension of stimuli are facilitated if people are provided with some theme or goal (such as objectives or questions) at the time of processing [...]. Goals help individuals determine the relevance of incoming information, resulting in knowledge being encoded, interpreted, and organized in memory around the underlying theme or goal."

Instructions to attend to a stimulus, together with *personal relevance* (see, *below*, Paragraph 5.3), are causes of salience which are basically motivational, that is, related to the subject's will to attend the stimulus: They generate involvement with the stimulus, no matter if their origin is external or internal. Therefore, these remaining two classes of salience occurrences cannot be referred to "in-salience" - as it will be defined in Chapter Three (*below*, in

Proposition One) - but rather to "re-salience," (*below*, Paragraph 2.4.3) that is, to a complementary form of salience which is basically motivational (Guido 1998) - inasmuch as the attention they elicit is voluntary, directed to the satisfaction of a goal, rather than being passively caught by the stimulus.[139] Consequently, they will not be discussed in detail in the present review, but treated in general terms in the following paragraphs.

5.2   Instructions to Attend to a Stimulus and Salience

It has been maintained that a stimulus is salient when someone is asked to pay attention to it (Fiske and Taylor 1991, p. 250). *Instructions to attend to a stimulus* are the most direct form of manipulating attention. It has been used both in cognitive (e.g., Koffka 1935) and in social perception (cf. McArthur 1980). By explicitly instructing people to watch one person rather than another, Taylor and Fiske (1975, Experiment 2) demonstrated a causation effect generated by the differential prominence of the target stimulus (cf. also, *above*, Paragraph 4.3.1 on *Top-of-the-head phenomenon*), but not a preferential recall.

Instructions from the experimenter to observe a stimulus have also been used in marketing and consumer research. Alba and Chattopadhyay (1986), for example, operationalized salience in terms of the amount of time subjects were exposed to and thought about a brand (i.e., subjects in the high salience condition were instructed to concentrate on a brand for one minute). Likewise, Kirmani and Wright (1989) explicitly "coached" sample subjects about attribute importance by instructing them to treat a target attribute as an important decision criterion.

A consumer may be even forced to attend to a stimulus, when the external pressures towards the stimulus cannot be escaped.[140] Some marketing examples of this principle of forced attention are provided by such intrusive personal selling techniques - as door-to-door, foot-in-the-door, etc. - where the perspective buyer can barely avoid the "impositions" of the salesman.

5.2.1   The Inhibition Effect on Memory

An important effect - which has been studied by operationalizing salience as instructions to attend to a stimulus - is that of inhibiting memory for stimuli which *compete* with the salient one. In two related studies by Alba and Chattopadhyay (1985, 1986), salience - defined as prominence *or* "level of activation" of a stimulus in memory -[141] was directly set by the instructions of the experimenters (i.e., having subjects *think about* a particular brand or product category). All subjects were given some familiar "cue" brand and then were asked to recall all other brands in that category.[142]

It was shown that the level of exposure (i.e., the frequency and the recency of exposure) of product-related information (i.e., brand names) enhances salience (we would say "relevance" - cf., *below*, Chapter Three, Paragraph 2.1.9) - thereby increasing the ability of a consumer to learn and recall that information -, whereas memory for competing brands, including those that otherwise would be candidates for purchase, was impaired. Similarly, it was shown that thinking about a particular product category can suppress the retrieval of competitive product categories (e.g., deodorant sprays versus deodorant soaps). Moreover, such recall inhibitions were demonstrated across a number of different induction techniques for operationalizing salience.[143]

The inhibition effect on memory for non-salient stimuli could be synthesized by recognizing that salient cues (i.e., brand names) would expand the retrieval set in memory if they serve as reminders of previously unrecalled categories (*category cuing*); on the contrary, they would inhibit retrieval of non-salient cues if they represent instances of accessible categories (*part-category cuing*). Apart from brands and product classes, Alba and Chattopadhyay (1985) argued that it would have been relevant to study recall of *attribute* information, to test if increasing the salience of a single attribute can inhibit recall of other attributes, thus resulting in a reduction of their situational salience (cf. Myers and Alpert 1977; Ryan and Etzel 1976). This strategy would suggest that "advertisers may be able to inhibit consideration of threatening competitors and unfavorable attributes by making salient in their ads nonthreatening competitors and their own attribute strengths." (Alba, Hutchinson, and Lynch 1991, pp. 19-20).[144]

Alba and Chattopadhyay's "preferred explanation" for the reason why inhibition occurs was that, when a brand name is salient (e.g., when it is presented as a cue), this causes an increase in the associative strength between the brand and its product category, thereby impeding consumer attempts to recall other brand from the same product category. During memory retrieval, a salient brand would be continually and unavoidably resampled at the expense of remaining unrepresented brands. As a result, the number of other recalled brands may be reduced.[145] This explanation was originally advanced by Rundus (1973), who proposed that the probability of retrieving a brand name is determined by the strength of association between the product category and the brand name divided by the summed strengths of associations between the product category and all brand names (the so-called *ratio rule*).

Miniard, Unnava, and Bhatla (1989) challenged this appeal to the ratio rule, by contrasting the rather compelling results of Alba and Chattopadhyay with an experiment that provided weak support for their conclusions. They used as stimulus material specially prepared print ads, devoid of illustrations, which were randomly assigned to subjects depending on the treatment condition. They concluded that their weak results could most probably be due to methodological weaknesses in the context conditions of recall: For example, multiple participants for each experimental session, lack of pictorial stimuli in the sample ads, low strength of treatment induction, and high strength of pre-experimental salience (which was originally supposed null by Alba and Chattopadhyay). An alternative explanation was proposed by Guido (1996a), who suggested, following Posner (1978), that because salience was induced by a set of specific instructions, limits to conscious attention could have inhibited stimuli not matching the elicited schemata (see also, *below*, Chapter Three, Note 90).

5.3   Personal Goal-Relevance and Salience

Differently from *instructions to attend to a stimulus* which set a goal from outside the individual, *personal relevance* concerns the individual's inner goals and interests. However, either when the perceiver attends the stimulus because he is instructed to do so under external pressures, or when he attends the stimulus because he is personally motivated, attention is determined by individual goals, rather than by being spontaneously attracted by the stimulus. Both cases, therefore, can be defined as instances of re-salience (see, *below*, Chapter Three, Paragraph 2.4.3), a construct that is complementary to in-salience. Although this is not the focus of our research, because involvement - at the basis of re-salience - also acts as an important moderating variable of in-salience, its role will be discussed in the next chapter (see, *below*, *Proposition Four*).

Involvement regards a different principle of salience according to which an individual attends a stimulus because it is relevant to his personal goals (Fiske and Taylor 1991, p. 249; see, also, Haley 1968, 1971; and Jolibert and Baumgartner 1997, for a definition of personal goals). In social perception, for example, people attend to significant others (e.g., a boss, a date). In consumer research, involvement has been typically conceptualized in terms of an individual's motivation to process marketing stimuli (see, *below*, Chapter Three, Paragraph 2.2.3: *Involvement is a moderator of in-salience*), the predominant viewpoint being that consumers are more likely to engage in information processing under conditions of high rather than low involvement (e.g., Celsi and Olson 1988; Greenwald and Leavitt 1984; Haugtvedt, Petty, and Cacioppo 1992; Ratneshwar, Pechmann, and Shocker 1996; Zaichkowsky 1985).

As a cause of salience, involvement, in turn, is mediated by other variables that intervene on the perceiver's focus of attention. The social perception literature, for example, has named, in particular, two variables: Perceiver's point of view, and arousal. First of all, the perceptual orientation of the perceiver - that is, if he is an actor or an observer of a stimulus behavior - can differently influence involvement and, thus, salience. This attentional focus, in turn, has been shown to have important consequences for various judgments made by social perceivers (cf. Borgida and Howard-Pitney 1983).[146] Secondly, the effect of arousal on attention - which has been manipulated, for example, with the presence of props (i.e., cameras or audiences) - can reduce the range of cues attended to, thus increasing the salience of the most obvious or familiar cues (cf. Taylor and Fiske 1978, Table II, p. 262, and pp. 276-277).

Indeed, according to our hypothesis, the role of involvement in the occurrence of salience is primary, as it acts both as an antecedent of personal relevance and as a moderator in the interpretation process of the contextual incongruity between a stimulus and a perceiver's schema (see, *below*, Chapter Three, *Proposition Four*).

6. SUMMARY

The studies reviewed in this chapter supply an updated view of the marketing and consumer research regarding physically salient stimuli. We started by considering the nature of the process of perception at the beginning of which salience provides the attentional and interpretive resources to make a stimulus memorable. In an information processing model segmented by stages, a salient stimulus regards all of them: Sensation, attention, interpretation, and memory. Although most of the research on salience has been conducted with social stimuli, the soundness of the applicability of the essential findings of this literature to the marketing context has been convincingly demonstrated by providing empirical evidence. The common ground across the definitions of salience proposed in social and non-social contexts appears to be its nature of *prominence*. Thus, a salient stimulus is prominent when it has - under different aspects - a superior impact to that of other perceived stimuli.

By acknowledging this core, common meaning, Fiske and Taylor (e.g., 1991) have provided a list of disparate causes of social salience, which we have used as a framework to review the marketing and consumer literature in this field. Three are the contexts that dominate the different forms of salience recognizable in literature: First of all, an *immediate context*, where salience is explained by the principle of figure-ground. According to this, "people direct their attention to those aspects of the perceptual field that stand out - the figure - rather than to the background of the setting - the ground." (Sears, Peplau, and Taylor 1991, p. 45). In such a context, we considered the three cases of salience: (1) Figural stimuli, (2) Stimuli dominating the sensory field, and (3) Contextually novel stimuli. Specifically, first, we reviewed the literature on bright, moving, and complex marketing stimuli. Secondly, we considered physical factors affecting in-salience - such as intensity (together with clarity and size), position (together with spatial perspective), and frequency (together with duration). And, thirdly, we examined those marketing stimuli which appear in isolation - whether this isolation was obtained either by performing an additional operation on an item within a group of similar alternatives, or by directly manipulating the items by inserting a different type of item within a group of similar items, or by intervening in the structural organization within a group - focusing, in particular, on the learning of an item isolated against a crowded or homogeneous background (the so-called *von Restorff effect*).

Then, we examined salience in a *larger context*, explained by the principle of unusuality, according to which a stimulus is said to be salient when it violates a perceiver's prior knowledge and expectations he can derive from that knowledge. In such a context, we referred to the cases of: (1) Statistically novel, (2) Unexpected, (3) Out-of-role, (4) Negative, and (5) Extreme stimuli. Specifically, in reviewing the consumer literature for statistically novel stimuli, we considered two relevant dimensions, namely uniqueness (the degree to which a particular stimulus differs from other exemplars) and (lack of) familiarity (the degree of an individual's [lack of] prior experience with a certain stimulus). We focused, then, on nature, sources, and formation of consumers' expectations and discussed, in particular, the process of causal attribution that has been found to be affected by salient stimuli (*Top-of-the-head phenomenon*). A crucial topic to the extent of our following model (see, *below*, Chapter Three) is what we addressed in reviewing the incongruity literature, by considering those perceptual events that fail to confirm established expectations. The effects of unexpectancy and the executional strategies to improve it have a major part in the practical manipulations of salience. Consumer literature on other kinds of stimuli was then reviewed: Specifically, we examined a particular class of social stimuli, out-of-role behaviors (i.e., the mismatching of a person's social role, position, or identity); together with negative and extreme stimuli resulting, respectively, from the evaluative valence or extremity of the information.

Finally, we addressed the remaining *motivational forms of salience*, explained by the principle of involvement. This group of factors includes salience occurrences due to. (1) Instructions to attend to a stimulus, and (2) Personal goal-relevance - whose detailed review was beyond the scope of the present research (focused on perception-based definitions of salience - rather than memory-based ones - as those set by goal relevance). Instructions to attend to a stimulus and goal-relevance, indeed, act on perceiver involvement, a variable that is posed in our in-salience hypothesis as an alternative cause of salience (i.e., re-salience). Nonetheless, particular attention was given to an important *inhibition effect* on memory that was studied under the instruction condition.

Our review fleshes out the problem areas introduced at the beginning of this book - namely: (a) If perceptual forms of salience share a common nature and origin; (b) How consumers process marketing information; (c) How information is compared with schemata in memory; and (d) How the relevance of certain elements within a schema facilitates the memory of in-salient information - which will be addressed in the following model of in-salience (Chapter Three) and empirically tested in a multi-level experiment conducted within an advertising setting (Chapter Four).

NOTES

[1] According to Gardner (1982, p. 179): "Krech and Crutchfield (1948) are credited with the earliest definition of salience [in reference to memory]: 'Saliency refers to the fact that not all of a man's beliefs stand out with equal prominence in his cognitive field. He may be more acutely aware of certain of his beliefs than others, they may enter his thoughts more readily, they may be more frequently verbalized - they are, in a word, salient.'"

[2] Perception is not merely a function of sensory inputs alone, rather it is the result of two kinds of stimuli which interact to form the personal perceptions experienced by each individual. The first type of inputs is constituted by physical stimuli (which are at the basis of in-salience); whereas the other type is constituted by memory stimuli, that is, individual predispositions based on past experiences such as expectations, motives, goals, etc. (cf. Schiffman and Kanuk 1991, p. 157). In our model of salience (Guido 1998), the latter stimuli are at the basis of a complementary form of salience (namely, re-salience). For a detailed review of memory-based definition of salience, see Guido (1996a).

[3] "These ideas were further developed by Narayana and Markin (1975) who suggested that those brands which did not feature in a consumer's evoked set could be subdivided into an *inert set* (those the consumer was aware of but where their feelings for the brands were neutral - neither positive nor negative) and an *inept set* (those the consumer was aware of but where feelings for these brands was negative)." (Rice 1993, p. 85).

[4] Individuals confront a daily barrage of marketing messages: This creates a widening gap between available and usable information, a phenomenon known as *information overload*. Such a phenomenon has been evident for decades, but today this gap has grown (together with the gap between the information rich and the information poor). Past research estimated, for example, that the average American consumer is exposed to between 200 and 500 promotional messages every day (Britt, Adams, and Miller 1972; Bovee and Arens 1995); other studies on advertising effects reported as many as 1500 advertisements to which a consumer is potentially exposed every day (Bauer and Greyser 1968). As reported by Elliott and Speck (1998), network prime time is 24 percent promotional material, consumer magazines contain 50 percent advertising, and many newspapers are 64 percent advertising. However, consumers were found to perceive only 76 advertisements per day, and as few as 12 of these messages were remembered. Furthermore, only 30 percent of the noticed ads generated any active processing (i.e., consumers reported that the ads were informative, enjoyable, annoying, or offensive), suggesting that consumers process many promotional messages with minimal levels of involvement (Hawkins and Hoch 1992). Similarly, in a study using an eye-tracking camera, recording what consumers actually saw when exposed to commercials, one result was that in some 43 percent of the commercials, the sponsor's name was overlooked (Abrams 1983). The selectivity of perception was also demonstrated in a mass-merchandising environment, where the average supermarket, for example, exposes the shopper to some 7500 items (Robertson, Zielinski, and Ward 1984).

[5] For reviews of perception in marketing (see Hansen 1972), the reader may turn to such classic sources as Allport (1955), Dember (1960), Vernon (1962), or to briefer marketing-oriented presentations like Crane (1972) or Douglas, Field, and Tarpey (1967). More recent texts in the psychology of perception include: Atkinson (1988); Kitchin and Freundschuh (2000); and, with a

consumer orientation: Dubois (2000); Olson and Sentis (1986); Sirgy (1983); and a critical edition of *Consumer Psychology* (forthcoming) in four volumes.

[6] Some texts in consumer behavior present stage models of information processing (comprehensive of the process of perception). Among these, Engel, Blackwell, and Miniard (1997): Information Processing = Exposure + Attention + Comprehension (Categorization + Elaboration + Organization) + Acceptance + Retention; Loundon and Della Bitta (1993): Information Processing = Acquisition (Exposure + Sensation + Attention) + Perceptual Encoding; Peter and Olson (1998): Information Processing = Exposure + Interpretation (Attention + Comprehension); Sternthal and Craig (1982): Information Processing = Exposure + Reception + Cognitive Analysis.

[7] Two notable exceptions are some segments of the stimulus-acquisition process (the number of stores shopped, salespeople consulted, and so on) and some overt responses (such as brands purchased). Apart from such directly observed overt actions, the majority of information-processing activities must be inferred for determining their influence on other variables and measures.

[8] Perception has to do with the selection and organization of sensory data in the environment, whereas learning involves changes in behavior that necessitates meaning and order being given to sensory data.

[9] The stage model represented in Figure 1 and the above discussion suggest a linear flow from sensation to memory. However, these processes occur virtually simultaneously and are clearly interactive. That is, "our memory influences the information we are exposed to, attend to, and the interpretations we assign. At the same time, memory itself is being shaped by the information it is receiving." (Hawkins, Best, and Coney 1992, p. 221).

[10] Earlier writings that dealt with this distinction used the terminology of person (or social) perception versus object (or nonsocial) perception. Later, the term "cognition" has replaced the term "perception". This because the focus of psychologists in contrasting the two domains have shifted, over the last 40 years, from Gestaltist principles of perceptual organization to information processing orientation and its mediating cognitive activities.

[11] Heider (1958), however, preferred the term "thing" perception over "object" perception, since both things and persons could be the "objects" of perception.

[12] As reported by Ostrom (1984, p. 22): "A modest number of studies have compared peoples responses to social and nonsocial stimuli, but even at the empirical level, this work has not been brought together in a single source."

[13] "[... 1. The] *building-block* view: [...] the processes involved in dealing cognitively with nonsocial events are simpler and conceptually more fundamental than the processes involved with social events. The study of cognitive processing in the context of nonsocial stimuli provides a foundation on which the more complex social cognition principles can be built. This position is inherent in the writings of Heider (1958), Higgins et al. (1981), MacLeod (1951), Sherif and Cantril (1945, 1946), Simon (1976), and Tagiuri (1958, 1969). The kinds of variables that are viewed as supplementing nonsocial cognition principles are individual differences, affect, personal experience, and self-relevance. [2.] A second viewpoint, the *fundamentalist position,* argues that there are no intrinsic differences in the cognitive processes involved in social versus nonsocial cognition. Each person develops a wide variety of cognitive capacities and processing mechanisms to cope with the stimulus world, and these are available regardless of whether the stimulus events involve social or nonsocial objects. This position is present in the writings of Eiser and Stroebe (1972), Hastie, Ostrom, Ebbesen, Wyer, Hamilton, and Carlston (1980), Isen and Hastorf (1982), Kretch and Crutchfield (1948), McArthur (1980), and Peak (1958). [... 3.] A

third point of view is [... t]he *realist* position [which] is in many ways the opposite of the building block position. [...] Realists argue that the foundation of all cognitive processes derives from episodes involving social objects (as opposed to nonsocial objects). [... D]evelopmental psychologists have noted that immediately upon birth (and even before) the infant is immersed in a social environment. It is an environment in which other persons are perceptually salient, an environment that places social demands on the infant, and one that responds to the infant's actions in predictable ways. [...] It follows from the above that the stimulus episodes that should have the greatest impact on the initial development of cognitive mechanisms are episodes involving social rather than nonsocial objects. Strategies of encoding and retrieval, schematic and categorical representations, information integration styles, and response capacities all evolve primarily in response to processing social knowledge. It is only later that the infant must begin mastering its nonsocial world to obtain desired outcomes. This position has been advocated by Chandler (1977), Damon (1981), DeCharms (1968), Forgas (1981[...]), Gelman and Spelke (1981), Hoffman (1981), Piaget (1952, 1954), and Zajonc (1980). For some (but not all) of its advocates, this position shares with the fundamentalist viewpoint a belief in the continuity of processes between social and nonsocial cognition." (Ostrom 1984, pp. 24-26).

[14] For example, Hoffman (1981) summed up a list of eight differences mentioned by Glick (1978) and Gelman and Spelke (1981), and then added three more of his own. Bretherton, McNew, and Beeghly-Smith (1981) reviewed some twelve differences provided by Shields (1978) and add two more of their own.

[15] "[A]ttention often focuses on what is currently being encoded. If you are thinking about something external, it is at least temporarily represented in your mind. However, attention is not limited to the encoding of external stimuli; whatever occupies consciousness is defined as the focus of attention. Attention thus can also be occupied by information retrieved from memory. If you are thinking about something you remember, that memory is the focus of your attention. " (Fiske and Taylor 1991, p. 246).

[16] Among the cases of statistical novelty, Taylor and Fiske (1978, Table I, p. 260) also consider the case of "false feedback about the self" and, by referring to the impressive quantity of data collected by Duval, Wicklund, and their associates (e.g., Duval 1976; Duval and Hensley 1977; Duval and Wicklund 1972, 1973; Wicklund 1975), they maintain that the salience effect holds for self-perception. We believe, however, that these authors in their experiments were not manipulating salience (i.e., of the self), but rather an attributional state. Mowen (1983) advanced a similar criticism on labeling effects.

[17] The figure is formed by the contour, the common boundary between two visual fields (called areas). The contour can operate on both fields but not at the same time. A well-known example is Rubin's (1921/1958) ambiguous picture of vase/twins, in which it is not possible to perceive simultaneously the figure of a vase and the figure of two face profiles.

[18] This article was mistakenly reported by Gardner (1982) as "Simon and Feigenbaum (1962)".

[19] As acknowledged by Zaltman and Wallendorf (1983), "[p]eople frequently confuse intensity with brightness. Intensity is a physical value, and brightness is the perceived magnitude. For example, suppose that a 10-watt flashlight is used outside a house on a sunny day and inside the house in a dark room. Wherever the flashlight is used, the intensity of the light is the same, since the light bulb is the same. However, the brightness is different. Inside the dark room the light seems to be brighter than outside. The perceived magnitude is different because the environment is different." (p. 582). For a brief review on brightness studies, cf. MacEachren and Mistrick (1992).

[20] The term color in physics includes both chromatic color (such as blue or orange) and achromatic color (such as black or white). These two types of color are perceived differently.

Achromatic colors are described in terms of contrast, whereas chromatic colors are described in terms of hue, brightness, and saturation (Beck 1972).

[21] Saturation was found strictly related to the salience of a color in a study by Whitfield (1981, p. 87), where the salience of a stimulus was equated, following Rosch (1975) and Tversky (1977), to "its referential status and defined as the degree to which it constitutes a reference point within a category."

[22] Light sources and product surroundings can have a special relevance to product displays, as they sharply affect color perception. For example, the visual difference between fresh and cured meats or the effect of cosmetic products cannot be detected in a store without the use of artificial lights. Surroundings also influence color perception because, for the principle of *simultaneous color contrast*, a color surrounded by another color changes its appearance. This is why some department stores are decorated with neutral colors so that the true colors of products can stand out. In products such as food, simultaneous color contrast can make the difference between buying or not buying a product. For example, "when uncooked meat is surrounded by other nonmeat products (such as green vegetables), the color appears to be different from that expected. For consumers, this color variation means quality variation. Even the container in which the meat is package may affect its color." (Zaltman and Wallendorf 1983, p. 584). People tend to refuse to eat food that is a different color from that expected.

[23] "Another illustration of this phenomenon was an ice-cream study in which it was found that, when given a cream-colored sample and a white sample of ice-cream, consumers preferred the cream-colored product for its taste, even though it contained less butterfat and was therefore less rich in taste. Consumers were obviously reacting to the color and did not know it." (Mahatoo 1985, p. 53).

[24] Color is widely used in advertising to influence emotional behavior. It was shown that different combinations of colors can evoke different reactions (Hornik 1980). Percy and Rossiter (1983, p. 19) examining the effects of colored vs. black-and-white print advertisements found that color "may produce a basically affective type of processing that influences emotional response to, but not beliefs about, the product" (see, also, Dooley and Harkins 1970; Mitchell and Olson 1981; Shimp 1981).

[25] Sometimes, the effect of color to recall is quite detrimental rather than facilitating, especially under semantic conditions. "When semantic conditions occurs, color may interfere with or detract from elaborative processing. With less processing to interfere with under sensory processing, this detrimental effect may be reduced." (Childers and Houston 1984, p. 653).

[26] We shall argue, however, that contrast with the context is not sufficient for a stimulus to affect communication efficacy (that is, to be salient), since there must be an incongruity between stimulus and schemata possessed by perceivers. This should explain why, for example, in a study by Popper and Murray (1989), background color and size of the type used in an in-ad health warning were not sufficient to affect ad efficacy; it was, instead, the novelty of the ad format.

[27] Britt (1978) added that "[m]ovement is a form of contrast in two ways" (p. 66). Apart from its relationship with a static environment, movement produces contrast when it violates basic expectations of regular rhythm or smooth progression.

[28] "[... A] situation consisting of all the aspects inherent in another situation plus some more is more complex than the other. As an example, a department store with a narrow selection of dresses is a less complex dress-shopping environment than a large specialty store with a very wide selection." (Hansen 1972, p. 50).

[29] "Thus, the degree of complexity varies inversely with the degree to which several elements of a message elicit a single response." (Britt 1978, p. 64).

[30] Complexity of messages influences both persuasion and comprehension of persuasive material according to communication modalities. "With difficult messages, both persuasion and comprehension [...] were greater when the message was written as compared with videotaped and audiotaped. With easy messages, persuasion was greatest when the message was videotaped, moderate when audiotaped, and least when written, but comprehension was equivalent regardless of modality." (Chaiken and Eagly 1976, p. 605).

[31] On this point, Natchez and Bupp (1986) found that image ads were less complex than issue ads and that this lack of complexity lead to better processing of image commercial information. In their study, complexity was defined as a formal characteristic of commercials, that is the amount of visual and verbal information present in commercials per time unit.

[32] "Attention span has two meanings: (1) in the technical sense it is the number of objects or separate stimulus elements that can be perceived in a single, short presentation - but in common usage it means: (2) the amount of time that a person can continue to attend to one type of input." (Rice 1993, p. 80). Similarly to the span of attention, Cavanagh (1972) found that the number of items which could be simultaneously maintained in the span of memory increases as the size and complexity of the items decrease. Interestingly, he also found that the time to search through a full memory for item recognition does not seem dependent on the complexity of material.

[33] Elsewhere Berlyne (1971) noted that simple or redundant patterns are pleasing, but uninteresting, whereas patterns that are both pleasing and interesting are complex patterns with internal organizations. To the extent of our hypothesis (as will be developed *below*), it is interesting to notice the position of Mandler on the relationship between value and interest. According to Mandler (1982), clearly pleasantness usually involves schema congruity, whereas interestingness is more likely to require accommodation. He argued that "positive value is tied to schema congruity, while interestingness is related to schema incongruity. [...] The relations between positive value and interest will depend on the degree of arousal engendered by the interest creating incongruity and by the particular meaning analysis that is engendered by the situation." (Mandler 1982, p. 25).

[34] These results are evidently in contrast with the above-mentioned findings by Hawkins, Best, and Coney (1992), and Walker and von Goten (1989). To explain discrepancies, there could be also methodological restraints because, as stimuli become more complex (e.g., advertising stimuli), attentional responses are more difficult to measure meaningfully for the myriads of variables that should be controlled (Rothschild and Thorson 1983).

[35] "The research suggests, for example, that commercial onsets and scene changes within commercials elicit vigorous orienting behavior in viewers (Lang 1988), but that information presented concurrently or during the first two seconds following scene changes and commercial onsets is remembered much more poorly than information presented more than two seconds after them [...]. In addition, there is preliminary evidence to suggest that if the structural feature used to attract the viewer's attention is visual it interferes more with information presented visually than it does with information presented verbally [...]. Thus, you might want to maximize memory by presenting the information verbally following a visual structural feature or visually following an audio structural feature." (Lang and Lanfear 1990, p. 149).

[36] Similarly, it has been maintained that, when the environmental arousal potential is extremely low, it may result in a rise in arousal. This phenomenon has been ascribed to boredom or to a perceptual conflict occurring because the stimulation is close to the absolute threshold of perception (Berlyne 1960).

[37] An illustration of this confusion in literature is provided by Robinson and McArthur (1982, p. 237), who stated: "For example, the general principle that 'intense' stimuli are salient suggests that

just as a brightly lit person is more salient than a dimly lit one (McArthur and Post 1977), so should a louder speaking person be more salient than a quieter one."

[38] "The attention-getting property of commercials can be seen by observing one to two-year-old children who happen to be playing around a television set. They may totally ignore the programming. However, when a commercial comes on, their attention is immediately drawn to it because of its dramatic sound quality." (Mowen 1993, p. 79).

[39] "The more intense the stimuli are, the shorter the interval seems to be. [...] A reverse effect occurs, however, if the interval is defined by a continuous stimulus and the subject is asked to compare two equal intervals made up of stimuli of unequal intensity. The interval with the more intense sound seems to last longer than the interval with the less intense sound." (Cohen, as quoted in Bogart 1967, p. 118).

[40] Size may exert its influence in some other ways. For example, ad picture size "may produce a cognitive-perceptual type of processing whereby the product or its image in memory is given stronger focus with a larger picture, thus influencing primarily beliefs formation" (Percy and Rossiter 1982, p. 19). Or, also, the size of an advertising headline announcing a retail sale has been shown to positively affect consumers' perception of the magnitude of the discount, with large prints suggesting a larger discount and *vice versa* (Bellizzi and Hite 1987).

[41] In cases like this, the in-salience hypothesis proposes that, rather than being the contrast between ads, it is the incongruity between the microscopic ad in that context and the generic idea of print ads possesses by the perceiver in his own schemata that generates (in-)salience (see, *below*, Chapter Three, *Proposition One*).

[42] Displays and similar attention-getting devices have been shown to influence choice where consumers must choose among a large number of poorly differentiated alternatives, even if they fail to have any relevant meaning to the consumer (Schindler, Berbaum, and Weinzimer 1986; see, also, Shindler and Berbaum 1983).

[43] According to Britt (1978, p. 69), audience members will more likely attend to materials that are formatted on good design characteristics - namely, *balance*, *proportion*, *sequence*, *unity*, and *emphasis* - than those of poor design, with the exception of materials that attract attention because of their very bad design.

[44] "It would seem possible that even cues low in incongruity might be perceived as incongruent if they were made highly salient to the processor. Suppose, for example, that these low incongruity cues were positioned in a text-like message as discrete nonsequential cues (e.g. two incongruent items separated by two intervening congruent cues). The temporal distinct multiple exposures to the incongruent information might promote the detection and elaboration of the cues' incongruous qualities such as that DDP [i.e., Data Driven Processing] would be stimulated. By contrast, if these low incongruity cues were presented contiguously in the stimulus message, thereby appearing as a unitary mass of incongruent information, the processor might be especially likely to overlook this singular unitized instance of low incongruity information and process the information in a CD [i.e., Conceptually Driven] manner. Hence, contextual factors such as the positioning of incongruent cues within a message also are hypothesized to influence the choice of processing strategy." (Meyers-Levy 1988a, p. 170; see, also, *below*, Chapter Three, Paragraphs 2.4.5-2.4.6).

[45] A rather extensive literature exists on order effects (for reviews, see Elio and Anderson 1984; Debren, Fiske, and Hastie 1979; Einhorn and Hogarth 1987; Jones and Goethals 1972; Lichtenstein and Srull 1987; Wyer 1974; Wyer and Carlston 1979). Order effects exists both for items in memory - e.g., recall of product attributes (Hoch 1984) - and for items in

perception - e.g., position of a television commercial in a commercial string (Webb and Ray 1979).

[46] Along with new attention to the amount of TV "clutter" (all nonprogram material, such as commercials, promotional announcements for stations/programs, public service announcements, etc.) is a sense of threat for the choice that may not be optimal, because of the competition for key positions and the tremendous increases in the cost of commercial time (Webb and Ray 1979).

[47] However, both theater operators and national advertisers seem cautious and reluctant about using this promotional tool (cf. Mowen 1993, p. 88). On the one hand, theater operators fear aggravating customers; thus, corporations that own large numbers of theaters screen the ads to make sure that they are appropriate (by making highly lavish productions) and avoid a hard sell. On the other hand, many national advertisers fear associating their products with violent or sex-laden movies.

[48] "[S]alience can hinge on seating position in a group; the person directly opposite you should be especially salient because that person dominates your visual field [...]. Thus, if you want to have maximum impact on the leadership of a meeting, sit opposite the chairperson at the head or foot of a long table; if you want to fade into the background, sit on the sidelines." (Fiske and Taylor 1991, p. 250).

[49] "Fiske, Taylor, Etcoff, and Laufer (1979) report that subjects recalled a greater proportion of verbal statements made by the character whose perspective they were instructed to take while reading a story. The research provided a comparison of the effects of subject perspective (physical vantage point attributed to a character) and subject role (actor or observer) and found that the visual perspective produced much larger effects on recall memory for verbal material than subject role in a narrative about a traffic accident." (Hastie, Park, and Weber 1984, p. 160).

[50] "Comprehension and learning can be aided by increasing the redundancy of information. Recent research evidence indicates that people will retain more information if they are exposed to fewer items but with greater redundancy (i.e., more extensive/repetitive forms) of coverage" (Dholakia, Mundorf, and Dholakia 1991). Indeed, repetition by itself does not imply the salience of the stimulus, but rather - as maintained by our *Proposition One*, see Chapter Three, *below* - also the *context* in which it occurs determines its effectiveness: Several studies have found that when the target ad is repeated in a cluttered environment, repetition may not affect memory and judgments. This finding has been attributed to the interference introduced by the cluttered environment (e.g., Kumar 2000) and inside a clutter (Pieters and Bijmolt 1997), but recently it has been proposed that it is the nature of the environment in which, for example, an ad is repeated that affects the occurrence of a type of processing, either item-specific or relational (Malaviya, Kisielius, and Sternthal 1996; Malaviya, Meyers-Levy and Sternthal 1999; Meyers-Levy 1991).

[51] "[... R]esearch has identified three unintended effects of repetition. First, repetition may affect the amount of attention paid to an ad. Thus, high levels of repetition may lead to "wearout," wherein lower amounts of attention are paid to each additional exposure and recall ceases to improve (Craig, Sternthal, and Leavitt 1976). However, alterations in presentation, such as when an ad is repeated in different media, may effect the rate of wearout. For example, when a television version of an ad is followed by a radio version, people actively reprocess the former during exposure to the latter (Edell and Keller 1989). Second, repetition may have adverse effects on a consumer's affective reactions to a message, perhaps by producing boredom or annoyance or by affording greater opportunity for counterargumentation (Calder and Sternthal 1980). Both effects are undesirable from an advertiser's perspective. A third outcome is undesirable from a consumer's perspective. That is, messages that become familiar through repetition also have a tendency to be perceived as more valid, independent of their actual validity (Bacon 1979; Hasher, Goldstein, and Toppino 1977)." (Alba, Hutchinson, and Lynch 1991, p. 21).

[52] For example, it has been maintained that heavy advertising should heighten recall of both the brand name and the attributes associated with it (see, for a review, Alba, Hutchinson, and Lynch 1991).

[53] Apart from interference produced by associations, which may cue competing concepts, it has been shown that frequent stimuli (such as written or spoken words), which are orthographically or phonologically similar to other less frequent stimuli, cause an inhibitory effect (referred to as *neighborhood frequent effect*) on the perception of these latter stimuli (see, e.g., Grainger et al. 1992), thus promoting further hindrance.

[54] "Indeed, some current advertisements seem to rely heavily on the persuasive power of attribute frequency. In these ads, consumers are introduced to the target product and then are told of the many "extra" gifts (read: trinkets) they will receive upon purchase. In addition, the target product is decomposed into its component parts (most of which are obligatory features of that product class) which are then discussed individually. In the end, emphasis is placed on the number of benefits the consumer can receive with a single purchase." (Alba and Marmorstein 1987, pp. 14-15).

[55] Originally, in a matrix containing 25 alternatives, they found that the salient one was *over four times* more likely to be chosen (Schindler and Berbaum 1983).

[56] Zinkhan (1986), however, criticized laboratory experiments by Schindler, Berbaum, and Weinzimer (1986) to the extent they offered fairly high internal validity at the cost of low external validity. He proposed "a more naturalistic setting", such as a simulated store, where to observe the effect of salience on choices under time pressure.

[57] "For example, McKinnon, Kelly, and Robison (1981) hypothesize effects of point-of-purchase signage which are due to the price or benefit messages which are explicitly communicated by the signs. And it is also possible, as Chevalier (1975) suggest, that end-aisle display may increase sales simply because consumers interpret them as indicating a special bargain." (Schindler, Berbaum, and Weinzimer 1986, p. 505).

[58] "If there are important differences between the alternatives, then these differences will be used to reject alternatives from the evoked set. But if the consumer regards the alternatives as similar, then there will be little basis for rejecting an alternative from the evoked set, and the evoked set will tend to fill up with the first seven or so alternatives perceived. Thus, if an attention-getting device causes one of these otherwise similar alternatives to be thrust into consciousness ahead of the others, it will have a very great likelihood of being included in the consumer's evoked set." (Schindler, Berbaum, and Weinzimer 1986, p. 505).

[59] "Johnson et. al (1990) found that placement of a novel word in an array with three familiar words (essentially making the novel word a distinctive stimulus) enhanced the localizability of the novel word but inhibited the localizability of the familiar ones. The authors called that result *novel popout*, describing it as 'the covert, rapid and automatic orientation of attention towards a perceptual trouble spot in an otherwise fluently perceived visual field' (p. 410)." (Webster 1997, p. 393, enphasis added). This inhibition effect has been documented also with stimuli perceivers are instructed to attend to (Alba and Chattopadhyay 1986; see, *below*, Paragraph 5.3: *The inhibition effect on memory*), but a reverse effect has been reported (i.e., superior learning for an item and enhanced memory for an entire list) under three major conditions (Cimbalo, McQuestion, and Wittig 1980; Webster 1997). Specifically, a task must involve: (a) A serial memory; (b) A simultaneous presentation of the items on the list; and, (c) An isolated item centrally located in the list: Not complex, but rather very simple, so as to act as an anchor point, and not "intensively" distinctive (e.g. nude photos in a set of line drawings).

[60] He wrote: "If the findings of this investigation are to find practical application, it would seem advisable to provide for about 25% white space to obtain a maximum attention. Due to the fact that most of our periodicals are crowded with pictorial and printed copy, and since the human eye can attend to only a small number of items simultaneously, it would seem desirable to segregate certain items to aid the limitations of the human mind." (Brandt 1942, p. 239).

[61] An isolated item is an item of one type embedded within a series of items of another type. A massed item, on the contrary, is one preceded by terms from the same element type.

[62] Von Restorff referred to a stimulus which is isolated as a *vivid* stimulus, rather than a *salient* one (see Wallace 1965). Vividness, however, in modern research, is considered a perfectly different construct from salience (see, e.g., Nisbett and Ross 1980, p. 45; Kisielius and Sternthal 1986).

[63] Mowen (1993) reported (p. 122, emphasis added): "Experiments have shown that a unique item in a series of relatively homogeneous items is *recalled* much more easily, because the effects of *proactive* and *retroactive* interference are minimized. [...] The practice of many students who use markers to high-light important words and phrases in a chapter also exemplifies the von Restorff effect." An explanation for this and the inhibition findings could be possibly traced in Metcalfe (1993).

[64] "The neural trace was the construct employed to explain isolation. Each item in a list sets up a neural trace. When items are similar, as in a homogeneous list, their traces lose some of their individuality and form an aggregation. The aggregation provides a background against which the trace of a particular different item can stand out. Von Restorff suggested that the item became isolated in the trace system. The processes of organization occurring within the trace system follow the same laws as the organization of perceptual excitations. Thus, by the 'law of similarity' a distinct item against a homogeneous background will be better retained, because there is an aggregation of the traces of the homogeneous items causing any single item to lose its identity. The trace of the isolated item becomes the 'figure' which stands out against the aggregated homogeneous traces, the 'ground.'" (Wallace 1965, p. 418).

[65] Thus, placing more than one distinctive stimulus in a stimulus display cancels the advantage provided by the single, distinctive stimulus (see Webster 1997, for a review).

[66] "The perception of another person's behavior can [...] be described in terms of the salience of that behavior. According to Gestalt psychology, perception is influenced by the context in which the stimulus is observed; for example, a dark gray ring on a white background is more salient (contrast effect) than a dark gray ring on a black background (assimilation effect). As applied to interpersonal relations, the concept of salience can be used to explain what is known as the Actor-Observer Effect. Jones and Nisbett (1972) found that for the observer, an 'actor's behavior is the figural stimulus against the ground of the situation' (Jones and Nisbett 1972, as found in Bem 1972, p. 42). In other words, the actor and his or her behavior are salient to the observer because these features stand out against the background situation." (Park 2000).

[67] Although each of these studies was theoretically measuring a concept similar to prior knowledge, the measures used were considerably different (Brucks 1985). From an operational point of view, it seems necessary to distinguish between two constructs: (1) What people perceive they know about the product or the product class; that is, their degree of confidence in their knowledge (*subjective knowledge*); and (2) What people actually know; that is, what knowledge they have stored in memory (*objective knowledge*). It is likely, however, what people perceive they know depends on what they actually know as well as their self-confidence in the amount and type of knowledge held in memory (Park and Lessig 1981).

[68] "*Familiarity* is defined as the number of product-related experiences accumulated by a consumer, and *expertise* is the ability to perform product-related tasks successfully. In general, *product experience* is a necessary but insufficient condition for consumer expertise." (Rao and Monroe 1988, p. 254, emphasis added).

[69] Knowledge structures, in general, and schemata, in particular, will be discussed in the next chapter.

[70] According to Berlyne (1960), the attention-getting properties of a stimulus can be divided into two classes: (1) *Physical properties* (e.g., brightness, color, size), which depend on the intensity of the stimulus; and (2) *Collative properties*, which depend on comparison or collation of the stimulus with its surrounding environment. Berlyne (1958) found that subjects focused more on recurring novel pictures than a recurring picture that became more and more familiar. By varying the degree of discrepancy between novel and familiar stimuli, moderately novel objects attracted more fixation than extremely novel ones.

[71] Enhanced recall for novel information has been found with bigrams (Smith 1973), nonsense syllables (von Restorff 1933), words (Jenkins and Postman 1948), complex action sequences in written prose (Bower, Black, and Turner 1979), courtroom trial evidence (Reyes, Thompson, and Bower 1980), written descriptions of personal behavior (Srull 1981) and filmed sequences of interpersonal behavior (Hastie 1980).

[72] The *repetition-variation hypothesis*, introduced by Schumann, Petty, and Clemons (1990), segmented variation strategies into two basic categories: *cosmetic variation*, in which certain non-substantive features of the ads arc altered while the basic product message is kept the same; and *substantive variation*, in which there is a conspicuous change in message content (i.e., arguments, attributes). While, in general, involvement is a moderator factor in the impact of variations on overall attitude, comparison to repeated same executions shows that varied ad executions imply that attention and encoding variability contribute independently to brand name memory and that encoding variability effects are obtained even when attention differences are controlled (Unnava and Burnkrant 1991b).

[73] Novelty can also regard *imagery processing*, that is an information processing mode that uses one of more of the five senses (MacInnis and Price 1987). This form of processing, currently used in experiential marketing (Schmitt 1999), seems to act directly on consumer behavioral intentions (BI). Fitzgerald Bone and Scholder Ellen (1990) argued that the "situational distinctiveness" of the imagery content is a factor which influences the imagery/BI relationship (together with "self-relatedness" and "plausibility"). Distinctiveness, which takes into account the imagined scenes' uniqueness, was considered as bounded at the lower end by mundane and at the upper end by bizarre. They maintained that is unlikely to enhance the relationship between imagery and BI presenting a product both in a mundane, common situation (because the association between the situation and the brand may be drowned out and unavailable), and in a bizarre, very distinctive situation (for the lack of links between the product and the situation which could actually occur in the consumer's life, despite the fact that novel situations positively influence advertisement and brand recall). Therefore, they hypothesized that "imagery which is plausible and moderately distinctive will create greater BI than imagery which is plausible and indistinctive or implausible and highly distinctive." (p. 450).

[74] Zajonc (1968) supported this assumption by drawing on primitive forms of attention: "[O]n the contrary, it is more likely that orienting toward a novel stimulus in preference to a familiar one may indicate that it is less liked rather than it is better liked. Ordinarily when confronted with a novel stimulus the animal's orienting response enables it to discover if the novel stimulus constitutes a source of danger. It need not explore familiar stimuli in this respect. Novelty is thus commonly associated with uncertainty and with conflict - states that are more likely to produce

negative than positive affect. [... Q]uite clearly [...] exploration and favorable attitudes are in fact negatively related." (p. 21).

[75] This stimulus uniqueness should be thought more in "temporal" than in a "spatial" way. If uniqueness was perceivable in a spatial context (on the base of a physical environment), we should presumably speak of *contextual novelty*. On the contrary, if uniqueness was perceivable in a temporal context (on the base of prior experiences), we should presumably speak of (relative) *statistical novelty*. In our hypothesis, however, the elements of context and of prior experiences (schemata) are both present in both cases (see also, *below*, Chapter Three, *Proposition One*).

[76] By considering advertising uniqueness, Olney, Holbrook, and Batra (1991) found that TV commercial *viewing time* was explained by the advertising content, partially mediated by the emotional dimensions and the components of attitude toward the ad via two primary routes to viewing time: (1) Feelings and Uniqueness/Uniqueness Squared → Pleasure → Hedonism → Viewing Time; (2) Uniqueness → Arousal → Interestingness → Viewing Time.

[77] In particular, there are three hypotheses upon the salience of direct comparative ads, that are summarized by Pechmann and Stewart (1991, p. 48): "[T]he novelty hypothesis suggests that direct comparative ads might be attention-getting when the advertised brand has a very high market share, since ads of this type are still novel. According to the index hypothesis, direct comparative ads might also attract attention when a low share brand compared to a high-share comparison brand, because the brand might serve as an index. But according to the confusion hypothesis, when direct comparative ads feature brands that have moderate market share are at parity, consumers actually pay less attention to them because such comparisons are apt to be very confusing." Elsewhere, it has been shown that the relative newness of a brand in the marketplace is a mediator in determining the effectiveness of comparative advertising (Iyer 1988).

[78] "Two examples of differentiation based on a salient attribute are the Harvard Business School (the 'case method') and 7Up ('no caffeine'). These 'products' have achieved high levels of differentiation *relative to competition.* Indeed, the involvement achieved still depends on the product category and will obviously not be as high for the selection of a soft drink as for the choice of a business school to attend. However, the objective is to achieve involvement *sufficiently* high relative to other brands in the product category to gain some measure of competitive advantage. 7Up is an interesting example of a brand which was in the doldrums until it focused on its lack of caffeine: 'Never had it. Never will'. It was not only brand of soft drink without caffeine, but it was the first to focus aggressively on this attribute, which had become salient as the American public was exposed to the scientific controversy surrounding caffeine's possible harmful effects. Other brands then followed with no-caffeine products, but 7Up had by then built momentum and increased involvement." (Robertson, Zielinski, and Ward 1984, pp. 132-133). Likewise, for social stimuli, Taylor and Langer (1977) reported the same conclusions for people carrying "novel visual stimuli", i.e., pregnant women. They stated: "[T]he pregnant woman becomes a statistically novel sight, when she is in public view. She is no longer responded to on the basis of her individuality - now the most salient part of her anatomy will determine the nature of many of her interpersonal interactions." (p. 29; see also Langer et al. 1976).

[79] Where uniqueness is not represented by the prototypical brand in the category, an atypical, nichy product could be chosen. This is usually the beginning of many fashions.

[80] "Each month, QVC Network presents a program called *Extreme Shopping*. The primary goal of each program is to present a selection of rare, unusual, and expensive products. The premiere program opened with Muhammad Ali's boxing robe (priced at over $12,000), followed by Jane Mansfield's former mansion (priced at almost three and a half million

dollars - genuinely offered on television for immediate sale). As another part of this presentation, after offering a Volkwagen Beetle painted by Peter Max (priced $100,000), QVC offered Peter Max prints which were personalized and signed by the artist (priced at about $200)." (Stafford 2000).

[81] Repetition is a prime which could act in the opposite sense, by increasing the frequency, say, of a brand name. The use of repetition as a tool for creating salience can be better explained through recourse to our hypothesis which places incongruity between the stimulus and the context at the origin of the salience construct (see *below*).

[82] "One area of marketing that relies upon consumer curiosity and interest in variety is magazine publishing where news-stand sales depend heavily on the appeal of the covers of each issue." (Wilkie 1990, pp. 188-189). "*Novelty* and *curiosity* can [...] cause us to direct our attention toward an interesting stimulus. Marketers have long used such words as 'New!' 'Improved,' and 'Free!' to play upon this factor in attracting attention from potential customers." (*Ibid.*, p. 246). According to Loewenstein (1994), curiosity (or "the desire to know") arises when individuals become alerted to the existence of an information gap in a particular knowledge domain. "Curiosity prompt individuals to generate hypotheses about their knowledge gaps and motivates them to seek information that confirms or discomfirms these hypotheses (Klayman and Ha 1987). [...] In addition, when curiosity-resolving information becomes available subsequently, the individual implicitly reviews this information to examine its degree of fit with self-generated hypotheses. This type of review or 'reprocessing' of a message would likely lead to better recall and better comprehension of the new information (see Fazio, Herr, and Powell 1992; O'Brien and Myers 1985)." (Menon and Soman 1999, p. 7).

[83] Since contemporary civilized societies have developed a tools system for vigilance maintenance, humans have considerable free (leisure) time in which they try to avoid the resulting boredom by seeking experiencing in recreational, aesthetic, and other "leisure-time" activities (Woods 1981, p. 360). In advertising, for example, the *need for cognition* - an individual difference variable which has been defined as the intrinsic motivation to engage in problem solving activities - has been found to be positively related to longer ad processing and superior recall for brands and claims (Peltier and Schibrowsky 1994).

[84] According to Woods (1981). "If we follow Cabanac's (1971, p. 1107) logic this occurs because little variation exists in the pleasantness of visual stimuli, and hence there is little opportunity for a very 'shocking' visual experience; on the other had, in taste (foods) and tactile (body collision, pressure) stimuli, the opportunity for a very unpleasant experience is probable. Hence, people are more willing to inspect novel sights as compared to other novel stimuli." (p. 280).

[85] Examples of perceptual defense studies are provided by Crane (1972, pp. 215-217). It appears that "an individual's needs, moods, and interests may make him see some symbols sooner than we'd expect him to (vigilance), and prevent him from seeing other symbols as soon as we'd expect (defense). It also appears that even when he doesn't admit in so many words that he can recognize the symbols being 'shown' him, bodily reactions beyond his conscious control, such as the sweating of his palms, reveal that something is getting through. [...] Although there is little doubt that perceptions are affected by characteristics of both message and perceiver, these relationships are complex. [...] Subjects appear to be quick to recognize symbols that they find rewarding. [...] A high-valued symbol may not only be seen more quickly, it may also be seen as larger."

[86] It has been demonstrated that, through repeated exposure, positive affect tends to increase and perceived risk tends to decline (Baker et al. 1986; Obermiller 1985).

[87] Thus, it has been argued that the effects of awareness on choice cannot be separated from those of affect (Hoyer and Brown 1990).

[88] As noted by van Raaij (1991), some authors distinguish between the term *expectation* and the term *expectancy*. Newcomb (1972) argued that the term *expectancy* emphasizes a psychological state, some kind of preparatory adjustment to anticipated events or situations. Whereas, the term *expectation* commonly refers to the content of what is expected. However, most authors do not make this distinction and we shall consider these terms as interchangeable.

[89] From an economic perspective, Shackle (1952, p. 2) defined an expectation as an act of creating imaginary situations, associating them with future dates, and assigning scaled measures indicating the degree of belief that these situations will become true. From a social science perspective, Georgescu-Roegen (1958, p. 12) defined an expectation as "the state of mind of an individual with respect to an assertion, a coming event, or any other matter on which absolute knowledge does not necessarily exist." From an organizational behavior perspective, Vroom (1964, p. 17) defined expectancy as "a momentary belief concerning the likelihood that a particular act will be followed by a particular outcome."

[90] *Active expectations* are those which are easily available in memory, at high levels of consciousness and involvement, and may, therefore, be instrumental in the purchase of products. Alternatively, *passive expectations* are those which are part of a schema and resides passively in memory either permanently (generally as true beliefs, which are probably not processed until disconfirmed) or temporarily (which remain in memory only for a brief time period - e.g., the expectation that the store will be open and the liquor will be available) (see Kahneman and Tversky 1982b).

[91] We should make a distinction between *immediacy* and *anticipatory* on the basis of the appearance or "knowability" of the data. Immediate knowledge is related to data based on historical events, regardless of their certainty, whereas anticipatory knowledge is related to future events or stimulus occurrences.

[92] Einhorn and Hogarth (1985) made a major contribution to the uncertainty literature by distinguishing between *risk* (when the probability distribution of outcome occurrence is known), and *ambiguity* (when it is only possible to rule out some of the plausible probability distributions).

[93] "Specifically, based on extant theory, imagery processing when combined with low levels of experience should result in more positivity bias, more expectancy-disconfirmation, and less satisfaction. In contrast, imagery processing when combined with high levels of experience should result in less of a positivity bias, less expectancy-disconfirmation, and more satisfaction." (MacInnis and Price 1990, p. 42).

[94] According to Tolman's (1932) seminal research, expectations are beliefs that a given response will be followed by some event (which acts as a positive or a negative reinforcer). Under this approach, expectations are part of a theory of learning that is called *operant conditioning*. Goal setting, aspirations, and plans, which are at least partly under one's own control, are examples of *intentional expectations*. Events that are outside one's control - e.g., because of a lack of resources, information, or time - are examples of *contingent expectations*.

[95] "Information sources can be categorized as social (parents, peers, friends), commercial (salespersons, advertising), or neutral (newspapers, magazines, government reports, consumer organizations). Advertising for new products purposefully attempts to create favorable informational beliefs (expectations) among consumers." (van Raaij 1991, p. 404).

[96] Extensive debate has centered on the definition of deception, with much concern about what information to consider (cf. Dover 1982). Inferential beliefs from information cues (i.e., attributes) which are salient from a Fishbeinian perspective (see, *below*, Chapter Three, Paragraph 2.1.10)

have been shown to strongly impact evolving cognitive structures (e.g., Glassman and Pieper 1980). In light of considerable evidence of inferential workings in information processing, marketers and advertisers must be prepared to accept responsibility not only for what they do say, but also for what they leave unsaid. There are several reasons why the indiscriminate and systematic targeting of cognitive heuristics may be unethical (Singer et al. 1991); it seems not enough that advertising could be considered deceptive only if advertisers use ad claims to reinforce or make salient false beliefs (cf. Russo, Metcalf, and Stephens 1981) since they are not obliged to correct all false consumer beliefs regarding the product class (Burke et al. 1988).

[97] In this sense, cue utilization is also an aspect of the "peripheral route" to persuasion in the Elaboration Likelihood Model (ELM) by Petty and Cacioppo (1986). In this seminal model, a cue is a superficial aspect of a message (e.g., a form or a spokesperson) used instead of arguments in order to persuade low involved consumers (see also, *below*, Chapter Three, Paragraph 2.4.6).

[98] "Expectations, that already exist in mind, tend to bias new stimuli in the direction of the existing expectations (anchoring). Existing knowledge structures serve as internalized frames of reference in which to encode incoming stimuli. An expectation is an important frame of reference (Craik and Lockhart 1972). Consumers may have a reference price in mind, and from this reference price (frame) they perceive (and recall) actual prices. New incoming information may not only change existing expectations insufficiently, but also an existing expectational frame may bias the perception of incoming new information." (van Raaij 1991, p. 406).

[99] In the search for a possible cause, the latter principle requires the attributor to take into account the whole "configuration" of factors present at the time of the observed effect. For this reason, it has been also referred as the *discounting principle* (Kelley 1973).

[100] Drawing on the work of Jones and Davis (1965); and Kanouse (1972).

[101] Illusory causal attribution was also assessed in natural settings, where variables are usually so closely tied one another that their effects are difficult to isolate and interpret (see Schwarz and Strack 1981).

[102] Alloy and Tabachnik (1984, p. 112) argued that "covariation perception is determined by the interaction between two sources of information: (a) the organism's prior expectations about the covariation between the two events and (b) current situational information provided by the environment about the contingency between the events."

[103] Analysis of variance and structural models revealed that schema-relevant recall, that is, information seen as representative of causal influence, was a plausible mediator; this was particularly true of relevant visual information. Fiske, Kenny, and Taylor's (1982) findings suggested that salience effect is due to: (a) The attentional advantage of inherently salient visual events, and (b) The influence of stored visual and non-visual schema-relevant information on causal judgments. Hence, none of the two alternative accounts of their data depended on recall; this made Hastie, Park, and Weber (1984) declare that "there is only *suggestive evidence* that recall mediates the effects of salience on judgments of causality." (p. 191, emphasis added).

[104] Fiske and Taylor (1978) proposed that "what may make information more available is either (a) Encoding through more than one mode, specifically both iconic and semantic encoding, or (b) Encoding which differs from the encoding of other stimuli, that is, images as opposed to semantic encoding." (p. 253).

[105] Pryor and Kriss (1977), and also Storms (1973), had similarly argued that attributions usually reflect not complex deductions but simply retrieval of that potential cause which is most available in memory.

[106] The *Perceptual organization hypothesis* suggested by McArthur (1980) remains, however, compatible with Robinson and McArthur's findings. In general, this hypothesis holds that salience manipulations influence the perceptual organization of stimuli in a manner which highlights the causal influence of the salient stimulus on the nonsalient stimulus, rather than vice versa.

[107] The incongruity we are dealing with regards the difference between one's expectations (based on prior experience or schemata) and external information (e.g., via audio *or* video). It should not be confused with *modality incongruence*, which concerns the extent to which two sensory channels (e.g., audio *and* video) communicate different information and, thus, the role on resource allocation among sensory inputs (e.g., Leigh 1992, Hung 2000; Kellaris and Powell Mantel 1996).

[108] What is relevant to our hypothesis (see also, *below*, Chapter Three, *Proposition One* and *Four*), in reference to products, is that they argue: "[W]hen making global evaluations of a set of alternatives, we assume that people go through a three-stage process: (1) identifying relevant attributes for consideration, (2) evaluating the level of each attribute, and (3) combining this information to form an overall evaluation of each alternative. Each stage can foster ambiguity. [...] Ambiguity at the integration stage is most likely to arise when the consumer faces uncorrelated attributes. [...] When attributes are uncorrelated or negatively correlated with each other, information processing demands will be much greater [...]. If the consumer does not exhaustively process the information or experiences slight fluctuations in attention [...], changes in evaluations occur because of greater sensitivity to the magnitude of individual attribute weights." (Ha and Hoch 1989, pp. 354-355).

[109] "*Elaboration* refers to the generation of associations to message information and its integration with prior knowledge" (Malaviya, Kisielius, and Sternthal 1996, p. 410).

[110] In research on complex verbal information, *theme* has been defined as the general focus of a story to which the plot adheres (Thorndyke 1977).

[111] A very interesting model - quite similar, under certain aspects, to Heckler and Childers' (1992) model - is the *Relevance-accessibility model* by Baker (1993) and Baker and Lutz (2000), according to which an advertising message appeal is most likely to influence brand choice when it is both *relevant* (i.e., able to easily achieve the choice objective) and *accessible* (i.e., when consumer involvement at the time of advertising exposure leads to its efficient encoding in memory). This model can be considered as an extension, under low-involvement conditions, of the *Accessibility-diagnosticity model* by Feldman and Lynch (1988) - see, *below*, Paragraph 4.5.

[112] O'Brien and Myers (1985) found that words that are unpredictable from a preceding context improve the memory recall for the passages that contain them: subjects took longer to comprehend lines with unpredictable words but this increased processing time facilitates recognition of such words.

[113] "Food is one product in which expectation and anticipatory attributes play an important role in consumer behavior. People are reluctant to taste products with colors, textures, or smells that differ from the ones they are used to." (Zaltman and Wallendorf 1983, p. 586).

[114] "The more heavily that audience members rely upon a past experience in regard to a message, the more likely they are to expect a recurrence of that experience when they are exposed to a message a second time." (Britt 1978, p. 174).

[115] Brennen and Brennen (1982) provide a pertinent example on this point: "[T]he statues of the gods in the primitive societies [...] seem to have one element always in common: they always have some unusual characteristic - disproportionately big eyes or mouths, eight legs, several

hands, and so forth - in contrast to Greek or Roman gods, who have rather human shapes. This basic similarity also exists between mythical animals from different societies. The griffin, phoenix, centaur, sphinx, manticore, Ganesha, and Ch'i-lin have one common characteristic: They are all creatures consisting of familiar parts in unfamiliar combination. This pattern can also be related to the role memory plays in such societies, since it is easier to remember unusual shapes than ordinary ones. However, once societies become literate, this task of memory is less important since one can remember the gods by reading the texts they have dictated rather than by their visual forms." (p. 155; see, also, Guido 1995).

[116] Not only can the pictorial part of an ad be subject to manipulations. Also the graphic part of the copy, such as typefaces, if carefully chosen, can add subtle connotative nuances to the denotative meanings conveyed by the words which employ them. Heavy type, e.g., may suggest strength, but most of these nuances reflect ways such typefaces have been used in the past (Crane 1972, p. 198b).

[117] "Although there has been considerable research documenting the impact of attention-drawing people upon causal attributions there is surprisingly little evidence bearing on the impact of attention-drawing behaviors. Given the impact of these variables upon impression formation, further research clearly seems warranted. One would expect, for example, that more causality will be attributed to actors who perform intense, novel complex changing, and unit-forming behaviors than to those whose behaviors are more subdued, ordinary, simple, static, and/or fragmented. And, given the shared distinctiveness illusory correlation effects documented in the research on impression formation, one would expect these effects to be especially pronounced when the actor's appearance, as well as his behavior, draws attention." McArthur (1981, p. 233).

[118] "Role theory is based on a dramaturgical metaphor. The study of a role - a cluster of social cues that guide and direct an individual's behavior in a given setting - is the study of the conduct associated with certain socially defined positions rather than of the particular individuals who occupy these positions. It is the study of the degree to which a particular part is acted appropriately (role enactment) as determined by this reactions of fellow actors and observers (the audience)." (Solomon et al. 1985, p. 102).

[119] Stereotyping involves considering a group of people in an unvarying pattern that lacks individuality (e.g., women, racial and ethnic stereotypes, senior citizen, baby boomers; cf. Wells, Burnett, and Moriarty 1992, pp. 42-45).

[120] "These predictions are based on expectations for behavior implied in common meanings. For example, a customer who walks into a clothing store is communicating consideration of a buying transaction or at least wants to browse. This behavior allows the salesperson to initiate the actions which correspond to a sales role. The salesperson's approach would not have the same meaning outside the store as inside, though in both cases a stranger is initiating conversation and perhaps asking questions of a somewhat personal nature. Once the shopper enters the store, he adopts the role of customer and a role-defined dyadic interaction familiar to both parties may begin" (Solomon et al. 1985, p. 103).

[121] Other research on the diverse persuasive impact of media has referred to the notions of different richness, involvement, and social presence of broadcasted vs. print media (cf. Chaiken and Eagly 1983). They are consistent, however, with the idea that the persuasive impact of modality is contingent on the valence of communicator characteristics.

[122] "It is important to note that, although social roles often become social identities, these two types of social positions are conceptually distinct. A person can enact a particular role but not identify with it (e.g. because role performance is forced by external pressure), and a person can identify with a social position (e.g. being short) that does not involve any role responsibilities." (Levine, Resnick, and Higgins 1993, p. 592). It is equally important to recognize- especially to the

extent of our dichotic theory (Guido 1998) - that social identities, as well as identity ideals and the global self, all exist in people's minds in the form of *schemata*. "For each identity (and role, etc.) there is an identity *schema* (role schema, etc.), which represents the person's store of identity-related knowledge - a collection of what-to-do information (derived from social interaction) when expressing an identity (such as bus driver). The nature and functions of schemas are well documented in the literature [...] and, as Mick (1988) noted, their position in consumer psychology is well established" (Kleine, Kleine, and Kernan 1993, p. 214).

[123] *Self-image* has been considered a multidimensional construct which implies various types of self, such as actual self, ideal self, social self, and sex role self (Onkvisit and Shaw 1987; see Graeff 1997 for a review). This can create a match/mismatch between the different types of self which - together with the *functional* match/mismatch (i.e., between the consumer's beliefs about brand utilitarian attributes/performance and the consumer's referent attributes) - influences attitudes and behaviors (Sirgy and Johar 1999).

[124] Salience can even affect the actors themselves. Frable, Blackstone, and Scherbaum (1990), for example, found that individuals who have social identities that are statistically rare and socially important (e.g. bisexual, wealthy) are more "mindful" during a dyadic interaction than are their "normal" partners, recalling more detailed information and taking their partner's perspective. Such a result is common to a number of studies where role expectations were manipulated. "Zadny and Gerard (1974) found that subjects' recall of items in a live skit varied depending on the role that was attributed to the target actor. Items were better recalled when they were related to the target's role (e.g., chemistry items when the target was a chemistry major) than when they were unrelated to the target's role (e.g., chemistry items when the target was a music major). These results could also be due to retrieval effects of role expectations, but it is likely that subjects selectively noticed and encoded items related to the target's role. Selectivity effects of manipulating the role of the target actor have also been found by Cohen (1977) and may be involved in Langer and Abelson's (1974) finding that therapists evaluate a target as more disturbed if previously told that the target is a 'patient' versus a 'job applicant.' Using a different paradigm, Andersoll and Pichert (1978) manipulated subjects' own role expectations by having them read a story containing information about a particular house from the perspective of either a burglar or a prospective home buyer. For the home buyer role at least the manipulation of role expectations appeared to have selectivity effects (as well as retrieval effects to be discussed later). Controlling for perspective at recall, a much higher proportion (at home buyer-related items were recalled when subjects had been initially assigned the home buyer role than when subjects had been initially assigned the burglar role)." (Higgins and King 1981, pp. 84-85).

[125] An extension of the study of Meyers-Levy (1988b) can be considered that of Widgery and McGuagh (1993), which confuses (as will be shown *below*, in Chapter Three, Paragraph 2.3) "salience" with the "importance" of message appeals.

[126] Price (1993) presented evidence to suggest that cognitive mechanisms other than information weighting may at least partially explain the negativity effect in the realm of product communications. Two experiments were described in which negative product test reports evoked "systematic changes in product attribute beliefs that were not explicitly targeted in the report. These indirect changes in cognitive structure were found to significantly mediate the relationship between the strength of the targeted attribute belief and attitude change. Changes in non-targeted attribute beliefs were weak and non-systematic when valence of the stimulus test reports was positive." (Price 1993, p. I).

[127] This conclusion considers the problem only from a cognitive perspective, whereas Homer and Yoon (1992) have demonstrated that also emotional responses to negatively framed appeals have a part in ad effectiveness. As suggested elsewhere (Burke and Edell 1989), advertisers can benefit from the arousal of negative emotions.

[128] "A piece of information is perceived as *diagnostic* if it helps the consumer to assign a product to one (and only one) cognitive category." (Herr, Kardes, and Kim 1991, p. 457, emphasis added).

[129] "Ads for sport gear, perfumes, vehicles, shoes, clothes, alcohol and soft drinks have used the adventure-and-danger theme as part of their appeal [...]. Most audiences of danger-inspired ads, however, enjoy danger images, rather than danger itself. [...] Advertising images, however, typically freeze the script and withhold release by depicting dangerous activities at the point when disaster may strike rather then at the moment of achievement. It seems that an emphasis on danger's negative potential contributes to its symbolic content, even as it evokes divergent readings by consumers with different social and existential values ([...] Csikszentmihalyi 1990)." (Curlo and Lerman 1999, p. 300).

[130] In a study on the optimal level of claim extremity, Goldberg and Hartwick (1990) predicted an interaction of "advertiser reputation and advertising claim extremity with (1) a positive relation between claim extremity and product evaluation for subjects given the positive reputation description, with change leveling off at higher levels of extremity, and (2) an inverted U-shaped relation for subjects given the negative reputation description, with maximum change occurring at intermediate levels of extremity. The obtained pattern of results [...] approximated that predicted" (p. 178).

[131] "[Advertising] must be so audacious that it gets written about in the newspapers, discussed in supermarkets, worried about in boardrooms or even joked about on talk shows" (Cornish 1987, as reported in Alperstein 1990, p. 16).

[132] As it will be explained *below* (Chapter Three, *Proposition Two*), attracting attention and maintaining attention are two different processes. Therefore, orienting response by itself is not enough to generate salience and salience effects, i.e., on memory. Thus, the in-salience hypothesis could be used to explain, for example, why opposite results have been obtained in past research on attractiveness and memory measures (e.g., Baker and Churchill 1977; Joseph 1982).

[133] Sexual material, however, may affect ad effectiveness in a less obvious way, that is misattribution of arousal. A good deal of research in social psychology supports the Schachterian prediction that sexual material may affect ad effectiveness by causing people to possibly misinterpret physiological activity caused by sexual content, thereby experiencing increases in such reactions as anger, aggression, sexual arousal, humor, and attitude change (see, for a review, Baron 1982).

[134] Employing the Freudian definition, *suggestiveness* is considered as any command or piece of information that triggers or arouses an idea in a person's mind (see Belch et al. 1982).

[135] This case is addressed in Chapter Three, Paragraph 2.1.1 (*below*): When the stimulus cue does not correspond to the information cue, the in-salience effect is lower (see, also, Peltier 1989).

[136] "In a study of advertisements for disposable razors, brand recall was higher among participants exposed to an attractive rather than an unattractive celebrity. According to Kahle and Homer (1985), when a celebrity's physical attractiveness is congruent with the degree to which the advertised product enhances attractiveness (e.g., a movie-star and a beauty product), the 'match-up' phenomenon of adaptive significance (see also Baker and Churchill 1977) would predict a positive impact upon product and advertisement evaluations. On the other hand, when there is incongruity between the product and celebrity attractiveness (e.g., a movie star and a kitchen product), evaluations will not be affected. Work reported by Kamins (1990) generally supports the 'match-up' hypothesis, confirming that for attractiveness-unrelated products, use of an attractive celebrity has no effect upon spokesperson, product or ad-based dependent measures." (Percy and Rossiter 1992, pp. 76-77).

[137] Although there are a number of variables that may impact on the likelihood of the implant affecting the purchase intentions - including interest in the product class, the number of exposures to the advertisement, and the type of copy contained in the advertisement - Caccavale, Wanty, and Edell (1982) tested only the type of copy contained in the ad.

[138] Key (1972) contended that it is not only "taboo four-letter words which are effective in manipulating the response of mass audiences, but other words, with taboo implications have also been shown to possess subliminal power. Words such as 'shot', 'whose', 'cult', 'pints', and 'taste', which differ by only one or two letters from certain taboo or emotional words, can also evoke strong, demonstrable emotional reactions." (p. 28). He also contended that the sexual suggestiveness of the consciously perceived elements of an advertisement enhances the effect of the subliminal elements.

[139] *In-salience* is defined as an incongruity in a certain context between a stimulus and a perceiver's schema, whereas *re-salience* is defined as a congruity in a certain context between a stimulus and a perceiver's goal (see Chapter Three, Section 2.1 and Paragraph 2.4.3, *below*).

[140] These cases are very similar to those discussed under spatial perspective, such as theater advertising (see, *above*, Note 47).

[141] It is interesting to notice, in this conceptualization, the particle "or" between the two definitions: It is not clear if it must be considered a conjunctive particle or rather a disjunctive one. It is the same problem we face in literature with other ambiguous definitions of salience. For example (emphasis added), Bettman and Sujan (1987, p. 142): "[...] framing often refers to making certain criteria more salient *or* available"; Nedungadi (1990, p. 264): "[...] when brand choice is memory based, it is brand accessibility *or* salience on that particular occasion that will determine the composition of the consideration set"; Zuckerman, Mann, and Bernieri (1982, p. 839): "Nonmotivational factors that may create the impression of false consensus include [...] availability *or* salience - one's own behavioral choice is readily retrievable from memory, thus exerting a strong influence on the estimates of behavioral choices in a group"; and so on (see also, *below*, Chapter Three, *Proposition Three*).

[142] Salience was *set* (Posner 1978) by providing instructions to subjects to consciously process some input (i.e., a brand name). "Salience was operationalized in terms of the amount of time subjects were exposed to and thought about the brand prior to recall. [... I]n thinking about it they could repeat the name to themselves, image the brand's packaging, or focus on ads they had seen for the brand." (Alba and Chattopadhyay 1986, p. 364).

[143] The salient cues were presented as a list of brands on a computer screen (Alba and Chattopadhyay 1985, Experiment 1); as single brands pictured onto separate slides (*Ibid.*, Experiment 2); or named in short passages typed on separate sheets of paper (*Ibid.*, Experiment 3). Salient cues were also brand names printed on the top of sheets of paper (Alba and Chattopadhyay 1986, Experiment 1); actual packages of branded products (*Ibid.*, Experiment 2); or brand names promoted in mock advertisements (*Ibid.*, Experiments 3 and 5) or in real television commercials (*Ibid.*, Experiment 4).

[144] However, Alba and Chattopadhyay (1985, p. 348) also maintained that: "There is reason to believe [...] that brand recall and attribute recall function differently. When recalling the attributes of a familiar product, consumers may recall their current brand or a prototypical case of the product class and use it as a very effective cue, thereby attenuating the effects of part-category cues. Such a strategy is not available for recall of brand names. Thus additional research is needed to investigate specifically the case of attribute recall." This research - to our knowledge - was never done, despite being mistakenly reported in a review by Alba, Hutchinson, and Lynch (1991). Results of our present research reveal that this inhibition

effect is strongly present also for product attributes (see, *below*, Chapter Four, Paragraph 4.1.3).

[145] "All this suggests that advertisers may be able to inhibit consideration of threatening competitors and unfavorable attributes by making salient in their ads nonthreatening competitors and their own attribute strengths." (Alba, Hutchinson, and Lynch 1991, pp. 19-20).

[146] Jones and Nisbett (1972) have argued that when actors seek to explain their own behavior, they give considerably weight to external, environmental (i.e., situational) causes; whereas observers place considerably more emphasis on internal, personal (i.e., dispositional) causes of the actor behavior. According to this explanation, therefore, aspects of the situation are phenomenologically more salient to actors, whereas characteristics of the actor and his behavior are more salient to observers.

Chapter 3

A MODEL OF INCONGRUITY-SALIENCE

All marketing stimuli, *initially*, exist in the consumer's external world and, therefore, they must be perceived to have an impact at all. Yet, only those stimuli that in a certain context are prominent to some extent to the individual consumer will have an impact on the outcomes of consumer information processes. The conditions under which this prominence has an influence on the marketing variables (inputs, stimuli) in the perceptual process, as well as its antecedents and its consequences on marketing, are the subject of a new model of salience which will be presented in some detail in this chapter.

Consumer literature has identified numerous ways in which salient stimuli can display their effects. Using schema theory and an information processing approach, our model of incongruity-salience - briefly referred to as the *In-salience hypothesis* - attempts to explain the conditions under which different marketing stimuli are able to produce communication outcomes (such as learning and memory). It will do this by supporting a redefinition of the concept of salience - as it has been used so far - and proposing a common source for the occurrence of salient stimuli. The in-salience hypothesis maintains that it is a contextual incongruity between a stimulus and a perceiver's schema that determines the occurrence of salience and the spread of its effects. Figure 2 synthesizes the basic proposition that will be illustrated here.[1]

Figure 2. An Incongruity-Salience Hypothesis

IN-SALIENCE			COMMUNICATION OUTCOMES
Stimulus	|		
Context	|→ Information Processing	→	Consumer Awareness
Schemata	|		

Source: Adapted from Guido (1993).

The in-salience hypothesis is part of a wider *Dichotic theory of salience* (Guido 1998) - whose development is under way (see Table 3) - which considers this construct as either the effect of an incongruity (i.e., in-salience), or the effect of the relevance (i.e., *re-salience*) of a stimulus when this is contextually congruent with a perceiver's goals. While the latter hypothesis will be only briefly illustrated here, the former will be adequately discussed.

The *In-salience hypothesis* represents an assimilation and extension of research in cognitive and social psychology, consumer behavior, and advertising theory, discussing, in particular: (1) If there is a common nature behind perceptual forms of salience; (2) How consumers process marketing information; (3) How information is compared with schemata in memory; and (4) How the relevance of certain elements within a schema facilitates the memory of information. The in-salience hypothesis is based on the view that the primary goal of marketing and advertising cannot be achieved if consumers are not at least aware of the marketing stimulus; this means that the stimulus must attract consumer's attention and must be interpreted in the same way as the marketer intended.[2] Unlike tactical research designed to determine specific executional cues of marketing and advertising campaigns, the in-salience hypothesis operates at a strategic level to identify the molar level of information that the marketer should communicate in any given situation. Thus, the model makes predictions about the conditions under which specific marketing stimuli will be perceived as salient and will be able to display their salience effects.

The focus of this chapter is on presenting three major assumptions (or axioms) upon which the model is built and four propositions that transform these assumptions into a theory of salience. Although these concepts could be applied with some limitations to perception in general, they will be discussed here within the framework of consumer behavior. The final part of this contribution will outline the implications of these propositions for the creation of consumer awareness.

Axiom One of the model states that salience cannot be defined in terms of its effects: By criticizing a theoretical position quite widespread in literature, the lack of validity of a definition of salience based on its effects is demonstrated. The key implication of this axiom is that a *stimulus* which is "salient", according to past definitions, cannot be discriminated by other stimuli which are only "vivid" or "involving," as also these constructs imply the capture of a disproportionate amount of attention. Axiom Two states that salience depends on the situation in which the stimulus occurs; salience does not exist in a vacuum, as an objective quality of the stimulus, but rather it depends on the *context* in which the stimulus occurs. Therefore, a stimulus can be salient only in certain places and in certain times. Finally, Axiom Three states that salience depends also on the perceivers of the stimulus; thus, a stimulus can be salient only in relation to the *schemata* possessed by an individual perceiver. It follows that a stimulus that is salient for a certain perceiver is not necessarily such for a different one.

Four propositions flesh these three axioms out. Proposition One states our definition of a perceptually salient stimulus: A stimulus is *in-salient* when in a certain context it is incongruent with a perceiver's schema. It follows that, for the occurrence of in-salience, the simultaneous presence of the following three elements is crucial: Stimulus, context, and perceiver's schemata. Proposition Two states that in-salience has to do with attention *and* interpretation. In an information processing model articulated in stages, in-salience is not merely the result of a figure-ground principle, but it implies a further stage, that of interpretation, in which the incongruity detected in a certain context is compared with a schema possessed by a perceiver. Proposition Three states that in-salience is a different construct from either activation, or accessibility, or availability (or, even, importance). While our theory recognizes the peculiar nature of in-salience, it also acknowledges that activation, accessibility, and availability have a role in the processing of in-salient stimuli as moderators of perceivers' schemata. Proposition Four states that personal relevance is a crucial moderating variable of in-salience. It acts as a moderator between the two types of salience (i.e., in-salience and re-salience). The major implication of the four propositions is that, once a stimulus has caught consumers' attention and has been perceptually encoded, in-salience generates *awareness*, i.e. a low-level form of memory impact and the goal of any marketing strategy.

Table 3. A Dichotic Theory of Salience

Type of Salience	IN-SALIENCE	RE-SALIENCE
Underlying Theory	*Incongruity-Salience Hypothesis*	*Relevance-Salience Hypothesis*
Type of Stimuli	*Perception-based*	*Memory-based*
Type of Cognitive Process	*Bottom-Up*	*Top-Down*
Type of Search Behavior	*Exploratory Search Behavior*	*Goal-Directed Search Behavior*
Type of Learning	*Incidental Learning*	*Intentional Learning*
Generative Causes	*Incongruity (Stimulus Contents or Weights)*	*Involvement (Personal Goals or Instructions)*
Hypothesis	*A stimulus is salient (in-salient) in a certain context when it is incongruent with a perceiver's schema*	*A stimulus is salient (re-salient) in a certain context when it is congruent with a perceiver's goal*
Type of Attention	*Involuntary Attention (or Passive Attention)*	*Voluntary Attention (or Planned Attention)*

Source: Adapted from Guido (1998)

The in-salience hypothesis is thoroughly discussed in reference to its complementary part (namely, *re-salience*) inside Guido's (1998) *Dichotic theory of salience*. It is argued that consumer awareness of the marketing stimuli can occur either when the stimulus is in-salient or when the stimulus is re-salient to the individual perceiver; that is, respectively, when the marketing/advertising stimulus is contextually *incongruent* with a perceiver's schema, or when the marketing/advertising stimulus is contextually *congruent* with a perceiver's goal (when a perceiver is involved with the stimulus). The former is basically a bottom-up process started by some external input; the latter is basically a top-down process started by some internal goal.[3] The former process is supported by *complexity theories* and, therefore, it will involve involuntary or passive attention. The latter process is supported by *consistency theories* and it will entail voluntary or planned attention.

Table 3 (*above*) summarizes the fundamentals of the *Dichotic theory of salience* which will be discussed in some detail - as for its model of incongruity-salience - starting from the following paragraph.

1.   AXIOMS

1.1   *Axiom One:* Salience Is Different from Its Effect

We assume that a *stimulus* can be correctly defined as "salient" (here, *in-salient*) only when salience as a construct is defined *a priori* and then memory for the stimulus, as a function of manipulated salience, is directly measured.[4]

This may seem obvious, but one trap of the salience construct is the temptation to be circular, to define as salient those stimuli that attract attention and are more memorable (cf. Fiske, Kenny, and Taylor 1982). In past literature, salience has been very often explained indirectly, by recurring to a number of paraphrases which have related its meaning to its effects. Specifically, one effect of salience has been used to define the construct itself: That of attracting attention (commonly referred to as *salience effect*). Davis (1990), for example, drawing on the studies of social cognition by Fiske and Taylor (1984), defined salience as "a property" of a stimulus "that attracts attention of perceivers" (p. 334). Also Lynch and Srull (1982), in a widely cited review on memory and attentional factors in consumer choice, explicitly mentioned "*salience effects*, in which physically salient events in the environment appear to capture a disproportionate amount of attention" (p. 31). Since the notion of salience - these authors refer back to - is Taylor and Fiske's (1978) notion linked to attention, such a definition of salience effects actually conceals a truism disguised as an empirical proposition. If a stimulus is salient because it captures a disproportionate amount of attention, the capturing of the attention cannot be anything but its effect, insofar as, *by definition*, a disproportionate amount of attention is the consequence of a salient stimulus.

Although attracting attention seems intrinsically related to the salience construct, this is not the only salience effect recognized in literature. The effect on attention, sometimes, acts as a mediator for other effects of salient stimuli, by which the salient construct has also been defined. We have already mentioned (see, *above*, Chapter Two, Paragraph 4.3.1), for example, a work by Taylor and Thompson (1982), in which salience has been defined as that "phenomenon that when one's attention is differently directed to one portion of the environment rather than to others, the information contained in that portion will receive disproportionate weighing in subsequent judgments" (p. 175). In this case, the definition of salience is linked to the causal connection between the *salience effect* (properly defined as the ability of salient stimuli to attract perceivers' attention) and its role in the following judgments. This result, known in literature as *top-of-the-head phenomenon*, together with the capacity of salient stimuli to facilitate their own learning (*von Restorff effect*), and to inhibit recall of competing stimuli (*inhibition effect*), is one of those three major effects of salience widely recognized in literature.

These salience effects (*top-of-the-head effect* on causal attribution, *von Restorff effect* on learning, and *inhibition effect* on memory) were all found apparently linked to the capacity of salient stimuli to attract attention of perceivers and elicit an accurate recall more easily.[5] However, the concept of salience to which past studies refer to is either different from one study to the other or often omitted in their research premises. Indeed, researchers conducting these studies usually gave salience a variety of meanings (e.g., accessibility, activation, availability, importance, capacity to attract attention, etc.), and only vaguely articulated the theoretical underpinnings of these terms. Therefore, while it is important to eliminate such definitions which circularly define salience through its effects, it seems also necessary to consolidate both the terminology and the measurement methodologies in salience literature to make these findings comparable.

The in-salience hypothesis proposes a more scientifically useful definition of salience that includes all the different perceptual antecedents of salience (i.e., both in a immediate and in a larger context) - apart from motivational antecedents, which are the subject of re-salience. It answers to the question of when a stimulus is salient by proposing a comprehensive cause - that is, a contextual incongruity between a stimulus and a perceiver's schema - which is able to explain the effects on attention and memory of the different salience manipulations presented in literature (including those based on the Gestalt figure-ground principle, unusuality, physical factors, etc.). By specifying the origin of the salience phenomenon, the in-salience hypothesis provides an aprioristic definition which enables us to discern between this construct and other similar ones - e.g., vividness - which could have the same effects on attention but not on memory (cf. Taylor and Thompson 1982). In conclusion, the definition of in-salience enables us to discriminate among different constructs - without confusing their cause with their effect - and to compare results presented in literature under different labels.

1.2   *Axiom Two:* **Salience Depends on the Context**

We assume that "salience" (here, *in-salience*) is dependent on the context in which the stimulus occurs. That is, salience is not an absolute quality of a stimulus, but rather its occurrence depends on the physical, situational environment in which the stimulus is perceived.

The role of the stimulus context is twofold and regards both the creation of the stimulus figurality and the activation of perceivers' schemata. First of all, the physical context is a necessary condition of perception, as it acts as a ground for the stimulus to be sensed (see, *above*, Chapter Two, Paragraph 3.1). Figurality, however, together with contextual novelty and other physical properties (such as position, intensity, size, etc.), is not a sufficient condition to make a stimulus salient. Such qualities, indeed, do not guarantee that a stimulus will be able to capture the perceiver's attention. Therefore, any definition that acknowledges these cases as positive examples of salience is fundamentally wrong. Since salience is not an absolute property of the stimulus, it varies in relation to contexts: The *same* perceiver in two different situations will not be equally attracted by the same stimulus.[6]

Figurality by itself does not imply salience. A new definition of salience cannot neglect that not everything that is perceived is, indeed, salient. That is, not every figural stimulus is able to gather the perceiver's mental resources required to process more deeply what comes to his attention. Figurality, in other words, is only a *pre-conscious* phase that allows people to distinguish each stimulus and to address the perceiver's attention to it. It is a continuous process that allows people to create a perceptual representation of the attended stimuli through the transformation by the sensory receptors of inputs into figures (Glass and Holyoak 1986). The conscious phase - the one concerning in-salience - occurs only subsequently. It is this latter phase - when a contextual incongruity between a stimulus and the perceiver's schema is detected - that constitutes the salience phenomenon.

Let's consider some examples regarding different instances of salience reported in literature. McArthur and Post (1977), in a widely cited study, have argued that brightness, motion and pattern complexity are conditions which allow a stimulus to stand out. Their manipulations were based upon Gestalt laws of figural emphasis in object perception (Berlyne 1970; Kahneman 1973; Titchener 1908), extended to the social field. We argue that such particular qualities (brightness, complexity, or movement) do not objectively imply the occurrence of salience. Figurality always comes from a contrast within a context: Inside a signboard, for example, a switched-off bulb attracts more attention than a lit-up bulb, although the latter is a more brilliant stimulus. The in-salience hypothesis, moreover, maintains that it is not the fact that the bulb is switched-off that makes the stimulus salient, but the possibility that its being switched-off is in contrast in that context with some mental schema possessed by a perceiver. In other words, while the switched-off bulb stands out thanks to its figurality, the fact that it attracts a perceiver's attention and that it is recalled would depend on the possibility that a perceiver - with a normal level of personal involvement[7] - could consider the bulb, say, burnt (that is incongruent, in a way, with the mental schema of "sign-board" he could have). Similarly, if we take the case of a "moving" stimulus, such as the one studied by McArthur and Post (1977) - that is, a person rocking on a rocking chair - compared to another stimulus - i.e., a person quietly seated -, while the perception of the stimulus will operate according to the Gestalt principles of figural emphasis, the interest and the focused attention which could come from such a stimulus would depend on the incongruity of the rocking movement in relation to the mental schema of "sitting person" possessed by a perceiver.

This interpretation is similar to that of statistically novel and unusual stimuli: Since rare and unfamiliar stimuli, as well as unusual ones, are rather infrequent in the perceivers' experience and, therefore, hardly represented in their schemata, it is easier for them to stand out and attract attention, thus resulting salient (cf. Fiske 1980). Also in this case, however, salience is not originated independently from the context in which a stimulus occurs. Indeed, if we simply maintained that only "novel" stimuli were able to capture attention, it would not explain why, sometimes, the most familiar stimuli are the ones more outstanding in certain environments (see, e.g., Zajonc 1968). This circumstance, actually, proves even more the importance of the context in which the stimulus occurs. A more familiar stimulus attracts attention when it occurs *in a novel context*, that is, in a context made of less familiar stimuli, which contrasts the perception of the stimulus object.[8]

Apart from figurality and novelty, also physical factors associated with a stimulus do not compulsorily imply the occurrence of salience. This position was clearly expressed by Reber (1985), who stated: "Salience [...] is not necessarily associated with physical factors such as intensity, clarity, size, etc." (p. 657). In analogy with figural stimuli, it is not the presence of physical qualities which makes a stimulus stand out, but the contextual relationship between the stimulus these qualities are associated with and the perceivers' schemata. This has been recently demonstrated by a paper in the field of print advertising, regarding manipulations of two layout components of an in-ad health warning. Rather than the physical qualities of the stimulus (in this case, the size of the type used and the background color of the ad), it was the novelty and the unusuality of manipulations the elements which produced the effects on attention (Popper and Murray 1989). The ad message, in other words, was not attended because it was large or colored, but because it was different in that context from consumers' expectations.

The context in which the stimulus is perceived performs also a second role in the creation of salience, that of influencing the activations of schemata. A particular schema, indeed, becomes active only in a given context (Barsalou 1987, 1989).[9] It has been convincingly demonstrated that schemata are unstable to the extent that different information is incorporated into the representations of a stimulus in different situations. We could talk, in such cases, of *context-dependent information* (Barsalou 1982). This argumentation has been supported, moreover, by a host of findings in literature (see, e.g., Anderson and Ortony 1975); therefore, for example, the same level of attention and memory is not aroused by reading the sentence: "The challenger was struck by a fist" in a column of a boxing match, rather than reading the same sentence in a report of an election debate.[10]

In synthesis, contextual dependency refers to variations in physical and situational circumstances that tend to cause differences in the accessibility of particular schemata for any perceiver. Different situations, events, and circumstances will vary with respect to the accessibility moderators (Higgins and King 1981).

1.3   *Axiom Three:* Salience Depends on Perceivers

We assume, finally, that "salience" (here, *in-salience*) is dependent on the individual perceiver. That is, salience is not an absolute quality of a stimulus, but rather its occurrence depends on schemata possessed by the person who processes the stimulus. We are not defining the term "individual" in the narrow sense of a particular person, but instead we are referring to members of various audiences. A conceptual schema is part of a mental set of an audience member. Thus, any experimental conclusion is based on composite findings about many individuals (see, *below*, Paragraph 2.1.5 on *Personal and modal schemata*).

This assumption stresses even further the conviction that salience is not an absolute property of a stimulus which acts independently from the conditions in which the stimulus occurs and is perceived. Together with the context, also the nature of the perceiver is essential for the occurrence of salience. A stimulus that attracts a perceiver's attention is not necessarily the same that attracts another perceiver's attention. On a shopping trip, for example, the announcement of a new dietetic product can be of some interest to a man with weight problems, but not to his fiancée who walks beside him (two different perceivers in the same spatial and temporal situation). The same announcement, moreover, can be of no interest to the same man a month later (same perceiver, different temporal situation), while he is lying pale and pasty in a hospital (different spatial situation), after having been let down by his fiancée.

In this "sad" example, we have imagined that a new dietetic product constitutes the stimulus.[11] Independently from the fact that the stimulus (the dietetic product) is salient because the man, the perceiver, is involved in weight problems (and has motives to be interested in the product) or rather because the man has noticed the product for its novelty (that is, its incongruity in relation to the idea he might have had about dietetic products on the market), the novelty by itself does not make the stimulus salient if it is not perceived as such by the individual. And, indeed, the attention of a different perceiver (in this example, the fiancée) could not be captured. Salience, in conclusion, cannot be separated from who the perceiver is.[12]

In past research, there has been usually a fundamental misunderstanding between what we call the *force of salience*, which is a property of the construct, and the *effect of salience*, which is a property of the receiver of the stimulus. While the force of salience is the potential effect inherent in a stimulus, the effect of salience is what manifests itself to the receiver. This separation becomes particularly important in the field of mass communication and marketing, where messages or products are addressed to a multitude of individuals. In this field, differently from interpersonal communication (where the receiver is known), it is necessary to operate a distinction on the nature of perceivers. Following Eco (1979), we call *addressee*, the model perceiver (whose attention has to be captured by the authors of the communication), and *receiver*, the real perceiver (whose attention is actually captured).[13] If we suppose that the communication is the advertising message, the addressee is a textual strategy for the type of interlocutor (e.g., the consumer) that the author of the ad (e.g., the copywriter) has in mind. The copywriter imagines a certain consumer, whose reactions to the ad he accounts for, and elaborates a message that is potentially salient for that model perceiver. By incorporating the device of the addressee in the structure of the ad, the copywriter is actually trying to give particular interpretive directions to his model perceiver. In this way, he establishes the force of the ad.

Nevertheless, once the message has been launched, the effects of the ad on receivers could not correspond to its planned force, since there are as multiple effects as many empirical perceivers.[14] It is on the receivers - who are the real perceivers - that the effect of the salient message depends. Therefore, an effect without the existence of a real perceiver does not exist. The in-salience hypothesis maintains that, in general, what will make an addressee a receiver is the availability and the accessibility of schemata which act as a base of comparison between the stimulus in that context and the information possessed by the perceiver. In synthesis, perceiver dependency refers to the individual differences in the availability and accessibility of particular schemata that are independent of any variations in the individual circumstances or contexts of perception (cf. Higgins and King 1981).

The bulk of the remaining portion of this chapter is devoted to presenting four major propositions of the in-salience hypothesis. The final part of this contribution outlines the implications of these propositions for the attainment of consumer awareness.

2. PROPOSITIONS AND IMPLICATIONS

2.1   *Proposition One:* A Stimulus Is In-Salient when It Is Incongruent in a Certain Context with a Perceiver's Schema

We define *in-salience* as an incongruity between a stimulus in a certain context and a perceiver's schema. It is the simultaneous presence of these three elements - stimulus, context, and schemata - which is the base of the consumer information process and the cause of any of its communication outputs. This definition of in-salience recognizes all the basic axioms stated above, namely: (1) The separation of the salience construct from its effects; (2) The role of the context in the perception of the stimulus; and (3) The role of the perceiver and the subjectivity of his experience based on schemata activated in the context of perception.

Only one other definition of salience in past literature would seem equally adherent to the premises made above, namely the most recent definition proposed by Fiske and Taylor (1991). Unfortunately, it has as a major drawback that of being quite indefinite. According to Fiske and Taylor (1991), salience to a perceiver is "the extent to which particular stimuli stand out relative to others in their environment" (p. 246). Next, by comparing salience to vividness, they add: "Whereas salience is determined by the relation of an object to its context, vividness is inherent in a stimulus itself" (p. 254). This latter factor, however, together with the use of the word *extent*, makes this definition quite ambiguous and hard to operationalize. Omitting the reference to the cause of this comparative prominence means defining as salient any figural stimulus able to influence perceivers simply at a pre-conscious level. On the contrary, it is the incongruity perceived between a stimulus in a certain context and a receiver's schema which enables us to determine the (in-)salience effects. In other words, not just any stimulus which is noteworthy or figural is salient, but a salient stimulus - that is, one which is able to influence attention and memory - can result from a contextual incongruity with a perceiver's schema.[15]

Operationalizations of in-salience, therefore, would be more easily achieved by marketers than before, with the practical advantage of knowing that the effect of this incongruity will result in higher degrees of consumer awareness. In past studies, on the contrary, the use of different definitions of salience did not grant the desirable effects on attention and memory (that is, consumer awareness), because the myriads of salience manipulations used did not refer to a common background. The main challenge of this approach is, indeed, to explain all the different cases of salience other than involvement (see, *above*, Table 2) by recurring to an incongruity model. Moreover, it is maintained that (in-)salience and incongruity are just *one* field of research - when using this approach based on schema theory and information processing. It is proposed, thus, to unify the terminology regarding in-salient and incongruent stimuli.

Hereafter, the three basic components of in-salience will be defined and discussed.

A. The Stimulus

The two major sources of influence in perceiving are (1) External events, objects, and situations, and (2) Internal influences, such as personal goals, interests, and drives. Either one may largely influence the perceptual mode. Generally speaking, the information processing starts with a *stimulus* - some kind of informational input, which may emanate from within the individual or from outside.[16]

In-salience is basically a bottom-up process that starts from physical, external stimuli.[17] In a consumer setting, these physical stimuli take the form of marketing stimuli. Stimuli are *cues* (Markin 1974, p. 242). Cues are features of complex percepts that possess a particular association or meaning, are learned, and often lead to misperceptions (see, e.g., Tom et al. 1987, *above*, in Chapter Two, Paragraph 3.2). A cue is an extremely flexible concept for describing aspects of a percept that may prove meaningful to a respondent. This flexibility makes cue a useful notion in dealing with a variety of non-verbal aspects of marketing and advertising. If a cue is exclusive to a particular object (e.g., the round-shaped bottle to Coca Cola), it is sufficient information for a percept. If the cue is common to more than one object, it is unreliable. Many cues used in marketing are not exclusive to a particular product, hence, they may lead to erroneous inferences or misperceptions.[18] Cue is also a useful notion in an experimental context: It suggests elemental or basic features of a percept that a researcher can add to or subtract from it in the course of devising manipulations.[19]

2.1.1   Stimulus Cues vs. Information Cues

Perception basically involves the process of categorization. In this process buyers make frequent use of cues. The active person is literally bombarded with stimulation at any given moment. However, only part of it gets through as information. This differentiation between stimulation and information sets a distinction between two types of cues individuals are faced with. A *stimulus cue* is a conspicuous stimulus somewhere in the sensory field toward which attention can be drawn or directed, whereas an *information cue* is a bit of information about a marketing stimulus.[20]

This separation is critical to marketers in their trying to make a stimulus in-salient. Indeed, not only do they need to draw the attention of consumers (i.e., addressees), but they also need to transfer to them certain pieces of information about the product. Marketing communication, including a large part of advertising, is not sought out *per se*. It operates to maximize consumer awareness and must incorporate elements that will direct search (call attention) to the product or to specific aspects of it. To succeed, it must transfer attention to an unsought message (information or motivating stimulus). Therefore, where an ad must seek out an audience member, the aim should be to maximize feature prominence (attention getting elements) of the information content advertisers want to convey to consumers, and to exclude the other advertising components. In the past, the concern of advertisers was to generate high levels of awareness for their advertisements rather than memory for any one piece of product/brand information. And, however, recalling that an advertisement showed a bull in a china shop without remembering the advertised brand or the product being offered for sale has less value than knowing that "Merrill Lynch is bullish on America."[21]

From this separation between stimulus cues and information cues, it follows an important corollary of the in-salience theory. If the in-salient stimulus is one which is able to display its effects on attention and memory, the best way for advertisers to pursue their goals is to *make the in-salient stimulus cue coincide with the information cue*. Indeed, when the piece of information (i.e., the information cue) they want to transfer to their audience is constituted by a stimulus (i.e., the stimulus cue) which is contextually incongruent with a perceivers' schema, the effects on attention and memory for that piece of information will be the greatest. A perfect coincidence between stimulus cues and information cues occurs, specifically, in the so-called *interactive pictures* (Lutz and Lutz 1977), where the brand name and the picture are one thing, conveying the same meaning or two different ones; or even in the so-called *suggestive brand names* (Keller, Heckler, and Houston 1998; Sen 1999), which are defined as brand names that convey relevant attribute or benefit information in a particular product context (such as PicturePerfect televisions, Mop'n Glow floor cleaner).[22]

The in-salience hypothesis, therefore, has the advantage of guiding advertisers in selecting modalities by which to convey the core of their message. If we consider an advertisement as "an organized collection of separate stimuli, rather than a single stimulus" (Leigh 1984, p. 6), the best solution for advertisers is to present their message (that is, their information cue) within the same in-salient stimulus (that is, *as* the stimulus cue), rather than to use two different cues in the same ad. Although little research has been done on the comparative attentional and memory value of schema-incongruent stimuli versus other stimuli in the same ad (for a specific application, see Peltier 1989), it seems apparent that there is no advantage in stimulating consumers to spend more time processing a stimulus cue in an ad containing a *separate* information cue, also for the existence of an inhibition effect for non-in-salient stimuli (cf., *above*, Chapter Two, Paragraph 5.2.1: *The inhibition effect on memory*).[23] This attentional focus on the stimulus cue, does not result, indeed, in higher memory scores for information cues such as product class, brand name, and product attributes, than if the stimulus cue was not in-salient.

2.1.2   Cue Normalizing and Cue Resisting

Our first proposition does not suggest that every individual who detects a cue incongruity be, in turn, motivated to process such a stimulus. Not every stimulus which is in-salient (that is, contextually incongruent with a perceiver's schema) necessarily implies processing consequences on attention and memory.

First of all, an incongruent cue could not be detected at all by the potential perceiver (i.e., the addressee). Apart from the case in which the incongruity is so weak as not to overcome a person's sensory threshold, this happens because an average audience member tends to perceive what he wants to perceive in any given message. That is, the product of perceiving is determined not only by the cues available but also by the degree to which the individual tends to eliminate a certain number of cues while arriving at a perceptual product. *Cue normalizing* refers to the absorption of a cue by a perceiver into his visual, audio, or verbally logical schema of the majority of the cues in the message. This happens regardless of how well the cue actually fits in the rest of the message the audience member is examining. As we said, people usually see what they expect to see, and what they expect to see is based on their schemata (Neisser 1976). Past experience, which often determines what is attended to, can prevent attending to messages that are not expected or which members of the audience are not accustomed to (see Britt 1978, pp. 88-89, for examples).[24] In a marketing context, people tend to perceive products and product attributes according to their own expectations.[25]

This effect of "assimilation to expectancies" occurs if the stimulus either does not deviate so much from expectancies or is rather ambiguous. The available evidence in personality literature indicates that when a cue is relatively ambiguous, perceivers selectively attend to those stimuli that they expect to find and these exert a disproportionate influence upon their impressions; on the other hand, when behavioral stimuli are unambiguous, those that deviate markedly from expectations draw more attention and have a stronger influence upon impressions than the expected ones (McArthur 1981). Either chronically accessible or activated schemata can influence impression formation by way of affecting a perceiver's expectations (see, *below*, *Proposition Three*).[26] A large portion of the things the perceiver fails to notice will make no difference. Some smaller cues simply may be transitional stimuli from one cue to another. However, occasionally *even in-salient cues* may fail to be registered either accurately or at all by an audience. This discussion refers precisely to these cases.

There are two extreme cases under which an incongruent cue is resisted, thus failing to induce information processing and hampering the display of a message's in-salience effects. *Cue resisting* refers to the removal of a cue from further consideration by a perceiver, such that it is either selectively ignored or overlooked. This occurs when the cue is too inappropriate to be normalized - i.e., either it is too insignificant to change the overall meaning of the message, or it is too complex or novel - and yet too evident to escape an initial glance.

The first case occurs when one's choice of processing strategy is contingent upon the level of cue incongruity (Hastie 1980; Meyers-Levy 1988a). Cues that are low in contextual incongruity may fail to motivate processing because their modestly aberrant content may be perceived not as incongruent but rather as fairly irrelevant to the stimulus-implied schema (Alba and Hasher 1983). Thus, cues that are modestly atypical, but not in clear opposition to the schema, may fail to invoke the associative activity that characterizes processing of in-salient stimuli (see also, *above*, Chapter Two, Paragraph 4.2).

The second case of cue resisting refers to such phenomena as perceptual blocking and perceptual defense (see, *above*, Chapter Two, Paragraphs 3.2 and 4.2). In the case of perceptual blocking, the in-salient stimulus is so complex that the perceiver screens it out. This process protects individuals from being bombarded with stimulations from the external world. In the case of perceptual defense, on the other hand, the in-salient stimulus is so novel (read, threatening) that it is not processed, even if exposure has taken place. This concept deals to a great extent with built-up attitudes, values, and other cognitive elements that cause a person to react at the moment of stimulation. The individual has developed certain attitudes about an issue and, if a stimulus is quite contradictory to his previous attitude or expectations, it could be rebuked and cast aside from conscious perception.

2.1.3   Moderate Incongruity

From the previous considerations, it follows that there is a range in stimulus intensity that is the best for in-salience occurrences. This result has also been found in past literature on incongruity. A growing body of evidence suggests that categorization processes are important not only in information processing, but also in consumer judgments and affect formation (see, e.g., Alba and Hutchinson 1987; Cohen and Basu 1987). Although congruence is envisioned as a continuum, researchers have focused on three discrete points: Congruity, moderate incongruity, and extreme incongruity.[27]

According to Mandler's (1982) *Model of schematic processing*, congruity between the configuration of a cue (e.g., those features that constitute a "beautiful home") and its expected values (e.g., those attributes stored in memory as a schema of "beautiful home"), results in the assimilation of the stimulus (which is seen as familiar and acceptable) and in a positive evaluation that does not cause physiological arousal or true affect. Moderate incongruity produces relatively more positive affect, resulting from the cognitive effort required for assimilation within the evoked schema.[28] Extreme incongruity, finally, is hypothesized to result in one of two processing responses (accommodation or schema switching) and several evaluative outcomes.[29]

Meyers-Levy and Tybout (1989), Ozanne, Brucks, and Grewal (1992), and Stayman, Alden, and Smith (1992) found support for Mandler's (1982) theory in a consumer-behavior context by examining the effects of congruity, moderate incongruity, and extreme incongruity between a cued product-category schema and a set of new product attributes.[30] These findings advocate our idea of a common origin between salient and incongruent stimuli - a link between salience and incongruity that can be explored through the theory of in-salience.

B.   The Context

In the in-salience model, the meaning of *context* is twofold: In a strict sense, it represents the physical environment in which the stimulus takes place; and, in a larger sense, it includes both external and internal factors - regarding the situation and the individual - that can moderate the act of perceiving. So wide-ranging are the kinds of influences which can be included under this heading, that it is debatable whether the label "context" is really helpful. The term "context," however, was also used in the past to include the broad environmental setting and emotional state in which an act of perception takes place, as well as the "sensory" context, i.e., other or earlier part of a scene which may influence the interpretation of the stimulus a person is currently perceiving (Humphreys and Bruce 1991, p. 95).

In a strict sense, context may be described as a number of potential stimuli, some of which are perceived as differing from the background (Restle 1961). The totality of these stimuli pre-consciously activates a perceiver's schema (Barsalou 1987, 1989), so that the individual is able to detect any incongruity between a particular stimulus in that context and the activated schema. While the former part of this process is automatic and uncontrollable (Higgins and Bargh 1987, p. 376), the latter part is usually conscious and regards both perceiver's attention *and* interpretation; thus, results can be measured in terms of memory for the in-salient stimulus (see, *below*, Implications). Evidence for this chain (context → schema → in-salient stimuli) has also been provided in consumer literature, although under different labels. Yi (1990), for example, discussed the effects of *contextual priming*, by defining ad context "the materials that precede or surround the target ad, such as articles in magazines, ads for other products, and station identifications on radio or television" (p. 215). Specifically, he maintained that contextual materials may activate particular product attributes and prime consumers' interpretations of product information, which, in turn, can affect consumers' evaluations of the advertised brands (see also, *below*, Paragraph 2.3.1 on *The role of activation*).

In a larger sense, context embraces both personal and situational factors. This broad classification relates to the internal characteristics of the individual and to the physical characteristics of the environment. *Personal factors*, on the one hand, regard the individuals and include their personalities and life styles, their motives (goals, interests, and drives), and their attitudes (brand-specific and general attitudes).[31] Each of these is affected by the others (Mahatoo 1985, p. 16). All of them can be summarized by the concept of *involvement*, which acts as a moderating variable for in-salience.[32] *Situational factors*, on the other hand, regard both the physical setting made by stimuli other than the focal one (competing stimuli, related events, etc.),[33] and the temporary characteristics of the individual that are induced externally or by the environment (the perceiver's task, mood, stress, lack of time, etc.).[34] Even when the significance of context is confined to its narrower sense, it is possible to demonstrate the ubiquity of contextual influences (see, *below*, Paragraph 2.2.4).[35]

C. Schemata

The notion of *schemata* is long established. It can be traced back to Head (1920) and Piaget (1926), but its contemporary use spawned by the famous, classic book *Remembering*, written in 1932 by Sir Frederic Bartlett of Cambridge University, from which the author of the current research drew his original inspiration for this study. Bartlett (1932) defined a schema as "an active organization of past reactions or of past experiences, which must always

be supposed to be operating in any well-adapted organic response" (p. 201).
Two distinct components of Bartlett's definition of the schema construct
provided the infrastructure that today's theoreticians use to define the basic
tenets of schematic information processing. First, he proposed that schematic
information processing is active at the *automatic level* of human processing.
Second, he stated that schemata are *masses* of organized past experiences that
are cognitively structured to represent combinations of information units.

From Bartlett' subconscious and holistic view of schematic processing, a
number of current definitions for the schema construct have been advanced in
the literature.[36] In recent years, together with schema, terms such as *prototype*
(Cantor and Mischel 1977; Posner and Keele 1970; Reed 1972; Rosch 1978),
construct (Higgins and King 1981), *theme* (Ostrom et al. 1980), *script* (Schank
and Abelson 1977), and *stereotypes* (Hamilton 1979) have also been proposed.
There are, of course, important differences among these conceptions, not all of
which have been fully articulated; yet, they all have been used to describe "an
organized representation of prior knowledge that guides the process of current
information" (Alloy and Tabachnik 1984, p. 114).

To develop an all-encompassing definition of schema is an especially
difficult if not impossible task. It is useful, however, to specify as completely as
possible the theoretical domain of the construct under investigation (Churchill
1979). For this purpose, the definition of schemata by Peltier (1989) can be
extremely effective. Schemata are defined here as "unconscious cognitive
representations that consist of general knowledge structures gained through
past experience that contain expectations for describing interrelationships
between a stimulus domain and previously formed categorical organizations of
that stimulus domain" (p. 10).

2.1.4   Characteristics of Schemata

This definition addresses a number of important dimensions for
identifying the conceptual domain of the schema construct. First, schemata are
abstract cognitive representations that operate through automatic activation.
Consumers can actively process schematic information, but it is the
unconscious operation of the schema that gives rise to the specific conscious
contents of the mind. Second, schemata are knowledge networks developed
over a lifetime of experiences that store specific attribute information used to
simplify the world into a more conceptually manageable framework. They
provide rules of thumb for constructing global cognitive responses from limited
information.[37] Third, schemata are categorical by nature and contain an
individual's cognitive organizations or categorizations of a given stimulus
domain.[38] These categories describing a particular schema are then organized in
a pyramidal fashion.[39] Fourth, schemata provide expectations or preconceptions

of the appropriate characteristics of a stimulus domain and the rules and procedures for applying these expectations. These schema-driven expectations are the cognitive devices used to appraise the congruity of a stimulus configuration.[40]

2.1.5   Personal and Modal Schemata

An important point is that raw stimuli and perception of the stimuli are quite different. The raw stimuli are composed of sound waves, light waves/particles, bits of chemicals, textures, and levels of temperature, whereas the interpretation of those stimuli results from information processing. Different perceivers may assign divergent meanings to exactly the same stimulus because its perception is influenced by their expectations and, first of all, by their schemata. As mentioned *above* (Axiom Three), we cannot assume that because two people receive exactly the same stimulus, say a message, they will perceive it in a similar manner. The basic insight that emerges from this approach is that no one ever shares an identical schema with another person, and so his experiences of reality will be unique and separate (cf. Kelly 1955).[41]

However, the laws of statistics allow researchers to define *modal schemata*, whose elements (i.e., stimulus attributes) are common to the majority of people in a spatial or temporal situation (cf. Fishbein and Ajzen 1975, p. 219; see also, *below*, Paragraph 2.1.10.1). Such shared schemata allow operationalizing the schema construct and making it valuable in marketing applications (see, *below*, Chapter Four, Paragraph 2.1, *Part One*). In the most generic application, for example, the advertiser would be encouraged to develop an ad featuring positively evaluated attributes associated with a product, which are shared by the largest portion of a user group: This strategy increases the likelihood that that ad will be relevant to the greatest number of people in a consumers' group. Such an approach is the one at the basis of *positioning*, i.e., providing products with attribute features (e.g., packaging, color, form, names, and theme) that induce the perceiver (consumer) to take note of them.[42] Success in positioning is dependent on the marketers' accurate information about the pertinent schemata that are employed by consumers in their product selection, and on their capacity to give the product those *re-salient* characteristics that fulfill expectations within the schematic context.[43] In general, because of this expectancy generalization, "a manufacturer must promote his product as the *only* product that can meet a particular need. Effort must be made to point out the differences between his product and that of a competitor and why the consumer can meet his wants most successfully with this product." (Britt 1978, pp. 174-176).

2.1.6 Types of Schemata

Within particular content domains, researchers have made specific claims about the nature of these mental structures and their functions as parts of a larger information processing system. According to Hastie (1981), three distinct conceptions of schemata are represented in recent cognitive theory: *Central tendency schemata, template schemata,* and *procedural schemata.* First, and simplest, are *central tendency schemata* (or *prototypes*), which have been defined somewhat differently in the past. The term has been referred either to a member of a stimulus set that is located at the statistical center of the distribution of items in the set (Posner 1969), or to a member of a category with the most attributes in common with other members of the category and the fewest attributes in common with members of other contrasting categories (Rosch and Mervis 1975). Second are *template schemata* (or *charts*), which are filing systems for classifying, retaining, and coordinating incoming sensory data (Sokolov 1975; see, also *below*, Paragraph 2.2.5). Third, and most complex, are *procedural schemata* (or *scripts*), which have reference to classes of similar action sequences in which the constituent behavioral elements are tightly interrelated.[44] All of them are useful examples of schemata employed by the in-salience theory.

2.1.7 Instantiation

Schemata and related knowledge structures have figured prominently in cognitive research in recent years. Although many of these experimental endeavors were conducted without the use of schema theory as conceptual focus, an empirical finding that has become clear is that information that can be *instantiated* into a schema is more memorable than information that can not. A schema is instantiated "whenever a particular configuration of values are bound to a particular configuration of variables at a particular moment in time" (Rumelhart 1984, p. 165).[45] Specifically, instantiation occurs when a stimulus configuration can be associated with an activated schema.[46] Instantiation does not necessarily mean that the information contained in a stimulus configuration matches that of the schema activated for processing it. It only requires that the stimulus can be *interpreted* from information contained in a schema. Consequently, information that is unable to be instantiated into a schema cannot be characterized as in-salient or non-in-salient because it cannot be interpreted in terms of expectations contained in the current knowledge structures of the perceiver.

2.1.8   Information Congruity Theory

When an individual confronts a particular stimulus configuration he searches his cognitive network to locate any relevant knowledge that might be useful for processing the incoming information. Upon activation of a relevant schema that is dependent on the context in which perception occurs, the individual will attempt to match the attributes of the stimulus configuration with the attribute requirements associated with that schema. *Information congruity* is defined as the degree to which the attributes associated with the stimulus configuration match the expectations that the activated schema allocates for those attributes. *Incongruity*, here, refers to the extent a structural correspondence is not achieved between the entire configuration of attribute relations associated with a stimulus and the configuration specified by the schema (Mandler 1982).

Given a long-standing principle in psychology, according to which individuals attempt to form and maintain internal consistency for their knowledge (see, for a review, Peltier 1989, p. 22), in light of incongruent stimulus information, individuals can turn to three basic attentional strategies for maintaining their schema consistency. They can: (1) Ignore the incongruent information; (2) Assimilate the information into a current schema (e.g., the unexpected event can be attributed to temporary or situational causes, or the meaning of the incongruity can be distorted or changed); or (3) Modify their schemata to form a new internally consistent representation (accommodation or schema switching - see, *above*, under *Moderate incongruity*; also, Coupey and Jung 1996). The last two strategies suggest that incongruent information requires more attentional resources for processing it than for information that confirms our expectancies. Numerous researchers have supported the notion that incongruent information receives more processing and produces more elaborate and recallable memory representations than does congruent or expected information (see, for review, Hastie, Park, and Weber 1984, p. 175).

However, it has been also shown that enhanced memory for incongruent information would not be found when people have strong expectancies and schemata (Stangor and Ruble 1989). This happens because people not only search, but they often have some sort of expectation or hypothesis about what they will find. For example, if consumers expect a leading brand to have superior characteristics than those of "unknown" brands, then they will be "set" to have evidence of poor quality in the unrecognized brand. Hence, these people can be said to "perceive" inferior quality even though, in the absence of brand identity, they might discover the same features in a well-known brand. *However*, the process by whatever name involves judgment (or prejudgment) is not "perception" at all but rather "inference" (Woods 1981, pp. 242-243). The inferred knowledge of the product is actually decided prior to any actual experience with it and, indeed, is based on inadequate feature detection, hence, it is not perception (see, *above*, Paragraph 2.1.2 on *Cue normalizing and cue resisting*).

2.1.9   Spreading Activation

When an individual perceives a stimulus, the incoming data are matched against a schema which is contextually activated. When input data are received, the perceiver constructs an episodic network (a chart) that provides an organized image of the perceived stimulus in terms of specific, known information. If there is a good fit between the incoming information and the activated schema, the individual will use the schema to fill in the gaps in the episodic network. Thus, the final impression is a combination of actual input information and information inferred from the schema (cf. Schneider and Blankmeyer 1983).

Considerable research and theory in consumer behavior has been based on the notions of categories or schemata possessed by consumers (e.g., Cohen and Basu 1987; Loken and Ward 1990; Meyers-Levy and Tybout 1989; Stafford, Walker, and Blasko 1996; Sujan and Bettman 1989), yet very little consideration has been given to the processes through which schemata are retrieved from memory (Ulhaque and Bahn 1992). Although various models of schema development and retrieval have been proposed (e.g., the *Hierarchical-network model* by Collins and Quillian 1969; the *Feature-comparison model* by Smith, Shoben and Rips 1974; the *Spreading-activation model* by Collins and Loftus 1975) - and although, also recently, the same cognitive phenomena have been addressed from a different perspective, alternatively referred to as connectionism, parallel distributed processing (PDP) models, or neural networks -[47] we shall focus here on spreading activation models. The reason being that the spreading activation, or network models, have better fared under the scholarly scrutiny of various researchers (Ashcraft 1989; Chang 1986).

According to the spreading activation model by Collins and Loftus (1975), a concept - for example, a brand - can be represented in memory as a node of a network, with attributes of the concept represented as labeled relational links between the node and other concept nodes. These links are pointers, and usually go in both directions between two concepts. The search in memory between concepts involves tracing out in parallel along the links from the node of each concept specified by the input stimuli. The spread of activation constantly expands, first to all the nodes linked to the first node, then to all the nodes linked to each of these nodes, and so on.

There could be multiple paths of various strengths between concept nodes. For example, Ferrari could be one such node in a consumer's memory while different attributes of Ferrari automobiles (fast, luxury, sporting, red, etc.) could be connected to the node Ferrari by associated pathways (see Figure 3). Another brand of sport cars (e.g., Porsche) may share some of the attributes with Ferrari (e.g., luxury) while it may also have some unique attributes of its own. The attribute "luxury" is thus linked to both Ferrari and Porsche. The more attributes two brands have in common, the more links there are between the two nodes, and the more related in memory the two brands will generally be. When a brand is activated, for example when attention is focused on Ferrari, the activation spreads out in a decreasing gradient along the links emanating from the activated brand. This activation may reach the node "Porsche" via the attribute node "luxury". When a path is found between two brands - i.e., two spreading activation intersects - a decision regarding them could be made (Collins and Loftus 1975).

Figure 3. A Possible Network Model of Memory for Ferrari

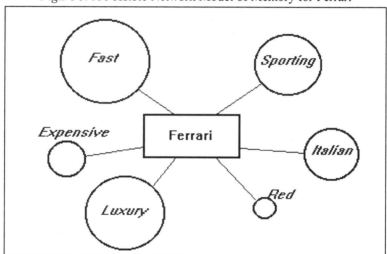

Brands or nodes have an activation value associated with them that reflects the current relevance of the node in memory (Anderson 1983). The links between nodes have weights associated with them that are determined by the strength of associations between the connected nodes. For example, if "fast" is regarded as the most relevant attribute of Ferrari, then the link, associating node "fast" to node "Ferrari", will have more weight associated with it reflecting the strength of association between the two nodes. On the other hand, if Ferrari is not thought of as an "expensive" car then the weight of the link associating node "Ferrari" to node "expensive" will be relatively low, or there will be no such link. *Relevance*, here, is defined as the weight of an attribute of a brand. In Figure 3 (*above*), the relevance of each attribute is represented by the size of the area of the circles indicating brand attributes.[48]

This point is important to the extent of our theory because *the nature of the incongruity related to an in-salient stimulus regards both the content and the weight (i.e., relevance) of the stimulus.* We argue that a stimulus can be in-salient not only when an aspect of it (i.e., an attribute) is contextually incongruent with one of the attributes in the perceiver's schema (i.e., it does not match it), but also when it has a different relevance - that is, a different weight - than that represented in the perceiver's schema. It follows that, for example, ad repetition can be a cause of in-salience, because it changes the weight associated to an attribute in the schema activated by the perceiver. The significant alterations that are brought about in the structure of consumer perceptions may take the form of shifts in the relative relevance of the attributes that are suggested by advertising. This is clearly consistent with *Agenda-setting theory* (Sutherland and Galloway 1981; Moran 1990; Schleuder, McCombs, and Wanta 1991). For example, if stories about energy receive repeated headlined coverage in an important newspaper, energy will be more relevant in readers' mind than if it had received occasional single-column mentions on inside pages (see, e.g., Obermiller 1995).[49] As noted by Ghorpade (1986, p. 26): "Advertising may be most effective in telling consumers what issues, attributes, or values to think about when making product decisions (agenda setting) rather than telling them what to think of those products or brands (persuasion)."

Under free-elicitation techniques, such as those used to operationalize "salient" beliefs in attitude-behavior models, it is reasonable to argue that the first, most accessible attributes will be those which are the most relevant - i.e., with the biggest weights - within each product schema (see, in particular, the next paragraph). Relevance, in other words, determines the accessibility of an element of a schema (e.g., a brand attribute), such that more relevant elements are more accessible for retrieval. A question such as "What attribute or product feature is the first one you think of when I say Ferrari?," is in effect measuring a pure form of agenda - i.e., the relevant attributes of Ferrari listed in rank order. This finding stresses the necessity of distinguishing between different constructs (i.e., salience, relevance, and accessibility - see *Proposition Three, below*), because in past literature the accessibility deriving from relevance has been usually referred to as "salience" (see, e.g., Fishbein and Ajzen 1975). On the contrary, the causal chain in a consumer environment is that (in-)salience influences a product's attribute relevance and this, in turn, influences accessibility (see, also, MacKenzie 1986).

2.1.10   The Concept of Salience in Attitude Research

Due to its relevance in literature, we reserve a space here for discussing the (memory-based) definitions of salience in attitude research. Basically, we shall consider two models: Fishbein and Ajzen's (1975) *Theory of Reasoned Action*, which treats salience as accessibility (operationalized as activation); and Fazio's (1986) *Process model*, which treats salience as prominence. These models have become so popular in their field that they have made widespread the meanings of salience they used, even if - we argue - they could be the subject of some criticism.

2.1.10.1 Fishbein and Ajzen's Theory of reasoned action. In Fishbein and Ajzen's (1975) *Theory of reasoned action* of attitude-behavior relationships - which extended Fishbein's (1963, 1967) *Learning theory* of attitude formation and change - salience is related to beliefs.[50] According to this theory, a person's *attitude* - which is postulated as one of the best predictors of a behavioral intention - "is a function of his *salient beliefs* at a given point in time" (p. 222, emphasis added). "Attitude" is defined here as an individual's internal evaluation of an object, such as a branded product. "Beliefs" are the subjective associations between any two discriminable concepts. As these ideas are applied to the typical marketing research study, the attitude object of interest is a brand and the related concepts are the product attributes. That is, marketing researchers have been mainly concerned with consumers' beliefs about attributes of a brand. According to the interpretation of Mitchell and Olson (1981), in the Fishbein and Ajzen's (1975) conceptualization, "salient beliefs" are those beliefs "activated from memory and 'considered' by the person in a given situation" (p. 318). Salience, in this view, is therefore considered as *activation in memory*, that is, activation of the associations (beliefs) made by the individual. The model then specifies the relationship between the set of salient beliefs about a concept (often terms *cognitive structure*) and the overall evaluation of (or *attitude toward*) the concept.[51]

Differently from Mitchell and Olson's (1981) interpretation, we argue that - if we directly go back to the text of Fishbein and Ajzen (1975) - we notice that the significance these authors originally gave to the term *salience* is much more related to the concept of *accessibility* rather than that of *activation* (Guido 1996a).[52] The failure to recognize dependency of salience on the context in which choice alternatives are perceived is argued to be a major limitation of the Fishbein paradigm (Scholten and Faia-Correia 1994; see, also, Shavitt and Fazio 1991). Fishbein and Ajzen (1975) maintain that: "Although a person may hold a large number of beliefs about any given object, it appears that only a relatively small number of beliefs serve as determinants of his attitude *at any given moment.*" (p. 218, emphasis added). This small number of beliefs that primarily determines a person's attitude toward an object are "the beliefs that are *salient* at any given point in time" (*Ibid.*, emphasis added). The authors explain this limitation, relying on research on information processing (e.g., Mandler 1967; Miller 1956; Woodworth and Schlosberg 1954) which suggests that each individual is able to attend to or process only five to nine items of information at a time.[53] This cognitive limitation should explain also Fishbein and Ajzen's reference to a specific period of time ("a belief is salient *at any given point of time*"), by recognizing that, as the time passes, salient beliefs are also subject to change; they may be strengthened or weakened or replaced by new beliefs (Barbaranelli and Guido 1998). In particular, Ward and Reingen (1990) recall Fishbein and Ajzen's (1975) suggestion that "individuals' sets of salient beliefs are subject to memory limits, and thus if previously unconsidered or nonsalient beliefs become more salient, others are likely to be dropped." (p. 260). The first consideration we can make, therefore, in support of our remark about Fishbein and Ajzen's approach to salience as accessibility, derives from the fact that salience, in these authors' view, is *contingent* to the moment in which attitude is determined. A salient belief, therefore, can be an antecedent of attitude *only as long as it is accessible in that particular moment.*

A second, more conspicuous consideration in support of our position derives from the modalities used by the authors to operationalize the concept of salience. In order to identify a person's *salient beliefs* about a given object or action, Fishbein and Ajzen (1975) suggest eliciting them "in a free-response format by asking him to list the characteristics, qualities and attributes of the object or the consequences of performing the behavior. It has been argued that salient beliefs are elicited first, and thus, consistent with the considerations above [cognitive limitations that impede processing], beliefs elicited beyond the first nine or ten are probably not salient for the individual." (p. 218). They also add: "Unfortunately, it is impossible to determine the point at which a person starts eliciting nonsalient beliefs.[54] Recommending the use of the first five to nine beliefs is therefore merely a rule of thumb." (*Ibid.*). Lutz (1991) provides a practical interpretation for this method to operationalize salience. After noticing that, in contrast to previous theories (e.g., Rosemberg 1960), Fishbein's model is quite situation-specific and deals with more stimulus-bound attributes, he suggests determining these *salient attributes* "by asking respondents in a free-response format, 'What comes to mind when you think of (the attitude object in question)?' The things an individual mentions in response to this question are taken to be the salient attributes of the attitude object - that is, *those aspects of the object of which the individual is aware without prompting.*" (pp. 326-327, emphasis added).[55] Consequently, both in Fishbein and Ajzen (1975) and in Lutz (1991), it is evident that their use of salience has to do with "accessibility" rather than "activation", because salient beliefs (attributes) are *already active* in relation to the attitude object (they do *not* need to be *activated*) and, therefore, they are *accessible* in an automatic manner. We would argue, according to our hypothesis of salience, that such beliefs (attributes) belongs to the same schema of the attitude object, that is, to the same packet of information, examples, weights, evaluations, etc. which forms that individual's schema.

In supporting this position, Fishbein and Ajzen (1975) stress the fact that, in dealing with salient beliefs, they look for something that is already "available" to the individual and it is "accessible" in that moment;[56] they do not want something that is made up ("activated") under the influence of the experimenter's techniques. They recognize that the elicitation procedure itself may produce changes in a person's belief hierarchy, such that previously nonsalient beliefs may become salient once they have been elicited and, in turn, change a person's attitude. In their words, "while listing his beliefs about an object, the person may recall some information he had forgotten or make a new inference on the basis of existing beliefs. The previously nonsalient beliefs may now become important determinants of his attitude. It follows that under these circumstances, the first few beliefs elicited will be highly related to the person's attitude as it existed prior to the elicitation of beliefs, but they may have a somewhat lower relationship to his attitude following elicitation." (Fishbein and Ajzen 1975, p. 219). This explains that salient beliefs must be "accessible" because they are available before elicitation; they must not be "activated" through any external manipulation, such as a contextual priming (e.g., Yi 1990) or a repetition process (e.g., Alba and Chattopadhyay 1986).

2.1.10.2 Modalities of free-elicitation techniques. Olson and Muderrisoglu (1979) have argued that, despite Fishbein and Ajzen advocating the use of free-elicitation techniques to operationalized salient beliefs, they have practically proposed procedures that do not allow treating salience as accessibility, but rather as activation because they influence, in some way, the elicited responses. According to these authors, Fishbein's (1967) original approach does not imply a completely *free* elicitation technique, as it provides subjects with rather specific instructions regarding the type of concepts desired: For example, "tell me what you believe to be the characteristics, qualities, and attributes of ..., etc." (Fishbein and Ajzen 1975; Kaplan and Fishbein 1969). Also marketing elicitation procedures usually imply asking consumers to state the "product characteristics" that come to their mind, rather than giving them freedom. Therefore, given this emphasis on product characteristics, Olson and Muderrisoglu (1979) argued that it is not surprising if, in marketing research, the typical multi-attribute model questionnaire includes belief ratings only about relatively abstract product attributes. It should be acknowledged, indeed, that other types of cognitive representations may be related to attitudes (cf. Abelson 1976; Calder 1978). These entail concrete visual images and scripts (Schank and Abelson 1977) as well as relatively concrete attributes (e.g., color, see Geistfeld, Sproles, and Bradenhop 1977). Therefore, only a totally unrestricted type of elicitation task is likely to generate these other types of concepts. The rationale of the *top-of-mind* recall technique proposed by Olson and Muderrisoglu is summarized in the following instructions given by the experimenter to the subject: "I will first tell you the name of the product. Then you tell me all the things that come to your mind about this product, as *rapidly* and *completely* as possible." (Olson and Muderrisoglu 1979, Appendix, p. 274, emphasis added).[57]

The operationalization of salience as "activation" rather than "accessibility" has important consequences on the stability of responses obtained by free elicitation. If the elicited salient beliefs - in their order - are not stably accessible beliefs for the subject, but rather situational activated beliefs, they could not be the ones who actually influence the subject's attitudes. The data reported by Olson and Muderrisoglu (1979), in a test-retest experiment, suggested caution in interpreting elicitation orderings in this manner, because of the lack of stability of results.[58] Olson and Muderrisoglu criticized Fishbein's operationalization of salience for relying heavily on the ordering of elicited concepts and maintained that to be confident in the theoretical interpretation of the order of elicited concepts, one should be confident first of the stability of that order. Finding that roughly 50 to 60 of the concepts elicited in a second trial were also elicited in a previous trial, they suggested restricting the definition of salience, rather than ranking ordering, only to those concepts that are reliably elicited over a multiple probing. Finally, they noticed that, in their two trials, the number of similar concepts elicited was substantially fewer (3 or 4) than the number of salient attributes typically theorized in the marketing and psychological literature (5-9 or more; cf. Fishbein and Ajzen 1975; Wilkie and Pessemier 1973).

In summary, salience in the Fishbein and Ajzen's model - and in its applications[59] - has been theoretically considered as "accessibility", but usually operationalized as "activation". We argued that salience for Fishbein and Ajzen means accessibility, rather than activation, because: (1) It varies according to the associations that are retrieved each time; and (2) It was not originally intended to take into account associations "activated" by external interventions. Moreover, differently from what we find in other attitude models (e.g., Fazio 1986), under Fishbein and Ajzen's hypothesis, salience has nothing to do with the same concept developed in social cognition (Taylor and Fiske 1978). In conclusion, this notion of salience duplicates the concept of accessibility and does not stress adequately the nature of "prominence" which is part of a useful determination of the salience construct.

2.1.10.3 Fazio's Process Model. The salience concept has also been used in another stream of attitude research. In the seminal work of Fazio on the attitude-behavior relationship (see, in particular, Fazio and Zanna 1978; Fazio 1986), salience has been referred as to the *prominence* of certain specific features of an object. In his *Process model*, Fazio and his colleagues suggested a process by which attitudes guide behavior. In this model, *attitude* is defined as a *learned association* between an evaluation of an object and the representation of that object in memory.[60] The strength of this association is defined as the *attitude accessibility*. Fazio focused on the proposition that the attitude accessibility may be the critical variable moderating the attitude-behavior relationship (Fazio 1986), as it expresses the likelihood that a previously formed attitude will be *activated from memory* (retrieved) in a behavioral situation. The stronger an attitude is held (that is, the more accessible it is), the more likely it is to be spontaneously retrieved when the individual encounters the object in a behavioral setting. The model maintains that, only if the attitude is retrieved, can it play its important role in guiding the individual's behavior.[61]

This stream of research is particularly relevant from an advertising perspective because non-evaluative dimensions of attitudes may be subject to advertising influence. In a brand choice context, this model suggests that highly accessible attitudes are more likely to be activated from memory and thus are more likely to influence brand perceptions and thereby brand choices than are less accessible attitudes. It may be possible, therefore, for an advertiser to influence the attitude-behavior relation by increasing the attitude accessibility, by means, for example, of *repeated processes*, such as the repeated supply of ad information, making attitudes based on indirect experience as accessible - and, possibly, as predictive - as those based on direct experience.

The attitude-to-behavior process is initiated when an attitude is activated, or spontaneously retrieved from memory. This attitude, whether favorable or unfavorable, serves to direct the processing of information about the attitude object: Salient attitudes are thought to give rise to *selective perception*,[62] that is, to make the individual attend information in the environment (or in memory) that is *consistent with* the activated attitude. Moreover, similarly to the above-mentioned *Theory of reasoned action* (Fishbein 1967; Fishbein and Ajzen 1975; Ajzen and Fishbein 1980), the perceptions of the object itself are combined with perceptions of norms operating in the situation to yield a definition of the event.

One caveat of this hypothesis is that the process of activation may not always be determined in this automatic fashion, since some behavioral situations may prompt or cue individuals to view their attitudes as relevant to behavioral decision (Borgida and Campbell 1982; Fazio 1986). Under these circumstances, individuals would be expected to activate their attitudes in a very deliberate, conscious, and reasoned manner. Fazio and his colleagues have presented considerable empirical support for a number of these cases (Fazio 1989; Fazio et al. 1982; Fazio, Powell, and Herr 1983; Fazio et al. 1986; Fazio and Williams 1986; Houston and Fazio 1989; Powell and Fazio 1984).

In these instances, the accessibility of an attitude seems originated by the salience (*prominence*) of the features of some contingent factor. Fazio, Powell, and Williams (1989) maintain that "if the object-evaluation association for a given product was weak and, hence, the chronic availability of the attitude was relatively low, then the immediate perception was likely to be influenced by *momentarily salient* thoughts or features of the objects." (p. 284, emphasis added). The momentarily salient factors that might operate include the object position (i.e., a product - a candy bar - being at the front of a display rather than in the back), the object attributes that were recalled from memory (the product's characteristics), the current inner state of the subject (how hungry the subject was), the recency of an experience (how recently the subject had eaten a particular food), the subject's past experiences (what snack foods the subject recalled as having stored at home), and the like.

In summary, according to this model, the accessibility of an attitude can be either the result of: (a) An automatic process, when the strength of the link between the attitude object and its evaluation is high (that is, an attitude is highly accessible in memory); or (b) A deliberative process, when certain situational salient variables are able to activate an attitude which is not otherwise available, mainly due to its low accessibility.[63] Although attitudes remain one of the most extensively investigated topics in social psychology, researchers have traditionally de-emphasized the role of contingent features of attitude objects in the elicitation of an attitude. Olson and Zanna (1993), for example, in a review on attitudes and attitude change, deliberately excluded the effects of salient events on attitudes, though recognizing they could be one of "many fascinating applications of attitude research to social problems" (p. 118; see, also, Petty, Wegener, and Fabrigar 1997).

We argue that the dichotic structure of this model could impede the clear understanding of the mechanism that leads to the activation of a pre-existing attitude by making it salient. The role of attitude accessibility can be put in the right perspective by recognizing that: (a) Attitude accessibility is not the only non-contingent variable acting on the strength of a pre-existing relation between the attitude object and its evaluation, rather it is only one of several indicants of such a strength. Raden (1985), for example, provides a through review of research on a number of strength-related dimensions of attitude, such as the *confidence* (or *certainty*) with which the attitude is held,[64] its *centrality* to the individual, its *importance*, its *relevance*, and its *extremity*. Moreover: (b) A conclusive definition of attitudes does not yet exist (Olson and Zanna 1993), therefore we do not really know if attitudes must be treated as associative networks of interconnected evaluations as maintained by Fazio (1990b), or else as knowledge structures (e.g., Kruglanski 1989), or even as simple evaluations (Eagly and Chaiken 1993; Ajzen and Fishbein 1980). As a matter of fact, Fazio himself seems to have shifted the focus of his theory by providing his new integrative *MODE Model*, which stresses *m*otivation and *o*pportunity as *d*eterminants of how attitudes influence behavior (Fazio 1990a).

In line with these findings, we argue that the activation of an attitude can be always explained by considering that it is generally the simultaneous presence of three elements - stimulus (motivation), context (opportunity), and individual's schemata (ability) - which allows an attitude to be salient. The association intrinsic in an attitude - between the attitude object and its evaluation - can be seen as part of more general schemata possessed by the individual and activated according to one or more stimuli present in a certain context. *Functional theories of attitude* recognize the importance of these factors, as they stress the role of stimulus characteristics (the attitude object itself), situational characteristics (the context), personality characteristics (the structure of the individual mind), and their interactions in the operational developments of attitudes (see, Shavitt 1989, for applications in consumer settings). In particular, the relevance of the role of context has been discussed both in social (Shavitt and Fazio 1991) and in consumer settings (Shavitt and Fazio 1990). Grounding on previous research which demonstrated that variations in the context for judging an attitude object (a product) can make either affective or cognitive considerations more salient and, therefore, more important in evaluating the object (the product), Shavitt and Fazio showed that consistency of judgments made in two different contexts increases when the same attributes are salient in both occasions. Despite the operationalization of salient attributes carried out in these studies, which could be the subject of strong criticism as salient attributes were, in some cases, mistakenly chosen according to their assumed importance,[65] the results demonstrate our view: That the stimulus used (the attitude object) activates a different attitude (therefore, a different schema) which matches the context of the situation in which the object is encountered.

Therefore, behavior in any given situation could be (if we agree with the *Process theory*), a function of the individual's immediate perceptions of the attitude object, as activated attitudes are able "to filter or bias an individual's immediate perception of the object, which influences the individual's definition of the event and thereby frames or influences subsequent behavior with respect to the object." (Berger and Mitchell 1989, p. 270).

2.2 *Proposition Two:* In-Salience Affects Attention *and* Interpretation

We argue that an in-salience occurrence concerns not only the attention stage of the perception process, but also the interpretation stage. It is through this further stage that any in-salient stimulus can display its peculiar effects on memory.

Traditionally, the concept of salience has been explained according to the *figure-ground principle* (see, *above*, Chapter Two, Paragraph 3.1), as the extent to which a stimulus stands out and is noticed (e.g., Sears, Peplau, and Taylor 1991). Proposition Two of our theory goes beyond this definition by maintaining that a stimulus which is figural (that is, which is sensed according to the figure-ground segregation) is not necessarily in-salient, as it can be easily assimilated in a perceiver's schema. Not every stimulus which is figural or noteworthy is in-salient, but the one that is incongruent in the context of perception with a perceiver's schema. Such a stimulus not only attracts consumers' attention, but also induces them to interpret the incongruity, thus producing its effects.[66]

In a general conception of cognitive economy (Bettman 1979), consumers - and individuals in general - cannot process or store all the vast amount of information available in their environment because of their limited capacity;[67] therefore, even when something is attentively observed, it does not mean it results salient, because it must be interpreted. Consider how many packages we pass on a store shelf without consciously perceiving them, how many ads we fail to process, and so forth. Our sensory system makes a wide range of stimuli from the external environment available, but we perceive only some elements of that world and ignore the others. For marketers, understanding how marketing stimuli can be in-salient to consumers, that is, how stimuli are selectively processed and recalled, offers guidance for designing ads, packages, and display that "break through the clutter" to gain attention and memory - the latter result being important because the range of consumer decisions that are memory-based is much broader than that of purely stimulus-based (Lynch, Marmorstein, and Weingold 1988). Thus, easy-to-remember items are more likely to be employed in marketing decisions than are more difficult-to-recall items (Costley and Brucks 1992).

In the following paragraphs, we shall illustrate, first, our critique of the figure-ground principle as an adequate explanation of the salience concept and, second, the position of the in-salience theory synthetically expressed by Proposition Two.

A. Criticism to the Figure-Ground Principle as an Explanation of Salience

The features of figure-ground organization were originally studied by Rubin (1921), who noted that people direct their attention to those aspects of the perceptual field that stand out (the figure), rather than the background of setting (the ground). Rubin and the Gestalt psychologists proposed that figure-ground segregation represents an innate and unlearned organizing property of the sensory system.

In recent years, the figure-ground principle has been taken as an explanation of the salience phenomena (Fiske and Taylor 1991, pp. 248-249). Although partially acceptable, this solution does not provide a sufficient interpretation of all the salience occurrences. There are at least three classes of reasons that show the figure-ground principle is *not* an exhaustive explanation of the salience phenomenon. First, perception of in-salience is not innate; second, figure-ground only attracts attention, whereas an in-salient stimulus maintains attention too; third, figure-ground as the sole explanation of salience neglects the role of involvement as a moderator.

2.2.1 Perception of In-Salience Is Not Innate

Several kinds of evidence have argued that information can be picked up only if there is a developing format. According to Neisser (1976), infants would be unable to perceive because they would have no initial format enabling them to obtain information. Infants in earliest life have a need for information. Being informed is similar to being active: It is concurrent with being alive and conscious. Any contact of sensory organs with the environment provides information. When the infant begins to try to act voluntarily, information is needed in order to act. This argument appears to be circular: "Life begins with action that provides information, but then action requires information. This is exactly what happens. Perception (obtaining information) and activity are intrinsically related." (Woods 1981, p. 176).

The perception of in-salience assumes a network of developed schemata.[68] On this topic, particular regard deserves a controversial paper by Colombo et al. (1986), who went along the former definition of salience. It suggested that increased attention in infants could be attributed to automatic attentional processes (such as those started by the figure-ground segregation), rather than to higher order processing (such as the relational processes forecasted by the in-salience theory). Previous research had inferred relational processing from infants' increased attention to stimuli containing different elements following habituation to a series of stimuli containing identical elements, whereas they found that infants also preferred the different-element stimuli without prior habituation. Infants' performance on this task was then attributed to stimulus salience (e.g., figurality) rather than relational processing (e.g., in-salience). We argue, however, that such results can be easily exposed to criticism. First, the authors do not explain what salience is: It could be exactly the same as relational processes. Second, they most probably used the same group of children in the second experiment (given that, in both groups, one child was always fussing!), therefore children could have already learned the stimulus array. And, finally, previous research (Caron and Caron 1981; and, also, Caron, Caron, and Glass 1983) has found strong support for the salience view of schematic information organization.

In conclusion, the figure-ground principle cannot account by itself for the occurrence of in-salience, because a network of schematic memory must already be in place. This is true also for re-salience - that is, that type of salience which results from processes started up by the individual rather than by external stimuli (see, *below*, Paragraph 2.4.3). There is convincing evidence that instructions and personal involvement can direct what people look at in a visual scene (see, for review, Coren and Ward 1989, p. 440). For example, Yarbus (1967) recorded eye-movement patterns while observers looked at pictures with different intentions in mind. Clearly, people look at different places in order to find information relevant to different questions. It was demonstrated that scanning eye movements must be planned prior to their execution and upon perceiver's expectation about the stimulus (Haber and Hershenson 1980). "People scan the visual world actively and purposely. They know where to look and they know what to look for" (Rabbitt 1984, p. 287). People are constantly exploring the visual field with high-speed ballistic movements called *saccades*. They can rapidly learn to inspect spatial locations in optimal order to detect target stimuli that may be present. Although this is a fairly automatic process for adults, it does not appear to be fully developed until children are about 6 or 7 years of age (e.g., Cohen 1981; Green, Hammond, and Supramaniam 1983). Also in top-down processes, therefore, the role of perceiver's preexisting schemata for the identification of salient stimuli maintains its crucial importance.

2.2.2   In-Salience Requires Maintaining Attention

The common assumption, according to which all figural stimuli are salient as long as they stand out and attract attention, seems arguable to us. If this was the case, each of the infinite figures (objects, people, etc.) that a person perceives continuously in the course of a day - in his endless activity of monitoring of the living environment - should be considered salient, at least for an instant! Clearly, not everything figural is "salient": It is not sufficient for a stimulus to *capture* attention; it is also necessary for it to *maintain* attention.

Attracting attention and maintaining attention are really quite different processes (Wilkie 1990, p. 239). To maintain attention on a particular stimulus, individuals must concentrate on it and use some degree of will power to keep their attention from drifting elsewhere (Aaker, Batra, and Myers 1992; Menon and Soman 1999).[69] Considering the distinction made above between stimulus cues and information cues, this different processing has important implications for marketers. In advertising, for example, those stimuli that may be highly successful in *attracting* attention to an ad (such as sex or music) might then hinder *maintaining* attention to the brand and its message (since the viewer is now enjoying his further thoughts about the sexual or musical stimulus that attracted his interest).

For the occurrence of in-salience, figurality may be necessary in capturing *attention*; however, to maintain attention, what is essential is the perception of an incongruity in some particular context with an existing schema. And, this further, inferential step requires *interpretation* (cf. Marcel 1983). A model of attention and interpretation could be useful to elucidate this point. In light of incongruent information, attention and interpretation are central procedural factors associated with the tendency to maintain internal consistency with schemata. Figure 4 (*below*) displays a synthesis of different cognitive models as proposed by Glass and Holyoak (1986). As is evident from this illustration, *figurality is only a pre-conscious process* that enables people to distinguish each stimulus and to address the perceiver's attention to it. It is a continuous process that allows people to create a perceptual representation of the attended stimuli through the transformation of inputs into figures by means of the sensory receptors.

According to the model, all inputs are processed by the sensory receptors, but only a privileged one has a further processing directed by the *executive decision mechanism*, which manages and controls the operations of the other mechanisms that constitute the information processing system. Next, the sensory information concerning the processed input passes through a *dimensional-analysis mechanism*, which yields representations in terms of perceptual dimensions by means of three visual dimensions (i.e., shape, brightness, and location). Then, the *figure construction mechanism* integrates the dimensional values to yield a perceptual representation of a definite image. The perceptual representation enters awareness at the level of a *comparison mechanism*, which compares the perceptual representation of the attended stimulus with the schemata stored in memory, in such a way the perceiver's executive mechanism can decide if, and what action, it wants to start. The stimulus influences the action to be taken but does not determine it, because other factors, internal or external, will influence the response.

Figure 4. Overview of Attention and Interpretation

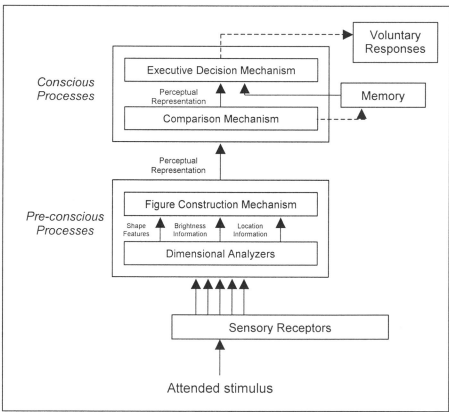

Source: Adapted from Glass and Holyoak (1986).

All the hierarchy of processing that leads to comparison and executive mechanisms is, therefore, pre-conscious, because it is directed towards bringing information about the attended stimulus into consciousness. The conscious phase, the one concerning attention and interpretation (i.e., the assignment of meaning to sensations), which creates *awareness*, occurs only subsequently (see, also, Marcel 1983). This latter phase, therefore, is the one to scrutinize in order to assess the origin of the salience phenomenon.

It is individual interpretation, not objective reality, which influences the perception of an in-salient stimulus.[70] People make meaning of stimuli by abstracting their relevant essential structures, which they substitute for the original stimuli.[71] The familiarity and simplicity of the abstracted structure then make it workable for everyday undertakings (cf. Wyer and Srull 1986; see also, *above*, Note 26). Three basic processes - organization, categorization, and inference making - are involved in interpretation (e.g., Wilkie 1990); each of them can imply misinterpretation. The first stage is to determine which of the huge numbers of molecules in the environment actually belong together (*perceptual organization*). Such organizing tendencies may even destroy reality (Hansen 1972, p. 48). In a stimulus object perceived as a whole, a number of disturbing elements may be neglected and missing elements may be added. Second, once a stimulus has been sensed, the problem becomes one of identifying it (*perceptual categorization*). That consumers may interpret the same stimulus differentially is a major problem for marketers. Classic examples of differences in categorization can be found in cross-cultural marketing.[72] Third, after a stimulus has been categorized, people are often interested in thinking more about it (*perceptual inference*). What is missing in the external stimulus is inferred from their schemata (Wyer and Srull 1980).[73] As assumed in Axiom Three (*above*), the role of the perceiver is crucial in perception and, ultimately, in choice. An interesting theory of human behavior (Boulding 1956), in its simplest form, states that consumers behave in accordance with what they know, what they think they know, and what they think they ought to know. Thus, consumer behavior stems from consumers' images, say, for products, and these images, in turn, from products' in-salient attributes (see, *below*, Chapter Four).

In synthesis, to manipulate in-salience, it is necessary to refer both to the attention and to the interpretation stages of the perceptual process. During and after attention to a stimulus, consumers attempt to gain an understanding of what it is and how they should react to it. In this interpretation phase, they retrieve from long-term memory a schema pertinent to the stimulus that can be used to help interpret it.[74] Although the principles of perceptual organization are applied unconsciously, the interpretive process occurs - almost always, for in-salient stimuli - consciously. That is, when attempting to comprehend and understand the nature of a stimulus, consumers may be aware that they are engaged in the task. During this process, the personal involvement of the consumer is one of the major moderating variables in the interpretation of how the stimulus is. In high-involvement situations, in particular, consumers will actively analyze the stimulus.

2.2.3   Involvement Is a Moderator of In-Salience

The maintenance of attention is much more determined by personal factors than by stimulus characteristics (Wilkie 1990, p. 239). In our discussion of selectivity, we have argued that, to maintain attention on a particular stimulus, individuals must usually concentrate on it and use some degree of will power to keep their attention from drifting elsewhere. Whether or not they will choose to concentrate on a stimulus will depend primarily on their personal goals, interests, and drives - and how well the stimulus is capable of satisfying them - in a word, it will depend on *involvement*.

By definition, in our theory, involvement is part of the context in a larger sense (see *above*, B. *The context*). We have used this term to summarize all the personal factors that can influence the processing of incongruity. In addition, involvement has been taken as the cause of *re-salience*, that is, the prominence of those stimuli which are personally relevant to an individual or, in other words, congruent with an individual's personal goals.

A well-known definition of involvement, which contains the viewpoints of many researchers, was provided by Zaichkowsky (1985), who defined involvement as "[a] person's perceived relevance of the object based on inherent needs, values, and interests." (p. 342). Involvement is here a motivational state that is a function of both situational and intrinsic sources of personal relevance derived from cues, contingencies, and prior knowledge.[75] It was found to influence both the amount, the direction, the focus of attention, and the depth, the breadth, the effort of comprehension during interpretation (Celsi and Olson 1988; see, also, Finn 1988; Jolibert and Baumgartner 1997; Peterman 1997; Warrington and Shim 2000).

The in-salience theory maintains that figurality is not sufficient *per se* to generate in-salience because the mechanistic bottom-up process that it configures does not consider involvement as a component. On the contrary, there must be some level of involvement by a person before he allocates attentional effort to process the incongruity. Past research has shown that people generally spend more time processing incongruent information (see Peltier 1989, for review), although irrelevant incongruities are often ignored (Hendrick 1972). Consumers have a heightened awareness of the stimuli that meet their needs or interests and a lesser (or lack of) awareness of stimuli irrelevant to their goals. Thus, they are likely to note ads for products that meet their needs or they are familiar with and to disregard those ones they have no interest in. *The way in which in-salience leaves traces on memory depends on the individual level of involvement*. Greenwald and Leavitt (1984), in a widely referred article, have distinguished four levels of involvement: Each of these provides a differential strength to the in-salience effect.

Involvement, moreover, has also an emotional or affective component in itself (see, for a review, Zaichkowsky 1986; also Restall and Gordon 1993; Ambler and Burne 1999). We argue that *the emotional component of involvement acts as a moderator of in-salience through the vividness of a stimulus*. According to a widely-accepted definition of vividness by Nisbett and Ross (1980), a stimulus is *vivid* to the extent that it is "(a) emotionally interesting, (b) concrete and imagery provoking, and (c) proximate in a sensory, temporal or spatial way" (p. 45). The most remarkable and theoretically important difference between salience and vividness - also observed in empirical studies (Brosius 1989; Eisen and McArthur 1979; Taylor and Fiske 1975, Experiment 2; McArthur 1980) - is that, while salience is determined by the relation of an object to its context, vividness is inherent in a stimulus itself (Taylor and Thompson 1982).[76] A different conception of vividness arises from the *Availability-valence hypothesis* by Kisielius and Sternthal (1984), a cognitive elaboration model alternative to Taylor and Thompson's (1982) *Differential attention model* (although a reconciliation of these two models has been proposed by Kelley 1989 and, more recently, by Anand Keller and Block 1997). If, on the one hand, vividness has been typically viewed as a characteristic of the stimulus - thus, e.g., pictures are vivid and verbal statements are pallid -, the availability-valence hypothesis, on the other hand, interprets vividness in terms of the process it evokes. Viewed from this perspective, pictorial and verbal representations are vivid only to the extent that they evoke cognitive elaboration of stimulus-relevant information in memory.[77] In general, psychological research tells us that events or information that evoke emotional responses are more memorable than neutral events (especially when measured through uncued, free-recall tasks), unless the emotional response is truly extreme and a repression response occurs (see Friedstad and Thorson 1993, for a review). Future research should demonstrate that, no matter which definition of the construct is chosen, vividness acts as a moderator (as a component of involvement) of the in-salience effect.

Apart from involvement, other factors could act as moderating variables. These are situational factors comprised in our definition of context in a larger sense. For example, a crucial condition for the recall advantage of in-salient information is the availability of adequate *exposure time* devoted to explaining or assimilating its incongruity. If *processing time* is limited, indeed, the individual will not receive an adequate opportunity for bringing previously stored information into working memory and, therefore, will not develop the elaborate network of associative pathways that distinguishes in-salient information from non-in-salient (cf. Houston, Childers, and Heckler 1987; Pieters, Warlop, and Hartog 1997). Exposure time and processing time, however, are not necessarily the same thing. People can allocate attentional resources to a stimulus configuration even after exposure has been completed.[78]

B.   The In-Salience Hypothesis as an Explanation of Salience

We believe that it is the incongruity between a perceiver's schema and the stimulus perceived in a context that generates in-salience, and not the figure-ground. By criticizing the current definitions of salience, the in-salience hypothesis maintains that the contrast with the physical context secures only figurality to the stimulus - that is, a level of pre-attentive processing - but not in-salience which depends, in turn, on a further processing from the detection of an incongruity between the target stimulus and a perceiver's activated schema. In this process, both the context and the perceiver's schemata are crucial elements for the detection of the stimulus' figurality *and* in-salience; the way in which this is accomplished is explained in the following paragraphs.

2.2.4   The Role of Context

In a seminal paper, Neisser (1967) has argued that the process that segregates regions of a visual scene into figure and ground is a *pre-attentive* process. This suggests that when there are clear feature differences between the target stimulus and the distractor items (which makes its physical context; see Britt 1978, pp. 109-110), the target becomes readily visible because distractors are lumped together as ground and the target stands out as a figure without any further processing. However, Proposition Two (*above*), argues that figurality by itself cannot be considered a cause of in-salience, because in-salience, to display its effects, requires a further processing of the stimulus that stands out (a loud sound, a bright light, a sudden movement, etc.) and not a rapid adaptation. In most of the cases, instead, what occurs - after the attended stimulus has been analyzed and identified - is assimilation.

The executive mechanism in the brain detects, indeed, only unexpected changes in the stimulus (cf. Glass and Holyoak 1986). This is evident, for example, when we first walk into a room where a clock is ticking loudly. We perceive that sound, but soon we scarcely notice the ticking at all. Only if the tick of the clock suddenly stopped, might we notice the change. This continued processing of previously attended stimuli is called *monitoring*. One influential theory of monitoring is the *Matching model* proposed by Sokolov (1969, 1975). He argued that, in order to monitor stimuli, the executive mechanism of the brain constructs a representation of the current environment, which is constantly updated. This internal representation can be viewed as a chart that provides a set of expectations about the immediate future. For example, the tick of the clock will be entered on the chart at regular intervals. At each moment, the chart is compared with current environmental inputs. If the expected tick is matched at the appropriate time, no further processing is needed. But if the tick does not occur, the resulting mismatch between the environment and the monitoring chart will cause a signal to be sent to the executive, bringing attention to the source of the mismatch.

In synthesis, our attention is grabbed by *changes* in the stimulus.[79] Thus it can be attracted as much by a sudden silence as by a sharp, unexpected noise. However, if a stimulus persists unchanged (even a figural stimulus, such as a sharp noise, when it is repetitive), the senses adapt or "get used" to the condition so that it becomes the normal environment. Absolute and differential thresholds rise, so that greater intensities and differences are required for a response. This saves the receptors from possible damages and permits the individual to attend to a new stimulus, that is, a new threat or promise. This process, which is called *habituation* or *sensory adaptation*, prevents any figural stimulus to become an in-salient stimulus.[80] Adaptation level theories were first delineated in connection with color sensation, habituation being identified as a perceptual phenomenon (see, for a review, Woods 1981, pp. 272-276). Today it is recognized that any constant sensory input is subject to adaptation. A person not only adapts to colors, tastes, odors, and other sensory qualities, but also to such more complex experiences as interpersonal relationships.[81]

2.2.5   The Role of Schemata

Habituation appears to be the result not only of context, in a strict sense, but also of one's schemata. This can be illustrated with an example. A humorous advertisement may attract attention if it is surrounded by more conventional copy approaches; whereas, if many humorous advertisements are involved, the ability of one of them to attract attention would be reduced. In this situation, habituation would be a matter of *context* of the stimulus. However, if past experience has suggested that most comparable advertising avoided humor in its copy, then one using humor may attract attention even if it is not unusual in its present context. In this case, it was the culmination of past experience upon which a perceiver's *schema* was made that contributed to the establishment of a reference point.

The importance of context and schemata in determining the perception of a stimulus was stressed by Helson (1959, 1964) in his *Adaptation level model* which is relevant to our discussion. According to Helson (1964), the adaptation level of an individual determines how he will perceive a stimulus and is the result of: (1) The qualities of the stimulus (*perceived discrepancy*), (2) The environment in which the stimulus is perceived (*contextual variables*), and (3) The physiological, psychological, and background traits of the perceiver (*individual characteristics*). He suggested that it is not only the focal stimuli that determine perception, but also the contextual stimuli (background) and residual stimuli (past experience). The individual learns to associate a stimulus set with a reference point or adaptation level so that, when a stimulus deviates markedly from that level, attention is created.[82]

In conclusion (and extreme synthesis), context and schemata allow the stimulus to be perceived as incongruent and be recalled; figure-ground is only a pre-attentive condition and by itself cannot be considered an explanation of the salience construct.

2.3 *Proposition Three:* In-Salience Is a Distinct Construct From Activation, Accessibility, and Availability

We argue that the in-salience construct has a peculiar origin that makes it different from other similar constructs - namely, *activation*, *accessibility*, and *availability* - salience has been also referred to in past literature in relation to memory processes. In Chapter Two, we reviewed *perception-based* definitions of salience (regarding the salience of external stimuli, such as objects, persons, products, etc). However, when reviewing literature regarding *memory-based* definitions of salience (i.e., the salience of internal stimuli, such as concepts, attributes, beliefs, etc.) - which is not the focus of this research, as it would mainly regard the *re-salience hypothesis* - it comes out that salience has been usually defined as either the *activation* of a concept in memory, or its *accessibility*, or its *availability*.

We consider these definitions to be *unsatisfactory* as descriptions of the salience construct, because they do not emphasize the nature of *prominence* which is intrinsic in the notion of salience (see Guido 1996a, for a meta-analysis of marketing studies dealing with memory-based definition of salience). Nonetheless, these constructs do have a role in the occurrence of in-salience *inasmuch as they moderate the elicitation of the perceiver's schemata*. In other words, in-salience cannot be identified with either activation, or accessibility, or availability of a stimulus, because in-salience is the contextual incongruity between a stimulus and a perceiver's schema. However, activation, accessibility, and availability can intervene in the generation process of in-salience as moderating variables for the retrieval of perceivers' schemata.

Very often in consumer research (as well as in common language), another construct has been referred to salience - namely, *importance* - even though many authors have already called for avoiding confusion between these two concepts (e.g., Alpert 1980; Marks 1985; Myers and Alpert 1977; Olson, Kanwar, and Muderrisoglu 1979; Wilkie and Weinreid 1972).[83] Differently from activation, accessibility, and availability, the definition of salience as importance - frequently associated with product attributes - is manifestly wrong: Even if an attribute is critical in a situation of choice, this does not mean that, at the same time, it is salient in a given context to a certain individual (see, *below*, Paragraph 2.4.4: *Attribute relevance vs. attribute importance*).[84] There are several cases in which the salience concept used in consumer studies is mistakenly referred to as importance. Other studies in consumer literature seem to have confused the two constructs. In the context of attitude models, it has been already acknowledged that "importance" cannot be taken for "salience" and used to derive measures for it (Fishbein and Ajzen 1975).[85] Otherwise, this usually happens where there is no direct reference to past research on salience and when salience is operationalized on the basis of a set of attributes pre-selected by researchers (see, for example, Biehel and Chakravarti 1983; Boote 1981; Dick, Chakravarti, and Biehal 1990; Johnson 1990; Klein and Bither 1987; Niemi and Bartels 1985).

The concept of attribute importance has been thoroughly investigated by MacKenzie (1986): In keeping with previous research, he has broadly conceptualized "attribute importance" as "a person's general assessment of the significance of an attribute for products of a certain type" (p. 175).[86] We have argued (Guido 1996a) that the several consumer studies in which salience has been treated as importance may be due to the confusion fostered by three aspects of the construct which make it similar to salience - i.e., same effects on the extremity of evaluations;[87] same "agenda-setting" value in consumer choices;[88] and three similar antecedents.[89]

Considering the unsoundness of a definition of salience as importance - which deserves, however, more attention in future research on attitudes (see, *below*, Chapter Four, Paragraph 4.4.3) -, we shall limit our analysis, hereafter, to a discussion on the role of activation, accessibility, and availability in the occurrence of in-salience.

2.3.1   The Role of Activation

Activation occurs when a schema is elicited, consciously or unconsciously, by an external stimulus. Such a stimulus can either be instantiated in a pre-existing schema or - if it can not - can induce the generation of a new schema (Mandler 1982). Operationally, activation can be triggered by any external stimulation - the so-called *priming* (or *semantic preparation*, as it has been also called by Collins and Loftus 1975) - which initiates, consciously or unconsciously, the cognitive elaboration process.

Priming refers to a number of different processes, by which it is possible to increase the general accessibility of a schema, thereby enhancing its likelihood of being used to encode new information. It has been characterized as a passive, *unconscious* process,[90] and it has been primarily studied by cognitive psychologists interested in lexical analysis (e.g., Foss 1982; McKoon and Ratcliff 1979; Neely 1977). Priming tasks have provided sufficient empirical support to network models of memory (Ashcraft 1989): In priming tasks a prime stimulus, which is presented first, influences some later process on a target stimulus which follows the prime. Past research has examined different forms of priming the activation of a stimulus or of a schema (Higgins and King 1981). The most common modalities are those related to *order effects* (i.e., primacy and recency) and *frequency effect* (i.e., repetition) (see, *above*, Chapter Two, Paragraph 3.3).

Although not in the context of spreading activation (with the exception of Ulhaque and Bahn 1992), priming paradigm has been used in the area of consumer behavior - see, e.g., Chung and Szymanski (1997); Cowley (1999); Herr (1989); Karrh (1993); Meyers-Levy (1989b); Moran (1990); Nowlis and Simonson (1997); Pechmann and Ratneshwar (1994); Tversky, Sattath, and Slovic (1988); Williams, Cafferty, and DeNisi (1990); and Yi (1990) on the impact of priming on consumer information processing and judgment. A spreading activation explanation of priming involves the same tracing process that people adopt for memory search (Collins and Loftus 1975).[91] When a concept is primed activation tags are spread by tracing an expanding set of links in the network out to some unspecified depth. Thus, when another concept is presented, it can make contact with one of the tags left earlier and find an intersection. (One of the non-obvious implications of this view of priming is that links as well as nodes will be primed.) When a concept is processed (or stimulated), activation spreads out along the paths of the network in a decreasing gradient: Thus, activation is like a signal from a source that is attenuated as it travels outward. The longer a concept is continuously processed (either by reading, hearing, or rehearsing it), the longer activation is released from the node of the concept at a fixed rate.[92] Finally, activation decreases over time and/or intervening activity.[93]

In a marketing setting, *priming facilitates the detection of in-salience* because it evokes the appropriate schema of reference to process the stimulus[94] or it allows the creation of "charts," that is, schemata which act as cognitive maps *à la* Sokolov (1975). In the first case, a schema already exists in memory; in the second case, a schema is made up to process information. How, operationally, this is obtained is shown, *below*, in Chapter Four (Paragraph 1.2.3).

2.3.2   The Role of Accessibility

While activation derives from any activity that is external to the individual mind, accessibility is related to an internal factor, namely the perceiver's *perceptual readiness* with which a stored schema is utilized in information processing (Bruner 1957). In other words, while *activated* schemata can be either accessed (preexisting schemata) or possibly made up (new schemata), *accessible* schemata are already available in memory (preexisting) and accessed because of an individual's predisposition to use them (cf. Higgins and King 1981). That is why, Feldman and Lynch (1988) define accessibility as the *easy* with which an input can be retrieved from memory. In the marketing context, several studies have established that consumers are influenced by information readily accessible in memory (for a review, see Kardes 1994).[95]

In a seminal paper, Bruner (1957) suggested two factors as antecedents of accessibility: *Expectations* (the subjective probability estimates of the likelihood of a given stimulus), and *motivation* (the search requirements imposed by one's needs, tasks, goals, etc.). Such factors are quite similar to those we proposed for salient stimuli (both in-salient, and re-salient stimuli), respectively: Incongruity, and relevance (see, *below*, Paragraph 2.4).[96] However, unlike salience as well as importance, accessibility - especially in its *chronic* acceptation - is independent from contextual circumstances (see also, *above*, Note 9) and refers to schemata individuals develop over a lifetime and almost invariantly use to process reality (Ratneshwar, Mick, and Reitinger 1990).[97]

In reference to internal stimuli, salience has been often treated as accessibility - although, according to our hypothesis, this is inappropriate (see Guido 1996a, and *above*). This lack of differentiation is clearly evident, for example, in Nedungadi (1990), and Tybout and Yalch (1980): The former maintaining that brand accessibility or salience is dependent on the consumer environment;[98] and the latter manipulating attributional states of the individuals rather than the salience of labeling cues.[99] Furthermore, a recent study by Ratneshwar et al. (1997), on a selective-attention model which is quite similar to ours (based on stimulus, situational, and individual factors), has assumed two types of salience (named *habitual benefit salience* and *situational benefit salience*) which are, indeed, nothing other than our constructs of accessibility and activation (respectively) - thus producing similar results. Yet, it has been mainly in the field of attitude research that the concept of salience has been deceptively used to indicate the relevance of elicited attributes (see, *above*, Paragraph 2.1.10).

In the most generic applications of a model of attention and interpretation (see, *above*, Figure 4), the selectivity resulting from schema accessibility - at an input stage - causes people to notice some aspects of the stimulus object while not noticing other aspects. Subsequently, at a consolidation stage, only those aspects of the stimulus object that have been noticed are encoded and stored. It is interesting to observe that, when the attributes of the stimulus are similar to the content of more than one schema and the match to these alternative schema is approximately the same, the stimulus is likely to be identified with whichever schema is most accessible (cf. Higgins and King 1981). In this sense, *the chronic accessibility of certain schemata moderates the occurrence of in-salience* because, on a similar level of matching, it makes ready to be used in processing only certain schemata (i.e., chronically accessible schemata).

2.3.3   The Role of Availability

To be accessible for processing, a schema needs to be previously stored in memory. Availability is best defined as the condition for a subject to possess knowledge structures (i.e., schemata) which can be used on occasion to process incoming stimuli. Traditionally, the terms "availability" and "accessibility" have been distinguished in literature: The former has been referred to whether or not a construct is stored in memory, whereas the latter to the readiness with which a stored construct is retrieved from memory (Tulving and Pearlstone 1966). More often, however, researchers have started to use them interchangeably (e.g., Nisbett and Ross 1980). According to Higgins and King (1981), this overlap was originally introduced by Tversky and Kahneman's (1973) description of *availability heuristics*, where availability refers not only to the ease of *retrieving* construct instances, but also to that of *constructing* instances of novel classes and events.[100] However, the traditional distinction still seems useful in dealing with various memory measures (e.g., differences between free and aided recall), therefore, we shall continue to use and support this distinction.

Availability of schemata differentiates between subjects who have these schemata (i.e., *experts*) and subjects who do not (i.e., *novices*). For example, since they are not experts, salient decision criteria are not *accessible* to novices, because they are not *available* to them: That is, novices cannot use these criteria, because they do not possess those knowledge structures (cf. Alba and Hutchinson 1987, 2000).[101] The interpretation of salience as availability, which also occurred in consumer literature (e.g., Wright and Rip 1980, on coincidental overlaps among rival ad campaigns; and Bettman and Sujan 1987, on external events priming particular buying goals), seems due to the extent researchers wanted to stress this difference between knowledge structures possessed by expert *vis-a-vis* novice consumers.[102]

Availability of schemata is typically accrued through experiential information that is easily interpreted by any consumer who has accumulated use with products in the product class (see, *below*, Chapter Four, Paragraph 2.1.1, for an application regarding *users* and *non-users*). The study of the different knowledge structures of experts has yielded to characterize consumer expertise and its effects: It has been found that the content and organization of knowledge is the crucial factor underlying expertise, and it influences processing, memory, and choice (see Bettman 1986, for a review). While novices are usually limited to externally defined ideals for products (usually obtained by word of mouth or consultation with an expert), experts hold prototypical ideals embedded in rich knowledge structures that are based on experience with a product class (Beattie 1982). This allows experts to process and assess product information differently than novices in judging brand similarity to an ideal.

We argue that, *novices commonly attend to in-salient cues*, which are "prominent" but sometimes trivial, *whereas experts are able to attend to re-salient cues*, which are "important" in a context of judgment or choice. A strong stream of past research supports this proposition. For example, Hutchinson (1983) has shown that subjects with higher expertise tend to group items mainly by their functional equivalence rather than by their surface similarities. Moreover, Sujan (1985) has shown that experts' different processing depends on the degree to which information matches or mismatches their existing knowledge. Finally, Beattie (1983) has demonstrated that for product experts, salience can be achieved by providing information about product attributes that allows inferences to be made about product performance during information interpretation, whereas for novices, salience is attained by providing information about a simple experiencing product performance (cf., also, Kim, Kardes, and Herr 1991).[103]

Availability of prior knowledge has also been found to structure the memory for current information. In particular, experts tend to cluster information by brand and to cluster brands by functional equivalence (see Bettman 1986). Johnson and Russo (1984) have provided a framework for understanding these effects of prior knowledge on memory. They outlined three skills that experts are used to develop: Superior knowledge of existing products; greater ability to encode new information; and greater ability to select relevant information. According to these authors, the greater ability to encode will tend to enhance memory, while the superior knowledge of existing products and greater ability to be selective may actually lead to fewer items of information recalled if new information is presented.

In light of past research, we argue that *availability of schemata is a moderating variable for the occurrence of in-salience* and acts through the several differences in information processing between experts and novices reported in literature. A typical situation where this is evident is free elicitation of product attributes as occurring in attitude-behavior models. When a brand schema is elicited (e.g., Ferrari), and a subject is uncertain or does not know the product attributes, the lack of schema availability induces the subject to make inferences by activating similar schemata. In such situations, the formation of expectations of uncertain or unknown product attributes has been shown to be based on the levels of similar known attributes from the past, on other attributes of the same product, or on attributes of other products in the category.[104] In any of these cases, the result of the novice's processing in terms of in-salience can be extremely different among novices (who have each a personalized strategy for choosing a reference schema), and between them and a class of experts (who possess - on average - common schemata rich in important attributes).

In conclusion, schema availability, together with schema activation (accessibility), acts as a moderator of in-salience. If a schema is not available to be retrieved for processing a stimulus, another schema will be inferred. Schema activation, therefore, can regard either a schema that is available - that is, stored in memory - and made accessible on that occurrence, or a new schema that is made up - that is, inferred - to process information. In both situations, these constructs are *not* in-salience, but rather *moderators* of in-salience. In-salience, indeed, is the result of the processing of a stimulus encountered by an individual in the context of perception and matched against his activated schema.

2.4 *Proposition Four:* **Relevance Is the Crucial Moderating Variable that Links In-Salience to Re-Salience**

We argue that *personal relevance* - being "the essential characteristic of involvement" (Celsi and Olson 1988, p. 211) - is the crucial moderator of *in-salience*. In addition, because relevance is - by definition - at the origin of the *re-salience* construct, it acts as the bond between these two types of salience.

In-salience and re-salience are two complementary types of constructs (Guido 1998). *In-salience* is hypothesized as a perceived incongruity between a stimulus in a certain context and a perceiver's schema; whereas *re-salience* is hypothesized as a perceived congruity between a stimulus in a certain context and a perceiver's motive (goal, drive, or instruction to attend the stimulus). Therefore, whereas the former construct focuses on reflexive aspects of attention, by considering those *bottom-up processes* which start from the perception of novel or unexpected stimuli; the latter concentrates on selective aspects of attention, by contemplating those *top-down processes* which have origin in the relevant goals and drives of the individual. In other words, the former construct considers those cases in which attention is directed by a stimulus that could seem novel or unexpected; the latter, on the contrary, regards those cases in which a person directs his attention on the basis of his personal motives, goals or drives.[105] Research indicates that these two types of salience can be significantly referred to different types of attention (cf. Hansen 1972, p. 98).

2.4.1   Different Types of Attention

It is a prevalent view in literature that the concept of attention, deprived of a theoretical substantiation, "is too amorphous to be of much value" (Eysenck and Keane 1990, p. 97). Attention has been most commonly used to refer to the selectivity of information processing, as was emphasized by William James in late nineteenth century: "Everyone knows what attention is. [...] Focalisation, concentration, of *consciousness* are of its essence. It implies withdrawal from some things in order to deal effectively with others" (1890, p. 404, emphasis added). Attention, in brief, mainly regards conscious focus on a stimulus.[106]

For their impact on the salience of a stimulus, it is useful to distinguish three types of attention in consumer behavior (Wilkie 1990, p. 241): (a) Voluntary (or planned) attention; (b) Involuntary (or passive) attention; and, a mix of the previous two, (c) Spontaneous attention.[107] Considering the two extremes, attention can be activated either voluntarily or involuntarily. *Voluntary attention* involves the consumer in searching out information in order to achieve some type of goal. Such a search can be either active, wherein an individual actually seeks or solicits information, or passive, wherein the individual searches for information only from sources he is exposed during the normal course of events. A major aspect of voluntary attention is *selectivity*. Through selective attention consumers identify the stimulus on which they will focus attention, based upon whether or not it matches their goals.[108] Selectivity implies that the search is being carried out in terms of a context or frame of reference. The seekers (perceivers) have "something" in mind, some goal or expectation, and seek to obtain information about this concern. They focus their search on the basis of this "frame of mind" or schema. What they perceive may be influenced by this frame of reference: Features of the environment that do not fit into their schema of search may be ignored or overlooked (Neisser 1976, p. 54).

Unlike voluntary attention, attention can be placed upon a stimulus passively. *Involuntary attention* occurs when a consumer has little immediate need for the information and makes no conscious effort to obtain it, but some information (e.g., surprising, novel, threatening, or unexpected) may nevertheless enter the system. Such stimuli initially result in an autonomic response in which the person turns toward and allocates attention to them. This response, which the consumer cannot consciously control, is called an *orientation reflex*. Because most advertisements consumers are exposed to are unrelated to the immediate goals of the audience, marketers undergo some trouble to elicit the orientation reflex. Television advertisers have employed a variety of strategies to activate this reflex. For example, they have adroitly exploited either distinctive, nonverbal sounds provoking surprise or fear, or learned attention-inducing stimuli (that is, stimuli that people have been conditioned to attend to immediately) such as telephones and doorbells (see, *above*, Chapter Two, Paragraph 3.2).[109]

Between these two extremes lies *spontaneous attention*, a combination of the previous two types. Here a consumer is not concentrating too narrowly and is ready to attend to a new stimulus. On the other hand, no particular stimulus is forcing its way into consciousness. His attention, therefore, is "spontaneous" in that it simply arises at that point in time. This appears to be the most common case in consumer behavior, as attention moves from object to object, sometimes sparked by the individuals' personal goals and sometimes the stimulus features.

As we said, different kinds of salience can be referred to different types of attention. Specifically, re-salience has to do with voluntary attention: If consumers pursue personal goals, they always seek something that is congruous with their schemata. For example, if someone craves for ham, he looks for ham (top-down process: *Re-salient stimulus*, see *below*). In-salience, on the other hand, has to do with involuntary attention: If the same individual "scans" his kitchen for ham and finds cheese (bottom-up process: *In-salient stimulus*), he can end up eating a cheese sandwich.[110]

2.4.2   The Meaning of Personal Relevance

Table 2 (*above*) illustrates a parallel between the two hypothesized forms of salience. From our theory it derives that, while for in-salience the stimulus incongruity is at the origin of the construct, for re-salience a similar role is performed by personal involvement. Involvement, here, is hypothesized at the basis of the attentional and memory effects of re-salience.[111]

It is useful, at this point, to specify as clearly as possible the theoretical domains of the variable "involvement" and how it relates to motivation and relevance. Generally speaking, we can consider motivation, involvement, and relevance as different levels of specification of the same type of construct (i.e., motivation $\rightarrow$ involvement $\rightarrow$ relevance). *Motivation* to process information has been conceptualized by most researchers in terms of consumer's involvement with the informational stimulus (see, for a review, Celsi and Olson 1988, p. 210). Motives, indeed, are personal goals, internal drives, or external instructions, which induce an individual to process a stimulus.[112] Such motives, in turn, determine the level of involvement a subject possesses in relation to a certain stimulus. *Involvement* has been viewed - within the in-salience hypothesis - both as part of the context in a larger sense and as a moderator of in-salience effects (see, *above*, Paragraphs 2.1 and 2.2.3). Within the re-salience hypothesis, it determines whether or not a perceiver is likely to be aroused and attentive to process those stimuli that are congruent, in a certain context, with his personal motives.[113] In any case, a consumer's level of involvement with a stimulus is determined by the degree to which that stimulus is perceived as being personally relevant. *Perceived personal relevance*, in other words, can be ultimately considered as the essential characteristic of involvement (cf. Celsi and Olson 1988; Petty and Cacioppo 1981; Richins and Bloch 1986; Zaichkowsky 1985).[114] In accordance with Celsi and Olson (1988), we suggest that a stimulus is personally relevant when a consumer perceives it to be self-related (i.e., related to his personal motives) or in some way instrumental in achieving his goals or in satisfying his needs. More specifically, the personal relevance of a product is represented by the perceived linkage between a consumer's motives (self-knowledge) and product knowledge (attributes and benefits). Whenever product characteristics are associated with personal motives, goals and drives, the consumer will experience strong feelings of personal relevance or involvement with the product.

2.4.3   The Re-Salience Hypothesis

The re-salience hypothesis maintains that a stimulus is re-salient when it is contextually congruent with a perceiver's goal, drive, or instruction to attend to it. Perceivers' involvement (i.e., perceived personal relevance) is at the basis of this phenomenon.

When personally relevant knowledge is activated in memory, a motivational state is created that drives consumers' overt behavior, such as search, and cognitive behaviors, such as attention and interpretation processes. In addition, the type and intensity of personal relevance, perceived in that situation (context), also directs the focus of cognitive processing and thereby affects the interpreted meanings that are produced by attention and interpretation processes (cf. Celsi and Olson 1988). In sum, motivation to process a stimulus information is a function of the personally relevant schemata that are activated in memory in a particular situation.[115] As in the in-salience hypothesis, it seems that the three fundamental elements - i.e., stimulus, context, and consumers' schemata - are also present for re-salience.

In the pursuit of specific goals (e.g., to satisfy one's hunger), instances of particular schemata (e.g., restaurants, grocery stores) are actively sought out, thus increasing the accessibility of those schemata. Such increased accessibility imposed by goals would lead to relatively active processing. For example, active information processing is likely to be involved when subjects are instructed that their task goal in reading about a target product is to form an impression of the product or to remember the details of the information provided (cf. Higgins and King 1981).[116] A stimulus, then, results prominent (that is, re-salient) when it is congruent to the schema activated by the goal.[117]

2.4.4   Attribute Relevance vs. Attribute Importance

Finally, a further statement is needed to distinguish the theoretical domain of the *relevance* construct from that of *importance*. Other than to persons, in the in-salience hypothesis, relevance has been also referred to specific elements of a schema (e.g., attributes) and has been operationally defined as the weight possessed by each element within a schema. (In Figure 3, *above*, for example, the attribute "fast," within the schema of "Ferrari," would have been the most relevant attribute.) Under this framework, the difference between the relevance of an attribute and its importance is a subtle one: *Relevance is simply the prominence of an attribute in reference to other attributes of the same schema, whereas importance implies an evaluation of that prominence* to assess the significance of that attribute to an individual (cf. MacKenzie 1986; see also, *above*, Paragraph 2.3). For example, an attribute can be relevant - despite being absolutely trivial - thus having the biggest weight inside a product schema of a consumer (see, also, Brown and Carpenter 2000). Such a result can be obtained, say, after an ad campaign (via repetition of the same ad) which would bring that attribute at the first place of the hypothetical agenda of a consumer (see, *above*, Paragraph 2.1.9). This agenda-setting result would be obtained even without an evaluation of the personal significance of that particular relevant attribute.

However, *in a situation of choice*, such attribute relevance is *generally* discounted by the importance given to that attribute, by *evaluating* the significance that the attribute assumes in the context of a decision. Moreover, this is the common situation considered under the re-salience hypothesis, because selective attention requires a search and an evaluation of the match of the stimulus with a perceiver's goals. Thus, due to personal involvement, to be re-salient, a stimulus must necessarily be important, rather than simply relevant.[118] Therefore, in any particular context, *re-salient stimuli are those stimuli that match the most important attributes of a consumer schema.* Importance refers to the degree to which information relates to a concept the buyer values highly. Specifically, it is information that will serve a buyer's motives in making a choice.

We said "generally"; as a matter of fact, the crucial moderator here is a person's level of involvement with the stimulus. Under high-involvement conditions, the consumer engages in deliberate search and processing, including information evaluation (yielding/acceptance) of the importance of the stimulus. Under low-involvement conditions, instead, there is little or no search for information: Exposure and attention are involuntary or passive, so that evaluation of the stimulus could be absent.[119] As hypothesized in Proposition Four, the variable *involvement* acts as a moderator. In the same context of perception, when involvement is high (i.e., high personal relevance), a stimulus to be (re-)salient should match an *important* attribute of the perceiver's schema; whereas, when involvement is low (i.e., low personal relevance or, even, irrelevance), a stimulus to be (in-)salient should mismatch a *relevant* attribute of the perceiver's schema.[120]

This scenario is much clearer if we consider that consumers, of course, do not always possess well formed beliefs about attribute importance (see Alba, Hutchinson, and Lynch 1991, p. 19, for a brief review). If they did, salience would be internally driven (top-down process) and correspond to the importance consumers assign to the attributes. When they do not possess such beliefs, salience could be externally determined (bottom-up process), perhaps via repetition or by the format in which it is conveyed (cf. Finn 1988).

It should be apparent at this point that manipulations of attribute relevance and attribute importance from external sources (e.g., advertisers) can have very strong effects on consumer decision making.[121] In the most generic application, advertisers would be encouraged to develop an ad featuring positively evaluated attributes associated with a product which are relevant to the largest proportion of a users' group (see, e.g., Manfredo 1989). As mentioned in Note 53 (*above*), these have been referred to as *modal salient attributes*, an adaptation of terminology introduced by Fishbein and Ajzen (1975). This strategy increases the likelihood that the ad will be relevant to the greatest number of people in a consumer group.[122]

2.4.5   Top-down vs. Bottom-up Processes

The re-salience and the in-salience hypotheses configure two complementary, basic modes of information processing, one putting the emphasis on personal characteristics, and the other on external stimuli. In re-salient processing, apprehension of information is largely guided by preexisting schematic knowledge to form expectations about incoming cues which are congruent with perceivers' motives; on the contrary, in in-salient processing, apprehension involves a detailed analysis of the incoming information in an effort to assemble incongruent cues into a coherent representation. Thus, the view that emerges is that personal goals, drives, and instructions operate as the motivational devices of re-salience, whereas cue incongruity serves as a motivational device to prompt in-salience.

This separation of modes is akin to Norman's (1976) ideas that processing may at times be *conceptually-driven* (*top-down*) with expectations based on current schemata and, at other times, be *data-driven* (*bottom-up*) by the stimulus information. While it is understood that salience typically entails some degree of both modes of processing, these terms will be used to connote a relative emphasis on one of these two strategies.

In *conceptually-driven processing* (CDP), higher level conceptual processes, such as memories of past experiences, general organizational strategies, and expectations based on schematic knowledge and personal goals, guide an active search for certain patterns in the stimulus input. "An example of conceptually-driven processing is the feature integration stage of feature integration theory, where focal attention selects a locus in space and integrates the features there into a perceptual object, perhaps in conjunction with prior hypothesis as to what to expect." (Coren and Ward 1989, p 325). Top-down, conceptually-driven systems can be powerful but their success depends heavily on their ability to make intelligent choices of what objects to expect.

In *data-driven processing* (DDP), the arrival of sensory information at the receptors starts the process of information directly in terms of some fixed set of rules or procedures. In a sense, data themselves guide the processing, since the rules usually concern the registration of particular patterns in the data. An example of data-driven processing could be the first stage of pre-attentive processing in feature integration theory. Thus, a visual input starts as an image within the eye, the lowest step being brightness discrimination (see Figure 4, *above*), and continues through various physiological stages until the analysis has reached a specific classification or recognition of the incoming signals and produced the perceptual representation. In a similar way, speech analysis starts with the sensory coding and works its way to the interpretation of the meaning of the utterance. A bottom-up, data-driven system typically produces highly veridical representations (Glass, Holyoak, and Santa 1979).

These two processing strategies can be thought of as falling on a continuum in which both are often simultaneously activated (Anderson 1983). However, a relative emphasis is devoted either to CDP or to DDP depending on the level of involvement of the perceiver that facilitates the occurrence of either re-salience or in-salience. Consumers are neither largely "theory-driven" nor predominately "data-driven"; rather, they are continually compelled by the relation between prior knowledge (schemata) and marketing stimuli (events).[123]

2.4.6   A Reconciliation between Communication Theories

Since the task of perception is to gather sensor information together and interpret it in terms of a coherent framework, in-salience and re-salience could be a key for the comprehension of the inner mechanisms of perception. These two kinds of processing are both essential and complementary, each assisting the other in the completion of the overall job of being aware of the world. Our hypothesis on salience allows finding a point of contact between conflicting communication theories, namely *consistency theories* and *complexity theory* (see Aaker, Batra, and Myers 1992, Ch. 11, for a review), a reconciliation between assimilation and contrast which was attempted after Helson's (1959) adaptation level model. Moreover, it allows clarifying the debate in advertising research between brand salience and brand image (Miller and Berry 1998).

Our approach assumes that tendencies toward consistency and variety both exist and that the dominance of one over the other depends on the three basic elements involved: Stimuli, contexts, and individuals (i.e., schemata). When the stimulus is contextually incongruent with one's schemata (i.e., in-salient), the individual will end up with pursuing variety.[124] When the stimulus is contextually congruent with one's goals (i.e., re-salient), the individual will be motivated to reduce stimulation and seek harmony.[125] Processing could be primarily moderated by involvement (as predicted by our *Proposition Four*): Thus, if a consumer is embarking on a major purchase, he may search for re-salient information; whereas, if it is a routine purchase, he could be influenced by in-salient information. But processing could be also moderated by other situational variables - both external (e.g., time pressure) and internal (e.g., mood) - as predicted by *Proposition One* (see *above*, B. *The context*).[126]

As a whole, the *Dichotic theory of salience* (Guido 1998) - which considers both the *In-salience* and the *Re-salience hypotheses* - could be fruitful in the debate regarding dual-process models of persuasion (cf. Tesser and Shaffer 1990), such as Petty and Cacioppo's (1986) *Elaboration likelihood model* (ELM), and Chaiken's (1987) *Heuristic-systematic model* (HSM). This could be done supporting a multistable model like the one proposed by Apter's

(1989) *Reversal theory*, built upon the assumption that people are inherently inconsistent - so that, dealing with the same situation in different circumstances, they behave in different ways (cf. O'Shaughnessy and Guido 1996).

Specifically, the *Reversal theory* proposes that the individuals' subjective experience is *bistable*, rather than homeostatic - that is, it implies two points of equilibrium rather than one (like a switch that can be turned on or off). Therefore, in relation to a stimulus, individuals (e.g., consumers) can be in one out of two *metamotivational states* - either a *telic state*, directed to the achievement of a goal, or a *paratelic state*, related to the behavior itself. The key notion here is that each individual during his everyday life - and even for very short periods - can frequently shift from one metamotivational state to the other, without being in both states at the same time.[127] If people are in a telic state, achieving a goal becomes a primary objective; if, on the contrary, they are in a paratelic state, this will be only a secondary objective and the activity itself will be the primary goal. Indeed, the telic state is linked to a certain disposition towards avoiding high levels of arousal, typical of anxiety, and searching accomplishment/relaxation, whereas the paratelic state is linked to a certain disposition towards seeking high levels of arousal, typical of excitement, thus avoiding boredom. Therefore, due to their different characteristics, the paratelic state leads to playfulness; whereas the telic state leads to seriousness (see Potocky and Murgatroyd 1993, for a review).

Following this approach, we could hypothesize that, in relation to the level of arousal triggered by the degree of personal involvement and by other contextual factors, a person can frequently switch from a state in which he is inclined to attend to in-salient stimuli (e.g., a paratelic state) to another in which he is inclined to attend to re-salient stimuli (e.g. a telic state) - with the obvious, important effects this switching has on memory and persuasion (Guido 1993) in particular, and on marketing and communications in general.

2.5 *Implications:* In-Salience Generates Consumer Awareness

As a result of the above propositions, we argue that in-salience generates perceivers' *awareness* of the object stimulus. As is implicit in our definition of the construct, because any in-salient stimulus involves *both* attention *and* interpretation, it implies that the individual is also aware of it (that is, the consumer has memory for it).

Consumer awareness, in our model, is defined as a rudimentary level of knowledge (e.g., brand knowledge), possessed by a consumer, involving memory for the object stimulus. Awareness represents the lowest end of a continuum of brand knowledge that ranges from simple memory of the in-salient stimulus - as measured by recognition or recall - to a highly developed cognitive structure based on detailed information (cf. Hoyer and Brown 1990). Thus, the distinction between awareness and recognition/recall is a subtle one, the former denoting a state of knowledge possessed by the consumer and the latter a cognitive process resulting from awareness.

2.5.1   Retrievability in Memory of In-Salient vs. Non-In-Salient Stimuli

Awareness is the first consequence of the information processing triggered off by any in-salient stimulus (see Figure 2, *above*).[128] Awareness is the product of several mechanisms for pre-conscious and conscious processing that are arranged hierarchically under the control of the executive. The early mechanisms in the hierarchy operate automatically, in a strictly bottom-up manner, to construct a representation of some object or event in the environment. They are uninfluenced by the results of the comparison and decision mechanisms that follow them. As shown in Figure 4 (*above*), there are two levels of mechanisms above the level of sensory receptors: Dimensional analysis, and figure construction mechanisms. The resulting perceptual representation corresponds to the individual's awareness of the attended input (Glass and Holyoak 1986, pp. 46-47).

In Marcel's (1983) words: "Awareness is taken to be the prerequisite of an ability to acknowledge or 'comment upon' our percepts, thoughts, memories, and actions" (p. 240). Although "consciousness always has an object, that we are always conscious of *something*" (p. 241), a variety of levels of awareness exists, ranging from total lack of awareness (unconsciousness) to a highly tuned sensitivity to a stimulus (Reber 1985, p. 77).[129] It is rational, therefore, to think that consumers are *more* aware of some stimuli rather than others. From Propositions Two and Four, it derives that, *all being equal, consumer awareness is greater for in-salient rather than for non-in-salient stimuli*. Or also, since awareness is assessed by the retrievability of the stimulus in memory as measured by recall or recognition, it derives that, *on an equal ground, a stimulus which was in-salient is more retrievable in memory than one that was non-in-salient.*

This superior retrievability of in-salient stimuli over non-in-salient ones is consistent with previous studies in social cognition that found higher memory for incongruent stimuli than for congruent stimuli (see, *above*, Chapter Two, Paragraph 4.3). Major explanations can be traced back to two alternative theories, namely the *Depth of processing argument* (Anderson and Bower 1973; Craik and Lockhart 1972; and Lockhart, Craik, and Jacoby 1976), which considers in-salient stimuli more retrievable because of the increased time and efforts spent to process the more difficult-to-comprehend stimuli (leading to a wider and deeper memory network for those stimuli); and the *Perceptual distinctiveness of processing* (Eysenck 1979; Eysenck and Eysenck 1980), which considers in-salient stimuli more retrievable by virtue of their unexpected nature which makes them more perceptually distinct than non-in-salient stimuli (see also, *below*, Chapter Four, Paragraph 4.1.2).

2.5.2   Salience Effect as a Retrieval Bias

No matter which theory is chosen to explain memory superiority of in-salient stimuli, the effect of in-salience could be that of favoring the retrieval of information which is unrepresentative of all that is known (Alba, Hutchinson, and Lynch 1991) and unimportant for consumers' decision making.[130] Such a selective retrieval (which must be distinguished from similar processes, such as selective search or selective exposure, which involve a failure to learn information) acts as a bias by distorting interpretive and elaborative inferences built on knowledge in memory and, thus, influencing consumers' choices (cf., e.g., Schaefer 1989).

A bias is any systematic error in the process of perception. Two types of biases characterize, respectively, the occurrence of re-salient and in-salient stimuli: *Motivational biases*, which occur when perceivers' needs and values interfere with perceivers' ability to process information; and *cognitive biases*, which result from characteristic ways people have of simplifying and processing information and which occur even when perceivers are trying very hard to be objective (cf. Schneider, Harstorf, and Ellsworth 1979, p. 243; see, also, Forehand and Keller 1996). Differently from random errors or those that arise out of stupidity and ignorance, biases are systematic and predictable errors built in the cognitive system.

Like "snap judgments" that people make immediately and seemingly without conscious thought (Taylor and Fiske 1978; and also, *above*, Chapter Two, Paragraph 4.3), retrieval biases can be the effect of the salience of particular factors.[131] It is well known that memory retrieval for brands and attributes is largely determined by attentional factors, familiarity, the presence of retrieval cues, and the level of competitive interference (see, e.g., Burke and Srull 1988; Keller 1987, 1991ab). However, advances in categorization research and renewed attention to the way in which consumers actually make choices suggest that the same elements which influence attention and interpretation of the salient stimuli (i.e., *context* for in-salience, and *motives* for re-salience) have also a major role in the retrieval process (Holden 1993).[132]

Both the influences of context (or situation) and motives are captured by a model (Holden and Lutz 1992) that suggests that brand awareness is a function of the cues that are salient in the retrieval situation. Following the spreading activation approach, the model proposes that the brand can be considered as a central node in memory with links to it from various other nodes representing attributes, benefits, and other brands (see Holden and Lutz 1992, p. 105). Any of these nodes is posited to have the potential to act as a cue to the brand, the success of the cuing being dependent on the associative strength between the cue and the brand. It is further posited that the links to the brand may be direct or indirect. For instance, a situation may directly evoke a particular brand while other situations may lead to thought of some attribute which in turn leads (directly) to the evocation of a brand. Motives and context, therefore, facilitate not only the processing of the stimuli encountered (in this case, the brands) by enhancing awareness, but also their retrievability in memory as a function of that awareness.[133]

2.5.3   Measures of Awareness

As mentioned in Chapter One, the multiplicity of definitions adopted in literature and the use of considerably different measures for the salience construct has impeded so far the creation of a common theoretical framework, posing two problems for research in this area. First, each individual researcher having no generally accepted measure to use has had to develop his own measure or, rather, borrow one. Second, researchers have had difficulty in building upon previous work when developing theories, since it was uncertain whether all these measures were measuring the same construct. On the other hand, the in-salience theory allows us to unify different cases of (in-)salience and - what is more important - considering that - because salience is the result of both attention and interpretation (see, *above, Proposition Two*) - *salience should be correctly assessed not through measures of attention but rather through measures of memory.*

Thus, the retrievability in memory, which is posited to descend from awareness, is operationally measured through *recall* and *recognition* of the stimulus. Recall and recognition measures have a long and detailed history of use in marketing as indicators of consumer awareness (Rossiter and Percy 1987). For recall the individual must describe a stimulus which is not present; for recognition a stimulus must merely be identified as having been previously seen (Bettman 1979).[134] Many problems and refinements have surfaced concerning the use of recall and recognition in marketing (Zinkhan, Locander, and Leigh 1986). Fortunately, psychologists have been active in refining basic recall and recognition measures and in formulating variants to evaluate different aspects of memory processes (see, *below*, Chapter Four, Note 35). At the very least, it can be considered that both measures of memory tap on a communal content domain - acquired or learned information - and, thus, should covary to a significant extent (cf. Laurent, Kapferer, and Roussel 1995).[135]

It is worth noting, however, that recent research on the measurement of advertising impact - addressing the relative sensitivity of recall versus recognition tests (e.g., Singh, Rothschild, and Churchill 1988) - has found that these two measures are unequally affected by the salience effect on retrieval. In particular, such effect occurs most strongly on recall tests and may virtually disappear on recognition tests (Alba and Hasher 1983; Alba and Hutchinson 1987). Thus, while arguments may be made from a managerial perspective regarding the value of recognition tests to tap awareness and learning of ads, such tests may mask biases that exist in consumer choice situations that require the free recall of attribute information (Alba, Hutchinson, and Lynch 1991).[136]

2.5.4   Hierarchy of Effects

Despite the importance of consumer awareness on brand choice, researchers have given little attention to developing an understanding of awareness as a construct (Holden 1993). Indeed, focusing specifically on brand awareness and its propagation through advertising, the centrality of awareness and of its antecedents (in-salient and re-salient stimuli) can be easily documented. From an empirical point of view, numerous studies have shown that brand awareness measures are powerful predictors of consumer choice behavior (e.g., Axelrod 1968; Haley and Case 1979; Miller and Berry 1998; Nedungadi and Hutchinson 1985). From a conceptual point of view, furthermore, brand awareness has been recognized as preceding - and necessary to - brand evaluation (Howard and Sheth 1969; Holden and Lutz 1992; Nedungadi 1990).

As discussed in Chapter Two, Section One (*above*, Note 3), consumers can only select brands among those which they are aware of (i.e., *awareness set*); and they usually select among those brands to which they have a positive feeling (i.e., *evoked set*), discharging brands which are neutrally (i.e., *inert set*) or negatively (i.e., *inept set*) evaluated. Therefore, although awareness is not a sufficient condition for choice, it is a necessary condition. Among the seminal theories on consumer choice, Lavidge and Steiner (1961) have provided a model to outline the logical process of how a consumer arrives at brand purchase. Figure 5 (*below*) diagrams their *Hierarchy of effect model*, which consists of seven stages, beginning with "Unawareness" and culminating in "Purchase." As is evident from this structure, all the possible effects towards consumer choice are based on the awareness stage.

An important assumption embedded in this model is that consumer behavior consists of three major dimensions: Cognitive, affective, and conative. This view is widely accepted in the marketing literature (a popularized description is the "think-feel-do" view of consumer behavior), despite some exceptions (Vakratsas and Ambler 1999). In brief, the *cognitive component* refers to rational elements involved with mental thought, the *affective component* refers to our emotional or feeling states, and the *conative component* involves the tendency to action or behavior on our part. In terms of fixed order, the model suggests that the cognitive operations come first, followed by affective, and then conative ones. All of them can arise only when a stimulus comes out of the "limbo" of unawareness.

Figure 5. The Hierarchy of Effects Model

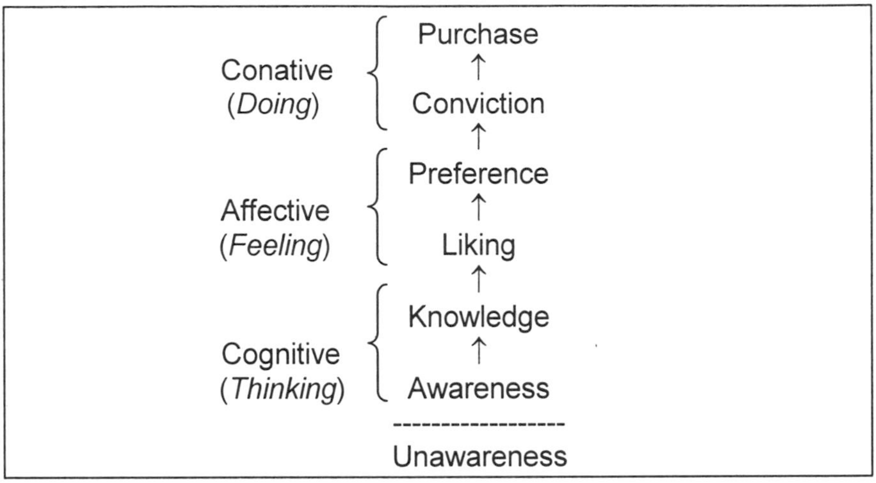

```
Conative      {   Purchase
(Doing)       {      ↑
              {   Conviction
                     ↑
              {   Preference
Affective     {      ↑
(Feeling)     {   Liking
                     ↑
              {   Knowledge
Cognitive     {      ↑
(Thinking)    {   Awareness
              --------------------
                  Unawareness
```

Source: Lavidge and Steiner (1961).

Despite the fact that the model's extensions and variations have occurred since the model's appearance (see, e.g., Brisoux and Chéron 1990; Preston and Thorson 1984), the awareness stage has always been reported as the first, insuppressible step towards consumers' final action. Even the major threats to the viability of the hierarchy - namely, models of *Nonhierarchical ordering* and of *Omitted hierarchy steps* - have recognized this. The former suggest that, even under low involvement, "*conscious* connections occur between the persuasive stimulus and something in the respondent's life" (Krugman 1966/67 - emphasis added - as reported in Preston and Thorson 1984, p. 61); the latter, involving minimal encoding and processing, recognizes that "Awareness steps are not really omitted. They simply require more methodological sensitivity to be detected" (Preston and Thorson 1984, p. 63).

Not only is enhanced awareness the result of in-salient stimuli, thus being the basis of any process of choice, but also their consequent enhanced retrievability in memory can bias consumer choices. Bettman's (1979) *Information processing model* provides a classic background for understanding the importance of in-salience and awareness on consumer choices. It maintains that, due to their limited information processing capacity, consumers rarely (if ever) undertake complex analyses of available alternatives when facing a choice; rather, they typically employ simple decision strategies (heuristics) which favor the more easily retrievable information in memory (see also, *above*, Chapter Two, Paragraph 4.3). In Bettman's (1979) model, information is acquired from the environment through two perceptual mechanisms: Scanning, and interrupt mechanisms. The scanner is continuously open to relevant information from the environment; the interrupt mechanism deals with messages that interfere with the process of making a choice. Cast in the light of our theory, the scanner is receptive to information "looked for" by the consumer (i.e., re-salient information), while the interrupt mechanism deals with messages that are "imposed upon" the consumer (i.e., in-salient information). However, both mechanisms can delay the making of a particular choice and can divert attention to a completely different area of choice (e.g., a more pressing problem).

The message for marketers from these ideas may be highly significant as it can help determine the advertising objectives and strategy that be adopted. Should market research indicate that the brand is in the *unawareness set* for a large proportion of the population then the task is to raise awareness in order to get it into the awareness set. Thus widespread media campaigns could be indicated with the aim of getting the brand known. If the brand were found to be in the *evoked set*, the promotional strategy would be defensive reinforcement. Otherwise, should it appear in the *inert* or *inept sets*, positive attempts would be made to change consumers' perceptions and attitudes towards the brand (Rice 1985). This approach to the topic has prompted some authors even to consider salience for a brand simply as "being in the consumer's consideration set" (Ehrenberg, Barnard, and Scriven 1997, p. 9):[137] "Salience-building brand advertising can therefore influence consumers' choices over time for brands which are not priced alike [...], if any of them are within the consumer's routinely acceptable price range. The advertising only has to keep the brand *sufficiently salient* to continue to be chosen as part of the consumer's habitual brand repertoire." (Ehrenberg, Scriven, and Barnard 1997, p. 30).

2.5.5   An Empirical Test of In-Salience

An experiment was conducted at the University of Rome, "La Sapienza," Italy, to test some of the basic propositions of the in-salience hypothesis. The experiment examined the model in an advertising environment by assessing differential effects on consumers' memory of both in-salient and non-in-salient messages in print ads. Applications and results are reported in the following chapter.

NOTES

[1] The effects of salience on communication outcomes mainly regards learning and memory, on the one hand, and attitudes and persuasion, on the other hand (Guido 1993). In this book, however, only the former outcomes will be discussed (Chapter Three) and tested (Chapter Four) through the use of the concept of consumer awareness. Future research on the effects of in-salience on attitudes and persuasion should not avoid considering Tesser's (1978) framework supporting schema theory applied to the attitude concept as a starting point. He wrote (p. 397): "There is not a single attitude toward an object but, rather, any number of attitudes depending on the number of schemas available for thinking about the object." Therefore, it is the schema (i.e., *evaluative framework* - cf. Cohen 1982) the perceiver is applying in processing the object that creates the incongruity and, thus, the in-salience effects in a given context (see, also, Millar and Tesser 1986).

[2] Interpretation is the same when the *force* and the *effect* of in-salience converge (see, *below*, Axiom Three).

[3] Following Janiszewski (1998), we distinguish between two types of search behavior. "Goal-directed search behavior occurs when consumers use stored search routines to collect information in a deliberate manner. In contrast, exploratory search behavior occurs when consumers are confronted with multiple pieces of information but have little stored knowledge about how to proceed with the information gathering." (Janiszewski p. 290).

[4] "A *construct* is a term specifically designed for a scientific purpose, generally to organize knowledge and direct research in an attempt to describe or explain some aspects of nature. Constructs have at least two types of meaning, systematic and observational [...]. *Systematic meaning* refers to the fact that the interpretation of what construct stands for depends on the theory in which the construct is embedded [...]. *Observational meaning* refers to the notion that a construct must be capable of being directly or indirectly operationalized if it is to have explanatory power [...]. If a construct has no observational meaning, it is merely a metaphysical term; if a notion has no systemic meaning, it is no construct but an observational term." (Peter 1981, p. 134, emphasis added).

[5] "Such findings have led to explanations which stress that, relative to non-salient stimuli, salient stimuli more often activate processing (see Pyszcynski and Greenberg 1981), are processed more deeply (Hastie and Kumar 1979), are encoded using multiple rather than single representations (Taylor and Fiske 1978), elicit more vivid imagery (Taylor and Fiske 1978), and are stored in more available locations in memory (Hastie and Kumar 1979; Pryor and Kriss 1977)." (Dix and Herzberger 1983, pp. 965-966).

[6] The vision that de-emphasizes the role of contextual effects in perception seems grounded on *feature theories*. According to these, the process of recognition of a stimulus begins with the extrapolation of its constitutive elements (for a face, e.g., its different features: a nose, two eyes, a mouth, a chin, and so on). This set of elements is then combined and compared against information stored in memory (Gibson 1969). Feature theories, which consider each element outside the context in which it is located, have not found strong evidence in experimental studies (see, e.g., Eysenck and Keane 1990, p. 47). By contrast, the importance of contextual effects has been convincingly demonstrated by Weisstein and Harris (1974), with their experiments on the detection of lines, in which the coherence of forms influenced the identification of the target line. Under this theory, the critical importance of context for the occurrence of salient stimuli is exalted.

[7] That is, for example, a person who is not an electrician. Otherwise, it would be a matter of re-salience.

[8] Also, re-salience, of course, could be an explanation.

[9] The only exception to this principle is constituted by *context-independent information*, that is, by those schemata that are *chronically* accessible to a perceiver (Barsalou 1982; and also, *below*, Paragraph 2.3.2).

[10] This position is supported, for example, by Stern (1988), who demonstrated in service advertising that either trite, ordinary symbols and bizarre, idiosyncratic ones can create brand awareness according to the advertising context in which they appear. In linguistics, moreover, the pragmatic concept of salience is the underlying principle for the *definiteness* of nouns (see Von Heusinger 1997, for a review). Taken together, the many studies from psycholinguistics, functional linguistics, and computational linguistics have identified a number of factors that affect the salience of the referent of a noun (Arnould 1998): i.e., recency, topicality, focus, semantic plausibility, parallelism, ambiguity, and others.

[11] At this stage of analysis, we do not mean to distinguish between the formal modalities of stimulus presentation (the advertising message) and the content of the stimulus itself (the advertised product).

[12] There is considerable evidence in several different areas for the operation of schema-like knowledge structures possessed by perceivers (see, e.g., Alba and Hasher 1983). The strongest evidence comes from studies showing that when people have different expectations about a target stimulus they interpret and recall it in different ways (see, e.g., Anderson and Pichert 1978; Bransford and Johnson 1972).

[13] In the following paragraphs, however, for reasons of simplicity, we shall not always distinguish between addressees and receivers.

[14] In the case of advertising message, therefore, more appropriately, we should speak of *text*, to refer to a planned force in reference to an addressee, and of *discourse*, to refer to the receivers' pragmatic achievement of meaning in reference to a text (Guido, M.G. 1999).

[15] The three components of in-salience (stimulus, context, and schemata) can be usefully compared to those of an alternative integrative framework on information processing for advertisements, the *Motivation-Opportunity-Ability (MOA) model* by MacInnis, Moorman, and Jaworski (1991) (Guido 1993; see, also, Andrews 1988; MacInnis and Jaworski 1989; Batra and Ray 1986; MacKenzie 1986; and Poiesz and Robben 1996, for discussing differences between MOA and ELM - see Chapter Two, Note 97, *above*). The MOA model provides an interpretation of these components as antecedents of brand information processing. In this perspective, the *stimulus* gives the Motivation to process a piece of information; the *context* gives the Opportunity to process it; and *schemata* support the Ability to encode it. Schemata, indeed, are best described as organized representations of prior knowledge (Alloy and Tabachnik 1984; Johnson and Katrichis 1988). Another similar model is the one proposed by Ratneshwar et al. (1997).

[16] "A tennis player actively playing a game of tennis is largely influenced by external sources, whereas a person engaged in fantasy or daydreaming is largely influenced by internal sources. A person absorbed in internal sources of information (memories) is less influenced by external events and vice versa. Young children, relatively free of internalized concerns, are much more attentive to external stimulation than older children or adults. However, one's internal state may cause him or her to direct perceptual activity outward; a thirsty person, for example, will look for a source of water." (Woods 1981, p. 183).

[17] Re-salience, instead, is basically a top-down process that starts from internal sources of influences (see, *below*, Paragraph 2.4.3).

[18] "Marketers who make changes in packaging or in any other product feature that functions to identify a product must be careful about the possibility of miscuing. [...] Supermarket or store brands commonly use this principle in their packaging. Their packages are often made to look like those of manufacturer brands in order to facilitate misidentification." (Woods 1981, p. 190).

[19] "There are, however, two difficulties with the cue concept when the focus is on meaning. First, the very idea of a cue grows out of a tradition in psychology - reinforcement and drive theory - which has often been hostile to the notion of mental process [cf., also, Aslin and Rothschild 1986, p. 566]. While the use of cue in a conceptualization does not presuppose or inevitably entail a behaviorist position, cue brings with it the idea of an involuntary or mindless response. The very flexibility of the cue concept can also be a drawback. Since virtually any and every aspect of an ad could potentially serve as a cue, we learn very little about the internal structure of an ad or about how different cues may have different effects. In this sense, to describe an element of an ad as a 'cue' provides very little information about what the role of that element may be in the creation of meaning." (McQuarrie 1990, p. 658).

[20] Information cue has been defined elsewhere as "advance information about where and when a stimulus event will happen" (Coren and Ward 1989, p. 453). In our discussion, however, the relation between stimulus cue and information cue will be similar to that between the form and the content of a stimulus.

[21] Analogously, Shiffman and Kanuk (1991, p. 160) noticed: "For years certain advertisers have used blatant sexuality in advertisements for products to which sex was not relevant because they knew such advertisements would attract a high degree of attention; however, such ads often defeated their own purpose because readers tended to remember the sex (e.g., the girl), but not the product or brand. Nevertheless, advertisers continue to use erotic appeals in promoting a wide variety of products from office furniture to jeans."

[22] More specifically, for a brand name to be deemed *suggestive*, "it must have well-defined associations or meanings that could be seen as relevant in a product setting. In other words, associations for a suggestive brand name must be both *salient* and *relevant* in a particular product context." (Keller, Heckler, and Houston 1998, p. 49, emphasis added).

[23] Notice that, by definition, *non-in-salient stimuli* are those stimuli that are contextually congruent with a perceiver's schema.

[24] Cue normalizing, together with in-salience and re-salience, is at the base of selective attention. This result has been implicitly recognized since 1964, when Berelson and Steiner noticed that: "Which stimuli get selected depends upon three major factors: the nature of the stimuli involved [i.e., in-salience]; previous experience or learning as it affects the observer's expectations (what he is prepared or "set" to see) [i.e., cue normalizing] and the motives in play at the time [i.e., re-salience]" (p. 100). Each of these factors, in turn, can serve to increase or decrease the probability that the stimulus will be perceived, and each can affect the consumer's selective exposure to and selective awareness of the stimulus itself (cf., also, Hansen 1972, p. 48).

[25] Cue normalizing can either cause problems to marketers or could be used effectively. Here two opposite examples are reported: "A common problem for secondary brands, which have relatively small market shares, is that consumers misinterpret their advertising as actually coming from one of the market leaders. Because the market leaders spend so much more money on advertising, consumers begin to expect that the messages they receive are coming from the major brands. Thus, when an advertisement is received from a secondary brand, the consumer may not pay enough attention to it to recognize that it is not a major brand doing the advertising." (Mowen 1993, p. 92). "An opposite tack, and one that has been used effectively in TV commercials, is to make the commercial seem so close to the story line of a program that viewers are unaware that they are watching an ad until they are well into it. For example, Ragu spaghetti sauce has run

commercials that look and sound more like family situation comedies (complete with laugh tracks and canned applause) than like ads that they attract and hold viewer attention. Similarly, advertisers are running print ads (called "advertorials") that so closely resemble editorial material that it has become increasingly difficult for readers to tell them apart." (Shiffman and Kanuk 1991, p. 159).

[26] Schemata are implicated in freeing up the cognitive system from having to analyze all aspects of a scene. For example, when viewing an everyday scene, such as an office or a sitting room, most people have clear expectations about what objects they are likely to see. Since there is no need to spend a very long time looking at expected objects, this frees up resources for processing more novel and unexpected aspects of any given scene. Because of this, unexpected objects tend to be remembered and recognized more easily, and exchanges of one unusual object for another (a cow for a car in a living room) are noticed far more often than are exchanges of one usual object for another (a chair for a table in a living room) (Friedman 1979). Moreover, unusual objects found in a visual scene are looked at longer (Antes and Penland 1981; Friedman 1979), even when perceivers are motivated to distribute their attention equally over the scene (Friedman and Liebelt 1981).

[27] "Much research (e.g., Sujan 1985) has applied the model developed by Fiske and Pavelchak (1986), who suggest that more holistic processing occurs when there is congruence with a primed product-category schema and that more attribute-level processing occurs when an incongruent instance is encountered." (Stayman, Alden, and Smith 1992, p. 242). Unlike Fiske and Pavelchak (1986), Mandler (1982) has hypothesized a schema-level rather than an attribute-level response model to incongruity (see, *below*, Paragraph 2.1.8 on *Information congruity theory*).

[28] The increase in positive evaluation may be due to reduction in uncertainty - that is, as learning about a stimulus increases, aversion tension due to familiarity decreases. However, Anand, Holbrook, and Stephens (1988) suggested that enhanced affect may also stem from subject's rewarding themselves for task performance (i.e., correct recognition of old and new stimuli).

[29] "First assimilation may not be possible and restructuring (accommodation) of the cued schema may be attempted. If unsuccessful, the affective evaluation will be strongly negative because of the 'unavailability of an appropriate response to the environment' (Mandler 1982, p. 24). If accommodation is successful, the 'resultant phenomena affect will be intensely positive or negative, depending not on the fact of arousal but on the current state of evaluation' (Mandler 1982, p. 24). Another response to extreme incongruity involves 'schema switching,' in which the 'solution is one of finding a different schema that fits the available evidence' (Mandler 1982, p 23). This response produces positive evaluations when congruity with a positively balanced schema is established. Evaluations associated with schema switching are hypothesized to be weaker than those produced by accommodation but stronger than those that result from assimilation." (Stayman, Alden, and Smith 1992, p. 242).

[30] "Meyers-Levy and Tybout (1989) found that, if the product was held constant subjects exposed to a moderately incongruent product description (even with a negative attribute) evaluated the product more favorably than those exposed to either a congruent or an extremely incongruent description. Ozanne et al. (1992) found that subjects exposed to a moderately incongruent new product engaged in more search than did subjects exposed to either congruent or strongly incongruent new products." (Stayman, Alden, and Smith 1992, p. 243). Finally, Stayman, Alden, and Smith (1992, p. 252) extended these findings and found that "schema processing may influence consumers' evaluations of their experiences with a product by affecting both the nature of expectations regarding the product and the types of disconfirmation judgments that are made during a trial."

[31] According to Axiom Three of the in-salience theory, schemata are also part of personal factors, as they are made up of perceivers' current knowledge and personal experiences. However, given their importance in the model, they are considered separately.

[32] Involvement, moreover, is taken as the source of the other complementary type of salience, namely *re-salience* (see, *above*, Table 3).

[33] The importance of the context in the form of "specification of the strategy space" (e.g., Grant and Quiggin 1998) has been stressed by all the strategic studies on the so-called *meeting-place problem* started by Schelling (1960) regarding the use of *focal* (or *salient*) *points* in decision making (see, also, Akerlof 1991; Colman 1997; Metha, Starmer, and Sugden 1994; Slemrod et al. 1997). Bacharach (2000) and associates have combined this body of work with the decision framing studies by Tversky and Kahneman (e.g., 1981), arguing that, if an option is salient, this is because the agent's own, spontaneous frame makes it so, by making it an odd one out on some dimension of that frame. In their words, for example, if a single white job applicant stands out among a set of candidates, his salience depends upon the selector's frame containing the dichotomy white/colored. Bachrach's *Variable frame theory* (VFT) included in coordination problems the psychological effects beyond rational choices and investigated the phenomenon of Buridanic choice (that is, when an agent is unable to identify a strictly best option): This can happen either when an option is believed to be "equal best"; or when the agent knows there is a unique best, but it may equally be any of some set (like in a lottery - see Schindler and Berbaum 1983); or when the principles for deciding are weak and/or the time and other resources the agent has for deciding are inadequate. According to Bacharach (2000): "Decision theorists have implicitly assumed that rational agents deal easily with Buridanic problems of the first two types, by 'tossing a coin'. However, agents may not always have a means of randomizing; moreover, in 1994 evidence was beginning to emerge that consumers faced with Buridan problems choose in another way: they choose an 'odd one out', even if the odd feature is known to be functionally irrelevant, like the yellowness of a chicken identical in taste and price to all the others (Carpenter et al. 1994). More recently, it has been found that in choosing from a row of identical items on a supermarket shelf, customers tend to take one in the middle, and in choosing from a set of equivalent routes, one that is outermost (Christenfeld 1995)."

[34] Many authors in the past have considered among the external factors influencing perception also the "stimulus factors," that is, such properties of the stimulus which "cause it to receive attention" (Wilkie 1990, p. 231). These would include size, intensity, color, movement, position, isolation, format, and so on. Such a definition reproposes in different terms the problem of salience. Their common origin is recognized in our model of in-salience, although we do not consider their salience as an objective quality of these stimuli.

[35] Chakravarti and Lynch (1983) provided a framework for exploring context effects on consumer judgment and choice processes. Context was found to influence overt judgments in at least three potential ways. That is, influencing: (1) Which aspects of the stimulus are selected for processing; (2) The scale values, i.e., the subjective, encoded representations of the stimulus cues; and (3) The judgment function that translates private evaluations to overt ratings.

[36] "Rumelhart and Ortony (1977) define schemata as 'memorial representations of categories that contain attributes typically associated with a particular object or concept category and reflect the interrelationship among these attributes'. Similarly, schemas have been defined as 'cognitive structure(s) that consist in part of the representation of some defined stimulus domain. The schema contains general knowledge about that domain, including a specification of the relationships among its attributes as well as specific examples or instances of the stimulus domain' (Taylor and Crocker 1981). In considering the unconscious nature of schematic processing, Brewer and Nakamura concluded that schemas are 'unconscious cognitive structures and

processes that underlie human knowledge that have been organized to form qualitative new structures' (Brewer and Nakamura 1984). Finally, schemas 'consist of elaborate sets of expectations about what is currently being or about to be processed, they appear to guide the encoding process in a relatively automatic way' (Mandler 1979)." (Peltier 1989, pp. 9-10). To remain within the terminology used by Berlyne (1957; 1958; 1960) - which was to a large extent an extension of Piaget's studies - schemata are "neuronal models of expectations" developed by individuals in the course of their lives (cf. Kahneman 1973, p. 53). They might include hypotheses and examples about the usual values of the stimulus, its variability, the conditions in which the stimulus shows up. Neisser (1976) says the following of schemata: "A schema is not merely like a format; it also functions as a plan. Perceptual schema are plans for finding out about object and events, for obtaining more information to fill in the format [...] the schema determines what is perceived [...] because information can be picked up only if there is a developing format ready to accept it." (p. 55). Finally, a paper by Hastie (1981), which distinguishes among the interpretations given to the term, can be extremely useful for present purposes. He states: "the critical features of the concept of a schema are that it is an abstract, general structure that establishes relations between specific events or entities; and, that any specific event or entity can be evaluated as congruent, or irrelevant with reference to the schema." (p. 41).

[37] "Conceptually, there are two such options. First, as is evident from Tesser's [1978] discussion, if attribute information is not found in memory the schema can facilitate continued processing to locate appropriate knowledge. Conversely, if the stimulus configuration itself represents only a subset of the total information contained in the schema, any missing attributes not found in the stimulus domain can be inferred from the schema. Thus, the stimulus configuration is 'matched against a schema, and the ordering and relations among the elements are imposed on the elements of the stimulus domain' [Taylor and Crocker 1981]." (Peltier 1989, p. 12).

[38] Categories are sets of features or attributes that are typically associated with a particular stimulus object that reflect similarities and define interrelationships between their members. "The literature often distinguishes between *categories* as taxonomic organizations of objects or words versus *schemas* as spatially or temporally organized structures" (Stayman, Alden, and Smith 1992, note 1, p. 240).

[39] "At the top of this hierarchy very abstract or general categories called *prototypes* can be found. A prototype is a category member with the greatest number of attributes in common with other members of the category and the fewest number of attributes in common with members of contrasting categories (Hastie 1981). [...] More specific bits of information associated with a target schema are embedded within the general categories. At the lowest level in the hierarchy a number of specific examples or instances of the schema, labeled *exemplars*, are stored into memory. [...] As is evident from the above discussion, exemplars are more flexible components of schematic categories than are prototypes. Prototypes are basically an average of all the exemplars for a given schema." (Peltier 1989, pp. 13-14, emphasis added). "Exemplars are known good examples of the category. Prototypes are abstract images embodying features or attributes most commonly associated with members of the category. The prototype need not to be identical to any particular exemplar." (Sujan 1985, p. 31). See, also, Sujan and Bettman (1989).

[40] The major consequence of this final dimension of schemata is that they facilitate the perception, interpretation, and memory of situational information, whereas an important by-product of their operation is a systematic bias or distortion. "In sum," as argued by Alloy and Tabachnik (1984, p. 141), "organisms both assimilate incoming information to their preexisting expectations and accommodate their expectations to the objective data of experience. That is, both make sense of and impose sense upon the world, simultaneously."

[41] "For example, if I use the word 'father', this will immediately trigger the reader's unique personal construct of 'father', a construct that will have been formed over a long period of time, based on the reader's experience of fathers. If they had a good, positive relationship with their own parents their construct would be very different to that of a person who had been regularly beaten and abused by their father, which in turn may be very different from that of a person who was orphaned at an early age. In other words your construct of 'father' is uniquely your own, and this will influence the perceptions, reactions and responses every time that word is used." (Rice 1993, p. 96). Furthermore: "A simple example of a [modal] schema might be 'something for lunch.' Each individual would have his or her own unique schema or mental image of 'something for lunch,' but many people would have quite similar schema because of their common backgrounds. A group of secretaries at work would have much in common: 'Something for lunch' would be nearby, inexpensive, light, and quickly served. However, the members of the group might have different taste requirements, and hence a restaurant catering to this trade would position itself accordingly. (Location as well as a light, varied menu would be positioning elements.) A group of homemakers (employed exclusively at home) would have a different 'something for lunch' schema from that of secretaries, but with elements in common - low in calories, quick and easy to prepare, appetizing, and on-hand." (Woods 1981, pp. 180-181).

[42] Woods (1981, p. 180, note 2): "Positioning represents an intent and the associated procedures directed at giving a product a strong, clear image for a particular use within some use domain. [...] The name 'positioning' was created by Robert P. Kolesik."

[43] Implications for marketers are significant in setting up global strategies able to work in the same way for consumers of different cultural contexts (cf. Aaker and Segupta 2000; Clark 1990; Choi, Nisbett, and Smith 1997; Du Preez, Diamantopoulos, and Schlegelmilch 1994; Giora 1999; Leach and Liu 1998; McCort and Malhotra 1993; Tse and Gorn 1993); that is, for example, the case of a pan-European approach to advertising campaigns (e.g., Guido 1991, 1992).

[44] "Ads[, for example,] can be viewed as scripts, that is, as prototypic rhetorical structures that present new information within a conventional format. Moreover, different kinds of ads, by having their own traditions of structure and content, involve different kinds of scripts: the before-after comparison, the expert testimonial, the slice of life, and the celebrity endorsement. Through experience, consumers probably develop strong expectations concerning the events, actors and objects associated with a particular type of ad." (Speck, Schumann, and Thompson 1988, p. 70).

[45] We do not distinguish here between *instances* and *analogues* of a schema. This distinction made in social perception, however, could have interesting consequences also in the cognitive field (see Higgins and King 1981, p. 73).

[46] On the contrary, "[w]hen the stimulus configuration does not trigger the activation of a related schema, it must be interpreted outside of the perceiver's current knowledge structure. This is a very robust finding that was first uncovered by Ebbinghaus (1885) and corroborated many times since, across a multitude of contexts" (Peltier 1989, p. 19).

[47] Such approaches, which feature formal mathematical models of cognitive processes, are enjoying increasing popularity (Hintzman 1990). Differently from the standard theory, connectionist approaches to schemata assume that schemata are implicit and created at the time an individual needs them. In short, schemata are not "things" stored in memory; rather, they are simply patterns of activation across a vast network of units connected in a constraint satisfaction system (cf. Brown 1992).

[48] "When a node is activated the spread of activation is modulated by the weights associated with each link, i.e., closely associated nodes produce higher activation transfer as compared to weakly associated nodes. Reder and Anderson (1980) found that the amount of activation spreading from a given node along a pathway is a function of the strength of that pathway relative

to the sum of strengths of all paths emanating from that node." (Ulhaque and Bahn 1992, p. 783). Anyway, in our simple model, the area of the circle represents a different attribute relevance, whereas the length of the arc does not have any particular meaning.

[49] This notion of relevance is much more similar to the concept of "psychological salience" as it was first introduced by Hartley (1946), who pointed out that salience phenomena imply manipulation of cognitive elements that have been established by learning. "[W]hen Hartley first introduced the concept of psychological salience, he illustrated it with a suggestion that Hitler did not so much increase anti-Semitic attitudes in Germany as bring already existing antisemitic attitudes into more prominent use for defining the everyday world. This, of course, increased the probability of anti-Semitic behavior. While the shift in salience does not tell the whole story, it seems to be one of the dynamics operating in response to massive repetition. Although a rather simple dynamic, it may be a major one when there is no cause for resistance, or when uninvolved consumers do not provide their own perceptual emphases or anchors." (Krugman 1965, pp. 353-354).

[50] The *Theory of Reasoned Action* (Fishbein and Ajzen 1975; Ajzen and Fishbein, 1980) is one of the most established models in the attitude-behavior literature, accounting for the formation of behavioral intentions as a basis for predicting behavior. This theory, which is an extension of Fishbein's (1963, 1967) *Learning theory* of attitude formation and change, has been, in turn, extended by a further model, Ajzen's (1991) *Theory of planned behavior*. All models assume that the proximal cause of behavior is one's intention to engage in that behavior, but each of them adds a further predictor for a person's intention. According to the *Theory of reasoned action*, a behavioral intention depends on two predictors: A person's *attitude toward the behavior* (the original determinant of Fishbein's *Learning theory*) and a person's *subjective norm* (i.e., his perception of the social pressure put on him to engage in a certain behavior); whereas, according to the *Theory of planned behavior*, there is a further predictor to consider, that is a person's *perceived behavioral control* (i.e., his perception of how easy or difficult it is to perform that behavior). Therefore, a behavioral intention is theoretically represented as a weighted sum of these predictors. Other independent variables have been added to improve the model, such as *past behaviors* (cf. Bentler and Speckart 1979; Caprara, Barbaranelli, and Guido 1998a) and the theory has been effectively tested in a number of contexts - including marketing and consumer settings - to predict a variety of intentions and behaviors (see, for a review, Eagly and Chaiken 1993).

[51] The original formulation which has been employed (Fishbein 1967) is the following:

$$A_o = \sum_{i=1}^{n} b_i e_i$$

where:

A_o = the overall evaluation of (or *attitude toward*) concept *o*;

b_i = the strength of the association between the attitude concept, *o*, and the *i*th concept (that is, the strength of the belief - expressed as a subjective likelihood - that the attitude object possesses the *i*th attribute);

e_i = the evaluation of the *i*th concept; and

n = number of salient beliefs.

In a marketing setting, the attitude object is usually a brand (for example, a branded candy bar), the *i*th concept is a *salient* product attribute according to an individual consumer (e.g., nutritious), the e_i is the evaluation rate of that attribute on a good-bad dimension, and *n* is usually the number of salient product attributes. When considering other predictors (e.g., subjective norm), similar salient beliefs should be elicited and evaluated (cf. Gibbs 1977). Fishbein's model belongs to the general class of *multiple attribute models*: The essential thrust of these models (also, Rosemberg 1960) is that attitudes can be predicted on the basis of brand attribute perceptions, typically weighted by the value importance of each attribute. According to Mitchell and Olson (1981, p. 319): "The basic theoretical proposition of Fishbein's attitude theory is that beliefs *cause* attitude. Because attitude is determined by a set of salient beliefs, changes in attitude must be mediated by changes in those beliefs. Therefore, to change a person's attitude toward a concept, one must modify the salient beliefs about that concept (Fishbein and Ajzen 1975, Ch. 6)." Beliefs can be modified by (1) changing the strength of a salient belief (b_i); (2) changing the evaluation of a belief (e_i); (3) creating a new salient belief; or (4) making a salient belief nonsalient (for salience change strategies, see Lutz 1991, p. 328).

[52] *Activation* is defined as an elicitation triggered by an external stimulus, whereas *accessibility* is defined as a perceptual readiness with which a stored construct is utilized in information processing (see *Proposition Three, below*).

[53] "Thus, in most applications of the Fishbein model, free responses from a smaller number of people (say, 20 or 30) are combined to discover the *modal salient attributes*, that is, those five to nine attributes that are mentioned most often. These attributes are then used in constructing questionnaires to measure the b_i, and e_i elements associated with each attribute." (Lutz 1991, p. 327).

[54] [Nonsalient beliefs are those beliefs that do not influence attitudes.]

[55] The reason why Fishbein and Ajzen (1975) deal with *salient beliefs*, while Lutz (1991) deals with *salient attributes* to operationalize the same concepts can be found in the quasi-identity between salient beliefs and salient attributes that is realized in this attitude model. In the Fishbein's (1967) model, belief can be regarded as the individual perceived likelihood that buying the brand will lead to some consequence. Lutz (1975) noted that not all beliefs an individual holds with respect to using a particular brand are necessarily beliefs about the *consequences* of using that brand but, in practice, beliefs tend to be in the form of consequences. Therefore, e.g., in consumer research, *product attributes* (e.g., "whitens teeth," "nutritious," "pleasant taste") have often been regarded *as beliefs* about the consequences of using a brand.

[56] Availability has to do with what was already stored in memory; accessibility has to do with how easily it can be retrieved (Tulving and Pearlstone 1966). Of course, what is not available cannot necessarily be accessible. However, intrusions in available information driven by free-recall techniques could alter the detection of accessible information.

[57] They found that "20 to 30% of the stable concepts elicited on [... different] trials were more concrete image or script type responses, while the remaining 70-80% were the more abstract product attributes. As a brief example, a common script type elicitation for the toothpaste brand probes was the description of a scene or scenes from a familiar television commercial. Attitude theorists and applied marketing researchers should begin to consider such cognitive elements and attempts to determine their effects on attitude formation and choice behavior." (Olson and Muderrisoglu 1979, p. 273).

[58] "The test-retest correspondence of the elicitation rank orders were uniformly positive but not extremely strong (all tau's < .50)." (Olson and Muderrisoglu 1979, pp. 273-274).

[59] Although various methods for establishing attribute salience have been used (Manfredo 1989; Myers and Alpert 1977; Sampson and Harris 1970; Wilkie and Pessemier 1973), the basic technique advocated by Fishbein (1967) is an elicitation procedure.

[60] This definition is quite consistent with the unidimensionalist view of attitude which excludes beliefs, intentions, and other cognitive elements (Lutz 1991).

[61] Fazio's work also demonstrated that attitudes based on direct experience were more predictive of behavior than attitudes based on indirect experiences (Fazio and Zanna 1978).

[62] "Perception", here, refers to "the individual's current feelings about, or appraisal of, the object as experienced in the immediate situation." (Fazio, Powell, and Williams 1989, p. 280).

[63] In addition, a further condition of attitude salience, due to order effects, is the *salience of initial attitude* (see, e.g., Fazio 1981; Ross 1975; Ross and Shulman 1973). In this case, an attitude is salient because it was the first formed by the subject; it has, therefore, a salient feature in its primary position in time.

[64] In the Berger and Mitchell (1989) study, however, *attitude confidence* displayed a pattern of results which was different from that of *attitude accessibility*.

[65] Salience is not an objective quality of an attribute, but it varies according to the context, the stimulus, and the perceiver. It is difficult to agree, therefore, with Shavitt and Fazio (1991) when they report: "For some attitude objects, certain attributes should *naturally* be salient when one makes a general evaluation. In evaluating a candy bar, for example, taste-related attributes should *normally* be salient." (p. 508, emphasis added). In this case, for example, taste-related attributes can be a statistically important variable, but nothing guarantees that they are salient variables too, in the sense that they are prominent.

[66] McArthur (1981), in a widely quoted paper, used interchangeably the terms *attention-getting*, *salient*, and *figural* to denote those stimuli which are selectively attended (note 2, p. 201). However, to say that a stimulus is *not* (in-)salient - but it is, say, figural - is not only a question of definitions. It means that such a stimulus will *not* have the power to display those effects, for example, on memory - and, in general, on communication outcomes - which are peculiar of in-salient stimuli.

[67] As reported by Gibson (1966): "In an eventful environment with sights and sounds and smells and touches all around, the individual cannot register everything at once, and his perception must therefore be selective." (p. 309).

[68] Adults know that persons can move about at will, but that ordinary chairs cannot. On the contrary, young children must learn this difference. Golinkoff and Harding (1980, reported in Ostrom 1984, p. 25) offered data on infants (at 16 months) who showed no surprise when either persons or chairs moved in the absence of external forces. However, by the age of 24 months, infants began to show surprise when chairs moved about at will. Such developmental differences appear to occur in other areas as well. A review paper by Lane and Pearson (1982), on how persons develop differential attention in their life, was the topic of commentaries by Hagen and Wilson (1982), by Jeffrey (1982), and by Odom (1982). One theme in these commentaries was that the concept of stimulus differentiation, together with the concept of stimulus salience, could explain existing data on attention development. Such commentaries, indeed, were addressed in a subsequent paper by Lane and Pearson (1983), who concluded, more generically, that there was "as yet no framework capable of explaining all data on attention development." (p. 227).

[69] "We discussed getting attention as the *stopping power of* an advertisement; keeping attention is the *pulling power* of an ad - it keeps pulling the reader or viewer through to the end of the message. [...] Interest is a momentary thing; it dies easily as attention shifts. A major challenge in advertising is to maintain interest until the point of the message is reached. Because of the scanning and browsing behavior of many readers and viewers, maintaining interest is more difficult than arousing it." (Wells, Burnett, and Moriarty 1992, p. 245).

[70] "Note that interpretation involves both a *cognitive* or factual component and an *affective* or emotional response. *Cognitive interpretation* is a process whereby stimuli are placed into existing categories of meaning. This is an interactive process. The addition of new information to existing

categories also alters those categories and their relationships with other categories. [...] *Affective interpretation* is the emotional or feeling response triggered by a stimulus such as an ad. Like cognitive interpretation, there are "normal" (within-culture) emotional responses to an ad (e.g., most Americans experience a feeling of warmth when seeing pictures of young children with kittens). Likewise, there are also individual variations to this response (a person allergic to cats might have a very negative emotional response to such a picture)." (Hawkins, Best, and Coney, 1992, pp. 231-232).

[71] "Memory schemas can implicitly color the present learning environment by affecting how individual neurons code information (Merzenich and deCharms 1996). In marketing, these schemas have been found to affect how consumers interpret sensory product experiences." (Braun 1999, p. 319).

[72] "When applied to advertising, this implies that not only it is entirely possible to obtain different percepts from different people through the use of ambiguous communications elements (i.e., pictures, words, and symbols), but it is equally possible to obtain the same responses from all (or almost all) of an audience through a highly structured advertisement." (Woods 1981, p. 229). "A cardinal rule for the marketer is to keep the discrepancy between the perceived reality and the objective reality as small as possible or, ideally, non existent. There is no greater ideal for the marketer than to hope that the consumer will perceive a brand exactly as it is, assuming of course that the product's quality is very high." (Mahatoo 1985, p. 51).

[73] Considerable evidence supports the view asserting that specific world knowledge can be used to interpret perceptions by making inferences about what might have led to the sensory data (Bruce and Green 1990; Gregory 1973; Shepard 1990). Shepard (1990) goes so far as to argue that: "What we see is [...] a reflection of what our minds bring to the act of perceiving" (referred in MacEachren and Mistrick 1992, p. 92).

[74] Attention and interpretation are virtually interactive (see, also, Chapter Two, Note 8, *above*). As reported by Krech and Crutchfield (1948): "What is true about our experiences with objects and people is also true about our experiences with events and ideas. [...] Man is an organizing animal. [...] We cannot say to ourselves, 'Hold off any interpretation until you collect all the facts.' As soon as we experience *any* facts, they will be perceived as organized into some sort of meaningful whole. This is a universal characteristic of the cognitive process and not a weakness of the impatient or prejudiced individual." (p. 86).

[75] Holbrook and O'Shaughnessy (1984) developed a classification of the different types of motivational/affective constructs related to involvement. They divided these constructs (i.e., desire, drive, emotion, mood, attitude, want, sentiment, and personality) according to whether they are: (1) Active or reactive; (2) Specific or general; and (3) Acute or chronic (cf. Aylesworth and MacKenzie 1998).

[76] This distinction which has emerged has most important consequences on the persuasive potential of salience and vividness. While there is rich evidence of the persuasive impact of salience, the effect of vividness on attitudinal judgments is a controversial issue. Much of the experimental data indicates that the vividness effect is illusory, that is it often has no consequences on attitudinal judgments (Taylor and Thompson, 1982). However, other research suggests that vividness can enhance or undermine the favorableness of attitudinal judgments, leaving the question open to different interpretations (see Kisielius and Sternthal 1986, for a review of the vividness controversy).

[77] Moreover, such elaboration may either enhance or undermine advocacy-consistent judgments, depending on the favorableness of the information elaborated (see, e.g., McGill and Anand 1989).

[78] Exposure time is the interval that a subject is given to examine a stimulus. If the individual remains attentive to the stimulus throughout this period then exposure and processing time are essentially identical (Just and Carpenter 1976). If upon removal of the stimulus the individual continues to think about the incongruity then processing time will exceed exposure time. In either case, before in-salience can occur, subjects will either need a sufficient amount of exposure time to an incongruent stimulus or they must at least rehearse the incongruity over in their minds.

[79] "A change in a stimulus will attract attention. Such change may be accomplished (a) by moving up or down one of the sensory dimensions, (b) by stopping or starting stimulation, (c) by altering an object's attributes. The change may occur in either time or space or both." (Crane 1972, pp. 209-210). "The amount of *change* can be thought of as the difference between the emerging and the original situations. The importance of change depends on whether or not it is noticed, which in turn depends on the magnitude of the change and on whether the change is expected. [...] When a change is expected, it will have little or no effect, whereas unexpected changes will be very consequential. The effect of unexpected changes is considered in the variable *surprise* [...]. *Surprise* depends on the contiguity of situational aspects in the past. The more frequently an aspect has occurred together with a certain other aspect, the more the second aspect will be expected when the first is perceived; consequently, the more surprising the absence of the second aspect will be. On the other hand, the less frequently they have been encountered together, the more surprising it will be to meet them together." (Hansen 1972, p. 50).

[80] "Strictly speaking, the environment is never completely static, but the change must exceed the 'differential threshold' before it is observed: and generally, the more change the more likely it is to be observed." (Hansen 1972, p. 50). "In situations where there is a great deal of sensory input, the senses do not detect small intensities or differences in input. As sensory input *decreases,* however, our ability to detect changes in input or intensity *increases,* to the point that we attain maximum sensitivity under conditions of minimal stimulation. This ability of the human organism to accommodate itself to varying levels of sensitivity as external conditions vary not only provides more sensitivity when it is needed, but also serves to protect us from damaging, disruptive, or irrelevant bombardment when the input level is high." (Shiffman and Kanuk 1991, p. 147).

[81] Helson (1973, p. 170) has cited evidence of the influence of adaptation on response behavior, on perception (information), and on affectivity.

[82] "Helson studied the adaptation-level construct in various contexts - among them, light intensity, colors, and lifting tasks. He found empirically that a weighted average of the logarithm of the various stimuli - focal, contextual, and residual - provided a reliable predictor for the adaptation level. The inclusion of the logarithm suggests that a very intense stimulus may not dominate the adaptation level to the exclusion of the others. Helson indicated that adaptation levels can be found for such stimulus properties as beauty, prestige, significance, quality, and affective value." (Aaker, Batra, and Myers 1992, p. 330).

[83] "In research studies, the concept of salience is frequently confused with other concepts. Salience is often used inappropriately by researchers to refer to the importance of concepts rather than to their activation potential. Salient concepts may very well differ in their importance. While dimensionality refers to the number of dimensions used in evaluation and thus can be seen as a 'content-free' measure of structure, salient concepts are those particular concepts which are activated. Thus, measures of salient concepts require analysis of the content of activated memory rather than a mere count of their number. Clearly there is potential for confusion among the terms salience, salient concepts, dimensionality, and importance." (Marks 1985, pp. 52-53).

[84] As noticed by Ortony et al. (1985, p. 5): "[R]elevance is a characteristic of attributes with respect to task and object domains rather than with respect to objects themselves, while salience is a characteristic of attributes with respect to objects themselves."

[85] We have already seen how salience, in these models, has been mainly referred to the accessibility of concepts, such as beliefs (see, *above*, Paragraph 2.1.10). Considering that sometimes it has been argued that some beliefs are more *important* than others in determining a person's attitude, Fishbein and Ajzen (1975) have raised the question "whether it is possible to use *subjective estimates of importance* to identify *salient beliefs*" (Fishbein and Ajzen 1975, p. 221, emphasis added). To answer this question, they said it is necessary to distinguish between several possible interpretations of "belief importance". They initially ruled out the possibility of measuring salience by using the concept of "value importance" as developed by Rosemberg (1956), which refers to *the amount of satisfaction or dissatisfaction derived from an attribute that is associated with a given object* (see Fishbein and Ajzen 1975, Ch.2), because this definition equates importance to the evaluation of the associated attribute - and there is considerable evidence that this evaluation is not related to belief salience (e.g., Fishbein 1963; Kaplan and Fishbein 1969; Zajonc 1954). Then, they considered how the term "importance" has been most frequently referred; in particular, three main definitions: (1) The perceived importance of an attribute for the person (which is highly related to the polarity of the attribute's evaluation); (2) The perceived importance as a defining characteristic of an object (which is closely related to the subjective probability of an association between object and attribute); or (3) The perceived importance as a determinant of a person's attitude (which, in contrast to the other interpretations, has been found to be unrelated to the position of the beliefs in question in the belief hierarchy; see, Kaplan and Fishbein 1969). Yet, it appeared that (Fishbein and Ajzen 1975, p. 221): "None of the different interpretations of belief importance can be used to derive measures that will identify salient and nonsalient beliefs", Salience, therefore, cannot be assessed with measures of importance.

[86] This definition was chosen over another (see, Alpert 1971; Myers and Alpert 1968, 1977), considered less general (as it applied only to a particular set of brands - not all brands - in a product class), which defined importance as "the importance of an attribute in determining a person's attitudes towards a set of brands" (MacKenzie 1986, note 1). We argue that, in its formulation, this definition should be discarded as a truism, since it defines "importance" with the same concept it is trying to explain.

[87] Clearly, the definition of MacKenzie (1986) relates importance to the evaluative aspect component of expectancy-value models of attitude, such as Fishbein and Ajzen's (1975, see *above*). In the attitude models, the *evaluative aspect* of the attribute is constituted by the $|e_i|$ component (see, *above*, Note 51). According to Fishbein and Ajzen (1975, p. 228), "attributes that are important are typically evaluated more positively or negatively (i.e., they are more polarized) than attributes that are unimportant." In other words, importance "will tend to be related to *polarity* of evaluation" (p. 228). As maintained by MacKenzie (1986, p. 175): "[... A] ttributes judged to be either extremely good or extremely bad would also be extremely important, and attributes judged to be only slightly good or slightly bad would only be slightly important." This effect has also been demonstrated in social psychology for salience (as *prominence*), by recognizing that evaluations of salient people are more extreme than evaluations of less salient people: "Taylor et al. (1977) ran a series of experiments in which they varied the 'solo' status of black group members; some groups had an even mixture of white and black members, other groups had only one black member. The 'solo' black was clearly more salient than were the blacks in the evenly divided groups. A pleasant black group member was evaluated more favorably when 'solo' than when in an evenly divided group, and an unpleasant one was evaluated more negatively." (Sears, Peplau, and Taylor 1991, p. 45). The influence of momentary salience (e.g., the sex composition of a group) on judgments and attitudinal responses had also been addressed to in other studies (e.g., Shomer and Centers 1970).

[88] Attribute importance can dramatically affect the outcome of a choice in a selection/evaluation process based on non-compensatory strategies (i.e., lexicographic or elimination-by-aspects), because it determines the order in which the attributes are considered. This effect has been also found for attribute salience (Sutherland and Galloway 1981, see *below*). By affecting the weight that a stimulus possesses in the mind of consumers, salience can change the position that a stimulus has in consumers' priorities.

[89] It has been hypothesized (MacKenzie 1986, Figure A) that the importance of an attribute mentioned in an advertisement is, indeed, the result of the characteristics of the ad (the stimulus cues), the characteristics of the message recipient (his schemata), and the factors influencing the message recipient's opportunity to cognitively elaborate on the ad (the context).

[90] Although, in general, neither the social-psychological nor the consumer literature have distinguished between active and passive processing, the cognitive literature has provided a detailed analysis of this distinction. Posner and Warren (Posner 1978; Posner and Warren 1972; Warren 1972) have discriminated between: (1) *Set* that is an active, conscious process in which conscious attention is controlled and deliberately directed toward an expected event (Posner 1978); and (2) *Priming* that is a passive, unconscious process which involves automatic and uncontrolled activation of schemata (Higgins, Rholes, and Jones 1977; Warren 1972). Tulving and Schacter (1990) called *priming* an exposure-induced change in subjects' performance *unaccompained* by awareness. This separation between active and passive processes is important because - given the specific limitations of active processes - it has diverse consequences on the perception of incongruent stimuli (Guido 1996a). According to Posner (1978), since conscious attention is limited in its capacity, this critical feature reduces the efficiency with which different types of stimulus can be processed. Consequently, (a) When conscious attention is directed to a schema, subjects' processing of stimulus information matching the schema is facilitated *but* their processing of stimulus information not matching the schema is inhibited or impaired (i.e., benefits with costs). In contrast, (b) When a schema is primed or activated without conscious attention being directed to the activated schema, subjects' processing of stimulus information matching the schema will be facilitated *without* inhibiting their processing of stimulus information that does not match the schema (i.e., benefits without costs). Posner (1978, p. 91) proposed three criteria a process must meet to say it is *automatic* (that is, occurring despite an intention to prevent it); it may take place: (1) Without intention; (2) Without giving rise to conscious awareness; and (3) Without producing interference with other ongoing mental activity.

[91] An alternative explanatory construct for priming is the *Last-in-first-out memory bins model* by Wyer and Srull (1980).

[92] "Only one concept can be actively processed at a time, which is a limitation imposed by the serial nature of the human central process [...]. This means that activation can only start out at one node at a time. But it continues in parallel from other nodes that are encountered as it spreads out from the node of origin." (Collins and Loftus 1975, p. 411).

[93] A more elaborate account for priming, which is an extension of the spreading activation model, has been proposed by Posner and Snyder (1975), who argued that the effects of context on comprehension require a second stage of elaboration (see Hastie, Park, and Weber 1984, for a review).

[94] *Appropriateness* is defined here as any consumers' schema that the author of the marketing communication feels is adequate for addressees to interpret the stimulus message.

[95] According to Menon and Wanke (1998): "Relatively new, however, is the idea that consumers may use this accessibility or experienced ease of retrieval as a diagnostic input in their decision-making, independent of the actual content of the information retrieved [... See,

also, *above*, Chapter Two, Paragraph 4.5]. What this literature suggests is that the information accessibility is itself diagnostic for judgments independent of the actual content of the information." (p. 264) Therefore, they promoted a discussion on the theoretical underpinnings of the mechanism behind accessibility, the conditions under which the relative diagnosticity of information accessibility and content may vary, and different domains and tasks for obtaining these effects.

[96] Yet, it was not the purpose of social psychologists to treat accessibility as a synonym of salience; Higgins and King (1981), who extended Bruner's work on accessibility determinants, specifically indicated *salience* as a factor enhancing the accessibility of a schema in memory, together with the *recency of activation*, the *frequency of activation*, and the *relationships to other accessible constructs*. It is interesting to notice that these authors studied the notion of accessibility in reference to the "schemata" used to identify a stimulus, rather than directly in reference to stimuli. (For the sake of precision, Higgins and King (1981, p. 71) used the concept of "constructs" - i.e., "coherent information about some entity typically derived from specific instances or occurrences" - rather than the more general concept of "schemata".) Higgins and King (1981) also maintained that salience which affects accessibility is, in turn, dependent on both the *prominence* and the *distinctiveness* of the schema. They hypothesized that "[t]he prominence of [... a schema] is determined by the qualities of its attributes" (Higgins and King 1981, p. 80) and, therefore, if the attributes of the stored schema are striking (because of their greater intensity, complexity, vividness, etc.), then that schema is more attention grabbing and, in turn, more accessible. This proposition, however, does not seem sufficiently supported due to the lack of available data. By admission of the same authors: "There has been very little experimental research concerned with the accessibility of stored constructs deriving from the prominence of their inherent attributes or instance." (Higgins and King 1981, p. 80). Drawing on their research, Schneider and Blankmeyer (1983), in a study on prototype salience, operationalized salience through a set of direct instructions (similarly to Kirmani and Wright 1989). Basing themselves on the classic model of Cantor and Mischel (1977) on personality prototypes (which were defined as normative conceptual schemata), Schneider and Blankmeyer (1983) argued that perceived trait and behavior relationships among prototypes relevant stimuli should have been strengthened when the relevant prototype (e.g., extroversion, introversion) was salient: "Quite clearly," they stated, "when a particular cognitive structure is salient, people tend to see the world through glasses tinted by that structure" (Schneider and Blankmeyer 1983, p. 721).

[97] Kelly's (1955) seminal work on the psychology of personal constructs (i.e., schemata) postulated that individuals develop over a lifetime a set of schemata that are applied in a relatively invariant manner to anticipate, structure, and understand environmental information. These *permanent* or *chronic* schemata, that help individuals to select information for elaborative processing, may be influenced by relatively temporary expectancies generated (or experimentally induced) by the task context (cf. Asch's original work on impression formation, 1946; and, more recently, Hastie and Kumar 1979; Srull 1981). For example, researchers operationalized chronic construct accessibility on the basis of frequency and primacy in traits and demonstrated that information relevant to a trait was capable of provoking automatic attentional responses (Bargh 1982; Higgins, King, and Mavin 1982). In addition, because of the individual's "structural" readiness to perceive some of the stimuli and not others, chronical accessible schemata enable people to pick up and process construct-relevant information even when processing resources are limited, such as under time pressure or overload conditions - e.g., faster paces of presentation in TV commercials (Bargh and Thein 1985; Ratneshwar, Mick, and Reitinger (1990). Ratneshwar, Mick, and Reitinger (1990) have argued that *chronically accessible* attributes are likely to have some inherent similarities to "salient" and "important" attributes. They stressed, however, from a methodological point of view, a considerable diversity and a lack of convergent validity in

assessing attribute chronicity by measures of attribute importance, like those, for example, suggested by Jaccard, Brinberg, and Ackerman (1986). Their preliminary conjecture was that, in an attitude judgment context, attribute chronicity is more closely related to the notion of "salience" rather than that of "importance." They refrained, however, from suggesting their own definition of salience, making a reference only to a review on social perception by Higgins and Bargh (1987), in which salience was treated as the inconsistency of a piece of information within its current context (Taylor and Fiske 1978).

[98] Nedungadi (1990), in a study on memory-based choices, explicitly equated brand accessibility to salience. He divided the choice process into two stages: (1) Brand consideration (when retrieval and formation of the consideration stage occurs); and (2) Brand evaluation (when consumers deliberate about the brands included). In the first of these two stages, he distinguished between *brand availability* (that he also called "brand awareness") and *brand accessibility*, and maintained that, although brand choice is memory based, whereas availability is a necessary precondition, "it is *brand accessibility or salience* on that particular occasion that will determine the composition of the consideration set" (Nedungadi 1990, p. 264, emphasis added). Basing his approach on the spreading-activation analogy (Anderson 1983; Collins and Loftus 1975), he then argued that salience depends on three factors: (1) The strength of activation of the brand node in working memory (which is a function of the frequency, recency, and salience of brand instantiation and of brand evaluation); (2) The strength or association between the brand node and other active nodes (which is a function of semantic similarity and the typicality or the position of the brand within the category structure); (3) The availability of retrieval cues (such as three types of information: category, brand, and attribute). Nedungadi's concept of *salience*, therefore, is the same concept as *accessibility*, but it depends on *activation*. For example, a brand can be activated (e.g., primed) by direct reference to some cues in the consumer environment, such as the brand name or, also, storefront signs, product lists, package labels, and marketer-controlled influences (displays, point-of-sale material, coupons, etc.). A brand prime will increase the strength of activation of the brand node - which will spread to other related brands in the network (cf. McKoon and Ratcliff 1986) - and, in turn, it will increase the salience of the brand.

[99] Building on research examining salience as "prominence" (Taylor and Fiske 1978) and individuals' use of schema-consistent and schema-inconsistent data in self-perception (Bem 1972; Markus 1977), Tybout and Yalch (1980) suggested that, when a person's own behavior is salient, it serves as a basis for making self-inferences which guide future behavior. Salience, here, was referred as the *accessibility* of a behavioral cue ("i.e. cues easily brought to mind", Tybout and Yalch 1980, p. 407). To test this hypothesis, salience was operationalized through a labeling procedure in a voting context. Tybout and Yalch theorized that the salience of the labeling cue would be a function of two factors: (a) The cue's *consistency* with an individual's existing self-schema and (b) The *availability* of other schema-relevant cues (i.e., "cognitive generalizations about the self, derived from past experience, that organize and guide the processing of self-related information contained in the individual's social experience" (Markus 1977, p. 64). They suggested that relevant cues are salient only to the extent that they are highly available or easily retrievable as a function of recent processing, and concluded that it was the simultaneous presence of these two factors (consistency and availability) which determines the salience of a behavior and its possibility to serve as a basis for determining self-perceptions and future actions. Drawing on their work, Reingen and Bearden (1983) investigated the impact of salience upon the efficacy of labeling in influencing behaviors. The idea behind the labeling hypothesis is that providing people with labels helps them to develop a self-perception about the type of persons they are. Subsequently, people use these labels as guidelines for their behaviors. Results partially supported their predictions. Mowen (1983), commenting on Reingen and Bearden's (1983) operationalization of salience, correctly posed the following question: "['Was that] a manipulation of salience or a manipulation of something else?'" (p. 56), considering that salience is a hypothetical

construct which is difficult to measure directly. In accordance with Mowen (1983), we believe that the manipulation which occurred in both Tybout and Yalch's (1980) and Reingen and Bearden's (1983) studies was not one of salience but one of an *attributional state* (see Folkes 1988), in which people made either an external or internal attribution for their behavior. Therefore, the perception of the locus of causality could have either reinforced or cancelled the labeling manipulation. Results, therefore, could be explained without recurring to the use of a salience construct (such as, creation of a positive mood, activation of schemata, conformation to other people's judgments, and so on).

[100] Salience explained as *availability* - which in the context of heuristics has been defined as the ease with which specific instances can be brought to mind as a primary basis of judgment - is often the result of a confusion between the origin of salience and its effect on facilitating memory retrieval. The salience of a stimulus and its availability are clearly related. Yet, it is not clear if it is the salience that makes a stimulus available, or *vice versa*. On one hand, it has been argued that things that have been recently primed become salient and are used in judgments involving ambiguous events. Sherman and Corty (1984, p. 211) noticed: "The influence of priming on availability has been interpreted in two ways. According to Wyer and Srull's (1980) 'storage bin' model, frequent or recent activation of a category leads to its being stored on top of the memory bin after its use. It is thus the first thing picked from the bin at subsequent memory search. Higgins and King (1981) proposed an 'energy cell' model in which frequent or recent priming increases the energy of the cells associated with the activated category. Highly energized cells are more available for use in processing information." In framing studies, a person deciding on a strategy for dealing with a given situation inevitably focuses on certain features of the situation and not others. These alternative ways of *interpreting* situations are called "frames", and their effects on decision-making are called "framing effects" (see, e.g., Van Schie and Van der Pligt 1995). Often there are rational grounds for identifying the relevant features. Sometimes, however, people have to choose when they simply do not have the information or expertise to know what features should be considered. According to Tversky and Kahneman's (1973, 1974) *availability heuristic*, people judge the frequency of events by the ease with which they can construct relevant instances of the event in question. Therefore, the relationship between salience and this tendency to generalize may be mediated by the construct of availability in memory. According to Hoch (1984, p. 660), "[a]vailability often has been equated with cue salience (Taylor and Fiske 1978). A common procedure has involved priming subjects to retrieve specific repertoires of thoughts (e.g., the friendly person stereotype) and then seeing what effects this has on memory and judgments (Higgins, Rholes, and Jones 1977; Srull and Wyer 1980)." Taylor and Fiske (1978) suggested that information connected with salient (read, *prominent*) stimuli may be more easily acquired and retained, because such information is encoded in more than one manner (e.g., both semantically and iconically) and stored in a more accessible form. Also, vivid information has been shown to be more likely to trigger inferential processes than abstract and remote information (Nisbett and Borgida 1975). All of which suggests that such kind of information is more available for use. According to Zuckerman, Mann, and Bernieri (1982): "There is both direct and indirect support for the link between salience and availability (Taylor and Fiske 1978). For example, a quantitative summary of 10 studies showed that salient information was better recalled than less salient information. In addition, salient stimuli were perceived as more causally prominent and more evaluatively extreme than less salient ones." (p. 844). On the other hand, it has been argued that, when dealing with internal salient stimuli (that is, with memory inputs), rather than with external salient stimuli (that is, with stimuli from the outside environment), salience can be the result of a chronic accessibility of some available construct, triggered by the perceptual readiness of the perceiver. Propositions Two and Three of our model could help overcome this indeterminacy.

[101] As Alba, Hutchinson, and Lynch (1991) have noticed: "The especially distressing aspect of all this is that salience effects are most likely to influence product novices and other vulnerable segments of the population [...]. Experts are less likely to conform to an advertiser's framing of a

problem and can remember nonsalient information more completely [...]. Novices, on the other hand, find it more difficult to challenge an advertiser's claims and will preferentially recall salient attributes, especially after delay. Thus, salient manipulations influence those consumers who are least capable of making optimal decisions." (p. 21).

[102] In consumer literature, not only has the differentiation between accessibility and availability not always been maintained, but also, in a series of studies, salience has been defined as *availability*. Two papers, in particular, have spread this definition of salience as availability, namely Wright and Rip (1980) and Bettman and Sujan (1987), both on the effects of problem framing, which has been referred "to cognitive activities, conscious or automated, that structure a decision problem" (Kirmani and Wright 1989, p. 173), requiring the consumer to deal also with "the product attributes (if any) to be considered." (*Ibid.*). These studies showed that unobtrusively primed information affects the recall and usage of particular attributes during product choice. By surreptitiously priming a common dimension, consumers were guided into making decisions in terms of that dimension. They maintained that framing, which "relates to the attributes that consumers focus on and consider *important*" (Bettman and Sujan 1987, p. 142, emphasis added), often "refers to making certain criteria more *salient or available*. Thus, the effects of framing should be apparent by an increased focus on those attributes relevant to the most available decision criteria in evaluation process, higher importance scores for these attributes, and/or an increased preference for alternative possessing such attributes." (*Ibid.*, emphasis added). In a seminal work on this phenomenon, Wright and Rip (1980) demonstrated that repeated reference to certain product dimensions increases their influence in subsequent consumers' judgments, presumably inducing consumers to think only in terms of those dimensions. Salience *inhibition effect* (cf., e.g., Alba and Chattopadhyay 1986 - see also, *above*) extends this consequence one step further by *preventing* recall and, therefore, consideration of alternative dimensions. Other studies have shown that it is possible to influence more subtly the way consumers consider alternatives by increasing the salience of some facts without explicitly suggesting that they are very important (see, e.g., Reyes, Thompson, and Bower 1979, which considers memory as a moderator).

[103] According to Beattie (1983): "The salience of verbal information in advertising (copy) can also be manipulated through vividness. [...] Since visual components of an advertisement tend to be more perceptually salient than verbal components [Paivio 1971], it is obviously in the advertiser's best interest to capture immediate attention through vivid pictures. In designing advertising copy, though, salience can be achieved, and consumer attention maintained, by directing copy to fit consumers' prior knowledge, so that copy referring to product experience is more vivid for product novices. Copy referring to product attributes is particularly informative, and therefore vivid, to product experts." (p. 582).

[104] "Meyer (1981) was among the first to model how consumer expectations of uncertain or unknown product attributes are formed. The expectations of the attributes are weighted functions of the subjective mean, its variance, and their interaction. The subjective mean of an unknown attribute is a function of a weighted average of similar attributes of other products in the same category. Thus, similar to Tolman (1932), the expectation of a product's attribute level is formed as a combination of the attribute levels derived from similar products (in the same product class). In the same way, the expectation of the variance of a product's attribute level is formed as a combination of the variance of the attribute levels derived from similar products. In Meyer's (1981) approach, missing product information is inferred from the information available from other similar (competitive) products. This is an "other product" approach. Another strategy is to infer missing information from the other attributes of the same (partially described) product. Highly correlated attributes may influence inferences as well. This is the "same product" approach. Ford and Smith (1987) found a greater effect of the "same product" approach than of the "other product" approach. [...] It is expected that the degree of attribute intercorrelation

determines which strategy a consumer will select. With highly correlated attributes, the "same product" approach is more likely. With low correlations, the "other product" approach is more likely. Contextual information may also play a role for consumers in inferring the value of unknown information." (van Raaij 1991, pp. 407-408).

[105] We prefer to use the word "drives," instead of "needs," in that *need* is used to describe states of deprivation and does not necessarily imply a motivational state that is explicitly present in the term *drive*. The standard view here is to treat need states as producing drives states that motivate behavior (Reber 1985, p. 217). To appreciate the problem, one must realize that there are needs for which there are no drives, such as the need for oxygen, for the distress felt when holding the breath is not a drive for oxygen but a drive to reduce carbon dioxide levels.

[106] A less-developed, difficult field of research regards *nonfocused attention*, where stimuli are attended to without deliberate or conscious focusing of attention. Findings are still contradictory in such areas as subliminal stimulation (Beatty and Hawkins 1989) or preconscious awareness (Janiszewski 1988).

[107] Another important distinction is that between *focused attention*, in which certain stimuli are selected from others, and *divided attention*, in which concurrent stimuli must be attended to at the same time. In the case of salience, it is evident that the kind of attention a stimulus is able to capture is the focused attention, in which all the receiver's mental and cognitive resources are directed towards one stimulus.

[108] "Thus, someone who is interested in buying a car, some furniture, or an expensive camera will actively seek information about the product. When reading newspapers, he or she will be on the lookout to find advertisements and articles that deal with the product sought. Conversely, if the marketing communication is not perceived as matching a goal, the consumer will tend not to focus attention on it. [... T]his is a major problem for advertisers on television and radio. Consumers may be exposed to the message but simply decide not to attend to the information contained in the communication." (Mowen 1993, p. 86).

[109] "With both voluntary and involuntary attention, cognitive capacity is allocated to the stimulus. When the individual attends to the information, he or she will reveal physiological arousal. The arousal may result in an increase in blood pressure, a change in brain wave patterns, a quickening of breathing, a slight sweating of the hands, and dilation of the pupils, among other things." (Mowen 1993, p. 86). Arousal, and its optimal level, has been the central theme of the clinical study of salience (cf., e.g., Berlyne 1960; Bettman 1979; Hansen 1972; Mandler 1982; McArthur 1981).

[110] It is interesting to consider a variant of this example: When a consumer is not looking for anything in particular and, by his continuous monitoring of the environment (spontaneous attention), he finds a slice of ham and decides to eat it, was that stimulus *re-salient* or *in-salient*? According to our definition of involvement, which includes both goals and drives, it was re-salient. As a matter of fact, while goals can be situational, some drives are constantly present (they are like chronically accessible schemata). Eating is a drive always present, but other more trivial ones can be found. For example, monitoring and seeing a packet of detergent reminds someone that he must wash his clothes. Therefore, some stimuli adapt to such schemata.

[111] We should have called this form of salience *involvement-salience*, similarly to the *incongruity-salience* of the in-salience hypothesis. This would have resulted in no advantage in the abridged form of the terms (since both would have been named *in-salience*). We preferred, therefore, the name *relevance-salience* (or *re-salience*) to specify the personal degree of involvement of this type of construct.

[112] *"Motivation* is the reason for behavior. A *motive* is a construct representing an unobservable inner force that stimulates and compels a behavioral response and provides specific direction to that response." (Hawkins, Best, and Coney 1992, p. 295).

[113] Sternthal and Craig (1982, p. 93) named this congruence the *pertinence* of information that affects the extent to which a stimulus is attended.

[114] Although it has not been clearly conceptualized, personal relevance has been shown to be associated with increased tendencies toward persuasion, and related to high recall of messages, message-relevant thinking, and stronger attitude-behavior consistency. On attribute-specific ads, the effects of personal relevance would be a greater probability of increasing the attention paid to ads, solidifying or creating positive attitudes toward intentions to purchase, and inducing or reinforcing purchase intention and behavior (see, also, Sperber and Wilson 1994).

[115] This approach on involvement in information processing - which emphasizes a person's subjective experience or feeling of personal relevance - is similar to the one proposed by Richins and Bloch (1986) and, especially, by Celsi and Olson (1988), who referred to this motivational state as *felt involvement.*

[116] Given the moderating role of involvement, the influence of motivation on schema accessibility can also result in relatively passive information processing (see, *below*, next paragraph). Moreover, such passive or unconscious processing, as reported by Higgins and King (1981), was a major focus of the so-called "new look" in perception (Allport 1955).

[117] *"Relevant* stimuli are chosen; that is, certain magazines are chosen from a magazine rack and certain food advertisements are read in a newspaper. *Irrelevant* stimuli are those not sought out, as illustrated by newspaper advertisements a reader does not intend to find or read." (Britt 1978, p. 92).

[118] This is opposite, of course, to what is hypothesized by the in-salience hypothesis, where relevance is a sufficient condition.

[119] Using an opposite terminology, Mahatoo (1985, p. 58) called this construct "relevance" rather than "importance".

[120] In other words, importance is needed for re-salience, relevance is enough for in-salience. To be salient, of course, means having peculiar effects on consumer awareness, attention and memory.

[121] MacKenzie (1986) has noticed: "Researchers have traditionally treated the weights attached to product attributes primarily as pre-determined, exogenous factors in their research This practice appears to be based on a belief commonly held by researchers (e.g., Lutz 1979, p. 329) and at least tacitly held by advertisers (see Wright and Barbour 1975) that advertising and other marketing efforts cannot easily influence the weights attached to product attributes because those weights are based on stable, deep-seated cultural norms and values. The existing empirical evidence, however, suggests that attribute [...] weights are not as stable as one would expect were values and cultural norms their sole determinants. For example, persuasive messages (Gardner 1983), situational factors (Miller and Ginter 1979), contextual factors like the number of levels or values an attribute takes on (Currim, Weinberg, and Wittink 1981), and the order of presentation of attribute information (Anderson and Hubert 1963) have all been observed to influence attribute [...] weights on occasion." (p. 174, omissions were made to overcome the lack of distinction between relevance and importance in the text). Apart from relevance, other contextual variables that have been found to influence memory effects are meaningfulness, familiarity, and similarity (Mahatoo 1985, p. 85).

122 Marketing research has assumed that advertising effectiveness can be enhanced by *attribute-focused advertising*, i.e. ads which emphasize the specific product attributes desired by a consumer group, although only recently have studies emerged to provide partial evidence that such attribute-specific advertising increases audience attention (Haley 1983). For example, in tourist marketing, past research has demonstrated that the tourist-attracting attributes, which were successful in promotional programs, were different according to the perceived image of the promoted place and to target consumer segments. They recommended that advertisements should focus on attributes that strengthen the positively held image of each area (Manfredo 1989).

123 There could be, indeed, gender differences. Meyers-Levy (1988b), for example, examined the effects of the level and salience of cue incongruity on males and females choice of processing strategies. She found that, unless motivated by unequivocal evidence of incongruity, males favored the use of conceptually-driven (CD) over data-driven processing (DD). Females, however, reliably employed data-driven processing even when cue incongruity was less easily detected. "Cue incongruity is often used in advertisements directed at consumers. [...] Given the frequent use of incongruity in ads, it is not surprising that consumer researchers have examined the effect of cue incongruity on processing. Similar conclusions obtain as those implied by the social cognition studies. For example, Sujan (1985) found that when product information was entirely consistent with subjects' pre-conceptions, processing appeared to be CD in that it centered on the rehearsal of subjects' prior product knowledge. But when the message contained incongruent information, individuals' processing appeared to be more DD: Relative to subjects in the former condition, those exposed to incongruity engaged in greater cognition and produced both more attribute specific thoughts. These effects, however, emerged only among subjects who were experts concerning the product category. Apparently because novices' limited knowledge of the category impaired their detection of the incongruity, novices were not motivated to employ DDP. The preceding analysis suggests that message inclusion of incongruent information may not always stimulate DDP. People may fail to detect cue incongruity for a variety of reasons and therefore may not engage in DDP." (Meyers-Levy 1988a, p. 169).

124 Under the in-salience hypothesis, it seems improper to speak of *variety seeking*, since we can seek only what is in our schemata, what is congruent with them. Rather, *variety seeks us*: what is incongruent with our schemata is, indeed, in-salient.

125 From a study by McGuire (1968) this reconciliation of theories seems quite reasonable and a non-monotonic relationship is suggested between psychological motives and cognitive variety. He concluded that he "would readily agree with Maddi [1968] that the organism probably likes a little bit, but not too much novelty and surprise, with this optimal point shifting predictably with personal and situational characteristics." (p. 259).

126 Forgas (1998), for example, recently presented a dual-process model of attributions, similar to previous psychological models (Chaiken, Liberman, and Eagly 1989; Gilbert and Malone 1995; Petty and Cacioppo 1986). Specifically, Forgas (1998) hypothesized that people in a happy mood would be more likely to make the fundamental attribution error (i.e., overstimating the influence of dispositional factors and understimating the power of situational forces on other people's behavior) than people in a sad mood, because of differences in level of mood-induced cognitive processing styles. "This is somewhat analogous to Petty and Cacioppo's (1986) dual-process model of attitude change. People who focus on the most salient, easily accessible features of the person and his or her behavior tend to make dispositional attributions for other people's behavior, and are like those who take the effortless, peripheral route to attitude change. In fact, research has shown that people in positive moods tend to pay less systematic attention to stimulus information and adopt a more flexible, heuristic-dependent processing style (Bodenhausen 1993). On the other hand, people who actively seek to process all the stimulus details they can observe, usually make the effort to consider the context in which the behavior occurred, and are similar to those who take the central route to attitude change. This idea has also been supported by research

which shows that people in negative moods are more motivated to pay careful and systematic attention to stimulus details (Schwarz and Bless 1991)." (Park 2000).

[127] According to the *Reversal theory*, there are three mechanisms leading an individual to *reverse* his metamotivational state: (1) Contingent events, internal (e.g., memories) or external (e.g., events); (2) Frustration, that comes when an individual is unable to obtain the right satisfaction in the state in which he is; and (3) Satiation when, after spending a certain length of time in one state, an individual change his state, even in the absence of contingent events or frustration.

[128] In the *Dichotic theory of salience*, awareness is the effect of the information processing triggered off by *in-salient* as well as *re-salient* stimuli (Guido 1998). This position is implicit altogether in many marketing and consumer behavior texts (see, e.g., Table 1, *above*). One for all, for example, in advertising, is the one given by Wells, Burnett, and Moriarty (1992, p. 245), who maintain that: "Interest [here read "salience"] is usually created by one of the two things - personal involvement [i.e, re-salience] or something intriguing [i.e., in-salience]. [...] Advertisers who are trying to develop a message that stimulates interest will speak to the personal interests of their target audience as well as do something to elicit curiosity."

[129] "The distinction between conscious and unconscious cognitive processes is not absolute. That is, there may be several degrees between the two extremes of 'complete awareness' and 'absolutely no awareness.' Adams (1957), after reviewing a number of studies dealing with different aspects of the unconscious control of behavior, concludes that at least four different conditions can exist: (1) Subjects may know the specific nature of the cue being introduced, (2) subjects may know the general nature of the cues, (3) subjects may believe that cues are being given but not know anything about the nature of the cues, and finally (4) subjects may not believe that any cue is being given. Cognitive elements may be unconscious for one or more of the following reasons: 1. Behavior can occur completely without cerebral or cognitive activity. 2. Cognitive processes can operate at a low level of arousal so that awareness does not occur. 3. Suppression of cognitive elements can occur. 4. Cognitive processes can involve concepts to which no verbal counterparts correspond." (Hansen 1972, p. 118). See Krishnan and Trappey (1999) for a historical overview of nonconsciousness in marketing research.

[130] We should make a distinction here, again, between *unrelevant* and *unimportant* stimuli. If re-salient stimuli are always important to a perceiver's goals, in-salient stimuli could be relevant and, at the same time, *un*important for the achievement of the optimal consumer choice (see, *above*, Paragraph 2.4.4: *Attribute relevance vs. attribute importance*).

[131] "The fact that a concept is salient in a choice-process does not imply that the individual is also aware of it. A number of factors may cause salient concepts to remain more or less unconscious." (Hansen 1972, p. 92). Here a brief florilegium about the discussed topic of conditioning without awareness. (A) "When pure-form behaviorists and cognitivists compare approaches, one of the debates they cannot resolve is the role of awareness in conditioning. Their debate is unresolvable because it is grounded in fundamental differences at the level of metaphysical commitments [...]. In behaviorism, mental events are considered nonscientific and are not the focal point of research; hence, for the behaviorist, the awareness issue is simply not of interest. The steadfast cognitivist, in contrast, perceives the awareness issue as pivotal. For example, Brewer (1974, p. 3) views "the hypothesis that events in conditioning come about in an automatic, unconscious fashion" as the central tenet in conditioning theory. He then dismisses six decades of conditioning research by arguing that whenever effects are observed, they will be accompanied by conscious awareness on the part of subjects about what was expected of them. Between these incommensurable positions is a body of work in which awareness is used as a progressive construct for enhancing understanding." (Allen and Janzewski 1989, p. 32). (B) "We can distinguish two basic types of awareness. The first can

be called *self-awareness*. One form of self-awareness is the knowledge of how one's behavior is influenced by the environment; in a Pavlovian conditioning paradigm, this means that the subject is aware that he or she has acquired and is performing a conditional response because of an acknowledged relationship between a conditional and unconditional stimulus. This type of self-awareness is related to, but distinct from, a second basic type of awareness: *External awareness*. One form of external awareness in Pavlovian conditioning experiments, implicit in the example given above, is an awareness of the relationship between the conditional and the unconditional stimuli, two elements in the environment. This form of awareness is called *contingency awareness* (Page 1973), something quite distinct from self-awareness where the causal link between the conditional-unconditional stimulus association and the conditional response is known. An awareness of the relationship between the conditional and the unconditional stimuli may lead to another form of external awareness: awareness of the experimental hypothesis. This is called *demand awareness* (Page 1973). [...] Focusing on demand awareness, Kahle, Beatty and Kennedy (1987), Brewer (1974), and Page (1973) have argued that Pavlovian conditioning procedures do not produce any real conditioning of adult human behavior: Behavioral change is merely a by-product of demand awareness. The argument is that behavioral changes seen in subjects following conditioning result from the subjects developing contingency awareness, then ascertaining what kind of behavioral change the experimenter wants to see, and then acting cooperatively." (Gorn, Jacobs, and Mana 1986, p. 415). Although there is some different view on the issue (Gorn, Jacobs, and Mana 1986), "[t]he question of whether awareness is necessary for conditioning is too vague to be answered experimentally at the present time", as McSweeney and Bierley (1984, p. 628) have concluded, reviewing developments in classical conditioning. (C) "The classical (and still widely popular) view of sensory events is that stimuli impinge on certain receptors and cause sensations. These sensations are 'processed' in the brain and produce 'perceptions.' Strangely enough, few questions are raised as to whether the affective quality or 'feeling' that occurs along with this stimulation is any different from the 'information' in the stimulus. For example, it is assumed that the sensation of being burned is of the same order as being informed that one has picked up a hot object. Gibson (1966), in calling attention to this assumption and to the duality of sensation, has revolutionized our thinking on this topic. The distinction between the information component and the affective or feeling component of sensory input gives rise to the question of what it is that we are aware of and what it is we experience - information or affect? [...] It has been found that awareness is not necessary in order to be informed or use information. Bindra (1976, pp. 109-110) notes the following: 'A stimulus may not generate a specific clear percept - an awareness or experiencing of it - and yet may influence behavior.[...]' [Mittal (1988), e.g., defines habit in terms of non-awareness.] He further comments as follows: 'It is also possible at least for responses that have become habitual that the production of a response can be achieved without any percept or image.' Gibson (1966 p. 2) writes the following: '[...] it is surely a fact that detecting something can sometimes occur without the accompaniment of sense impressions. An example is the visual detection of one thing behind another [...] there will be many examples of the principle that stimulus information can determine perception without having to enter consciousness in the form of sensation.' From Bindra and Gibson support the position that, at least as far as an information component is concerned, there need not necessarily be awareness. However, what about the affective feeling component? To 'feel' something is to be aware. Evidence on pain suggests that the intensity of felt pain or even the awareness of pain [...] - need not have a direct stimulus correlate. Thus, people are aware of pain under some circumstances, but not aware of it under others, even though in both instances the injuries or other physical damage are similar. The evidence indicates that sensory inputs (i.e, energy events) that the person is unaware of either as affect or as information may occur in other words, events that people are unaware of may occur in their lives, and these do not 'qualify' as experienced events." (Woods 1981, pp. 387-388).

[132] "First, the role of *situation* in influencing brand evocation is important. Generally, the influence of situation on choice has been considered to be mediated by an influence on the weighing of attributes in the multi-attribute model (e.g., Miller and Ginter 1979). However, research from the categorization literature [...] has suggested that contextual factors can change the graded structure of a category. [...] In addition and somewhat belatedly, consumer researchers have begun to recognize the importance of *motives* in consumer choice. Rossiter and Percy (1987) noted that ads should link brands to the category need in order to be effective. In a similar vein, Warshaw (1980) noticed that brand attitudes are better able to predict behavior if intentions towards the product category are known." (Holden 1993, p. 383, emphasis added).

[133] A stimulating clue for future research could be to imagine, for retrieval of information in memory, a cause similar to in-salience of physical stimuli. In line with Krech and Crutchfield's (1948) original definition of salience (see, *above*, Chapter Two, Note 1), retrieval of in-salient stimuli could be hypothesized as a contextual incongruity between those stimuli in memory and the perceiver's *images*, rather than *schemata* (see, for reviews on imagery, Childers and Houston 1983; MacInnis and Price 1987; Paivio 1971; Unnava, Agarwal, and Haugtvedt 1996; Unnava and Burnkrant 1991a).

[134] The recall-versus-recognition issue is also related to the concept of involvement. Recall seems to be a more appropriate measure of awareness for products which elicit high involvement; recognition, for the other cases (Singh and Rothschild 1983).

[135] The dichotomy between *in-salience* and *re-salience* applies also to kinds of learning involved: Whereas in-salience seems related to *incidental learning*, re-salience appears related to *intentional learning*. Incidental learning, under experimental conditions, occurs when subjects are not told that their memory would be tested; whereas had subjects been told that recall or recognition would be required later, there would be intentional learning. "The reason for using incidental learning is that since the subject is not trying to learn the items, there is no temptation to process or encode a given word in any way other than that specified by the experimenter. If the subject knows he must subsequently recall the item, then he may well try to commit it to memory in other ways, forming images or associations or perhaps just repeating it to himself." (Baddeley 1991, p. 161).

[136] "Rossiter and Percy (1987) make an important observation that measures of recognition of the brand name may not necessarily reflect the recognition process that takes place in the choice situation. They note that in the choice context, brand awareness may be mediated by recognition of one or more of a number of elements of the product, for example, the package, the colors, the brand logo, etc. Furthermore, measures of ease of recognition (Alba and Hutchinson 1987) may be more appropriate." (Holden 1993, p. 383).

[137] According to Ehrenberg, Barnard, and Scriven (1997, p. 9): "Salience is broader than any single measure of brand performance. It depends on virtually all the different possible measures of performance correlating. Compared with Brand B, if Brand A has more salience than B, it has more people who: - Are 'aware' of it (for just about *any* awareness measure); - Have it in their active brand repertoires (for frequently bought products); - And/or have it in their consideration sets (i.e., brands they *might* buy); - Are familiar with the brand; - Feel it has brand assurance (e.g., retail availability, after-sales service, etc.); - Have positive attribute beliefs about Brand A; - Regard it as value for money; - Harbor intentions to buy and/or to use it in the future (and do so); - Would buy-A-if-their-usual-brand-was-not-available; - Choose A in a named product test; - Note and recall its advertisements (by and large); - Talk more often and more richly about it in focus groups; - Are 'loyal' to A (by any measure of loyalty). For directly competitive and substitutable brands, all the different measures tend in practice to correlate well." White (1999) has strongly criticized this approach, by considering

it an over-simplistic view based on the unwillingness to accept the insights of psychology and, in particular, of qualitative research.

Chapter 4

CONSUMER AWARENESS OF PRINT ADVERTISEMENTS

In this last chapter, we propose a research design aimed at assessing the validity of the *In-salience hypothesis* in stimulating consumer information processing which, in turn, results in consumer awareness. Since the in-salience model is a general model which could be validated with any kind of marketing stimuli (products, ads, salespersons, etc.), it was necessary to choose - preliminarily - a limited setting for an operative testing of its propositions. Drawing on research on brand personalities as consumers' schemata (Caprara and Barbaranelli 1996, 2000; Caprara, Barbaranelli, and Guido 1998b; Caprara, Barbaranelli, and Guido, forthcoming/ab), we determined to assess consumer awareness for *in-salient print ads*. Specifically, consumer awareness was tested in terms of ad message recall by manipulating in-salience of ad claims for three major branded products.[1]

We limited perception analysis to print advertising, rather than considering advertising in general (printed and broadcasted), to restrict the current field of investigation to *visual phenomena*. On the one hand, this limitation should not invalidate the basic principles behind the general framework of in-salience, on the other, it should allow a simple operationalization of the construct in our laboratory experiment (cf. Hornik 1980; Rosbergen, Pieters, and Wedel 1997). In the intentions of the experimenter, this application was *not* planned as an exhaustive test of the in-salience theory, because this theory - as it was proposed and developed in Chapter Three - is wider in its scopes and valences, thus, applicable in many cognitive fields. Rather, this study was thought of as a means of providing support to the basic propositions of the theory in a particular marketing setting, that of advertising.

This chapter is structured in the following fashion. First, we shall describe the research objectives regarding unsolved issues in the salience literature and provide specific hypotheses - that derive from our in-salience theory - to address these issues. Second, we shall discuss the methodology used for the experiment that was designed and implemented to test the relevant hypotheses. Third, we shall present results and data analysis of the experiment in two related studies regarding in-salience effects, ad exposure time, schema activation, memory decay, and relevance levels. Finally, we shall discuss the findings of these studies and present implications, limitations, and future research.

1. MESSAGE IN-SALIENCE IN PRINT ADVERTISEMENTS: EFFECTS ON CONSUMER PROCESSING AND MEMORY

One of the fundamental postulates of the *In-salience hypothesis* is that - for the existence of in-salience and, thus, consumer awareness - three elements are necessary: A stimulus, a context, and a schema. In this study, these factors were *in-salient ad claims* as the stimulus, *print advertising* as the context, and *brand personalities of the advertised products* as schemata.

1.1   Research Objectives

The literature reviewed in Chapter Two provides full details into how salience has been treated in the past and the role it has been given inside consumer processing of information. Although there has been a considerable amount of research exploring the salience construct - especially in social cognition -, the concept of salience has always been maintained separate from the concept of incongruity (the latter being usually considered as one of the possible instances of salience). Truly, salience has been treated as an umbrella concept, covering different constructs from accessibility to availability, from activation to importance. The in-salience model presented in Chapter Three, indeed, enables us to address many of the numerous questions and problems past research on salience has left unanswered and unsolved. Furthermore, it facilitates the putting together of the two streams of research regarding, respectively, salience and incongruity; by demonstrating the communalities between these two corpora, it provides the fundamentals for the development of a new comprehensive theory.

The experiment presented in this chapter examined some of the major problem areas addressed by the theory through the basic propositions introduced in Chapter Three. The objective of this application was to test the in-salience model in an advertising setting so as to explore how consumers process in-salient and non-in-salient information presented in print ads and to assess their impact on learning and memory. Operationally, the main focus of this study was to look at the effect of in-salient and non-in-salient advertising claims on top-of-mind and free recall of information contained in the copy.[2] This information included those attributes (so-called *markers*) used to identify a brand and affirm its image. Such an issue is particularly important to advertisers when trying to develop promotional strategies that are designed to strengthen memory responses for their brands. Top-of-mind and free recall have their greatest impact on consumers' memory for brands to be evaluated; thus, if each of these memory tasks is differently affected by in-salient and non-in-salient information, it would be extremely useful to evaluate this differential impact.

In reference to the four basic propositions advanced by the *In-salience hypothesis*, we focused on as many research objectives. The first, general objective was that of assessing whether in-salient information presented in ads stimulate consumers to spend more time processing the ads and whether this attentional focus results in higher awareness. The second objective regarded the stages of the perception process: Special attention was directed towards the relationship between stimulus in-salience and ad exposure time to determine whether viewership length can be considered as a possible moderating variable. Moreover, in an unlimited exposure time condition, time was tested as a moderator of memory strength for in-salient and non-in-salient information. In establishing the third objective, research attention was allocated to other constructs similar to salience, namely activation (or accessibility) and availability, in order to demonstrate that, when a particular schema has common elements available to all perceivers, the activation of such a schema can improve the memory effects of in-salient stimuli based on those common elements. Finally, as for the fourth objective, having defined relevance as the weight of the elements (e.g., attributes) in a schema, it was tested as a moderating variable of the effects of in-salience on memory for those common elements in perceivers' schemata on which in-salient stimuli were based.

These four research objectives formed as many experimental levels that were covered in two studies of one compact experimental design, as explicitly reported in the research hypotheses discussed below.

1.2 Hypotheses

The following hypotheses were constructed after the fundamental propositions of the in-salience theory. They were the product of a careful analysis of the previous work done in this area by consumer and social behavior researchers as well as the result of an examination of past literature within the specific field of information processing and memory.

1.2.1 Experimental Level One

Experimental Level One is linked with Proposition One of our theory: A stimulus is in-salient when it is incongruent in a certain context with a perceiver's schema. In-salience implies a memory advantage of in-salient stimuli over non-in-salient ones. Applying this to an advertising setting, we can hypothesize that an in-salient message (that is, a message which communicates an attribute of a brand which is incongruent with the brand schema possessed by a perceiver) is better recalled than an non-in-salient message (that is, a congruent one). Thus, an ad claim which apparently communicates a brand attribute that is incongruent with the brand schema (e.g., the brand image or part of it) is better recalled than an ad claim which is congruent.

The three fundamental elements postulated by Proposition One of the in-salience theory were as follows: The *stimulus* was an ad message; the *context* was set by a print advertisement; and the *schema* was the image of the brand possessed by perceivers. We assumed that schematic incongruities enhance the possibilities for the in-salient message to be noticed and processed, thus creating awareness. In our research design, *consumer awareness* represents the lowest end of a continuum of brand knowledge that ranges from simple recall of the stimulus message to more detailed brand information (cf. Hoyer and Brown 1990). Therefore, it follows that:

Awareness

> H1:   Recall is higher for in-salient messages than for non-in-salient messages.

1.2.2   Experimental Level Two

Experimental Level Two is linked with Proposition Two of our theory: In-salience has to do with attention *and* interpretation. In an information processing model made up of stages (i.e., sensation, attention, interpretation, and memory), in-salience is not merely the result of a figure-ground principle, as maintained by past research on salience. Rather than being a simple matter of sensation (whose effects are assessed at the level of attention), it implies a further stage, that of interpretation, in which the incongruities detected in a certain context are compared with schemata possessed by perceivers (whose effects can be appraised in terms of memory, rather than attention).

In an advertising setting, receivers presented with in-salient ad claims are supposed to engage in cognitive elaboration aimed to solve the incongruity contained in the ads. As the resulting in-salience derives from perceivers' interpretation of the stimuli (i.e., a further stage in the process of perception), we hypothesized that with the increase of ad exposure time, consumers have more opportunities to process the in-salient stimuli. This longer processing effort would result in higher recall for the in-salient messages contained in those claims. Therefore:

Ad Exposure Time

H2*a*: As the amount of available ad exposure time increases, the memory advantage for in-salient messages over non-in-salient messages is increased.

It was hypothesized that, with the availability of adequate exposure time, the receiver has a sufficient opportunity to scan the advertisement to the degree necessary for establishing an elaborate memory network linking the in-salient stimulus to the other elements in the ad and compare it with his schemata.[3] The work by Houston, Childers and Heckler (1987) on picture-word inconsistencies (i.e., conveying different attributes) provided partial support for this claim. They found significant recall superiority for the inconsistent combination only when subjects were given fifteen seconds of ad exposure time. No significant effects were found after less than five seconds or ten seconds of ad exposure time. These authors suggested that their conflicting results might be due to the dual-code nature of consistent information (Paivio 1971), or to the redundancy of that information.[4] But an alternative explanation, advanced by Peltier (1989), is that subjects were not given sufficient time to process the entire ad. If they had been allowed to view the ads for longer than fifteen seconds or for a time interval that they themselves would have selected, the authors' findings might have turned out differently.

It was predicted that the use of in-salient claims in advertisements would result in longer processing of ads; we further hypothesized that this memory superiority would hold over time. If the assumption that in-salient information creates more associative links connecting it to other cognitive elements is correct, and that the links associated with in-salient and non-in-salient information fade at a constant rate (see Anderson and Bower 1973 and, *above*, Chapter Three, Paragraph 2.1.9 on *Spreading activation*), then the memory network for in-salient information should continue being stronger over time (given that the time delay is not so long as to obscure all memory traces). Hastie (1980) found this to be true over time delays of five minutes, twenty-four hours, seven days, and fourteen days. Srull (1981) found similar results for time delays of three minute and forty-eight hours.

In our study, the relationship between information in-salience and memory decay was examined as a means of testing the degree to which in-salient and non-in-salient information remained in an individual's accessible memory network over time, by hypothesizing that:

Time of Measurement

H2*b*: Recall after a twenty-four hour delay is higher for in-salient messages than for non-in-salient messages.

While there have been studies that looked at the memorability of congruent and incongruent information over time (e.g., O'Brien and Myers 1985; Sujan, Bettman, and Sujan 1986), the same attention was not given to studying the memory for peripheral information over time. Short-term memory for an advertisement without an equally effective long-term impact provides limited advantages to advertisers. This issue is particularly important when considering the huge amounts of time and money spent by organizations to inform, persuade, and remind target audiences of the products they offer.

1.2.3   Experimental Level Three

Experimental Level Three is linked with Proposition Three of our theory: In-salience is a different construct from: (1) Activation (or Accessibility), and (2) Availability. In past literature, these concepts were usually considered as synonyms of salience. On the contrary, the in-salience theory maintains that they are improperly referred to as they do not allow the proper expression of the nature of "prominence" intrinsic in the salience construct. The *In-salience hypothesis* overcomes this limitation by stressing the existence of an incongruity between the stimulus in a context and a perceiver's schema (which allows such a stimulus to be prominent compared to the other stimuli). It recognizes, at the same time, that *activation, accessibility*, and *availability* have a role in the processing of in-salient stimuli as moderators of perceivers' schemata.

In the context of an ad for a branded product, we hypothesized representing a perceiver's schema by the brand image for the advertised brand. We assumed that all consumers share some common elements (i.e., attributes) within their schemata; for example, if a Ferrari is perceived as a sports car, it is possible that the majority of the users believes that Ferrari is "fast." Moreover, some attributes (as "fast," in our example) can be so closely linked with the brand image that they can be also shared by non-users of the product (we can assume, for example, that also people who do not possess a Ferrari believe that it is a "fast" car). For other attributes, however, or for more complex products, or also for simple products in the context of complex judgments, there should be differences in knowledge structures between novices and experts (e.g., the latter being usually users of the product). Therefore, the *availability* of a schema - or of certain elements of a schema - was posed as a necessary condition for the occurrence of the in-salience effects in receivers of the message.

However, to this end, it is necessary not only that the schema is available but also that the schema is activated (that is, accessible) when the stimulus that advertisers want to make "in-salient" to receivers is presented. Indeed, the activation of another schema, which is substantially different from that hypothesized by the authors of the stimulus claims (e.g., the copywriters) might result in a lack of an in-salience occurrence. Therefore, *activation* - and the consequent *accessibility* - of the schema were posed as the other necessary condition for the occurrence of in-salience. In our study, since we assumed that the receivers' schema regarding the advertised product consists of a series of attributes possessed by the branded product which define its brand image (i.e., its brand personality - see, *below*, Paragraph 2.1.2), it was hypothesized that by cuing a brand schema through a *prime* we could increase the effects of the in-salient claims. As stated above (Chapter Three, Paragraph 2.3.1), a prime refers to any process by which it is possible to increase the general accessibility of a schema, thereby enhancing the probability of the occurrence of an incongruity between the stimulus claim and the activated schema.

Because schematic inconsistencies promote increased processing efforts, if we select - in the making of the stimulus cues - only those schema elements (i.e., attributes) which are commonly available to both users and non-users, it follows that:

Priming

H3:   Activation of the brand schema increases the memory advantage of in-salient messages over non-in-salient messages.

In synthesis, for the occurrence of in-salience, first, a schema must be available. That is, a consumer must have an *a priori* knowledge structure in place before any expectation for a message used in an advertisement can be established. If the receiver has no prior expectations concerning the advertised brand, then there is in essence neither in-salient nor non-in-salient information because there is no basis on which to judge the in/congruity of that stimulus.[5] Thus, there must be an available schema that a consumer can tap when processing the elements of an ad. Second, a schema must be activated (that is, externally induced) or must be accessible (that is, naturally ready) to establish expectations. Mere storage of schematic knowledge in memory is not a sufficient condition for obtaining the memory advantage for the in-salient information. Unless a schema is instantiated there is again no opportunity for assessing the in/congruity of a stimulus. The activation of a particular schema, indeed, depends on the context in which the stimulus occurs (e.g., Barsalou 1987, 1989; Palmer 1975; Yi 1990).[6] Thus, the target stimulus within an advertisement (in this case, the ad message) must not only be one the reader has a related schema for, but it must also be able, in that particular context, to embed an expectation. Finally, it is possible to induce the activation of a particular schema by using a prime. This process of priming may or may not occur naturally (cf. Sujan, Bettman, and Sujan 1986). A number of sources suggests, for example, that the pictorial component of an ad naturally acts as a prime, thus embedding expectations and, therefore, instantiating a schema (e.g.,

Peltier 1989; Stafford, Walker, and Blasko 1996; Yi 1990).[7] Researchers, however, could artificially have consumers' attention focused on the brand schema by cuing, for example, the brand image (to which, in our case, an in-salient ad message is referred) through a direct mention of one or more marker attributes which act as tags of the appropriate schema.[8] In a similar fashion, other studies in the past (e.g., Chung and Szymanski 1997; Cowley 1999; Meyers-Levy and Tybout 1989; Sujan, Bettman, and Sujan 1986) have externally induced the activation of a schema for cuing an incongruent stimulus.

1.2.4   Experimental Level Four

Experimental Level Four is linked with Proposition Four of our theory: Relevance is a crucial moderating variable of in-salience. Not only will recall be higher for an in-salient stimulus than for a non-in-salient one (H1), but also recall will be higher for an in-salient stimulus which is incongruent with an element of the perceiver's schema (i.e., a brand attribute) which is more relevant (i.e., which has a heavier weight within the schema) than another less relevant element.

We argued that, if the incongruity in the in-salient message occurs between the stimulus cue and a brand attribute which has a greater weight within a brand schema than the other brand attributes within such a schema, then the recall effect of the in-salient message will be greater. Let us say, for example, that the brand image of Ferrari is expressed by different attributes: Fast, luxury, red, etc. We can assess that, to the majority of consumers, the attribute "fast" is more prominent (relevant) within the schema of Ferrari than the attribute "red." It means that, on average, the attribute "fast" is more congruent with the image of Ferrari possessed by the majority of consumers than the attribute "red".[9] For any brand, therefore, we can develop a list of attributes according to their relevance, that is, their weights inside a modal brand schema.

We hypothesized that, when a claim is in-salient because of an attribute which is more relevant than another attribute used in another in-salient claim, then the former in-salient message has a memory advantage over the latter in-salient message. Therefore:

Relevance of In-salient Stimuli

H4:   When an attribute is more relevant (that is, when it has a greater weight than another attribute within the same brand schema), recall of an in-salient message regarding that attribute is greater.

1.2.5   Summary of Hypotheses

In the above paragraphs, we have defined four levels of experimental inquiry to test, in an advertising setting, the effects of in-salience on consumer awareness in terms of ad message recall. H1 predicted that in-salient messages would be better recalled than non-in-salient messages. H2*a* predicted that recall of in-salient messages in print advertisements would be higher than non-in-salient messages when viewers look longer at those ads; while H2*b* predicted that they would be more memorable even after a twenty-four-hour delay. H3 predicted that activation of the appropriate brand schema would enhance the memory advantage of in-salient messages over non-in-salient ones. Finally, H4 predicted that messages that are in-salient because of a more relevant attribute would be better recalled than in-salient messages that are in-salient because of a less relevant attribute within the same brand schema.

2.   METHOD

2.1   Research Design

An experiment was designed to test the above hypotheses investigating the effects of in-salient stimuli, presented within print advertisements, on consumers' processing and memory. The experiment was the result of the four levels of inquiry corresponding to the above-mentioned experimental levels.

As stated in Chapter Three, for the existence and the development of its effects, in-salience requires three basic factors: Stimulus, context, and schemata. The *stimulus* used in this study was constituted by advertising claims containing messages that could be incongruent with the brand image (in-salient messages) or congruent with the brand image (non-in-salient messages). Specifically, the selected stimulus cues were those attributes commonly identifying the brand within consumers' schemata. The *context* of the stimulus occurrences was a specific task given to the subjects for evaluating a series of print advertisements. The *schemata* for product information were identified in consumers' brand images of three different branded goods: An investment product (i.e., Opel automobiles); a consumer product (i.e., Manetti & Roberts bath foam); and a service (i.e., Sip mobile phone service - at the time of this research, the only Italian provider of such telephone services).

The study was implemented in two main stages, as reported below. In *Part One*, amongst the general research strategies for examining the structure of consumer memory for product information (cf. Mitchell 1982; Olson and Muderrisoglu 1979), following the most commonly accepted model of memory, the *Associative network model* (e.g., Wickelgren 1981), we assessed consumers' brand schemata as brand images, within the construct definition of brand personality (Reynolds and Gutman 1984). For each stimulus brand, we measured the relevance of a series of attributes in defining the brand image according to both users and non-users. In *Part Two*, drawing from previously developed attribute lists, we selected some of the attributes equally shared by both users' and non-users' brand schemata to be employed in the manipulation of in-salient ad claims. The executional strategy selected for the creation of in-salient stimuli was *resonance* (McQuarrie and Mick 1992), which consists in the development of alternative combinations of wordplay with relevant pictures that create ambiguity and incongruity. Analysis was, then, conducted to assess in-salience effects on consumers' processing and memory - namely, to measure top-of-mind and free recall of ad message which were in/congruent with those schemata in the context of print advertisements.

A.   *Part One*: **Measurement of Brand Schemata**

The purpose of the first part of this study was to examine the average knowledge structures possessed by users and non-users of three branded products. Such brand schemata were used by the experimenter as a basis for the creation of in-salient ad claims (in *Part Two* of the study, *below*). This section contains a description of the measurement procedures employed, the theoretical background, and the research design. Results and synoptic tables are also included and discussed.

2.1.1   Measurement Procedures

It is generally acknowledged that the issue of how to develop valid measures of consumers' knowledge structures can be approached only by having first a theory of memory to draw on and a conceptual definition of the hypothetical construct one is trying to measure. To get around this problem, it has been argued that the measurement of the hypothetical knowledge structures should depend on the type of information processing activities that are to be explained (Mitchell 1982).

To examine the research issues of this study, we used two heterogeneous sets of subjects, *users* and *non-users* of each of the three stimulus brands, to elicit their evaluation of the relevance of certain attributes for describing their brand images. This involved identifying individuals who differed in knowledge within such particular domains and then examining how their performance differed on the specific task. As most previous research, we employed rating scales anchored to researcher-specified attributes, an approach which is partly based on the classic *Associative network model* of memory (e.g., Wickelgreen 1981): By giving specific lists of attributes, the researcher activates particular nodes in memory and then the subject expresses his measure of the particular weight associated with that node.

We refrained to use a free elicitation procedure to prompt brand attributes. This was done for two main reasons: First, to overcome a problem free-elicitation techniques could cause. Specifically, as mentioned above (Chapter Three, Paragraph 2.1.10.2), Olson and Muderrisoglu (1979) argued that, in marketing research, the typical multiattribute model questionnaire (e.g., Fishbein and Ajzen 1975) advocates the use of free-elicitation techniques to operationalize salient attributes that practically propose procedures that provide subjects with quite specific instructions regarding the type of concepts desired: For example, "tell me what you believe to be the characteristics, qualities, and attributes of ..., etc.", rather than giving them freedom. It should be acknowledged that other types of cognitive representations might be related to the target objects (cf. Guido 1996a). Second, we did not use free elicitation to adhere to the lexicographic tradition at the basis of the theoretical definition of schema we chose for this study, namely brand image in the acceptation of brand personality (see *below*). This does not mean, however, that in future research other different procedures for measuring knowledge structures should not be employed (such as those, for example, proposed by Mitchell 1982). On the contrary, their use should be recommended to a further test of the rationale of our theory.

2.1.2   Brand Image as Brand Personality

Schemata have been defined as packets of information centered around concepts. In a consumer setting, schemata can be thought of as networks of attributes centered on a brand. A simple model for the schema of Ferrari possessed by an individual is illustrated in Figure 3 (*above*) as a network of circles centered around the brand, with the area of each circle representing the relevance of a specific attribute and the arcs between circles representing the linkages with the concept.

We assumed consumers have schemata for any specific brand selected for this study and that they partly share information contained in those packages. We attempted to operationalize these communalities by using the conceptualization of schemata as *brand images*. The concept of brand image, however, is an unstable one (Dobni and Zinkhan 1990; Poiesz 1989; Reynolds and Gutman 1984); therefore, we adopted among the formal definitions of the construct one which could provide an unequivocal interpretation - also in the light of a consolidate research tradition such that in the personality literature.

By selecting *brand personality* as brand image, we put the principal emphasis of our conceptualization on personification. This practice has long been recognized in marketing (Arons 1961; Martineau 1958), but it became especially popular in the 1980s (Bettinger, Dawson, and Wales 1979; Debevec and Iyer 1986; Hendon and Williams 1985). Brands are assumed to have personality images just as people do (Arias-Bolzmann, Chakraborty, and Mowen 2000; Fox et al. 1998; Tom and Eves 1999): For example, a recent Benson & Hedges Cigarette campaign has employed the rhetorical figure of personification (Pullack 1997). These brand images are not determined by the physical characteristics of the product alone, but by a composite of other factors such as advertising, price, word-of-mouth, news media reports, stereotypes of the typical users, and other marketing and psychological associations (Sirgy 1985).[10]

In social perception, psychologists who have studied personality descriptions typically subscribe to a *trait approach* to studying and measuring human personality and believe that every person can be calibrated on the extent to the possession of certain traits (such as being aggressive, warm, etc.). This approach is usually attributed to the psychologists Gordon Allport, H. J. Eysenck, and Raymond Cattell, who have developed, since the late 1930s, a model which reduces the infinite number of trait adjectives by which people can be measured to five basic underlying dimensions or *Big Five factors* (see, for complete reviews of these studies, Digman 1990; Goldberg 1993; McCrae and John 1992; Wiggins and Pincus 1992). The most common labels of these five factors are: (1) *Extroversion/Introversion*, the preference (or not) for social interaction and for activity (whose examples of prototypical attributes are adventurous-cautious, sociable-reclusive, *et similia*); (2) *Agreeableness*, the orientation toward compassion and caring about others, and away from antagonism (e.g., good-natured-irritable; gentle-headstrong); (3) *Conscientiousness*, the preference for goal-oriented activity, namely the degree of organization (e.g., responsible-undependable; tidy-careless); (4) *Emotional Stability* (or *Neuroticism*), the ability to cope effectively with negative emotions (e.g., composed-excitable; calm-anxious); and (5) *Openness to Experience* (or *Intellect*), the tolerance for new ideas and new ways of doing things, experientially oriented (e.g., sensitive-insensitive; intellectual-unreflective; refined-crude; imaginative-simple).[11] The Big Five solution is the meeting point of two traditions of research: The lexicographic and the factorial traditions. Both are based on the *Sedimentation hypothesis* by Cattell (1945) - stating that the most important individual differences in human transactions will come to be encoded as single terms (usually, attributes) in many of the world languages. The resulting five factors, indeed, proved to be relatively generalizable across different nationalities. Also in the Italian lexical context, which regards our study (as it was conducted in Italian, with an Italian sample), the emergence of the Big Five factor structure has been convincingly demonstrated (Caprara and Perugini 1994).

Similarly to persons, also brands have been seen as characterized by personality profiles defined by a series of attributes (Aaker and Fournier 1995; Berry 1988; Durgee 1988; Endler and Rosenstein 1997; Plummer 1984/85). However, in both industry and academia, most attribute batteries have not been scrutinized over the years. For example, Linquist (1974) was frequently cited as the basis for selecting attributes because his review summarized the image dimensions specified by researchers in nineteen articles; and yet, some of these dimensions were empirical and some others were conceptual, thus simply suggestive of dimensions that could or could not be meaningful to consumers. To overcome these difficulties, the Big Five model and the various lexicographic studies provide an important referent in that they give the advantage of reducing, through factor analysis, the thousands of attributes by which it is possible to describe personality to relatively few prototypical attributes, the so-called *markers* (related to the major latent dimensions of each brand personality). Markers enable us to communicate the meaning of the dimension they belong to without ambiguity, thus reducing the risk of confusing dimensions (Goldberg 1992).

However, as noted by Aaker (1997), a satisfactory method of selecting adjectives for measuring brand personality has not yet been defined. Her study focused on a general cross-category framework investigating brand personality dimensions underlying 114 traits used to describe 37 different brands. After sorting out a number of descriptors of brand personality, a five-factor solution was found; yet, only three of these factors appeared in the Big Five model. Recent research in the Italian marketing context (Caprara and Barbaranelli 1996, 2000; Caprara, Barbaranelli, and Guido 1998b; Caprara, Barbaranelli, and Guido, forthcoming/ab; Caprara, Barbaranelli, and Zimbardo 1997) confirmed the hypothesis that the Big Five model and its prototypical attributes (i.e., markers) can be plausibly extended from human personality to brands and products, but suggested to explore the existence of other qualitative dimensions apart from the Big Five,[12] as well as the possibility for the same markers to be applied indifferently to all brands.[13]

2.1.3   Procedure

There are different methods of learning about the personality consumers associate with a brand. Some of them are more direct and quantitative, while others are more indirect and qualitative. Among the quantitative techniques available, perhaps the simplest is to have consumers rate a brand on various personality adjectives. Different brands, thus, could be "profiled" (that is, compared) on these personality adjective scales.[14]

We measured three branded products - namely, Opel automobiles (henceforth OPEL); Manetti & Roberts' bath foam (henceforth MRBF); and

Sip mobile (a.k.a. cellular) phone service (henceforth SMPS) - for the image possessed by users and non-users of these products by using lists of prototypical attributes.[15] The experiment was conducted at a major Italian university (University of Rome, "La Sapienza"), using lists of attributes in Italian, and an Italian sample. The purpose of this section of our research was to measure the level of relevance of each attribute in defining the personality image of the brand. Parallel studies on the same lists of attributes were conducted to measure, through factor analysis, the Big Five dimensions for those brands (Caprara and Barbaranelli 1996; Caprara, Barbaranelli, and Guido 1998b).

The sample consistency and the questionnaire content were slightly different according to the brand tested. Table 4 summarizes these distinctions.

Table 4. Subjects and Attribute Lists

	OPEL	MRBF	SMPS
Subjects in the pilot study	Thirty (15 users and 15 non-users); 70% men and 30% women. Age: 20-50.	Sixty (30 users and 30 non-users); 100% women. Age: 25-50.	One hundred and fifty (75 users and 75 non-users); 67% men and 33% women. Age: 16-60.
Attribute lists in the pilot study	300 polarized Big-Five attributes divided in 5 lists; judged on a 5-point semantic scale.	315 Big-Five attributes divided in 5 lists; judged on a 5-point Likert scale.	300 (200 Big-Five attributes + 100 extra Big-Five attributes) divided in 10 lists; judged on a 4-point Likert scale.
Subjects in the main study	One hundred and fifty (75 users and 75 non-users); 70% men and 30% women. Age: 20-50.	Three hundred (150 users and 150 non-users); 100% women. Age: 25-50.	Six hundred (300 men and 300 women); 70% men and 30% women. Age: 16-60.
Attribute lists in the main study	40 polarized Big-Five attributes.	40 Big-Five attributes.	50 attributes (30 Big-Five and 20 extra Big-Five) in 2 lists of 25 attributes each.

Note. OPEL = Opel automobiles; MRBF = Manetti & Roberts bath foam; SMPS = Sip mobile phone service.

For each of the three branded products, research was articulated in two stages: In the pilot stage, subjects evaluated the relevance level of a number of attributes (about 300 attributes for each manipulation) in representing the personality of the stimulus product. Lists were compiled on the basis of a pool of attributes which were found suitable for describing human personality in an Italian extension of the Big Five model (Caprara and Perugini 1994).[16] The attribute order was casualized and attributes inserted in lists of 60 items each (30 items each in the SMPS manipulation). Following this pilot stage, the first 40 attributes (50 attributes in the SMPS manipulation),[17] which were rated as the most relevant in describing the personality of each stimulus product, were used to rate the relevance level in the main stage. None of the pretest subjects took part in this stage.

2.1.4   Results and Discussion

Results are summarized in Tables 5-7 (*below*). These tables provide, on average, the consumers' perceived relevance of an attribute in representing the personality of a specific branded product. For a sample equally divided between users and non-users of the products, there were only few items that presented significant differences in their perceived relevance according to the two types of subjects.[18]

Such findings were taken as maps of the personality images possessed by consumers for the stimulus products. As mentioned above, parallel research was carried out to isolate, through factor analysis, those groups of attributes which were more strictly associated with each other, so that they could imply a latent dimension explaining this similitude. Results of this research showed three condensed dimensions for the OPEL: Conscientiousness/Stability, Extraversion/ Agreeableness, Openness; three condensed dimensions for the MRBF: Stability/Conscientiousness, Extraversion/Openness, Agreeableness; and two condensed dimensions for the SMPS: Stability/Agreeableness/Conscientiousness, Extraversion/ Openness.[19] These findings were used in the selection of attributes for the in-salience manipulation (*below*).

Table 5. Relevant Attributes in Description of Consumers' Image for Opel Automobiles

Variable	Users		Non-users		Total		F	p
	M.	Std Dev.	M.	Std Dev.	M.	Std Dev.		
Solid/Fragile	4.52	.61	3.97	.82	4.16	.80	16.88	.0001
Safe/Unsafe	4.24	1.00	3.81	.87	3.95	.94	7.33	.0076
Reliable/Unreliable	4.44	.84	3.71	.95	3.95	.97	21.39	.0000
Strong/Weak	4.32	.77	3.68	.89	3.89	.90	18.95	.0000
Tidy/Untidy	4.18	.85	3.71	.87	3.87	.89	9.90	.0020
Prudent/Imprudent	4.22	.79	3.61	.86	3.81	.88	17.59	.0000
Serious/Frivolous	3.95	.96	3.68	.76	3.77	.84	3.70	.0562
Stable/Unstable	4.18	.92	3.56	.88	3.77	.94	16.07	.0001
Constant/Inconstant	4.25	.76	3.47	.88	3.73	.92	27.17	.0000
Careful/Careless	3.98	.94	3.59	.92	3.72	.94	5.90	.0163
Farsighted/Shortsighted	4.04	.70	3.52	.82	3.70	.82	14.28	.0002
Controlled/Impulsive	3.96	.83	3.56	.74	3.69	.79	8.91	.0033
Friendly/Hostile	3.98	.77	3.54	.80	3.69	.81	10.07	.0018
Honest/Dishonest	4.14	.70	3.47	.86	3.69	.87	22.85	.0000
Nice/Mean	4.08	.66	3.48	.90	3.68	.87	17.23	.0001
Relaxed/Tense	3.90	.79	3.52	.81	3.65	.82	7.46	.0071
Sincere/False	4.12	.75	3.39	.80	3.64	.85	28.32	.0000
New/Old	4.06	.91	3.41	1.06	3.63	1.06	13.62	.0003
Developed/Underdevel.	4.18	.77	3.34	1.01	3.62	1.01	26.81	.0000
Determined/Undeterm.	4.00	.88	3.39	.87	3.60	.91	16.07	.0001
Generous/Selfish	3.92	.83	3.41	.76	3.58	.81	13.93	.0003
Cheerful/Sad	3.88	.69	3.42	.88	3.57	.85	10.48	.0015
Attentive/Oblivious	3.80	1.01	3.45	.76	3.57	.86	5.47	.0207
Energetic/Sluggish	3.82	.92	3.44	.83	3.57	.88	6.47	.0120
Quiet/Nervous	3.86	.90	3.39	.91	3.55	.93	8.95	.0033
Refined/Coarse	3.94	.87	3.31	.95	3.53	.96	15.16	.0001
Patient/Anxious	3.76	.89	3.37	.73	3.50	.81	8.19	.0050
Calm/Agitated	3.68	1.02	3.37	.86	3.47	.92	3.81	.0526
Modern/Ancient	3.82	.87	3.29	.97	3.47	.97	10.44	.0015
Funny/Boring	3.94	.79	3.16	.98	3.42	.99	23.77	.0000
Cordial/Distant	3.62	.83	3.27	.79	3.39	.82	6.17	.0141
Competitive/Uncompet.	3.64	.98	3.25	1.05	3.38	1.04	4.69	.0319
Sensible/Insensible	3.55	.81	3.25	.59	3.35	.69	6.38	.0126
Lively/Dull	3.66	.92	3.20	.98	3.35	.98	7.61	.0065
Hot/Cool	3.84	.94	3.10	.78	3.34	.91	25.30	.0000
Affectionate/Unaffect.	3.55	.79	3.01	.81	3.19	.84	14.72	.0002
Innovative/Conservative	3.24	1.02	2.99	1.21	3.07	1.15	1.57	.2119
Fanciful/Unimaginative	3.32	.87	2.90	1.04	3.04	1.00	6.08	.0148
Original/Traditional	3.38	1.31	2.84	1.11	3.02	1.20	7.01	.0090
Unconventional/Conv.	2.71	.97	2.79	.95	2.76	.95	.24	.6261

Note. *d.f.* = 1,149

Table 6. Relevant Attributes in Description of Consumers' Image for Manetti & Roberts Bath Foam

Variable	Users		Non-users		Total		F	p
	Mean	Std Dev.	Mean	Std Dev.	Mean	Std Dev.		
Well-known	4.42	.83	4.31	.87	4.37	.85	.83	.3624
Famous	4.44	.84	4.30	.90	4.37	.87	1.28	.2593
Natural	4.40	.82	4.00	.98	4.20	.90	9.78	.0020
Soft	4.35	.82	3.76	1.06	4.06	.94	19.25	.0000
Favorite	4.24	.93	3.79	1.08	4.02	1.01	9.98	.0018
Suitable	4.29	.69	3.54	1.02	3.92	.86	37.27	.0000
Classic	4.02	.93	3.79	1.09	3.91	1.01	2.58	.1094
Efficient	4.28	.84	3.49	1.15	3.89	1.00	30.72	.0000
Balanced	4.19	.96	3.57	1.13	3.88	1.05	17.46	.0000
Sensible	4.12	.95	3.62	1.05	3.87	1.00	12.49	.0005
Comfortable	4.13	.92	3.59	1.10	3.86	1.01	14.18	.0002
Regular	4.03	1.03	3.59	1.14	3.81	1.09	8.22	.0046
Feminine	4.05	.95	3.44	1.10	3.75	1.03	17.59	.0000
Loyal	4.01	1.02	3.48	1.31	3.75	1.17	10.15	.0017
Fair	3.90	.97	3.55	1.20	3.73	1.09	5.14	.0244
Responsible	3.91	1.08	3.52	1.22	3.72	1.15	5.72	.0177
Competitive	3.97	1.04	3.38	1.22	3.68	1.13	13.54	.0003
Productive	3.95	1.10	3.39	1.14	3.67	1.12	12.49	.0005
Quiet	3.78	1.06	3.40	1.15	3.59	1.11	5.93	.0158
Rational	3.72	1.12	3.43	1.27	3.58	1.20	2.94	.0877
Lively	3.88	.91	3.18	1.10	3.53	1.01	24.10	.0000
Great	3.88	.89	3.16	1.04	3.52	.97	27.59	.0000
Conscientious	3.75	1.07	3.28	1.24	3.52	1.16	8.25	.0045
Optimist	3.84	1.12	3.17	1.20	3.51	1.16	16.73	.0001
Determined	3.68	1.12	3.26	1.24	3.47	1.18	6.35	.0125
Spontaneous	3.78	1.13	3.14	1.17	3.46	1.15	15.41	.0001
Joyful	3.70	1.06	3.19	1.19	3.45	1.13	10.28	.0016
Comprehensive	3.69	1.12	3.20	1.15	3.45	1.14	9.30	.0026
Dynamic	3.75	1.10	3.10	1.13	3.43	1.12	16.88	.0001
Altruistic	3.65	1.22	3.21	1.38	3.43	1.30	5.71	.0178
Energetic	3.71	1.07	3.06	1.15	3.39	1.11	17.13	.0001
Sober	3.51	1.12	3.27	1.11	3.39	1.12	2.31	.1300
Innovative	3.69	1.11	3.09	1.22	3.39	1.17	13.22	.0004
Romantic	3.71	1.22	3.02	1.26	3.37	1.24	15.48	.0001
Methodic	3.41	1.10	3.26	1.10	3.34	1.10	.93	.3360
Conventional	3.40	1.11	3.05	1.17	3.23	1.14	4.72	.0309
Discounted	3.23	1.07	3.18	1.21	3.21	1.14	.09	.7573
Patient	3.33	1.13	3.02	1.15	3.19	1.24	3.71	.0553
Mild	3.38	1.24	3.00	1.23	3.19	1.24	4.74	.0306
Fanciful	3.38	1.25	2.81	1.22	3.10	1.24	10.62	.0013

Note. *d.f.* = 1,199

Table 7. Relevant Attributes in Description of Consumers' Image for Sip Mobile Phone Service

Variable	Users Mean	S.D.	Non-users Mean	S.D.	Total Mean	S.D.	F	p
Comfortable	3.53	.70	3.42	.75	3.48	.73	1.61	.2055
Communicative	3.37	.91	3.49	.72	3.43	.82	1.68	.1958
Expensive	3.31	.78	3.40	75	3.36	.77	.96	.3272
Easy	3.22	.86	3.27	.78	3.25	.82	.32	.5729
Modern	3.21	.79	3.27	.77	3.24	.78	.35	.5555
Efficient	3.15	.72	3.18	.71	3.17	.72	.17	.6796
Active	3.07	.80	3.14	.81	3.11	.81	.62	.4311
Productive	3.20	77	3.00	.83	3.10	.80	4.70	.0309
Innovative	2.99	.86	3.20	.83	3.10	.85	4.51	.0345
Dynamic	3.03	.87	3.12	.87	3.08	.87	.85	.3559
Compact	3.17	.81	2.99	.97	3.08	.89	3.06	.0812
Near	3.11	.80	3.01	1.01	3.06	.91	.78	.3786
Accommodating	2.91	.82	3.04	.88	2.98	.85	1.83	.1771
Right	3.15	.88	2.79	.99	2.97	.94	10.76	.0012
Updated	2.83	.87	3.07	.86	2.95	.87	5.48	.0199
Resolute	3.01	.84	2.85	.90	2.93	.87	2.56	.1103
Incisive	2.89	.87	2.75	1.01	2.82	.94	1.83	.1769
Agreeable	3.03	.88	2.51	.98	2.77	.93	23.95	.0000
Informed	2.77	.94	2.71	.92	2.74	.93	.38	.5349
Sociable	2.81	.92	2.66	1.01	2.74	.97	1.93	.1657
Laborious	2.68	.90	2.73	.94	2.71	.92	.17	.6756
Sharp	2.63	.80	2.73	.82	2.68	.81	1.14	.2867
Expansive	2.68	.98	2.61	1.09	2.65	1.04	.40	.5278
Free	2.82	.96	2.43	1.04	2.63	1.00	11.65	.0007
Constant	2.75	.94	2.49	.87	2.62	.91	5.93	.0155
Determined	2.64	.99	2.60	1.07	2.62	1.03	.09	.7641
Ordinate	2.74	.78	2.48	.98	2.61	.88	6.57	.0108
Competitive	2.63	.98	2.56	1.04	2.60	1.01	.33	.5680
Resolute	2.61	.94	2.56	1.08	2.59	1.01	.18	.6744
Resistant	2.68	.85	2.44	.81	2.56	.83	6.20	.0133
Solid	2.60	.86	2.30	.90	2.45	.88	8.58	.0037
Coherent	2.55	.94	2.30	1.02	2.43	.98	5.00	.0260
Rich	2.45	.96	2.41	1.03	2.43	1.00	.10	.7471
Balanced	2.59	.84	2.21	.94	2.40	.89	13.50	.0003
Responsible	2.48	.87	2.27	.94	2.38	.91	3.79	.0523
Stable	2.53	.85	2.21	.88	2.37	.87	10.57	.0013
Creative	2.39	1.10	2.35	1.04	2.37	1.07	.09	.7613
Protective	2.46	1.01	2.22	1.01	2.34	1.01	4.22	.0408
Loyal	2.38	.99	2.27	.99	2.33	.99	.98	.3228
Special	2.34	.92	2.29	.94	2.32	.93	.29	.5924
Strong	2.46	.98	2.15	.90	2.31	.94	8.20	.0045
Decorous	2.53	.99	2.05	.96	2.29	.98	18.26	.0000
Private	2.36	.97	2.17	.94	2.27	.96	3.21	.0743
Cordial	2.48	1.03	2.06	.90	2.27	.97	14.08	.0002
Original	2.25	.97	2.25	.97	2.25	.97	.00	.9883
Harmonious	2.20	.99	2.01	.93	2.11	.96	2.82	.0941
Impeccable	2.20	.88	1.95	.86	2.08	.87	6.00	.0149
Discrete	2.11	.94	1.92	.92	2.02	.93	3.21	.0743
Exemplary	2.12	.93	1.88	.87	2.00	.90	5.37	.0211
Generous	2.05	.94	1.78	.80	1.92	.87	7.02	.0085

Note. $d.f. = 1,299$

B. *Part Two*: Effects of In-salient Ad Messages on Consumer Awareness

In the second part of the study, we selected from the previously developed tables a number of attributes to be used in the in-salience manipulation for assessing in-salience effects on consumers' processing and memory of ad messages. This section contains a description of the research design used, the sample employed, collection procedures, ad development pretests, variables, and scoring system.[20]

2.1.5   Experimental Design

The experimental design for this second part of the study was a 2 (*message in-salience*: in-salient, non-in-salient) X 3 (*ad exposure time*: five seconds, fifteen seconds, and unlimited) X 2 (*schema activation*: primed, unprimed) X 2 (*time of measurement*: immediate, delayed) X 3 (*relevance level*: three attribute ranks) within group fractional factorial design. Message in-salience, time of measurement, and relevance level were the within group factors, chosen to improve the external validity of this study. Time of measurement and relevance level were the fractional factorial components (Kirk 1982): In order to simplify experimental procedures, only subjects in the unlimited exposure time condition received the memory decay and the relevance level manipulations.

The design for the experiment is diagrammed in Table 8 (*below*). The purpose behind using a within group factorial design, rather than a between group factorial design, is that exposing subjects to both in-salient and non-in-salient messages should create a more externally valid experimental setting by providing subjects with an environment where in-salient and non-in-salient information had to compete with each other for "viewing time" and "memory space." External validity was further increased by the fact that mass media such as magazines, television, and radio are much more likely to contain both types of ads rather than just one or the other.[21]

A fractional factorial design was employed for two main reasons. First, our experimental interests did not include an examination of ad memory over time under "forced" exposure time conditions (those conditions that restrict subjects to a maximum time limit for viewing an ad - e.g., five seconds). Time of measurement effects were of interest only when subjects were given the opportunity to self select the length of time that they wished to view an ad (unlimited exposure time). Second, the use of fractional factorial design was preferred in consideration of the prohibitive number of experimental cells needed for a full factorial design across all the six levels of attribute relevance and the three levels of ad exposure time - with and without the priming manipulation. Simplification of experimental procedures was a major advantage of this design (see Kirk 1982, for a complete discussion of the benefits in using a fractional factorial design).

Table 8. Experimental Design

In-salience Ad Exp.Time	Priming	Immediate Recall		Delayed Recall	
		In-salient Ads	Non-in-salient Ads	In-salient Ads	Non-in-salient Ads
5 Seconds	U			*Empty*	*Empty*
	P			*Empty*	*Empty*
15 Seconds	U			*Empty*	*Empty*
	P			*Empty*	*Empty*
Unlimited	U	1 2 3	1 2 3	1 2 3	1 2 3
	P	1 2 3	1 2 3	1 2 3	1 2 3

Note. P = Primed; U = Umprimed; 1, 2, 3 = Relevance levels. For each cell, n = 20.

2.1.6   Subjects

Totally, two hundred and forty Italian subjects (120 men and 120 women) participated in this second part of the study. They were all undergraduate students of an Italian state University. Participation was on a voluntary basis. Subjects were assigned to the experimental conditions by groups of ten (5 males and 5 females).

2.1.7   Procedure

Upon arrival subjects were seated in front of a projection screen. They were told that they were doing concept testing for a main ad agency. Subjects were also told that the ads that they would be seeing were in an unfinished form and that they would be asked for their feedback after they had viewed all the ads. In the intentions of the experimenter, this task set the context of schema activation.

Subjects were shown the print ads via a slide presentation. The use of slides enabled the experimenter to control for the amount of time that each subject was exposed to an ad. To control for advertisement order effects, presentation orders of in-salient and non-in-salient ads were randomly assigned to the subject groups. The four different orders that were used in the experiment are shown in Table 9 (*below*).

The order of ads in Order One was developed on the basis of the relevance ranks of the attributes used in ad claims. It started with the first two levels of OPEL, then there were the second two levels of MRBF, and finally the third two levels of SMPS. Then, there were the second two levels of OPEL, the third two levels of MRBF, and the first two levels of SMPS. Finally, there were the third two levels of OPEL, the first two levels of MRBF, and the second two levels of SMPS. Once this order was determined, the in-salience force of the messages was alternated, with the first claim having an in-salient message, the second a non-in-salient message, the third in-salient, and so on, until all eighteen ads were assigned. Order Two used the same order of ads, the only difference was that in-salient claims replaced non-in-salient claims and vice versa. This was done so that each pair of ads (in-salient/non-in-salient) was seen in the same order. Order Three was the opposite of Order One and Order Four was the opposite of Order Two. Because fatigue was a likely possibility in this study, it was felt that a reversed order would have balanced attentiveness across subjects.

Upon completion of the slide presentation, subjects were administered the dependent measures. To test memory, subjects were given a booklet in which their responses pertaining to the ads they viewed were to be recorded. They were first asked to complete written protocols where they were instructed to write down as many advertising messages as they could remember immediately, *without any thinking* (*top-of-mind recall*). Subjects should respond with the first thing that came to their minds, with very little thought behind it.

When subjects could no longer recall any more information (without pausing for thinking) they were instructed to turn to the next page - without being allowed to turn back - and try to remember as much as they could with respect to any of the specified brands (*free recall*). They were not required to recall this information in an ad-by-ad format but only to match messages with the brands (by the way, in all conditions, the brand name was part of the claim).

Table 9. Ad Orders

Order One	Order Three
OPEL/Safe (I)	SMPS/Solid (I)
MRBF/Determined (N)	MRBF/Natural (N)
SMPS/Creative (I)	OPEL/Original (I)
OPEL/Careful (N)	SMPS/Informed (N)
MRBF/Conscientious (I)	MRBF/Classic (I)
SMPS/Generous (N)	OPEL/Innovative (N)
OPEL/Friendly (I)	SMPS/Dynamic (I)
MRBF/Conventional (N)	MRBF/Joyful (N)
SMPS/Modern (I)	OPEL/Energetic (I)
OPEL/Energetic (N)	SMPS/Modern (N)
ORBF/Joyful (I)	MRBF/Conventional (I)
SMPS/Dynamic (N)	OPEL/Friendly (N)
OPEL/Innovative (I)	SMPS/Generous (I)
MRBF/Classic (N)	MRBF/Conscientious (N)
SMPS/Informed (I)	OPEL/Careful (I)
OPEL/Original (N)	SMPS/Creative (N)
MRBF/Natural (I)	MRBF/Determined (I)
SMPS/Solid (N)	OPEL/Safe (N)

Order Two	Order Four
OPEL/Safe (N)	SMPS/Solid (N)
MRBF/Determined (I)	MRBF/Natural (I)
SMPS/Creative (N)	OPEL/Original (N)
OPEL/Careful (I)	SMPS/Informed (I)
MRBF/Conscientious (N)	MRBF/Classic (N)
SMPS/Generous (I)	OPEL/Innovative (I)
OPEL/Friendly (N)	SMPS/Dynamic (N)
MRBF/Conventional (I)	MRBF/Joyful (I)
SMPS/Modern (N)	OPEL/Energetic (N)
OPEL/Energetic (I)	SMPS/Modern (I)
MRBF/Joyful (N)	MRBF/Conventional (N)
SMPS/Dynamic (I)	OPEL/Friendly (I)
OPEL/Innovative (N)	SMPS/Generous (N)
MRBF/Classic (I)	MRBF/Conscientious (I)
SMPS/Informed (N)	OPEL/Careful (N)
OPEL/Original (I)	SMPS/Creative (I)
MRBF/Natural (N)	MRBF/Determined (N)
SMPS/Solid (I)	OPEL/Safe (I)

Upon completion of these tasks, subjects in the delayed memory condition were asked not to discuss the day's activities with anyone and were told to turn at an assigned time on the following day. The turn times assigned to subjects were determined by their starting time on the first day of the study. Subjects in the immediate memory condition were asked demographic questions, debriefed, asked for secrecy, and dismissed.

2.1.8   Ad Development Pretests

Two pre-test studies were conducted for the purpose of creating test ads that would be appropriate for addressing the issues under consideration. The first of these pretests was used to select brand attributes from the lists developed in the first part the study. The second was used to design ad claims.

2.1.8.1 Attribute Selection. Before the in-salience manipulation could take place, it was necessary to select first from the lists the attributes to be introduced in the copy of the ads. A four-stage pretest process was developed to accomplish this objective. First, each list of brand attributes was divided into three sections according to relevance ratings (1-12, 13-26, 27-40, for OPEL and MRBF; 1-16, 17-32, 33-50, for SMPS). Second, those attributes within brand schemata for which there was a significant difference between brand users and non-users (p < .001) were excluded. Third, only those attributes amongst the remaining, which represented a Big Five dimension of brand personality were considered (cf. Caprara and Barbaranelli 1996; Caprara, Barbaranelli, and Guido 1998b). Finally, amongst the remaining attributes, six attributes per brand were selected (two for each section of relevance ratings, having divided each ranking list into three sections), provided that such attributes were the most comprehensible in an advertising context on the estimation of three experts judges. The attributes selected for ad claims' development (in order of decreasing relevance) were: (1) For the OPEL condition: safe (*sicura*, p = .0076), careful (*attenta*, p = .0163), friendly (*amichevole*, p = .0018), energetic (*energica*, p = .0120), innovative (*innovativa*, p = .2119), and original (*originale*, p = .0090); (2) For the MRBF condition: natural (*naturale*, p = .0020), classic (*classico*, p = .1094), conscientious (*coscienzioso*, p = .0045), determined (*determinato*, p = .0125), joyful (*gioioso*, p = .0016), and conventional (*convenzionale*, p = .0309); (3) For the SMPS condition: modern (*moderno*, p = .5555), dynamic (*dinamico*, p = .3559), informed (*informato*, p = .5349), solid (*solido*, p = .0037), creative (*creativo*, p = .7613), and generous (*generoso*, p = .0085). Figures 6, 7, and 8 (*below*) illustrate the memory models for the three chosen brands. Relevance - that is, the attribute weight - is represented by the (roughly sketched) areas of the circles, whereas the lines separating the circles indicate belonging to a different Big Five dimension (according to Caprara and Barbaranelli 1996; and Caprara, Barbaranelli, and Guido 1998b).[22]

Figure 6. Network Model of Memory for Opel

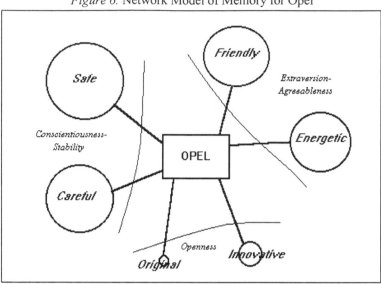

Figure 7. Network Model of Memory for Manetti & Roberts Bath Foam

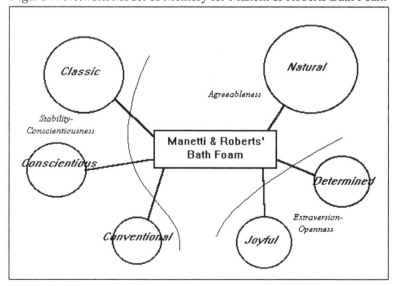

Figure 8. Network Model of Memory for Sip Mobile Phone Service

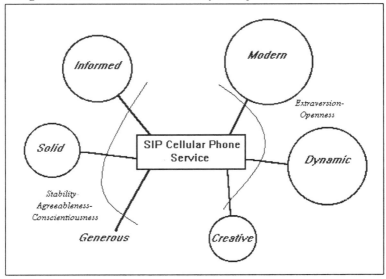

2.1.8.2 Claim Development. One of the most crucial aspects of this study was the development of the claims to be used in the test advertisements. After the previous pre-test study, which resulted in the selection of eighteen attributes, another pretest was designed to actually come up with the copy of the ad claims containing these attributes.

As we previously assumed that the coincidence of stimulus cues and information cues maximizes in-salience effects (see, *above*, Chapter Three, Paragraph 2.1.1), we were looking for a number of in-salient messages (i.e., the information cues to be recalled) incorporating the selected brand attributes (i.e., the stimulus cues). In order to increase the in-salience level of manipulations, we wanted a claim which contained as many different categories of "salience" as possible - considered in literature amongst the first two classes reviewed in Chapter Two. Therefore, we wanted a stimulus claim which was *figural* (i.e., the words of the claim in colored, complex patterns and, in contrast, a black and white picture); *contextually novel* (i.e., the headline isolated from the other elements of the ad); *statistically novel* (i.e., possibly different from everyday advertisements); *unusual* (unexpected, i.e., an apparently disparaging claim; furthermore, with a negative and extreme copy); *physically dominant* (i.e., both for its position and for its frequency - the latter effect being realized through the repetition of the same headline except for the attribute variation); a claim which was seen by subjects from the same vantage point of observation (all in front of a screen).

The ad executional strategy that appeared in our opinion to grant the maximum of simplicity, while pursuing the research objectives, was *advertising resonance*. Resonance is a technique that consists in the development of alternative combinations of wordplay with relevant pictures, which creates ambiguity and incongruity by producing an echo or multiplications of meanings (McQuarrie 1989; McQuarrie and Mick 1992, 1996, 1999; Stafford, Walker, and Balsko 1996; Tom and Eves 1999). As pointed out by Pollay and Mainprize (1984), a wordplay occurs when two or more different meanings coexist in an ad, and the literary surface is modified by a deeper implicit core. In technical terms, advertising resonance presents the consumers with an *incongruous polysemy*. Following Berlyne (1971), incongruous means that the structure of the advertised text deviates from expectations, while polysemy means that certain elements (or "symbolic signs," for semiologists - see Mick 1986) within the ad have been made to convey extra meaning that they would not ordinarily have when standing alone. For resonance to be possible, therefore, the verbal and visual elements have to combine to create extra meaning, and this extra meaning has to depart from normal usage.[23]

McQuarrie and Mick (1992, 1999) used multiple perspectives and methods to investigate advertising resonance.[24] Manipulation of resonance showed positive treatments in three domains: Liking for the ad, brand attitude, and unaided recall of the headlines. For the latter reason, it seemed particularly appropriate for this study.[25]

The relevant picture in our test ads was a simple picture of the branded products. Because inside the test ads there were only the picture and the brand claim (not even, for example, a character, an endorser, other background elements, etc.), it was important that the pictures used in the study were consistent with the copy of the claim. Indeed, the research question for this study was how *message* in-salience (that is, the apparent contextual incongruity between the message and the perceivers' schemata) stimulated recall and not whether there was incongruity between the ad claim and the other elements in the ad (i.e., the picture).

The wordplay was determined by conducting an exploratory pretest, on a group of twenty subjects (none of them employed in the main experiment), regarding different forms of the same claim - each embodying both the brand name and a marker attribute present in perceivers' schemata. In wordplay development, maximum impact was achieved through the use of a "surrealistic" technique, namely *paradox*, which employs intellectual antitheses (see, in particular, the informative review by Homer and Kahle 1986; and, also, Arias-Bolzmann, Chakraborty, and Mowen 2000).[26] The rationale supporting this form of art has not been clearly formulated (Alquie 1965), but basically surrealism has been historically an attempt to break the traditional mold constituting the objective world of science and logic through the use of incongruous stimuli (images and words).

To date, surrealism has been rarely a topic of interest in advertising research and consumer behavior literature. Perhaps, the most closely aligned body of knowledge was in the area of novelty effects. Furthermore, surrealism is only one special case of novelty, far more precise and limited than novelty. For the creation of the claim, we drew inspiration from Magritte's famous surrealist painting named *The Treachery of Image*, more generally known by its caption which says, behind a portrait of a pipe: "This is not a pipe" (*sic*).[27] In the claim development pretest, subjects were given different wording of a claim apparently expressing that a brand (e.g., Ferrari) *did not a have an attribute* (e.g., "it was not fast"), because - as it was stated in smaller letters below the picture - *it was beyond that stage* (e.g., "it was faster"). The latter line served to moderate the incongruity, by proposing a resolution for the mismatching (cf. Meyers-Levy and Tybout 1989).[28] The lines that worked better in the Italian language - in terms of free recall - were found to be those of this template:

"[BRAND NAME] is *not* [ATTRIBUTE]
...It's more than [ATTRIBUTE]."

Test ads were realized through the use of most of the "salience" techniques reviewed in Chapter Two and mentioned at the beginning of this paragraph (namely, figurality, contextual novelty, statistical novelty, unusuality, and physical dominance). Figures 9-10 (*below*) report black-and-white (English) versions of two test ads (i.e., an in-salient and a non-in-salient ad).[29] All the executional cues were the same in both conditions.

2.1.9   Independent Variables

We considered five independent variables: *Message in-salience, ad exposure time, schema activation, time of measurement*, and *relevance level*.

2.1.9.1 Message In-salience (in-salient, non-in-salient). Message in-salience was manipulated as a within group factor. In all the experimental conditions, each subject received both the in-salient and the non-in-salient ad claim manipulation.

In our model, in-salience is a case of incongruity (see review, *above*, Chapter Two, Paragraph 4.3.2). By definition, in-salience is a contextual incongruity between a stimulus and a perceiver's schema. Thus, as in-salience is defined, it is larger than either the principle of figure-ground or that of unusuality, because it explains both salience instances in an *immediate* and in a *larger* context (cf. Fiske and Taylor 1991).

Figure 9. In-salient Test Ad

Opel is NOT friendly

... It's more than friendly.

Figure 10. Non-in-salient Test Ad

Opel is friendly

… It's more than friendly.

Past literature on incongruity, relevant to this study, includes: O'Brien and Meyers (1985), who measured incongruity as the unpredictability of target words presented in paragraphs; Sujan, Bettman, and Sujan (1986), who manipulated incongruity in terms of inconsistent salesperson behaviors; Peltier (1989), who regarded incongruity as the degree to which a character presented in an ad did not match the receiver's expectations for that character; Houston, Childers and Heckler (1987), who measured incongruity as the degree to which pictures did not match the words used in ads - where pictures acted as a prime eliciting the schema that words were found not to match with; and, also, more recently, Lee and Mason 1999; Schmitt, Tavassoli, and Millard 1993; Stafford, Walker, and Blasko 1996.

For the purposes of this study, message in-salience was defined as the degree to which a claim presented in the context of evaluating a print advertisement did not match the perceivers' image for the advertised brand.

2.1.9.2 Ad Exposure Time (five seconds, fifteen seconds, and unlimited). Exposure time levels could be classified into two categories: Experimenter-controlled exposure time (five seconds and fifteen seconds), and viewer-controlled exposure time. The experimenter-controlled exposure time levels used in this study were selected for three reasons. First, they were consistent with the minimum and maximum amount of time allocated in the studies by Houston, Childers, and Heckler (1987) and by Peltier (1989). Direct comparisons of results, therefore, were made possible. Second, the minimum exposure time (five seconds) was in line with minimum values of exposure duration which do not alter motivation, ability, and opportunity to process commercial information (see de Heer and Poiesz 1998): Indeed, exposure duration less than four seconds were shown to impact differently those three variables.[30] Third, exposure times of five seconds and fifteen seconds were far enough apart from each other so as to stimulate significant learning and memory differences. This allowed for the testing of the hypothesis that the memory superiority for in-salient messages over non-in-salient messages decreases as exposure time decreases.

A viewer-controlled exposure time level was selected for inclusion in this study because it allowed for the testing of the hypothesis that in-salient messages stimulate better recall than non-in-salient messages when subjects were permitted for longer viewing time. An "unforced" exposure time factor is especially important for print advertisements in that readers have the locus of control with respect to readership of an ad. Opportunity to process brand information can be greatly enhanced because the message arguments are delivered at a rate conducive to processing them. Chaiken and Eagly (1976), for example, found enhanced comprehension of a difficult message with print versus broadcast media. Likewise, Anand and Sternthal (1990), de Heer and Poiesz (1998), and MacKenzie (1986), demonstrated that consumers pay more attention to brand information if given more time to examine it.

2.1.9.3 Schema Activation (primed, unprimed). We activated through the use of a *prime* the dominating factors among the Big Five which best described the brand personality (that is, the brand image possessed by receivers). In the intentions of the experimenter, this should have increased the recall of the in-salient claims by providing a correct basis of comparison for ad claims.[31] Activation should have increased accessibility of the brand schema, given that such a schema (as elicited by those marker attributes which were part of it) was assumed to be available on average to all subjects.[32]

The primes used to activate brand schemata were constituted by those markers which Caprara and Barbaranelli (1996) and Caprara, Barbaranelli, and Guido (1998b) found to be, through factor analysis, the highest-loading factors from the same lists of attributes developed in Part One of this study (see, *above*, Tables 5-7). Specifically, for the three dimensions of Opel, the markers used as primes were *reliable (affidabile), cheerful (allegra),* and *new (nuova)*; for Manetti & Roberts bath foam were *sober (posato), dynamic (dinamico),* and *soft (morbido).* For Sip mobile phone service were *solid (solido),* and *updated (aggiornato).* All these attributes were found to have the highest saturation values.

Before starting the experimental session, subjects in the "primed" condition were instructed to read the following lines on the cover of their answer booklet: "You are going to see a number of print ads for three branded products: Opel automobiles, Manetti & Roberts bath foam, and Sip mobile phone service. Opel is a brand that is perceived as reliable, cheerful, and new. Manetti & Roberts bath foam is a brand that is perceived as sober, dynamic, and soft. Sip mobile phone service is a brand that is perceived as solid, and updated." Following this introduction, they were shown the slides. Subjects in the "unprimed" condition were shown the slides without any former introduction.

2.1.9.4 Time of Measurement (immediate, delayed). A time-of-measurement variable was necessary to test the proposition that in-salient ad messages would be more memorable than non-in-salient ad messages in both the short term and the long term.

The choice of twenty-four hours as the appropriate time delay was made for a number of reasons. First, past research in information incongruity was examined to see if there were any common decay periods across these studies. Hastie (1980) used retention intervals of five minutes, twenty-four hours, seven days, and fourteen days. Srull (1981) used three minutes and forty-eight hours.[33]

Second, in the retention interval selection process we considered the properties of the dependent measures. Information recall has historically exhibited fairly steep decay curves (e.g., Bahrick 1964; Ebbinghaus 1885; Zielske 1959). Long retention intervals could therefore result in very low absolute recall scores. Added to this equation is the notion that forgetting is inversely related to the number of repetitions (Zielske and Henry 1980; also, Burke and Srull 1988). Few repetitions would therefore suggest rapid memory loss. The above discussion led to eliminate the seven-day and fourteen-day conditions from the list of potential delay periods. The overall rationale for this decision was based on the fact that subjects were not instructed to remember the information given to them; that this information was in printed form; and that subjects were given only one exposure.

Third, the final factor that contributed to the selection on twenty-four hours as the appropriate decay period revolved around current industry practices: A day-after test is the industry norm for measuring recall memory (cf. Guido, G. 1999). While recognition memory tests often use periods of time longer than twenty-four hours, longer delay times would not be appropriate for measuring recall. Forty-eight hours was therefore eliminated.

2.1.9.5 Relevance Level (level one, level two, level three). The level (or rank) of attribute relevance was determined according to the weight of the brand attributes in each brand schema. Attributes belonging to the same relevance level were selected according to their sectional rank in each brand schema, not according to their nominal value. As a matter of fact, schemata for different branded products could not possess the same number of attributes - to the detriment of a nominal value scale. The choice of ranks, on the contrary, could make brand attribute lists of different length comparable. The hypothesis to be tested here implied the assessment of the effects of attribute relevance on memory, where relevance is defined as the weight inside a *specific* brand schema.

2.1.10   Measurement of Dependent Variables

We considered two dependent measures of memory - *top-of-mind recall*, and *free recall* - to assess consumer awareness. Awareness, as mentioned above, was defined as a rudimentary level of brand memory involving, at least, recall of the ad message information. Thus, the distinction between awareness and recall is that the former denotes a state of knowledge possessed by the consumer and the latter a cognitive process resulting from awareness (Hoyer and Brown 1990).

Among the different memory measures reported in literature - considered that in this study the contextual situation (subjects' evaluation of the test ads) implied a high level of task involvement (e.g., Zaichkowsky 1994) -, *recall* was considered a more appropriate measure of awareness than recognition procedures (Singh and Rothschild 1983). Statistical analysis was performed on the results of top-of-mind and free recall. Aided recall and recognition measures of memory information were excluded as dependent variables. In aided recall, subjects receive one or more cues in an attempt to key their retrieval process to specific data pieces stored in memory and associated with that cue. In this study, since the ad message consisted of only two main elements (the brand name and one attribute), we had to take either one element or the other as a retrieval cue. Given the extreme simplicity of the stimulus material, we considered testing aided recall inconsequential.

Recognition measures were also excluded. In recognition processes, target items are provided to the respondents (usually with accompanying distractor items), and subjects must simply determine which items were included as part of the stimulus exposure. Hence, recognition requires only stimulus-based judgments. Although there are apparently conflicting results in the literature in relation to different memory retrieval tasks (cf. Peltier 1989),[34] empirical evidence suggests that recall and recognition scores covary (Singh, Rothschild, and Churchill 1988; Stapel 1998; Zinkhan, Locander, and Leigh 1986). Among the most popular general variants of memory models, both *Strength theory* and various versions of the *Dual-process theory* basically agree on the fact that measures of memory tap on a communal content domain and should covary with one another.[35] At the very least, it can be considered that both recall and recognition procedures were developed to measure facets of the same thing - acquired or learned information - and should covary to a significant extent.[36] In support of covariation among recall and recognition, it has been found that a number of temporal factors related to the stimulus exposure and the exposure-test interval affect recall and recognition performance in a similar way (Singh, Rothschild, and Churchill 1988). On the other hand, organizational properties of the stimulus, or properties that are imposed by the learning task, are known to have a pronounced facilitating effect on recall, but a much weaker effect on recognition. The effect of organization on recognition does, however, become more commensurated with the effect on recall as the exposure-test interval increases (Mandler 1980). In our study, therefore, previous considerations and reasons of simplicity suggested that only recall measures for assessing consumer awareness should be employed. In particular, we used: Top-of-mind and free recall.

2.1.10.1 Top-of-mind Recall. In top-of-mind recall, subjects respond with the first ad message that comes to their mind, without pausing for thought. It was demonstrated by past ARF research on copy validity that, in the area of salience, the highest performance came from this type of measurement (Haley and Baldinger 1991).

2.1.10.2 Free Recall. In free recall (also called "unaided recall"), individuals must generate relevant cues for retrieving target information as well as perform the necessary retrieval tasks from memory. This procedure entails providing only some limited aspect about the context or circumstances in which the initial encoding of the learned information occurred. It corresponded to pure memory-based judgments: Subjects listed as many advertising messages as they could remember.

2.1.11   The Scoring System

The purpose of our study was not strictly to test the memory for the ad *claim* (namely, e.g., "Ferrari is not fast... It's more than fast!"). On the contrary, the purpose of our study was to test the memory for the ad *message* (that is, the meaning of the claim, namely, e.g., "Ferrari is fast"). We thought, indeed, that to a marketer it was the communication of the meaning of the claim, rather than the form (in-salient or non-in-salient), that was important in any marketing promotion (see also, *above*, Note 22).

Consequently, in making the scoring system for the ad message recall we privileged recall of the right meaning of the claim above perfect recall of all the exact words of it. Only two elements of the claim were considered essential for scoring a right answer: First, recall of the brand name and of the attribute name used in a claim; and, second, a right match between the brand name and the attribute used.

Subjects were asked to recall as many ad messages as they could, without pausing to think. A pause was considered a suspension from writing of more than five seconds. Assistants of the experimenter, who were spread among participants, helped to ensure this timing was respected. Subjects pausing for more than five seconds were invited to turn the booklet page. Each recalled message would receive a maximum of two points, for a total possible recall score of thirty-six points for each subject. A maximum of eighteen of these points could be given to the nine in-salient ads and a maximum of eighteen points could be given to the nine non-in-salient ads.

Subjects received two points for writing exactly the right ad claim (i.e., the copy) which they had seen, one point for writing the right ad messages (i.e., brand attributes), and zero points for writing wrong ad claims or ad messages. Ad claims and ad messages were considered wrong: (1) When they were reported in the in-salient form even if they had been showed in the non-in-salient form, or vice versa; (2) When the brand name or the brand attribute name were not correctly reported; (3) When there wasn't a correct match between a brand name and a brand attribute; (4) When claims or messages that were not stated in the ads were reported.

Answers to in-salient message manipulations were counted separately from answers to non-in-salient message manipulations. For a correct definition of the constructs, the results for top-of-mind recall were incorporated in the results for free recall (i.e., results for top-of-mind recall were counted first separately, then as a part of free recall results), so that the former construct was considered as a timing specification of the latter one.

3. RESULTS

The hypotheses developed in Section One suggested that the use of an in-salient copy in print advertisements would result in a longer processing of the claims. It was predicted that this longer processing effort would result in higher (top-of-mind and unaided) recall for the messages contained in those ads. It was further hypothesized that this memory superiority would hold after a priming and over time, and that this memory superiority would decrease as exposure time decreases. Finally, it was predicted that, in reference to more relevant elements of a schema, memory effects of in-salient messages would be higher. Section Two discussed the method of the experiment that was designed to test these hypotheses. This section will present the results of this experiment, as follows: First, the success of the message in-salience manipulation will be examined; second, results for the experiment will be presented in two related studies, given the fractional-factorial design of this research. Tables containing summated recall scores, analysis of variance, and in-salience X independent variables interaction and simple effects will be also included.

3.1   Manipulation Check

One of the most important factors of this study is the degree to which message in-salience was properly manipulated. The results obtained would have been meaningless without showing support for the assumption that an in-salient ad copy was significantly different from a non-in-salient one.

In itself, the ad development process described in *Part Two* (*above*) increased our confidence that the in-salience manipulation would be successful. While these pretests increased the probability that in-salient and non-in-salient claims would be viewed as such by receivers, it was still necessary to conduct a manipulation check to further substantiate whether in-salience manipulations were indeed successful for subjects in the main experiment. This manipulation check was conducted on forty-eight subjects (eight randomly selected subjects for each experimental condition) after they finished the dependent measures booklet. To check in-salience, subjects evaluated only *the first part of each ad claim* (e.g., "Opel is not safe," or "Opel is safe"), by assessing the contextual incongruity between the partial ad messages and their brand schemata. In-salient messages had mean scores approaching one on a five-point Likert scale, with one being very incongruent, and non-in-salient messages had mean scores near five, with five being very congruent.

Table 10 shows the findings for this manipulation check. A paired t-test of means shows that in all cases the in-salient and the non-in-salient messages were significantly different from each other (p < .001 for all comparisons). It is apparent from these results that the message in-salience manipulations were successfully implemented.

Table 10. Manipulation Check: Ad Message In-salience Scores (t-Test of Means)

Attribute Claim	Manipulation	Mean	Std Dev.	d.f.	t	p
OPEL/Safe	In-salient	1.98	3.17	47	5.20	p<.001
	Non-in-salient	4.39	.87			
OPEL/Careful	In-salient	1.92	.68	47	12.71	p<.001
	Non-in-salient	3.78	.83			
OPEL/Friendly	In-salient	1.98	.74	47	9.07	p<.001
	Non-in-salient	3.46	.76			
OPEL/Energetic	In-salient	1.87	.73	47	14.86	p<.001
	Non-in-salient	4.29	.82			
OPEL/Innovative	In-salient	2.14	2.85	47	4.81	p<.001
	Non-in-salient	4.22	.72			
OPEL/Original	In-salient	2.08	.87	47	6.29	p<.001
	Non-in-salient	3.60	.96			
MRBF/Natural	In-salient	1.64	.67	47	16.59	p<.001
	Non-in-salient	4.21	.68			
MRBF/Classic	In-salient	2.37	.67	47	7.63	p<.001
	Non-in-salient	3.60	.70			
MRBF/onscientious	In-salient	2.02	.56	47	10.65	p<.001
	Non-in-salient	3.54	.74			
MRBF/Determined	In-salient	2.00	.71	47	6.59	p<.001
	Non-in-salient	3.00	.71			
MRBF/Joyful	In-salient	2.12	.73	47	10.18	p<.001
	Non-in-salient	3.92	.71			
MRBF/Conventional	In-salient	2.50	.68	47	6.16	p<.001
	Non-in-salient	3.58	.68			
SMPS/Modern	In-salient	1.50	.55	47	21.89	p<.001
	Non-in-salient	4.52	.68			
SMPS/Dynamic	In-salient	1.87	.57	47	15.72	p<.001
	Non-in-salient	4.00	.46			
SMPS/Informed	In-salient	1.64	.73	47	14.81	p<.001
	Non-in-salient	4.46	.71			
SMPS/Solid	In-salient	2.10	.63	47	8.01	p<.001
	Non-in-salient	3.35	.69			
SMPS/Creative	In-salient	1.96	.71	47	7.96	p<.001
	Non-in-salient	3.23	.80			
SMPS/Generous	In-salient	2.23	.72	47	6.43	p<.001
	Non-in-salient	3.33	.78			

3.2 Data Analysis

As stated above, the entire study was a 2 (message in-salience) X 3 (ad exposure time) X 2 (schema activation) X 2 (time of measurement) X 3 (relevance level) within group fractional factorial design. Message in-salience, time of measurement, and relevance level were the within group factors, while time of measurement and relevance level were the fractional factorial factors. Because of the different levels of inquiry contained in the study and its fractional factorial design, data analysis was conducted in two separate studies. Study One examined the relationship between message in-salience, exposure time, priming, and memory, and it was analyzed in a 2 (message in-salience) X 3 (ad exposure time) X 2 (schema activation) factorial design. Study Two addressed the relationship between message in-salience, memory decay periods, schema activation, levels of attribute relevance, and memory, and it was analyzed in a 2 (message in-salience) X 2 (time of measurement) X 2 (schema activation) X 3 (relevance levels) factorial design. A total of 240 subjects (40 per cell) participated in the study.[37]

3.2.1 *Study One:* The Roles of In-Salience, Ad Exposure Time, and Schema Activation

Study One examined the relationship between message in-salience, exposure time, priming and memory. It was a 2 (message in-salience) X 3 (exposure time) X 2 (schema activation) factorial design, where message in-salience was the within-group factor, whereas ad exposure time and schema activation were the between-group factors.

H1 predicted a memory advantage of in-salient messages over non-in-salient messages. In determining recall memory for in-salient ad messages and non-in-salient ad messages, a summated in-salient memory score (nine ads) and a summated non-in-salient memory score (nine ads) were calculated for each of the ad messages, for each of the subjects. The same procedure was repeated for top-of-mind and for free recalls (free recall results being *inclusive* of top-of-mind recall results).

Table 11 (*below*) contains summated recall scores for the hypothesis H1 (recall as a function of in-salience). As it can be seen from this table, significant main effects across exposure time were found for ad message top-of-mind recall (mean in-salient = 7.12; mean non-in-salient = 2.74) and free recall (mean in-salient = 7.69; mean non-in-salient = 3.10). Stimuli recall as a function of in-salience (H1) was supported for both top-of-mind recall (in parentheses) and, in general, for free recall.

Table 11. Means across Ad Exposure Time and Schema Activation: Summated
          Recall Scores

Ad Exposure Time	Priming	Immediate Recall		Marginals
		In-salient Ads	Non-in-salient Ads	
5 Seconds	Unprimed	(4.65)	(1.08)	(2.86)
		5.02	1.12	3.07
	Primed	(3.52)	(1.58)	(2.55)
		3.78	1.60	2.69
15 Seconds	Unprimed	(7.55)	(2.60)	(5.07)
		8.48	2.66	5.57
	Primed	(8.58)	(3.40)	(5.99)
		9.32	3.99	6.65
Unlimited	Unprimed	(8.86)	(4.51)	(6.68)
		10.11	5.07	7.59
	Primed	(9.57)	(3.26)	(6.41)
		11.08	4.17	7.62
Marginals		(7.12)	(2.74)	(Overall = 4.93)
		7.69	3.10	Overall = 5.53

Note. Top-of-mind recall is indicated in parentheses.

H2*a* predicted an interaction effect between ad exposure time and recall memory. Support for this hypothesis would be achieved by obtaining a significant in-salience X ad exposure time interaction, with higher levels of exposure time (unlimited and fifteen seconds) favoring in-salient ad messages, and lower levels of exposure time (five seconds) resulting in no advantage or favoring for non-in-salient ad messages.

Analogously, H3 predicted an interaction effect between activation of the brand schema and recall memory. Support for this hypothesis would be achieved by obtaining an increased recall for the in-salience X schema activation, with activation of brand schema favoring in-salient ad messages, and no activation resulting in no memory advantage. The favoring of non-in-salient ad messages in the latter case should be excluded because of the experimental use of brand attributes which were common to both users' and non-users' brand schemata (as measured in *Part One*'s attribute lists).

Results of the repeated measures analysis of variance, testing the in-salience X schema activation X ad exposure time interaction, are presented in Table 12 (top-of-mind recall) and Table 13 (free recall). These results show a significant exposure time interaction for ad message top-of-mind recall (F = 15.41, d.f. = 2,234, p < .001) and also for ad message free recall (F = 23.73, d.f. = 2,234, p < .001). To help determine the statistical pattern of this interaction, an analysis of simple effects was undertaken and it was found consistent with *a priori* expectations.

Table 12. Study One: Repeated Measures ANOVA - Top-of-Mind Recall

	M.S.	d.f.	F	p	η^2
In-salience	2310.02	1,234	445.03	.000	.655
Exposure	632.86	2,234	121.96	.000	.510
Activation	1.52	1,234	.29	.589	.001
Exposure X Activation	19.22	2,234	3.70	.026	.031
Exposure X In-salience	79.98	2,234	15.41	.000	.116
Activation X In-salience	1.10	1,234	.21	.645	.001
Expos. X Activ. X In-sal.	32.41	2,234	6.24	.002	.051

Note. *n* = 240.

Table 13. Study One: Repeated Measures ANOVA - Free Recall

	M.S.	d.f.	F	p	η^2
In-salience	2827.55	1,234	658.59	.000	.738
Exposure	935.93	2,234	200.36	.000	.631
Activation	7.75	1,234	1.66	.199	.007
Exposure X Activation	23.16	2,234	4.96	.008	.041
Exposure X In-salience	101.88	2,234	23.73	.000	.169
Activation X In-salience	.35	1,234	.08	.775	.000
Expos. X Activ. X In-sal.	33.10	2,234	7.71	.001	.062

Note. *n* = 240.

Table 14 provides a pictorial representation along with calculations of simple effects for each of the exposure time levels in top-of-mind recall. Significant simple effects consistent with *a priori* expectations were found under five seconds of exposure time (mean in-salient = 4.09, mean non-in-salient = 1.32, F = 149.56, d.f. =1,79, p < .001), fifteen seconds of exposure time (mean in-salient = 8.06, mean non-in-salient = 3.00, F = 183.09, d.f. = 1,79, p < .001), and unlimited exposure time (mean in-salient = 9.21, mean non-in-salient = 3.88, F = 132.99, d.f. = 1,79, p < .001). Although, in the latter case, the effect was proportionally weaker than that for the other two conditions, simple main effects significantly favored top-of-mind recall of in-salient ad messages. Also free recall of in-salient ad messages was favored (see Table 15) and simple effects resulted strongly correlated with top-of-mind recall simple effects: Under five seconds of exposure time (mean in-salient = 4.39, mean non-in-salient = 1.36, F = 158.03, d.f. = 1,79, p < .001); fifteen seconds of exposure time (mean in-salient = 8.90, mean non-in-salient = 3.33, F = 237.36, d.f. = 1,79, p < .001); and unlimited exposure time (mean in-salient = 10.59, mean non-in-salient = 4.62, F = 236.79, d.f. = 1,79, p < .001). Therefore, H2a was supported.

Table 14. Top-of-Mind Recall: In-salience X Ad Exposure Time Interaction and Simple Effects

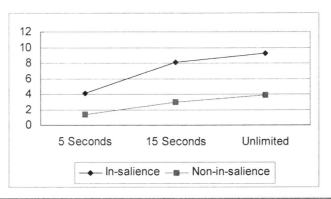

	Mean In-sal.	S.D.	Mean Non-in-sal.	S.D.	d.f.	F	p
5 Seconds	4.09	1.77	1.32	.95	1,79	149.56	.000
15 Seconds	8.06	2.54	3.00	2.29	1,79	183.09	.000
Unlimited	9.21	3.02	3.88	2.69	1,79	132.99	.000

On the contrary, it was not possible to support - in this experiment - H3 related to schema activation. The kind of priming used in immediate memory manipulations did not provide significant main effects for top-of-mind and free recall. The partial *eta*-squared statistic (η^2), used to describe the proportion of total variability explained by the grouping or factor variable, indicates - with its values next to zero - that schema activation explained very little of the total variability. As it results from Tables 12 and 13 (*above*), also tests for schema activation X message in-salience interaction were not significant. Tables 16 and 17 (see *next* page) show, despite these weak interactions, a memory advantage for primed ad messages over unprimed. It is most probable that this advantage was weak due to the kind of prime used in the experimental conditions of schema activation which could have generated a part-list cuing effect (see, *below*, Paragraph 4.1.3). In conclusion, however, these results did not support H3.

Table 15. Free Recall: In-salience X Ad Exposure Time Interaction and Simple Effects

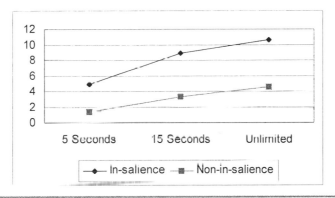

	Mean In-sal.	S.D.	Mean Non-in-sal.	S.D.	d.f.	F	p
5 Seconds	4.39	1.84	1.36	.96	1,79	158.03	.000
15 Seconds	8.90	2.37	3.33	2.30	1,79	237.36	.000
Unlimited	10.59	2.21	4.62	2.82	1,79	236.79	.000

Gianluigi Guido

Table 16. Top-of-Mind Recall: In-salience X Schema Activation Interaction and Simple Effects

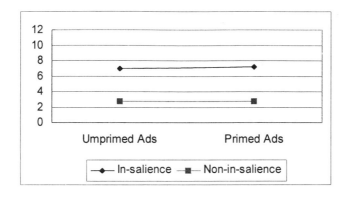

	Mean In-sal.	S.D.	Mean Non-in-sal.	S.D.	d.f.	F	p
Unprimed	7.02	3.10	2.73	2.73	1,119	185.64	.000
Primed	7.23	3.53	2.74	1.92	1,119	196.33	.000

Table 17. Free Recall: In-salience X Schema Activation Interaction and Simple Effects

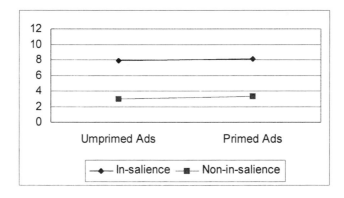

	Mean In-sal.	S.D.	Mean Non-in-sal.	S.D.	d.f.	F	p
Unprimed	7.86	3.02	2.95	2.70	1,119	318.55	.000
Primed	8.06	3.73	3.26	2.39	1,119	223.94	.000

3.2.2   *Study Two:* **The Role of Memory Decay and Relevance**

Study Two examined the relationship between message in-salience, memory decay, schema activation, relevance levels, and memory. It was a 2 (message in-salience) X 2 (time of measurement) X 2 (schema activation) X 3 (relevance levels) factorial design. Message in-salience, time of measurement, and relevance levels were the within group factors, whereas schema activation was the between group factor.

Analysis of the roles of memory decay and relevance was restricted to subjects in the unlimited exposure time condition (n = 80), as our experimental interests did not include an examination of ad memory over time under "forced" exposure time conditions (i.e., five or fifteen seconds). Tables 18 and 19 (*below*) show results of repeated measures analysis of variance for both top-of-mind and free recall.

Table 18. Study Two: Repeated Measures ANOVA - Top-of-Mind Recall

	F	d.f.	p	η^2
In-salience	210.61	1,78	.000	.730
Time of Measurement	359.98	1,78	.000	.822
Activation	.88	1,78	.350	.011
Relevance	127.23	2,156	.000	.620
In-salience X Time of Meas.	61.75	1,78	.000	.442
In-salience X Activation	12.74	1,78	.001	.140
In-salience X Relevance	99.40	2,156	.000	.560
T. of Meas. X Activation	.03	1,78	.863	.000
Time of Meas. X Relevance	52.50	2,156	.000	.402
Activation X Relevance	.25	2,156	.781	.003
In-sal. X T. of Meas. X Activ.	.31	1,78	.580	.004
In-sal. X T. of Meas. X Relev.	46.35	2,156	.000	.373
In-sal. X Activ. X Relev.	2.97	2,156	.054	.037
T. of Meas. X Activ. X Relev.	1.35	2,156	.263	.017
In-sal. X T. of Meas. X Activ. X Relev.	1.30	2,156	.276	.016

Note. n = 80.

As hypothesized by H2*b*, main effects of in-salience and time of measurement were extremely significant both for top-of-mind (F = 210.61, d.f. = 1,78, p < .001, η^2 = .730; and F = 359.98, d.f. = 1,78, p < .001, η^2 = .822) and free recall (F = 236.76, d.f. = 1,78, p < .001, η^2 = .752; and F = 424.10, d.f. = 1,78, p < .001, η^2 = .845). Memory decay favored in-salient messages over non-in-salient messages both in the immediate and in the delayed condition (after a 24-hour delay).

Table 19. Study Two: Repeated Measures ANOVA - Free Recall

	F	d.f.	*p*	η^2
In-salience	236.76	1,78	000	.752
Time of Measurement	424.10	1,78	.000	.845
Activation	.39	1,78	.533	.005
Relevance	174.56	2,156	.000	.691
In-salience X Time of Meas.	74.21	1,78	.000	.487
In-salience X Activation	10.90	1,78	.001	.122
In-salience X Relevance	109.14	2,156	.000	.583
Time of Meas. X Activation	.17	1,78	.681	.002
Time of Meas. X Relevance	63.76	2,156	.000	.450
Activation X Relevance	.30	2,156	.742	.004
In-sal. X T. of M. X Activ.	.25	1,78	.622	.003
In-sal. X T. of M. X Relev.	56.72	2,156	.000	.421
In-sal. X Activ. X Relev.	2.59	2,156	.078	.032
T. of M. X Activ. X Relev.	1.49	2,156	.228	.019
In-sal. X T. of Meas. X Activ. X Relev.	1.29	2,156	.277	.016

Note. *n* = 80.

Tables 18 and 19 also contain significant in-salience X time of measurement interactions (F = 61.75, d.f. 1,78, p < .001; and F = 74.21, d.f. = 1,78, and p < .001). These interactions are diagrammed in Tables 20 and 21 (*below*) along with a calculation of simple effects for the immediate and delayed conditions. These results supported our hypothesis. Both top-of-mind and free recall were significantly high for in-salient ad messages in the immediate condition (top-of-mind recall: mean in-salient = 9.21, mean non-in-salient = 3.88, F = 132.99, p < .001; free recall: mean in-salient = 10.59, mean non-in-salient = 4.62, F = 236.79, p < .001), and also in the delayed condition in-salient ad messages had a higher recall score than did non-in-salient ad messages (top-of-mind recall: mean in-salient = 2.58, mean non-in-salient = .95, F = 23.03, p < .001; free recall: mean in-salient = 2.80, mean non-in-salient = 1.19, F = 23.44, p < .001). Therefore, H2b was supported.

In line with results of Study One, priming effects were not significant. On the contrary, results strongly supported H4, which forecasted an interactive effect between attribute relevance levels used in in-salient ad messages and memory recall. Results of the repeated measures ANOVA showed a clear relevance level interaction for ad message memory for both top-of-mind (F = 99.40, d.f. = 2,156, p < .001) and free recall (F = 109.14, d.f. = 2,156, p < .001). This significant effect was also evident under delayed memory conditions.

To help determine the statistical pattern of this three way interaction, an analysis of simple effects for each of the three relevance levels was carried out for free recall considering, first, in-salience X relevance level interactions under immediate memory conditions (Table 22, *below*), and, second, in-salience X relevance level interactions under delayed memory conditions (Table 23, *below*). Significant simple effects consistent with *a priori* expectations were found under the first two levels of attribute relevance. Irrelevant messages (3rd relevance level) were the least recalled, whether they were in-salient or non-in-salient.[38] Therefore, by reducing the relevance level, it was possible to dissolve the memory advantage of in-salient messages; whereas, in general, as hypothesized, recall for non-in-salient messages was independent from relevance. In conclusion, H4 was strongly supported.

Table 20. Top-of-Mind Recall: In-salience X Time of Measurement Interaction and Simple Effects

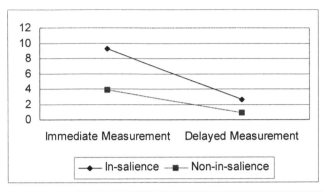

	Mean In-sal.	S.D.	Mean Non-in-sal.	S.D.	d.f.	F	p
Immediate Measurement	9.21	3.02	3.88	2.69	1,79	132.99	.000
Delayed Measurement	2.58	2.48	.95	1.51	1,79	23.03	.000

Table 21. Free Recall: In-salience X Time of Measurement Interaction and Simple Effects

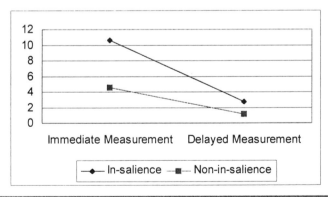

	Mean In-sal.	S.D.	Mean Non-in-sal.	S.D.	d.f.	F	p
Immediate Measurement	10.59	2.21	4.62	2.82	1,79	236.79	.000
Delayed Measurement	2.80	2.45	1.19	1.53	1,79	23.44	.000

Table 22. Free Recall: In-salience X Relevance Level Interaction and Simple Effects under Immediate Memory Conditions

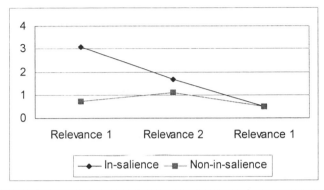

	Mean In-sal.	S.D.	Mean Non-in-sal.	S.D.	d.f.	F	p
Relevance 1	3.10	1.05	.74	.56	1,79	268.27	.000
Relevance 2	1.68	.87	1.09	.79	1,79	21.21	.000
Relevance 3	.51	.63	.49	.56	1,79	.07	.79

Table 23. Free Recall: In-salience X Relevance Level Interaction and Simple Effects under Delayed Memory Conditions

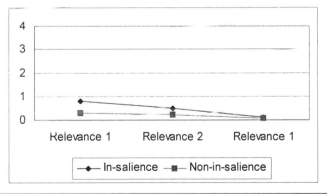

	Mean In-sal.	S.D.	Mean Non-in-sal.	S.D.	d.f.	F	p
Relevance 1	.81	.72	.30	.40	1,79	37.74	.000
Relevance 2	.48	.52	.21	.32	1,79	16.03	.000
Relevance 3	.11	.24	.09	.19	1,79	.50	.48

4. DISCUSSION

Results of the two studies empirically confirmed the main propositions of the theory of in-salience. All hypotheses were supported, with the only exception of schema activation that was found here statistically non-significant. Factors such as ad exposure time, memory decay, and relevance played a major role in the occurrence of in-salience. Consumer awareness as a consequence of in-salience was demonstrated by both top-of-mind and free recall measures.

The purpose of the current section is to integrate findings of the two studies regarding the four experimental levels addressed in Section One (*above*) into an overall discussion of the in-salience theory in an advertising setting. This would consider how ad-message in-salience influences consumers' processing and memory, and how this can help marketers and advertisers to develop ad campaign that maximize consumer awareness for their brands. The key issue in this discussion is awareness and how it is moderated by the use of different measures of memory (top-of-mind and free recall), ad exposure time, memory decay, schema activation, and relevance levels.

This section is structured in the following fashion. In the general discussion, we shall incorporate into the analysis the moderating effects of the different memory tests, levels of ad exposure time, measurement time, schema activation, and attribute relevance. Secondly, we shall discuss both theoretical and pragmatic implications of applying the in-salience theory in an advertising setting. Thirdly, we shall consider two general areas of potential limitations, i.e. threats to the internal and to the external validity of the study. Finally, we shall assess three useful areas of future research regarding, respectively, involvement and media effects, advertisement complexity, and attitudes and persuasion.

4.1   General Discussion

Prior to discussing results generated from our experiment, it may be useful to briefly review the research objectives we set. They were designed to address four main theoretical propositions advanced by the in-salience theory. As many experimental levels were considered: (a) Demonstrating that in-salient messages are better recalled than non-in-salient ones; (b) Showing that in-salience affects both the attention and the interpretation stage of an information processing model; (c) Examining how the activation of a schema affects the occurrence of in-salience; (d) Determining the role of relevance of certain schema elements (i.e., attributes) on the perceived impact of in-salient stimuli.

4.1.1   Experimental Level One

As hypothesized in H1 - linked with Proposition One of our model - by using the same attention-getting devices (same figure, same position, same patterns, etc.) in two types of ads which differed only in the use of a semantic device - i.e., resonance (Mick and McQuarrie 1992, 1999) -, ad message memory was increased with progression of ad exposure time. Because both in-salient ad messages and non-in-salient ad messages were "salient" according to the past definitions of the construct - because of figurality, physical dominance, etc. (e.g., Fiske and Taylor 1991) - the only difference which justifies the outstanding memory advantage for in-salient ad message is the presence of resonance, that is an in-salient device able to create a contextual incongruity between the stimulus and the perceivers' schemata for those brands.

Results confirming H1 are much more convincing when considering the task difficulty effect. Asking subjects to free recall claim information, for which they had seen only once, *without being aware* since the beginning that they had to recall those claims, created a testing situation where high memory scores could be very difficult to obtain.[39] The difficulty of the encoding and retrieval tasks played a tremendous role in shaping results. If we had considered only one brand - rather than three different brands - it would have been much easier for subjects to associate each attribute to the brand, thus avoiding overlapping of schema attributes (which were also found). In addition, thought time - which could occur even after an ad is no longer visually available - was limited here by the fact that subjects were continually confronted with other visual stimuli (i.e., other ads). In spite of this experimental complexity, results of both top-of-mind and free recall provided strong support for the incongruent nature of in-salient ad messages.

4.1.2   Experimental Level Two

In a perception model based on stages, the memory advantage of in-salient stimuli over non-in-salient ones can be explained by the fact that the in-salience effect on memory occurs not merely as a result of sensing a stimulus and assigning it to its contextually relevant place inside a perceiver's schema - which is a matter of attention -, but rather by the perceiver's experiencing an incongruity between such stimulus and its contextually activated schema - which is a matter of interpretation (as postulated by Proposition Two). In-salience, therefore, is the result of an increased processing effort caused by a contextual incongruity between a stimulus and a perceiver's schema. The *In-salience hypothesis* implicates that, when a consumer is not involved in a stimulus, *only a contextual incongruity between such stimulus and a perceiver's schema* can produce a significant effect on the perceiver's memory. A consistent finding across our studies showed that any stimulus which was in-salient was better recalled than a non-in-salient stimulus (i.e., a stimulus which was contextually congruent with the perceiver's schema).

This finding is consistent with previous results in social cognition research that found higher recall for incongruent stimuli than for congruent stimuli (e.g., Bodenhausen and Wyer 1985; Hastie 1980; Hastie and Kumar 1979; Srull 1981; and Wyer, Bodenhausen, and Gordon 1984). In explaining why in-salient messages were more recallable than non-in-salient ones, the *Depth of processing argument* (Anderson and Bower 1973; Craik and Lockhart 1972; and Lockhart, Craik, and Jacoby 1976) - as well as Hastie's (1980) *Associative storage and retrieval model* - could provide theoretical support. In-salient ad messages should have been more difficult to comprehend than non-in-salient ad messages were. Subjects should, therefore, have spent additional time processing in-salient ad messages as a tool for explaining this information acquisition dilemma. An increased processing effort suggests a longer period for that stimulus in working memory, leading to a wider and deeper memory network for that stimulus. More specifically, as the depth of processing increases, so does the subsequent probability for long-term retention. It would seem that ad messages were more memorable because of this increased processing effort devoted to them (Forehand and Keller 1996).

In relation to our results, this argument seems a more convincing explanation than a recall superiority for in-salient ad messages based on the *Perceptual distinctiveness of processing* (Eysenck 1979; Eysenck and Eysenck 1980), which would consider in-salient messages more retrievable by virtue of their unexpected nature that makes them more perceptually distinct than non-in-salient messages. The latter explanation is more valuable *irrespective* of exposure time (Craik and Lockhart 1972; Hastie and Kumar 1979; Lockhart, Craik, and Jacoby 1976), for both long-term memory traces (Eysenck 1979), and when memory traces do not closely resemble a number of other memory traces (Eysenck and Eysenck 1980); yet, it does not seem the case of our Study One. Results of our study clearly showed that the longer the exposure/processing time was, the higher recall of in-salient messages was. The memory advantage was found to increase with ad exposure time; it was observed immediately after subjects had seen the messages, and for stimuli which were repeated by virtue of their presentation order. *Depth of processing theory*, therefore, seems a better explanation than encoding distinctiveness under the conditions of Study One.[40]

As hypothesized in H2*a*, the recall superiority for in-salient ad messages increased with increased amounts of ad exposure time. This was substantiated in Study One by the significant effects found for in-salience (top-of-mind recall η^2 = .655; free recall η^2 = .738), exposure (top-of-mind recall η^2 = .510; free recall η^2 = .631), and exposure X in-salience (top-of-mind recall η^2 = .116; free recall η^2 = .169). These results are theoretically consistent with the depth of processing model discussed above. For a deeper memory network to occur for a particular in-salient stimulus, the longer the amount of exposure/thought time allocated to that stimulus is, the better recall is.

It was further predicted (H2b) that the recall superiority for in-salient ad messages would remain even after a twenty-four hour testing delay. This hypothesis was supported in Study One and corroborates other studies that also found that incongruent information was more memorable over time (Bellezza and Cheney 1973; Hastie 1980; Peltier 1989; Srull 1981). Time of measurement (together with in-salience) resulted strongly significant in explaining the total variability of the sample (top-of-mind recall η^2 = .836; free recall η^2 = .883). Anderson and Bower's (1973) *Human associative memory (HAM) model* can be used here to explain why this in-salient ad message recall advantage was still present after the one-day delay. Specifically, this model maintains that information in memory decays at a constant rate. If two pieces of information have a near identical pattern of associative pathways linking it to other cognitive elements in memory, memory for this information will fade at a similar pace. Therefore, since an in-salient ad message has a larger number of associative linkages attached to it, this should result in such an ad message being more memorable over time than a non-in-salient one.[41]

To summarize, two possible explanations were preferred in interpreting the recall superiority for in-salient ad messages for longer periods of exposure time and after a delay. First, since in-salient ad messages are more puzzling than non-in-salient ones, they require additional exposure time in an attempt to explain the information acquisition dilemma. This deeper processing, in turn, improves recall of in-salient ad messages. Second, because of the principle that information in memory fades at a constant rate, the recall advantage of in-salient ad messages remaines even after a twenty-four hour delay.

4.1.3   Experimental Level Three

Another research question - linked to Proposition Three of our model - regarded the impact of the activation of schemata on memory for an in-salient stimulus. It was hypothesized (H3) that the activation of an appropriate brand schema would have increased the advantage of in-salient ad messages over non-in-salient ones. Although this advantage was not statistically significant, results showed a slight prevalence of average recall for primed ads.

We believe that this statistical failure to give proof of the benefits of schema activation was due to the unfortunate choice of the prime used in the experiment. As mentioned above, the prime was set to be a disclosed statement containing those marker attributes which were found the best descriptors of each dimension of brand personality (Caprara and Barbaranelli 1996; Caprara, Barbaranelli, and Guido 1998b). Such attributes provided the highest saturation values in the factor analysis of all the attributes presented in the attribute lists (see, *above*, Tables 5-7).

Unfortunately, those markers were very similar to the attributes presented in the copy messages, so that they could have triggered a *part-list cuing effect* (cf., *above*, Chapter Two, Paragraph 5.2.1 on *The inhibition effect on memory*), hindering the effect of activation. This interpretation is supported by the fact that, in the lowest exposure time condition (five seconds), subjects recalled more attributes when they were unprimed (top-of-mind recall: mean in-salient = 4.65, mean non-in-salient = 1.08; free recall: mean in-salient = 5.02, mean non-in-salient = 1.12) than when they were primed (top-of-mind recall: mean in-salient = 3.52, mean non-in-salient = 1.58; free recall: mean in-salient = 3.78, mean non-in-salient = 1.60). Subjects, indeed, were found to mistakenly recall in primed ads those attributes used in the priming to elicit the activation of their brand schemata. A high percentage of answers had to be discarded because subjects recalled the attributes used in the prime as if they were showed in the copy of the ads.

Part list cuing effect is one of the most popular cases of retrieval block (see, for a review, Roediger and Neely 1982). Slamecka (1968, 1969) introduced part-list cuing effects in recall. In his paradigm, subjects studied a list of words and were then given part of the list and told to use these terms as cues to recall the remainder of the list. Free recall subjects compared recall of the target words (those not used as cues) to recall of the same words. The general finding was that under a wide variety of conditions the part-list cues impede recall, so that a word used to elicit recall of other items in its logic category hinders rather than facilitates recall of other words in the same category. As mentioned above, also in consumer literature, inhibition phenomena - such as part-list cuing - have been demonstrated with marketing stimuli, e.g. brand names (Alba and Chattopadhyay 1985, 1986). Priming (by prior selective attention in judgment and choice tasks) and framing (by varying current task goals) have been shown to influence information recall, and brand attitudes (Loken and Hoverstad 1985), as well as choice (Cohen and Chakravarti 1990).[42] Although three main theories have been advanced to explain the part-list cuing decrement - Watkins' (1975) *Cue overload approach*; Rundus' (1973) *Sampling-with-replacement model*; and Raaijmakers and Shiffrin's (1981) *Search of associative memory model*) -, the most parsimonious conclusion seems to be that the effect should be explained by properties of the retrieval system, with the encoding and storage assumptions made being relatively unimportant.

To summarize, we were not able to demonstrate statistically that the activation of a brand schema can substantially improve the in-salience effect on memory, because - with our priming manipulation - we probably run into a classic case of part-list cuing effect. Brand attributes used in the prime to cue the dimensions of brand personalities partially hindered recall of similar attributes used in ad messages. Future research should examine less intrusive modalities for priming brand schema activations (e.g., presentation of pictures, direct sampling, etc.), thus providing statistical evidence for this hypothesis.

4.1.4   Experimental Level Four

The final research question in this study - based on Proposition Four of our model - regarded the role of schema elements, namely brand attributes, in the significance of the memory advantage of in-salient ad messages over non-in-salient ad messages. It was postulated (H4) that, when an attribute is more relevant inside a brand schema, an in-salient message based on that attribute would be more fully recalled than another in-salient message based on another, less relevant attribute of the same brand schema. This should not happen for non-in-salient ad messages, as their recall would be independent from the relevance of the attributes on which they are based.

Results obtained in the experiment strongly supported this hypothesis. Relevance, together with in-salience, was a significant factor in explaining the memory advantage of ad message, even after a 24-hour delay. Considering three different levels of relevance, this effect is much more evident with the first level, which explains 58% of the total immediate recall of in-salient ad messages; while the second explains 32%, and the third explains a remaining 10%. These findings were doubled by particularly similar results on the delayed recall side (respectively, 58%, 34%, and 8%). On the contrary - as hypothesized - non-in-salient ad messages did not show a similar distribution. When used for non-in-salient claims, the same brand attributes were not recalled according to their assessed relevance. On average, the immediate recall for the three levels accounted for, respectively, 32%, 45%, and 22% of the total; and the delayed recall for, respectively, 48%, 35%, and 17% of the total. It is evident that the recall distribution for in-salient ad messages was proportional - in a decreasing fashion - to the relevance levels of the attributes used, whereas the recall distribution for the non-in-salient ad messages was much flatter and less dependent on relevance. These results can have important implications for marketers in their choice of ad formats where using brand attributes. Counterintuitively, our findings suggest that, if marketers want to associate more strongly an attribute to the brand and make their messages more memorable, they have to use an in-salient - apparently negative - claim in relation to the most relevant brand attributes.

From the analysis of simple effects (Tables 22-23, *above*), it is clear that those attributes in the last relevance level (namely, *innovative* and *original* for OPEL; *joyful* and *conventional* for MRBF; and *creative* and *generous* for SMPS) were less recalled both in the in-salient and in the non-in-salient conditions. As they were chosen among the last items in the attribute lists (see, *above*, Tables 5-7), they showed to be irrelevant in describing brand personalities. The Big-five model of personality, which was used for defining brand schemata possessed by perceivers, supplied only a limited number of attributes which could be hypothetically relevant for both social and marketing stimuli (that is, persons and brands). It is not surprising that those attributes which could be more strongly referred to the peculiar nature of the branded products were the most frequently recalled (*safe* for the car; *natural* for the bath foam; and *modern* for the phone service), rather than those which could be more strongly referred to aspects of the human personality. As a matter of fact, the attribute *solid*, which was employed as a stimulus for SMPS (but is commonly used to define the quality of a car), was very often erroneously referred to by subjects in their answers as if they had seen it in the OPEL ads.

Most probably, if we had chosen the attributes to be used in the experimental conditions among the non-big-five attributes, recall could have been improved. In this way, the initial discrepancy between the attribute and the schema would have been eliminated and it would not have been detrimental to the perception of the subsequent incongruity between the attribute in the ad and the receivers' schema. As a matter of fact, if an attribute had been *initially* incongruent within the brand schema (that is, the antithesis of a *relevant* attribute), then it could not have been contextually incongruent with receivers' schemata (that is, in-salient). For example, the attribute *generous,* used to define the phone service, had been incongruent (that is, not relevant) *from the beginning*: Most probably, it would not have ever been mentioned to define SMPS, if attributes had been freely elicited. Therefore, when used in a resonant ad, its negation (e.g., *the SMPS is not generous*) should not have attracted much attention, considered that from the beginning people would have not generally associated SMPS with generosity. This could have caused, in turn, non-significant results for recall measures.

Analogously, a settled attitude towards considering particular products either as extensions of the human personality (Wallendorf and Arnould 1988) or possessing an anthropomorphic characterization (Arias-Bolzmann, Chakraborty, and Mowen 2000; Tom & Eves 1999) could have had consequent effects in terms of brand images and memory. For example, the better results obtained for OPEL - which can be documented - should be explained by the greater, culturally consolidated anthropomorphism of cars than that of products like bath foams, or even services (like SMPS). This means that it is easier for a subject to identify the personality of car with that of a person (by using the same attributes), than to recognize a similar human personality in a branded bath foam or in a phone service. Each product seems to have a peculiar index of adaptability for the Big-five model of human personality in describing its brand image, and this should be the subject of specific future research.

In summary, we have demonstrated that, even with the limitations of the model of brand image chosen in this study to define receivers' brand schemata (namely, a *social* model of personality), the relevance levels of brand attributes, which are part of those schemata, influence recall of in-salient ad messages, with more relevant attributes being better recalled within in-salient ad messages than less relevant attributes. On the contrary, this relation does not apply to non-in-salient ad messages. In substance, the same brand attributes have different effects on recall according to the condition (in-salient vs. non-in-salient) in which they are presented in an ad.

4.2   Implications

The advantages of using the in-salience theory in an advertising setting can be best summarized in two areas regarding theoretical and marketing implications.

4.2.1   Theoretical Implications

From a theoretical point of view, this study is significant for two main reasons. First, it generally recognizes the possibility of the in-salience framework of putting together two streams of thought in cognitive psychology, that is, salience and incongruity models. Demonstrating this possibility in an advertising setting gives evidence of the birth of a new comprehensive theory. The in-salience theory proposes a unified source for the generation of salient stimuli (e.g., ad messages), in relation to the perceiver's expectations and the situational environment. This source of salience is the incongruity between the object *stimulus* perceived in a certain *context* and the existing mental *schemata* of the perceiver. In consideration of the existing confusion in the literature regarding terminologies and measures (Heckler and Childers 1992), this comprehensive theory has the further theoretical advantage of permitting the unification and consolidation of both the terminology and the methodologies required to explore, conceptually and empirically, the nature of incongruities that may influence the processing of complex marketing communications.

Second, this study is theoretically significant because it specifically extends research of the effects of salience and information incongruity on processing and memory beyond a person perception context (where it was usually confined in the past) to include other areas more germane to marketing. Earlier discussion pointed out that most of the research examining salience and stimulus congruity was in a person perception context (see, *above*, Chapter Two, Paragraph 1.2). In the person perception literature, results by Hastie (1980), Hastie and Kumar (1979), Srull (1980), and others, found support for a recall advantage for incongruent stimuli. The objective for studying the information congruity paradigm outside a person perception context was to determine whether an advertising setting could also be used to generate the memory advantage for advertising information. Results from the current research supported the notion that in-salient ad messages are more memorable than non-in-salient ad messages. It can be concluded, therefore, that the information congruity paradigm can be successfully adapted in a consumer behavior/advertising setting.

4.2.2   Marketing Implications

Together with theoretical implications, there are also a number of strategic benefits available for practitioners as well. From a marketing point of view, the improvement is threefold and regards the following strategic areas: Increasing exposure time of an ad; enhancing memory for an ad, and usage in other promotions.

The in-salience approach enable us, first, to identify executional strategies to be used for the creation of attention getting advertisements by offering a rationale which is able to guide marketers in the discovery of potential weaknesses of any specific ad. Both advertisers and consumer researchers have long been interested in developing a theoretical understanding of the mechanisms that lead to the production and execution of effective marketing communications. Such communications serve as informational inputs to consumers' decision-making processes and, therefore, are a key issue in any advertising strategy. However, while advertising practitioners have intuitively concentrated on creative efforts (Ogilvy 1983), consumer researchers have started to develop a theoretical understanding of the processes implied in consumers' memory and attitude towards ads, maintaining that creative efforts can be maximized through a comprehension of how consumers process and store ad information. In affluent societies, the use of marketing communication media places marketers in an overpopulated information environment, competing with hundreds of other advertisers for limited consumer attention (see, e.g., Burke and Srull 1988; Elliott and Speck 1998; Keller 1991b; Webb and Ray 1979). They must overcome the well-developed perceptual screening system consumers have incorporated into media fruition behaviors (Bettman 1979). This study has shown that the inclusion of information that is in-salient in a certain context with consumers' previously developed schemata can better penetrate the audience's perceptual screen and increase the amount of attention given to the ad (hence, the degree to which the information being presented is processed). Therefore, given the increasingly cluttered advertising media, enhancing in-salience can increase the ability for getting consumers to notice an ad and, ultimately, it can pay substantial dividends.[43]

Second, the in-salience approach allows enhancing memory for an ad. In advertising campaigns, the marketers' objective to generate advertisements which can have an impact on attention is equally important as that to create advertisements which can be easily remembered. Ad measures, such as first mentioned ad recall, Starch recognition tests, awareness levels, and degree of ad and brand knowledge, all emphasize the need to design ad campaigns that are memorable. This study has shown that memory is affected by the use of in-salient and non-in-salient ad messages and it can be strongly improved by the use of ad messages of the latter type. Furthermore, the in-salient use in advertising of brand attributes present in the receivers' schemata can help marketers to strengthen the prototypical traits of a brand image, thus developing or consolidating a brand positioning in the marketplace (Varaldo and Guido 1997; Guido 2000). Brand positioning is used to differentiate a company's offering from that of its competitors by means of a distinctive brand image (e.g., communicating benefits and uses of a brand, stating how it is better than its competitors', and why consumers should want to buy it). The enhanced processing of message information for in-salient ad claims may therefore help companies especially for new product introductions, or when a decision is made to change a particular ad campaign/position. The use of in-salient claims may generate additional benefits through their ability to stimulate enhanced processing of the messages communicated in advertisements. Specifically, in the search for comprehending inconsistencies, consumers may be stimulated to read extensive copy more deeply, thus accomplishing a knowledge objective which goes beyond the simple awareness factor to include memory for more detailed information.

Finally, the in-salience approach can be valuable for promotional tools other than magazine-type advertising. Direct mail campaigns and billboard advertisements could both benefit from it by stimulating consumers to examine more closely the advertising content inside. This is particularly important when considering, respectively, the large number of promotional messages that are delivered to consumers through the mail, and the limited amount of time consumers have for deciding whether they want to read a billboard message or not. In-salient advertising strategies could be also effectively used in Internet advertising, to sufficiently motivate consumers to click on an advertising banner to transport them to the advertiser's website.[44] Also in-store advertising may obtain advantages in a similar fashion. In-salient ad messages on product packages may be used as a memory cuing device for reminding consumers of claims and positioning information. Other point-of-purchase materials, such as in-salient ad messages on end-aisle displays, mobiles, and posters may stimulate consumers to read the messages supplied to them, which may therefore increase the subsequent probability of purchasing these products on display. Illustrated coupons containing in-salient claims may receive enhanced gazing time, which could help raise redemption rates by either increasing the probability that they will be clipped out and saved, or cueing consumers to getting messages. The above-mentioned promotions are all examples where enhanced exposure time to a promotional communication can improve the overall strategic value of a promotion. There are certainly other cases where in-salience benefits may accrue. The bottom line is that any communication may be improved, and memory may be increased, through the use of in-salient ad messages. In addition, wherever an in-salient ad message can be used in a promotional communication, it will have at least the ability of enhancing exposure time to a company's message (cf. Peltier 1989).

4.3   Limitations

As in almost any study of consumer behavior, there are a number of potential limitations that may have an impact on its experimental results.

4.3.1   Threats to Internal Validity

Potential threats to internal validity are: The effects of treatment manipulation, and the use of personality schemata.

Although the post-dependent measures manipulation check confirmed that in-salient and non-in-salient ad messages were viewed as such by subjects, the actual advertisements themselves could not have stimulated such a strong effect during testing. Specifically, the ads that were used in the experiment were only apparently incongruent with perceivers' schemata, as their in-salience could be solved in a wordplay (see, *above*, Note 22). Therefore, after repeated exposures to similar ads, subjects could no longer have perceived a real incongruity. This could have happened especially for subjects in the 15 second condition or in the unlimited exposure time condition who could have had more time to memorize this kind of wordplay. We used four ad presentation orders to minimize the effects of learning and difference in serial positions. The use of more than four ad orders may therefore have been a more effective in-salience manipulation device.

As for the use of brand personality schemata to approximate brand images, this choice could have weakened our results in terms of in-salience levels. Relating brand image to personality is intuitively appealing on many grounds.[45] Yet, associating brand image with personality is difficult. Most notably, by using personality attributes (i.e., Big Five attributes) rather than other attributes (i.e., extra Big Five attributes) to describe a branded product, the relevance level could have been low since the beginning. To describe SMPS, for example, an extra Big Five attribute such as *expensive* could have been more relevant (that is, more congruent) to the receivers' schema of SMPS than any other Big Five attribute.[46] Therefore, other definitions of brand image different from brand personality (which put emphasis, for example, on symbolism or on cognitive and psychological elements) are advisable for future research. Rather than having researchers to propose the list of attributes, researchers could elicit subjects to supply their schema relevant attributes freely, or ask them which attributes come to mind when they think of an ad for a product.

4.3.2   Threats to External Validity

Threats to external validity regard the possibly "unnatural" setting of the experiment.

Certain characteristics of our research were included to enhance its internal validity, but obviously they limited the generalizability of the results to natural advertising settings. Such limitations to external validity - though common in many consumer research methodologies that do not utilize field experiments (Burke and DeSarbo 1986) can be traced in different areas. Certainly the test ads contained much less information than the actual print ads. In addition, the exposure environment could seem artificial: The ads were not embedded in editorial material, exposure was forced and timed (except for the unlimited exposure time condition), and the effects were taken immediately after exposure. Whether similar mediation effects would be obtained after post-exposure delays of more than one day is not known. In natural settings, however, consumers' stored knowledge will interact with the advertised information. In addition, the same kind of wordplay, the large number of ads, and the absence of surrounding editorial material may have caused subjects to routinize their responses or to behave in other "unnatural" ways. Therefore, process-tracing methodology (such as verbal protocols or eye-movement recording) could be used in future studies to monitor the content of consumer information processing during the advertising review period. In sum, moving to more natural research settings and advertising stimuli will complicate the research design problems and will require more rigorous controls and measurements.

4.3.3 Other Limitations

There are a number of other limitations that may have had an effect on the experimental results. First, involvement or the level of brand familiarity: The use of more (or less) familiar brands might have led to different findings. Second, media type effects: A point medium was used, but in-salience effects might have been different across media. Third, stimulus complexity: Subjects received only a single exposure to each test ad. A more realistic situation would have been one where multiple exposures over time were used. Finally, the retrieval task: At first, subjects were not aware they had to recall ad messages. Because what it is recalled - and how it is recalled - may be highly dependent on the information processing strategy used (Mitchell 1982), different tasks would have probably caused differences in the organization and structure of information in memory.[47]

The limitations discussed above were not brought up to invalidate the results of the experiment designed here to test the effects of ad message in-salience on consumer awareness. The consistency of results across the different experimental conditions and dependent measures widely supported all the propositions tested. These limitations were only brought up to generate an understanding of possible moderating effects that may have dampened these results.

4.4   Future Research

A number of research questions regarding in-salience theory were answered through the completion and the discussion of results of the above experiment. However, there are many more potentially useful empirical issues that still need to be met in relation to the effects of stimulus/ad message in-salience on the processing and memory for information. Some of the most useful extensions of this research program can be summarized as below.

4.4.1   Involvement and Media Effects

Involvement was not manipulated in this study, as we chose to select schema elements (i.e., attributes) which were commonly available to both low-involved and high-involved consumers (i.e., users and non-users).

Future research should consider how consumer involvement moderates memory effects (cf. Borgida and Howard-Pitney 1983; Celsi and Olson 1988; Finn 1988; Park and Hastak 1994; Rosbergen, Pieters, and Wedel 1997) and if enhanced motivation reduces or eliminates the need for ad message in-salience by equalizing processing efforts. Enhancing involvement, indeed, should increase a subject's motivation to process information (namely, personal relevance).

The issue of involvement is strictly connected with the choice of the advertisement media.[48] When subjects are moderately or highly involved, opportunities to process brand information can be greatly enhanced because the message arguments are delivered at a rate conducive to processing them. In these regards, print media, as well as the Internet, provide a particular good context for the use of in-salient advertising strategies since they provide consumers the ability to search for information and to elaborate on it at their own pace (Ariely 1998; Deighton 1996). Chaiken and Eagly (1976), for example, found enhanced comprehension of a difficult message with print versus broadcast media (see also, Andreoli and Worchel 1978; Wright 1981). Likewise, MacKenzie (1986) and Anand and Sternthal (1990) demonstrated that consumers pay more attention to brand information if given more time to examine it. Our study used magazine type ads as the medium for testing ad message in-salience effects. Further research could sort out media effects by the use of in-salient stimuli in broadcasted media, such as television or radio, or in other promotional mix tools, such as personal selling and telemarketing. Other promotional devices, such as point of purchase displays and package design, may benefit substantially from the use of in-salient ad messages enhancing exposure time, and their potentially stimulating value could also be tested.

4.4.2   Advertisement Complexity

In-salient claims were found to stimulate additional gazing time for ad message information. This information was in the form of a magazine headline. An additional question is whether in-salient ad messages can also stimulate consumers to carefully read more complex body copy. This is a major concern for advertisers when trying to convey product specific knowledge for their brands beyond what is presented in the headline. For example, advertisers of "really new products" (Menon and Soman 1999) face the difficult task of motivating consumers to learn about radically new - and unfamiliar - product benefits and attributes. A similar challenge is faced by most web advertisements on the Internet, who must motivate consumers to actively interact in order to acquire appropriate information,[49] and by providers of information services, whose acceptance is affected by the kind of stimulation they provide (Dholakia, Mundorf, and Dholakia 1991).[50]

More generally, an important question to address for marketing theorists and practitioners is how additional stimuli included in an environment containing in-salient information are processed. That is, how an in-salient stimulus affects processing of other information (e.g., contained in an ad). We assumed that the maximum of in-salience effect can be obtained when the *stimulus cue* corresponds to the *information cue*. Yet, it would be interesting to know the impact of an in-salient cue on the information present in its environment and the possible moderating variables. Does in-salient information stimulate further processing of other stimuli? Or does it inhibit such processing (cf. Alba and Chattopadhyay 1986) by drawing attention away from other information? This means to find if the individual components in an ad (such as product class, brand name, ad message, etc.) are remembered better when paired with in-salient or non-in-salient information. The answers to these questions and similar ones will not only expand our knowledge about consumers' information processing and memory, but they will also assist marketers in the development of efficient and effective promotional offerings to fight the thousands of messages that bombard consumers every day.

4.4.3   Attitudes and Persuasion

Processing and memory for in-salient and non-in-salient ad messages were examined in this study, but not also attitudinal responses for this information. Increasing memory for ads, or motivating consumers to look at them longer, will be relatively unimportant issues if consumers negatively evaluate these ads. Learning and memory, by themselves, are only one area of the communication outcomes generated by in-salient information. The other main area is constituted by attitudes and persuasion (see Guido 1993, figure 1, p. 11) in the field of consumer choices.[51] As noticed by Lee and Mason (1999, p. 157): "Although much is known about the memory superiority of ads with incongruent information, their effect on consumer attitudes remains unexplored. Such study is warranted to address at least two important issues: Do different forms of incongruency affect attitude formation differently? And if so, do incongruent conditions that foster greater memory recall also have the same favorable effect on attitude formation?"

It seems that motivation is increased with re-salient (congruent) information; whereas persuasion is increased with in-salient (incongruent) information (cf. Jain and Maheswaran 2000). "In motivating, the message is related to and is congruent with people's beliefs and attitudes and reinforces these beliefs and attitudes. By comparison, the process of persuading tends to change the beliefs and attitudes of people. Persuading goes beyond relating the message to the audience members' beliefs and attitudes in such a way that they will tend to reevaluate their beliefs and attitudes." (Britt 1978, p. 42). A considerable impact on attitude changes has been found even with a single ad exposure (Gibson 1996; Holden and Vanhuele 1999; Pham 1997; Reardon and Moore 1996).[52] Future research on in-salience effects in this area (cf. Meyers-Levy and Malaviya 1999; Ang and Low 2000) could be very useful to researchers and practitioners alike, as it entails more direct consequences on consumers' buying behavior.

This issue of attitude effects is strongly connected with the existing relationship between the concept of *in-salience* and that of *importance*. Because of their concern with how consumers perceive and choose among alternative products and brands, consumer researchers are especially interested in the specific attributes or product characteristics that consumers consider important in some sense (Olson and Muderrisoglu 1979). In-salient attributes (such those, for example, we used in the ad messages of our study), by means of their effects on recall, could change their relevance - as perceived by consumers - especially in the long run, thus probably modifying their perceived importance in the context of a following consumer choice. Such a scenario could be the interesting subject of future research that should examine both the persuasion potential and the routes of in-salient stimuli on consumer decision processes.

5. CONCLUSIONS

The results of this study showed that in-salient and non-in-salient ad messages have a differential impact on information processing and memory and, in turn, on consumer awareness. Factors such as ad viewing time, memory decay, schema activation, and relevance were shown to play a major role in the generation of these results. Additional research is certainly needed before we will be able to fully understand how in-salience operates across a wide number of situational interventions. The research extensions discussed above are all areas that may bear fruits of continued empirical focus.

To summarize our discussion, we have shown that, in social science, a redefinition of the concept of salience is needed. Our *In-salience hypothesis* seems to provide a promising solution to this problem because, in general, it allows a common conceptualization for all the salience cases reviewed in the literature and, when applied to advertising settings, it supplies a comprehensive framework for consumers' processing of complex marketing communications. With our research design, we offered a limited empirical application of our theory which was able to assess consumer awareness generated in one area of the model's communication outcomes - namely recall memory - as resulting from the brand information processing sparked off by in-salient stimuli. Future research should corroborate the model's potential for improvements both in the theoretical and in the marketing field.

NOTES

[1] An earlier version of this study was presented at the *Marketing Communications Conference* of the American Marketing Association in Dublin, Ireland (Guido 1997).

[2] We shall call *in-salient* those stimuli contextually *incongruent* with a perceiver's schema; whereas we shall call *non-in-salient* those stimuli contextually *congruent* with a perceiver's schema.

[3] Taylor and Fiske (1981) operationalized this processing as the "looking at time" for a pictorial or written stimulus. Attention, then, was related to the amount of effort expended by an individual to process a specific piece of information and defined as the amount of time an informational stimulus is actively processed in short-term or working memory (see, also, Erber and Fiske 1984).

[4] Paivio's (1986) *Dual-coding theory* maintains that the imagery and verbal systems are both structurally and functionally distinct although they can function as integrated informational structures. He suggested that image and verbal codes are unequal in mnemonic value, "perhaps by a 2:1 ratio favoring the image code" (p. 77).

[5] When no schema is available for the brand, consumers might develop expectations by making inferences from schemata they find more similar or more accessible (see, *above*, Chapter Three, Paragraph 2.3).

[6] Yi (1990) pointed out these potentialities of ad context in altering the impact of a particular ad on brand evaluations. As mentioned above (see Chapter Three, Paragraph 2.1), he defined ad context "the materials that precede or surround the target ad, such as articles in magazines, ads for other products, and station identifications on radio or television" (p. 215). Specifically, he maintained that contextual materials may *activate particular product attributes* and prime consumers' interpretations of product information, which, in turn, can affect consumers' evaluations of the advertised brands. Similarly, an example of priming is provided by comparative ads: In such peculiar ads, the most famous brand acts as a prime for the interpretation of the other brand on the basis of the most salient (distinctive) attribute/s possessed by the brand.

[7] "Bolen (1984) suggested that artwork is the component of an ad that is processed first. Mitchell (1983) found that visual stimuli are accessed to construct a verbal understanding of an advertised brand. Research by Alesandrini (1982), Houston, Childers, and Heckler (1987), Lutz and Lutz (1977) led to the conclusion that interactive pictures can be used as an advanced organizer for creating expectations for the information to follow. Research in the area of picture versus verbal stimuli suggested that pictures are processed in a more holistic, more integrative manner and with more elaboration than words (e.g., Childers and Houston 1984; Edell and Staelin 1983; Holbrook and Moore 1981); eye fixation studies found that people focus on outlines of pictures and are influenced by such factors as color, size and shapes (e.g., Haber and Hershenson 1980; Mackworth and Morendi 1967)." (Peltier 1989, p. 43; see, also, Jarvenpaa 1990).

[8] As mentioned above (Chapter Three, Note 94), *appropriateness* is defined as any consumers' schema that the author of the ad claim (e.g., the experimenter, the copywriter) feels is adequate for receivers to process the stimulus message.

[9] Relevance, in the sense of weight, has been assessed in past research in other forms, under different names. For example, Fishbein and Ajzen's (1975) concept of salience is nothing else than relevance assessed in terms of easier availability of schema elements (i.e., salient beliefs or salient attributes). Or elsewhere, if it is assessed in reference to a specific end, thus requiring an evaluation of any schema element (e.g., any product attribute), then relevance has been treated as a synonym of importance (see Chapter Three, Paragraph 2.3).

[10] "In an attempt to provide an unequivocal interpretation of the very unstable concept of brand image, a consolidated research tradition has put the principal emphasis on personification of brands (cf. Dobni and Zinkhan 1990). However, this tradition has suffered due to the lack of both a common theory and a consensual taxonomy of personality traits. This has led to a proliferation of constructs, severely undermining the comparability of different approaches and even the credibility of the construct itself. Biehl (1993), for example, suggested that brand image is composed of the image of the provider (e.g., the manufacturer), the user, and the product itself. Farquhar and Herr (1993) argued that the associations evoked by brands include specific product attributes, customer benefits, usage situations and other summary evaluations. Coulter and Zaltman (1994) and Fournier (1995, 1998), using in-depth interviews, maintained that brands have meaning in themselves, and add meaning to a person's life, through their status as partners in a relationship with the consumer." (Caprara, Barbaranelli, and Guido, forthcoming/a).

[11] "Most recently, by re-analyzing factor solutions derived from human personality descriptions, Digman (1997) found second-order dimensions that account for correlations among the Big Five, resulting in two higher-level factors. According to Digman, these two factors represent the highest level of a hierarchical model of personality characteristics in which personality terms are arranged in order of increasing complexity, from the most specific behavioral response to the broader personality dimensions. The first dimension (named *Factor*) is defined by the common aspects of Agreeableness, Conscientiousness and Emotional Stability and represents such personality aspects as socialization, social interest, union, communion, and intimacy. The second dimension (named *Factor.*) is defined by the common aspects of Extroversion and Openness to Experience and represents such personality aspects as striving for superiority, individuation, personal growth, achievement of status, and desire for power. These two factors can, thus, be considered as meta-traits at a higher level of abstraction, which do not invalidate the soundness of the five-factor structure." (Caprara, Barbaranelli, and Guido forthcoming/a).

[12] It is an important empirical problem, for entities which are different from human personality, to ascertain if: (1) Their more socially relevant characteristics can be codified in the language and be universally shared; (2) Their verbal describers can be limited to a number of dimensions; (3) Some of their verbal describers can be considered as markers, therefore more capable of communicating - incisively and without ambiguity - the meaning of the dimension they belong to.

[13] "In conclusion, while it may be possible to describe brand personalities with only a few factors, it is unlikely that the same factors used to describe human personality are suitable for the description of brands. In this regard, our findings are in line with those of Aaker (1997), who observed that 'though some dimensions (or factors) of human personality may be mirrored in brands, others might not' (p. 348). The traditional repertoire of human personality may serve for construing a brand personality, but only to a certain extent. When applied to products and brands, the Big Five model needs revision and adaptation. Results show that only the two meta-factors, blends of the five main dimensions, are consistently replicated in

brand perceptions. Most importantly, moreover, adjectives used to describe those traits may 'shift' from one factor to another, according to the type of the selected stimulus brand." (Caprara, Barbaranelli, and Guido, forthcoming/a).

[14] "[T]his method of using scales and adjectives suffers from at least two disadvantages: the list of specific personality scales used might be incomplete (or some of them might be irrelevant), and consumers may be unable or unwilling to give their true opinions about a brand's personality through such "direct" elicitation techniques. [...] The hope is that they will be more able to get at some of these "unconscious" (or difficult-to-articulate) personality perceptions that a consumer may have about a brand. For example, if a reason for buying designer jeans is that consumers feel more socially accepted when they wear them because others wear them too, this is less likely to emerge in direct methods - where a logical, functional rationalization may be provided instead - but may well appear in these qualitative methods." (Aaker, Batra, and Myers 1992, p. 261).

[15] All these three stimulus products were sold, at that time, on the Italian market as, respectively, *automobili Opel*, *Bagno Schiuma Neutro Roberts*, *Servizio di Telefonia Mobile Sip* (such labels were used in the study).

[16] Only for the SMPS manipulation, the initial pool of 200 attributes describing personality under the Big Five framework was integrated with a pool of 100 attributes extra Big Five, which were selected from the dictionary to represent functional and instrumental characteristics of the stimulus object which could not be easily reflected by human personality dimensions. It must be noted, however, that for the in-salience manipulation in the second part of our experiment we chose only among the Big Five attributes.

[17] In the SMPS manipulation, among the 50 selected attributes, 30 were Big Five attributes, and 20 were extra Big Five attributes.

[18] All the significance levels were subsequently corrected according to the *Bonferroni inequality*, by multiplying the probability *p* for the number of statistical tests conducted on the same subjects (cf. Stevens 1990).

[19] Because data analysis on Big Five attributes and extra Big Five attributes for the SMPS manipulation was carried out separately, other two dimensions for the extra Big Five attributes were found and named Accessibility/Convenience, and Adequateness/Discretion.

[20] For the second part of this research, we followed an approach similar to that of Peltier (1989) in his brilliant dissertation on incongruity effects.

[21] Internal validity was enhanced as we chose not to use a mock magazine format for the ad presentation. The main benefit of placing stimulus ads amongst other information is, indeed, that a more externally valid design might be assumed. Alternatively, the benefit of the no magazine format is that internal validity would be enhanced by increasing the probability that the in-salience manipulation would successfully take place. Moreover, the use of a no magazine format is more consistent with past research procedures. Houston, Childers, and Heckler (1987) used a procedure very similar to this study. Researchers in social cognition directly manipulated congruity by asking subjects to form impressions of certain people and subsequently provided them with additional information that was either consistent or inconsistent with those impressions (e.g., Hastie 1980; Hastie and Kumar 1979; Srull 1981), thus increasing the probability that the congruity manipulation was successful.

[22] In these figures, the areas of the circles, representing different attribute weights, are not exactly proportional to the actual calculated values, as figures here are only approximated visual representations of the model.

[23] Resonance is but one example of a family of literary devices termed *rhetorical figures*. The best-known is metaphor (e.g., Dawar 1992; Hitchon 1991; Morgan and Reichert 1999; Ward and Gaidis 1990). Another is allegory, which conveys two textual meanings in one word (e.g., Stern 1989, 1990). Usually, resonance elicits humor, a construct that draws on the violation of the same principles of common sense (Kuhlman 1985), either principles of logic (nonsense humor) or principles of conduct (taboo humor) (cf., e.g., Alford 1982).

[24] A two-factor technique, similar to resonance, was developed by Menon and Soman (1999). They showed that generating curiosity about the new product increases the motivation to seek knowledge and leads to greater acquisition of new product information (an effect that is stronger when a product class cue is provided). They identified two factors that increase the effectiveness of curiosity-based advertising: A curiosity trigger stimulus (say, by featuring a novel or unexpected new product feature), *and* a relevant product class cue. These factors would allow consumers to generate focussed and meaningful hypotheses by helping them link the new information with the existence knowledge schema for the product class. They argued, moreover, that curiosity-generating strategies that provide curiosity-resolving information after a temporal delay would allow consumers greater opportunity to generate hypotheses and elaborate on the source of the curiosity.

[25] Generally speaking, an *ad message* and an *ad claim* can be considered interchangeable terms. Strictly speaking, an ad message is the meaning that the ad claim wants to communicate. In our study, we tested the memory effects of in-salient/non-in-salient ad claims in terms of recall of the ad messages. Indeed, what is important for the purpose of our research (and, usually, to marketers' purposes) is consumers' comprehension of the meaning of the ad claim. Moreover, we tested an in-salience construct that was *only apparently* incongruent with consumers' schemata, because incongruity was resolved as a copy wordplay. This, however, should not invalidate results, as in-salience (of claims and, indirectly, of messages) - even if it is only apparent - should have important effects on memory (see Meyers-Levy and Tybout 1989 on moderate incongruity).

[26] Other surrealistic techniques involve: isolation; modification; hybridization; change in scale, position, or substance; provocation of accidental encounters; double images; and conceptual bipolarity (Homer and Kahle 1986)

[27] Surrealist artists have often stressed the subconscious or nonrational significance of imagery by exploitation of chance effects, unexpected juxtapositions, and unorderly connections. For Magritte, in particular, "paintings were intended as an attack upon society's preconceived ideas and predetermined good sense. He considered his work successful when no explanation of causality or meaning could satisfy our curiosity. [...] In Magritte's paintings, events are perceived without the inner link usually associating cause and effect. Problems are solved by rearranging what we have always known, not by giving new information. Magritte used only familiar objects, brought together or combined in such a way as to evoke something else, something unfamiliar. It is the unexpected in Magritte's work (and that of other surrealists) that provides information, because what is fully expected tells us nothing." (Homer and Kahle 1986, p. 51).

[28] If there was not this concluding line, the in-salience would have been not only apparent, but real, thus avoiding achieving the effect sought by the resonance technique. To the extent of marketing implications, this effect was undesired.

[29] Strictly speaking, in the claim: "Opel is *not safe*... It's more than safe," the stimulus cue - i.e., the in-salient stimulus cue - is made by the words "not safe." Because we tested the recall of the matching between the brand (Opel) and the attribute (safe) - not just the manipulated attribute -, the information cue (that is, "Opel is not safe") does not perfectly coincide with the stimulus cue (the latter being included). We assumed that recall of the stimulus cues would be better if subjects should recall *only* the manipulated attributes (manipulated means, here, an attribute in the

resonant condition to be in-salient). Of course, recalling the attribute but not the brand would be less useful on a marketing point of view (see also, *above*, Chapter Three, Paragraph 2.1.1).

[30] According to de Heer and Poiesz (1998, p. 532): "To examine the impact of exposure duration on motivation, ability and opportunity to process commercial information, a study was set up in which each of twenty subjects viewed one hundred WWW-advertising pages under different conditions of exposure duration: 1, 2, 4, 6, and 8 seconds. It is surprising to note that, if exposure duration is shorter than 4 seconds, ability and motivation differ significantly, while the difference is not significant at an exposure duration of longer than 4 seconds. A related finding was that intercorrelations between the three information processing antecedents reached a maximum at 4 seconds. The assumed conceptual independence of the antecedents increases over time at an exposure duration longer than 4 seconds."

[31] It is important to notice how the effects of priming can interact with memory (cf. Srull and Wyer 1980; see also Higgins, Rholes, and Jones 1977; Stapel, Koomen and Velthuijsen 1998). Homer and Kahle (1986) used priming statements to provide audiences with cues that created expectations for subsequent *product-relevant information* in an advertisement and improved their recall. They hypothesized that, "because priming should make existing schemata salient and should facilitate assimilation, any schema-consistent information from an advertisement should be remembered more easily." (p. 53). They combined priming with incongruent (namely, surrealistic) ads, suggesting that such presentations should inhibit incorrect recall of information, facilitating accommodation by drawing attention to what is atypical. Results of assimilation and accommodation showed that priming improved memory for schema-congruent information. Homer and Kahle (1986) explained their results maintaining that "subjects presented with priming statements were better able to incorporate the ad's arguments into their existing schemata" (p. 54), in line with *Social adaptation theory*. According to Homer and Kahle (1986, p. 52): "Social adaptation theory (Kahle 1984; Kahle and Homer 1985; Kahle and Timmer 1983) a neo-Piagetian account of attitudes, values and other social cognitions, implies that cognitions function to facilitate adaptation to an individual's environment. Persons seek equilibrium with the environment by assimilating new information into existing schemata while accommodating mental structures to incorporate new, discrepant information. Individuals evaluate information in terms of its adaptive significance. If an individual decides a certain piece of information has achieved its potential in terms of facilitating adaptation (with one's environment), processing of that particular information will cease, and processing attention will be directed elsewhere." It has been shown that, in cases of product evaluations, when subjects are primed with an evaluative dimension prior to exposure to an ambiguous description of the product, evaluation of the product tends to be consistent with the prime (e.g., Dick, Chakravarti, and Biehal 1990; Levin and Gaeth 1988; Bettman and Sujan 1987; Kirmani and Wright 1989). Moreover, the effects of the prime are larger when there is a long interval between exposure to the description and judgment. This result is consistent with conclusions of a study by Alba, Marmorstein, and Chattopadhyay (1989): "As delay increases, memory for the original detailed information decreases, whereas higher-order interpretations made salient by the prime remain stable. Thus, over time, evaluations become dominated by and more consistent with the original interpretation of the object." (Alba, Hutchinson, and Lynch 1991, p. 20).

[32] In this chapter, for the sake of simplicity, we use the currently accepted term "prime" to indicate our manipulation process. However, according to Posner and Warren's (1972) discrimination between "prime" and "set" (see, *above*, Chapter Three, Note 90), our manipulation was actually a "set" - that is, a conscious process deliberately elicited through a direct statement.

[33] While significant results were found by both researchers across each of the retention intervals, two other factors had also to be considered (Peltier 1989): First, print material had much lower absolute levels of observable memory than film material. Second, subjects probably spent

more time processing this material than they normally would have because they were told to either form an impression of this information or to try to remember it.

[34] In general, relatively little is known about the differential impact, if any, of information congruity on free recall, aided recall and recognition for the information contained in advertisements. Two studies that attempted to assess recall and recognition of information presented along with incongruent stimuli resulted in conflicting conclusions: O'Brien and Myers (1985) found that both recall and recognition of information preceding unexpected target stimuli exceeded that for information preceding congruent stimuli. Conversely, Houston, Childers and Heckler (1987) found that, while recall was higher for product class information and brand names when they were presented with pictures and words that did not match, both recall and recognition of product attribute information were higher when pictures and words did match. As we noted, however, the former study can be taken as an instance of in-salience manipulation, whereas the latter is only an instance of incongruity.

[35] Psychologists have advanced these two general theories that attempt to delineate processes involved in recall and recognition. The once popular *Strength theory* holds that experiential episodes result in the retention of memory traces of varying strength, and that recall and recognition tasks, which involve the same underlying memory process, simply differ in the amount of trace strength required (Kintsch 1970; Murdock and Dufty 1972). The second, more dominant, model is the *Dual process theory* (Anderson and Bower 1972, 1974) which holds that recall involves two steps: memory search and recognition. To recall an item, a subject first generates a number of prospective candidates for recall during the search process and then decides, through recognition, that one of them is the stimulus item. The dual-process theory thus assumes that recognition is a subprocess of recall.

[36] According to Stapel (1998): "[A]ll recall comes from the much larger groups of people who recognise the advertising efforts. Average proved recall of print ads occurs among one out of every three recognizers. *Recognition* data indicate how many saw the ad. *Recall* figures tell us how many of them did become sufficiently interested to actually look and often read what the advertiser tries to tell them." (p. 41, emphasis added).

[37] As shown *above*, the memory scores for each of the memory retrieval tasks/ad components were in essence ratio scales built from the summation of discrete variable scores. Top-of-mind and overall free recall scores were summed over a 0-1-2 coding system. A number of researchers have shown that the F-test is robust to violations of the metric measures assumption when cell sizes of 30 or more observations per cell are used (see, e.g., Benepe 1949; Child 1946; Mandeville 1969; and Snedecor 1946; Snedecor and Cochran 1967). Therefore, to overcome possible threats to statistical conclusion validity, the experiment was designed to satisfy the above sample size requirement.

[38] Results for top-of-mind recall showed much similar trends.

[39] The congruity manipulation devices used in this current research were somehow a departure from the past. In social perception studies, researchers instructed subjects to form an impression for a particular person, and then were given impression consistent and impression inconsistent information about this person. They were then asked to think about this information. Therefore, in these research settings, information congruity was overtly manipulated. The use of an advertising environment, where an ad message had to stimulate its own congruity attention and assessment, suggests that an incongruity can cue schematic information processing in subtler ways (Peltier 1989).

[40] However, it would be interesting to test in future research the role of relevance (i.e., re-salience) in long-term memory, which could weaken the depth of processing explanation. This theory, indeed, tends to ignore the role of the retrieval environment in determining long-

term retention. In essence, it is the *personal relevance* of what has been learned to the demands of the memory test that could determine whether or not retention would occur in the long term. Under these circumstances, elaboration or extensiveness of processing and distinctiveness of processing need to be considered, as well as the depth of processing.

[41] It should be noted, however, that long periods of time without rehearsal could eliminate the accessibility of this information altogether (Anderson and Bower 1973).

[42] "Retrieval contingencies, moderated by memory accessibility of previously encountered brand-attribute information, had dramatic effects on choices (Biehal and Chakravarti 1986). Also, when opportunity for evaluative analysis is low and memory for semantic detail is poor, consumers may retrieve and use frequency counts of positive and negative attributes possessed by a brand in making judgments (Alba and Marmorstein 1987)." (Cohen and Chakravarti 1990, p. 247).

[43] The concept of ad exposure time also suggests which medium may benefit most from the use of in-salient messages (cf. Peltier 1989). Self-selected exposure time to an ad suggests that a consumer must have the locus of ad viewing control. Advertisements shown in a print medium usually allow consumers this locus of control, whereas a broadcast medium does not (assuming that the message is not recorded and played back at the viewers' discretion). Therefore, magazine ads, newspaper ads, direct mail pieces, billboards, and the like, will probably benefit most by the use of in-salient ad messages.

[44] As noticed by Menon and Soman (1999, p. 30): "Unlike television advertising in which information is disseminated in a temporally distributed manner, the information in Internet advertising is spatially distributed. This might increase the consumer's belief in finding the appropriate curiosity-resolving information and hence, make him or her more willing to accept the challenge of elaborating on it."

[45] "Both are multidimensional, and both appear to operate at the same level of abstraction. Personality has been said by some (Kassarjian and Sheffet 1975) to be best conceived of as a dynamic whole, which is consistent with the general sense that many have about brand image. Many consumer theorists are of the view that purchase behavior is determined by the interaction of the buyer's self concept with the 'product's personality', and in this context the definitional relationship is also especially apt." (Dobni and Zinkhan 1990, p. 115).

[46] The impact of in-salience is higher when we say that "SMPS is not expensive," or that the "MRBF is not foamy," rather than "SMPS is not dynamic" or the "MRBF is not conscientious," because the level of attribute relevance (that is, congruity with the products' schemata) is usually higher for brand specific attributes (i.e., extra Big Five attributes) than for personality attributes (i.e., Big Five attributes).

[47] Also it is not clear if the resulting structure from a single artificial task would have been similar to the memory structures that occur naturally from information acquisition from many different sources (e.g., advertising, neighbors, etc.).

[48] "Krugman (1965) was one of the first to note the major differences that exist in consumer processing of print versus broadcast advertising. In developing his *low-involvement-learning hypothesis*, Krugman (1965) noticed that print media require the active participation of the audience since reading printed words is a quite demanding cognitive task. Indeed, the *information-processing-parsimony hypothesis* (Holbrook 1978) argues that consumers try to minimize demanding cognitive endeavors and would be unlikely to read information of little interest to them. Greenwald and Leavitt (1984) also recognized the limited ability of print media to get a meaningful response from uninvolved consumers, 'with rapid page turning and only partial scanning of page contents [...], critical cues that could attract higher involvement may

simply be missed' (Greenwald and Leavitt, 1984, p. 590). Therefore, Buchholz and Smith (1991) concluded that print media have limited capacity to influence uninvolved or passive audience members who are disinclined to read a message." (Guido 1993, pp. 8-9).

[49] For example, "most Internet advertising is in a form (e.g. banners, buttons) that requires sufficient interest and motivation on the part of consumers to actively interact with the advertisement and access appropriate information (Kirsner 1997). Consequently, web advertisers are concerned about the fact that they have limited, if any, control over consumer exposure to the content of the advertising and hence consumers' education (Briggs and Hollis 1997)." (Menon and Soman 1999, p. 3).

[50] "Since the launch of PRESTEL videotex service by the British Post Office in 1969, videotex, audiotext, online database, pay TV, toll-free calling services (800 numbers), metered calling services (900 numbers), electronic mail, home shopping networks, home banking services, voice messaging systems, distance education programs and other 'tele-delivered' services have proliferated. [...] Information services tend to be audio or text-based, at least as far as the introductory and interactive portion of the service is concerned. People will pay attention to and use such services only if the interactive portion is interesting and involving. Information services can be made more acceptable to users by making such services lively, entertaining, and pleasant. Unfortunately, this simple lesson has not yet been learned by those designing information services: they continue to view such services in terms of technological advances and economic utilities. This view has not been much of a problem so far because information services have been confined mainly to business settings. As such services move out of the workplace and into homes, shopping malls, etc., the need to make these services lively and entertaining will intensify. To the 'kidvid' generation that has been raised on flashy and colorful entertainment programs from Sesame Street to MTV, information in a bland form is unlikely to be acceptable [see Greer et al. 1982]. Video and computer game manufacturers learned this lesson during the 1980s and improved the entertainment value of their games dramatically through graphics, motion, and sound. In desktop computers, Apple's Macintosh computer changed the concept of a user interface radically by introducing icons and graphics. In software, Microsoft's Windows includes a game designed to familiarize the user with the features of the program. Information service providers will have to incorporate these lessons and develop additional strategies to enhance hedonic valence, salience, and vividness." (Dholakia, Mundorf, and Dholakia 1991, who define *salience* as the "highlighting" of a particular segment in a total information package).

[51] A similar area of research is that of *choice context effects*, which refer "to the finding that the proportion of subjects choosing a particular product from a set is influenced by set composition in a manner apparently inconsistent with stable preferences." (Prelec, Wernerfelt, and Zettelmeyer 1997, p. 118). See, also, Huber, Payne, and Puto 1982; Meyers-Levy and Tybout 1997; Simonson and Nowlis 2000; Simonson and Tversky 1992.

[52] For example, "Vanhuele and Pham discussed the communication effects of what they call advertising 'fragments' (i.e., minimal messages often restricted to a brief mention of the brand name). These types of messages are increasingly pervasive in today's communication landscape (e.g., event sponsorships, product placements in movies, brand logos on the Internet, tv program endorsements; [...]). They presented an experiment which examined whether brief exposures to fragments carrying only brand names (e.g., 'Marlboro') can result in instantiation of the brands' core associations (e.g., masculinity)." (Pham 1997, p. 121). Gibson (1996) examined the potential of a single exposure of a television commercial, finding three important results: (1) A single additional exposure of a TV commercial can change brand attitude for an established brand; (2) The range of possible effects of a single additional exposure is huge, from very positive to very negative; and (3) The range of possible effects is not related to the product category.

References

Aaker, D.A., R. Batra, and J.G. Myers (1992), *Advertising Management*, 4th Edition, Englewood Cliffs, NJ: Prentice-Hall.

Aaker, J. (1997), "Dimensions of Brand Personality," *Journal of Marketing Research*, 24 (August), 347-356.

Aaker, J. and S. Fournier (1995), "A Brand as a Character, a Partner and a Person: Three Perspectives on the Question of Brand Personality," in *Advances in Consumer Research*, Vol. 22, eds. F. R. Kardes and M, Sujan, Provo, UT: Association for Consumer Research, 391-395.

Aaker, J. and J. Segupta (2000), "Additivity versus Attenuation: The Role of Culture in the Resolution of Information Incongruity," *Journal of Consumer Psychology*, 9 (2), 67-82.

Abelson, R.P. (1976), "Script Processing in Attitude Formation and Decision Making," in *Cognition and Social Behavior*, eds. J. Carroll and J. Payne, Hillsdale, NJ: Lawrence Erlbaum.

Abrams, B. (1983), "Sponsor Recall," *Wall Street Journal*, (March 24), 35.

Adams, J.K. (1957), "Laboratory Studies of Behavior without Awareness," *Psychological Bulletin*, 46, 383-405.

Ajzen, I. (1991), "The Theory of Planned Behavior," *Organizational Behavior and Human Decision Processes*, 50, 1-33.

Ajzen, I. and M. Fishbein (1980), *Understanding Attitudes and Predicting Social Behavior*, Englewood Cliffs, NJ: Prentice-Hall.

Akerlof, G.A. (1991), "Procrastination and Obedience," *American Economic Review*, 81 (2), 1-19.

Alba, J.W. (1983), "The Effects of Product Knowledge on the Comprehension, Retention, and Evaluation of Product Information," in *Advances in Consumer Research*, Vol. 10, eds. R.P. Bagozzi and A.M. Tybout, Ann Arbor, MI: Association for Consumer Research, 577-580.

Alba, J.W. and A. Chattopadhyay (1985), "Effects of Context and Part-Category Cues on Recall of Competing Brands," *Journal of Marketing Research*, 22 (August), 340-349.

Alba, J.W. and A. Chattopadhyay (1986), "Salience Effects in Brand Recall," *Journal of Marketing Research*, 23 (November), 363-369.

Alba, J.W. and L. Hasher (1983), "Is Memory Schematic?," *Psychological Bulletin*, 93 (2), 203-231.

Alba, J.W. and J.W. Hutchinson (1987), "Dimensions of Consumer Expertise", *Journal of Consumer Research*, 13 (March), 411-454.

Alba, J.W. and J W. Hutchinson (2000), "Knowledge Calibration: What Consumers Know and What They Think They Know," *Journal of Consumer Research*, 27 (September), 123-156.

Alba, J.W., J.W. Hutchinson, and J.G. Lynch, Jr. (1991), "Memory and Decision Making," in *Handbook of Consumer Behavior*, eds. T.S. Robertson and H.H. Kassarjian, Englewood Cliffs, NJ: Prentice-Hall, 1-49.

Alba, J.W. and H. Marmorstein (1987), "The Effects of Frequency Knowledge on Consumer Decision Making," *Journal of Consumer Research*, 14 (June), 14-25.

Alden, D.L. and W.D. Hoyer (1993), "An Examination of Cognitive Factors Related to Humorousness in Television Advertising," *Journal of Advertising*, 23 (2), 29-37.

Alden, D.L., W.D. Hoyer, and C. Lee (1993), "Identifying Global and Culture-Specific Dimensions of Humor in Advertising: A Multinational Analysis," *Journal of Marketing*, 57 (April), 64-75.

Alesandrini, K.L. (1982), "Strategies that Influence Memory for Advertising Communications," in *Information Processing Research in Advertising*, ed. R.J. Harris, Hillsdale, NJ: Lawrence Erlbaum, 65-81.

Alford, R. (1982), *The Evolutionary Significance of the Human Humor Response*. Paper presented at the Third International Conference on Humor, Washington, DC, August.

Allen, C.T. and C.A. Janiszewski (1989), "Assessing the Role of Contingency Awareness in Attitudinal Conditioning with Implications for Advertising Research," *Journal of Marketing Research*, 26 (February), 30-43.

Allison, R.I. and K.P. Uhl (1964), "Influence of Beer Brand Identification on Taste Perception," *Journal of Marketing Research*, 1 (August), 36-39.

Alloy, L.B. and N. Tabachnik (1984), "Assessment of Covariation by Humans and Animals: The Joint Influence of Prior Expectations and Current Situational Information," *Psychological Review*, 91 (1), 112-149.

Allport, F.H. (1955), *Theories of Perception and the Concept of Structure*, New York: Wiley.

Alpert, M.I. (1971), "Identification of Determinant Attributes: A Comparison of Methods," *Journal of Marketing Research*, 8 (May), 184-191.

Alpert, M.I. (1980), "Unresolved Issues in Identification of Determinant Attributes," in *Advances in Consumer Research*, Vol. 7, ed. J.C. Olson, Ann Arbor, MI: Association for Consumer Research, 83-88.

Alperstein, N.M. (1990), "The Verbal Content of TV Advertising and Its Circulation in Everyday Life," *Journal of Advertising*, 19 (2), 15-22.

Alquie, F. (1965), *The Philosophy of Surrealism*, Ann Arbor, MI: University of Michigan Press.

Alsop, R. (1988), "Advertisers See Big Gains in Odd Layouts," *The Wall Street Journal*, (June 29), 25.

Ambler, T. and T. Burne (1999), "The Impact of Affect on Memory for Advertising," *Journal of Advertising Research*, 39 (March/April), 25-34.

Anand, P., M.B. Holbrook, and D. Stephens (1988), "The Formation of Affective Judgments: The Cognitive-Affective Model Versus the Independence Hypothesis," *Journal of Consumer Research*, 15 (December), 386-391.

Anand, P. and B. Sternthal (1990), "Ease of Message Processing as a Moderator of Repetition Effects in Advertising," *Journal of Marketing Research*, 27 (August), 345-353.

Anand Keller, P. and L.G. Block (1997), "Vividness Effects: A Resource-Matching Perspective," *Journal of Consumer Research*, 24 (December), 295-304.

Anderson, D.R. and S.R. Levin (1976), "Young Children's Attention to Sesame Street," *Child Development*, 47, 806-811.

Anderson, N.H. and S. Hubert (1963), "Effects of Concomitant Verbal Recall on Order Effects in Personality Impression Formation," *Journal of Verbal Learning and Verbal Behavior*, 2 (December), 379-391.

Anderson, J.R. (1983), "A Spreading Activation Theory of Memory," *Journal of Verbal Learning and Verbal Behavior*, 22, 261-295.

Anderson, J.R. and G.H. Bower (1972), "Recognition and Retrieval Processes in Free Recall," *Psychological Review*, 79 (March), 97-123.

Anderson, J.R. and G.H. Bower (1973), *Human Associative Memory*, Washington, DC: Winston & Sons.

Anderson, J.R. and G.H. Bower (1974), "A Propositional Theory of Recognition Memory," *Memory and Cognition*, 2 (3), 406-412.

Anderson, R.C. and A. Ortony (1975), "On Putting Apples in Bottles: a Problem of Polysemy," *Cognitive Psychology*, 7, 167-180.

Anderson, R.C. and J.W. Pichert (1978), "Recall of Previously Unrecallable Information Following a Shift in Perspective," *Journal of Verbal Learning and Verbal Behavior*, 17, 1-12.

Andreoli, V. and S. Worchel (1978), "The Effects of Media Communication and Message Position on Attitude Change," *Public Opinion Quarterly*, 42, 59-70.

Ang, S.H., S.M.g Leong, and W. Yeo (1999), "When Silence Is Golden: Effects of Silence on Consumer Ad Response," in *Advances in Consumer Research*, eds. E.J. Arnold and L.M. Scott, Provo, UT: Association for Consumer Research, 295-299.

Ang, S.H. and S.Y.M. Low (2000), "Exploring the Dimensions of Ad Creativity," *Psychology and Marketing*, 17 (10), 835-854.

Antes, J.R. and J. Penland (1981), "Picture Context Effects on Eye Movement Patterns," in *Eye Movements: Cognition and Visual Perception*, eds. D. Fisher, R. Monty, and J. Senders, Hillsdale, NJ: Lawrence Erlbaum, 157-170.

Appel, V., S. Weinstein, and C. Weinstein (1979), "Brain Activity and Recall of TV Advertising," *Journal of Advertising Research*, (August), 7-15.

Apter, M.J. (1989), *Reversal Theory: Motivation, Emotion and Personality*. London: Routledge.

Arias-Bolzmann, L., G. Chakraborty, and J.C. Mowen (2000), "Effects of Absurdity in Advertising: The Moderating Role of Product Category Attitude and the Mediating Role of Cognitive Responses," *Journal of Advertising*, 24 (1), 35-49.

Ariely, D. (1998), "Controlling the Information FLow: On the Role of Interactivity in Consumers' Decision making and Preferences," Unpublished dissertation, The Fuqua School of Business, Durham, NC: Duke University.

Arnheim, R. (1974), *Art and Visual Perception*, Los Angeles, CA: University of California Press.

Arnold, J.E. (1998), "Reference Forms and Discourse Patterns," Ph.D. Dissertation, Stanford University, June, http://www.cis.upenn.edu/~jarnold/diss/chapter1.html.

Arons, L. (1961), "Does Television Viewing Influence Store Image and Shopping Frequency," *Journal of Retailing*, 37 (Fall), 1-13.

Asch, S.E. (1946), "Forming Impressions of Personality," *Journal of Abnormal and Social Psychology*, 41, 258-290.

Aslin, T.M. and M.L. Rothschild (1986), "An Introduction to a Cognitive-Behavioral Perspective of Consumer Behavior," in *Advances in Consumer Research*, Vol. 13, ed. R.J. Lutz, Provo, UT: Association for Consumer Research, 566.

Ashcraft, M.H. (1989), *Human Memory and Cognition*, Glenview, IL: Scott, Foresman and Company.

Assael, H. (1992), *Consumer Behavior and Marketing Action*, 4th Edition, Boston, MA: Kent Publishing Co.

Atkinson, R.C. (1988), *Stevens' Handbook of Experimental Psychology: Perception and Motivation*, New York: Wiley.

Auchincloss, D. (1978), "The Purpose of Color," *Graphic Arts Monthly and the Printing Industry*, 50 (11), 46-48.

Axelrod, J.N. (1968), "Advertising Measures that Predict Purchase," *Journal of Advertising Research*, 8 (march), 3-17.

Aylesworth, A.B. and S.B. MacKenzie (1998), "Context Is Key: The Effect of Program-Induced Mood on Thoughts about the Ad," *Journal of Advertising*, 27 (2), 17-31.

Bacharach, M. (2000), "Framing, Salience and Product Image Project Full Report of Research Activities and Results," (7 April), http://www.economics.ox.ac.uk/Research/Breb/FRAM/report.html.

Bacon, F.T. (1979), "Credibility of Repeated Statements: Memory for Trivia," *Journal of Experimental Psychology: Human Learning and Memory*, 5 (May), 3-17.

Baddeley, A. (1991), *Human Memory*, London: Lawrence Erlbaum.

Bahrick, H.P. (1964), "Retention Curves: Facts or Artifacts?," *Psychological Bulletin*, 61 (3), 188-194.

Baker, M.J. and G.A. Churchill, Jr. (1977), "The Impact of Physically Attractive Models on Advertising Evaluations," *Journal of Marketing Research*, 14 (November), 538-555.

Baker, W. (1993), "The Relevance Accessibility Model of Advertising Effectiveness," in *Advertising Exposure, Memory, and Choice*, ed. A.A. Mitchell, Hillsdale, NJ: Lawrence Erlbaum, 49-88.

Baker, W., J.W. Hutchinson, D. Moore, and P. Nedungadi (1986), "Brand Familiarity and Advertising: Effects on the Evoked Set and Brand Preference," in *Advances in Consumer Research*, Vol. 13, ed. R.J. Lutz, Provo, UT: Association for Consumer Research, 637-642.

Baker, W.E. and R.J. Lutz (2000), "An Empirical Test of an Updated Relevance-Accessibility Model of Advertising Effectiveness," *Journal of Advertising*, 26 (1), 1-14.

Barbaranelli, C. and G. Guido (1998), "Brand Specificity as a Moderator Variable in Purchase Intention Measurement," in *Studi dell'Osservatorio*, Dipartimento di Scienza dei Sistemi Sociali e della Comunicazione, Università degli Studi di Lecce, Galatina, Italy: Congedo Editore.

Barbeau, B.J. and W.J. Qualls (1984), "Consumers' Perceptions of Attributes and Behavioral Intentions: An Extended Comparison-Level Model," in *Advances in Consumer Research*, Vol. 11, ed. T. Kinnear, Provo, UT: Association for Consumer Research, 84-87.

Bargh, J.A. (1982), "Attention and Automaticity in the Processing of Self-Relevant Information," *Journal of Personality and Social Psychology*, 43 (3), 425-436.

Bargh, J.A. and R.D. Thein (1985), "Individual Construct Accessibility, Person Memory, and the Recall-Judgment Link: The Case of Information Overload," *Journal of Personality and Social Psychology*, 49 (5), 1129-1146.

Barlow, T. and M.S. Wogalter (1993), "Alcoholic Beverage Warnings in Magazine and Television Advertisements," *Journal of Consumer Research*, 20 (June), 147-156.

Baron, R.M. (1980), "Contrasting Approaches to Social Knowing: An Ecological Perspective," *Personality and Social Psychology Bulletin*, 6, 591-600.

Baron, R.S. (1982), "Sexual Content and Advertising Effectiveness: Comments on Belch et al. (1981) and Caccavale at al. (1981)," in *Advances in Consumer Research*, Vol. 9, ed. A.A. Mitchell, Ann Arbor, MI: Association for Consumer Research, 428-430.

Barsalou, L.W. (1982), "Context-Independent and Context-Dependent Information in Concepts," *Memory and Cognition*, 10 (1) 82-93.

Barsalou, L.W. (1987), "The Instability of Graded Structure: Implications for the Nature of Concepts," in *Concepts and Conceptual Development: Ecological and Intellectual Factors in Categorisation*, ed. U. Neisser, Cambridge, UK: Cambridge University Press.

Barsalou, L.W. (1989), "Intra-Concept Similarity and Its Implications for Inter-Concept Similarity," in *Similarity and Analogy*, eds. S. Vosniadou and A. Ortony, Cambridge, UK: Cambridge University Press.

Bartlett, F.C. (1932), *Remembering: A Study in Experimental and Social Psychology*, Cambridge, UK: Cambridge University Press.

Bassili, N.J. and M.C. Smith (1986), "On the Spontaneity of Trait Attribution: Converging Evidence for the Role of Cognitive Strategy," *Journal of Personality and Social Psychology*, 50, 239-245.

Batra, R. and M.L. Ray (1986), "Situational Effects of Advertising Repetition: The Moderating Influence of Motivation, Ability, and Opportunity to Respond," *Journal of Consumer Research*, 12 (March), 432-445.

Bauer, R.A. and S.A. Greyser (1968), *Advertising in America: The Consumer View*, Boston, MA: Harvard Business School.

Beattie, A.E. (1982), "Effects of Product Knowledge on Comparison, Memory, Evaluation, and Choice: A Model of Expertise in Consumer Decision-Making," in *Advances in Consumer Research*, Vol. 9, ed. A.A. Mitchell, Ann Arbor, MI: Association for Consumer Research, 336-341.

Beattie, A.E. (1983), "Product Expertise and Advertising Persuasiveness," in *Advances in Consumer Research*, Vol. 10, eds. R.P. Bagozzi and A.M. Tybout, Ann Arbor, MI: Association for Consumer Research, 581-584.

Beatty, S.E. and D.I. Hawkins (1989), "Subliminal Stimulation: Some New Data and Interpretation," *Journal of Advertising*, 18 (3), 4-8.

Beck, J. (1972), *Surface Color Perception*, Ithaca, NY: Cornell University Press.

Belch, M.A., B.E. Holgerson, G.E. Belch, J. Koppman (1982), "Psychophysiological and Cognitive Responses to Sex in Advertising," in *Advances in Consumer Research*, Vol. 9, ed. A.A. Mitchell, Ann Arbor, MI: Association for Consumer Research, 424-427.

Belk, R.W. (1988), "Possessions and the Extended Self," *Journal of Consumer Research*, 15 (September), 139-168.

Bellezza, H.P. and T.L. Cheney (1973), "Isolation Effect in Immediate and Delayed Recall," *Journal of Experimental Psychology*, 97, 213-219.

Bellizzi, J.A. and R.E. Hite (1987), "Headline Size and Position Influence on Consumers' Perception," *Perceptual and Motor Skills*, 64 (1), 296-298.

Bello, D.C., R.E. Pitts, and M.J. Etzel (1983), "The Communication Effects of Controversial Sexual Content in Television Programs and Commercials," *Journal of Advertising*, 12 (3), 32-42.

Bem, D.J. (1972), "Self-Perception Theory," in *Advances in Experimental Social Psychology*, Vol. 6, ed. L. Berkowitz, New York: Academic Press, 1-62.

Bentler, P.M. and G. Speckart (1979), "Models of Attitude-Behavior Relations," *Psychological Review*, 86, 452-464.

Berelson, B.R. and G.A. Steiner (1964), *Human Behavior*, New York: Harcourt, Brace, and World, Inc.

Berger, I.E. and A.A. Mitchell (1989), "The Effects of Advertising on Attitude Accessibility, Attitude Confidence, and the Attitude-Behavior Relationship," *Journal of Consumer Research*, 16 (December), 269-279.

Berlyne, D.E. (1957), "Conflict and Information-Theory Variables as Determinants of Human Perceptual Curiosity," *Journal of Experimental Psychology*, 53, 399-404.

Berlyne, D.E. (1958), "The Influence of Complexity and Novelty in Visual Figures on Orienting Responses," *Journal of Experimental Psychology*, 55 (3), 289-296.

Berlyne, D.E. (1960), *Conflict, Arousal, and Curiosity*, New York: McGraw-Hill.

Berlyne, D.E. (1966), "Curiosity and Exploration," *Science*, 153, 25-33.

Berlyne, D.E. (1967), "Arousal and Reinforcement," in *Nebraska Symposium on Motivation*, ed. D. Levine, Lincoln, NE: University of Nebraska Press.

Berlyne, D.E. (1970), "Attention as a Problem in Behavior Theory," in *Attention: Contemporary Theory and Analysis*, ed. D.I. Mostofsky, New York: Appleton-Century-Crofts, 25-49.

Berlyne, D.E. (1971), *Aesthetics and Psychobiology*, New York: Appleton-Century-Crofts.

Berlyne, D.E. (1973), "The Vicissitudes of Aplopathematic and Thelematoscopic Pneumatology (or The Hydrography of Hedonism)," in *Pleasure, Reward, Preference*, eds. D.E. Berlyne and K.B. Madsen, New York: Academic Press.

Berry, C. (1983), "A Dual Effect of Pictorial Enrichment in Learning from Television News: Gunter's Data Revisited," *Journal of Educational Television*, 9, 171-174.

Berry, N.C. (1988), "Revitalizing Brands," *Journal of Consumer Marketing*, 5 (Summer), 15-20.

Berscheid, E., W. Graziano, T. Monson, M. Dermer (1976), "Outcome Dependency: Attention, Attribution, and Attraction," *Journal of Personality and Social Psychology*, 34 (5), 978-989.

Bettinger, C.O., L.E. Dawson, Jr., and H.G. Wales (1979), "The Impact of Free-Sample Advertising," *Journal of Advertising Research*, 19 (3), 35-39.

Bettman, J.R. (1979), *An Information Processing Theory of Consumer Choice*, Reading, MA: Addison-Wesley.

Bettman, J.R. (1986), "Consumer Psychology," *Annual Review of Psychology*, 37, 257-289.

Bettman, J. R. and C.W. Park (1980), "Effects of Prior Knowledge and Experience and Phase of the Choice Process on Consumer Decision Processes: A Protocol Analysis," *Journal of Consumer Research*, 7 (December), 234-248.

Bettman, J.R., D. Roedder-John, and C.A. Scott (1986), "Covariation Assessment by Consumers," *Journal of Consumer Research*, 13 (December), 316-326.

Bettman, J.R. and M. Sujan (1987), "Effects of Framing on Evaluation of Comparable and Noncomparable Alternatives by Experts and Novices Consumers," *Journal of Consumer Research*, 14 (September), 141-154.

Biederman, I., R.J. Mezzanotte, and J.C. Rabinowitz (1982), "Scene Perception: Detecting and Judging Objects Undergoing Relational Violations," *Cognitive Psychology*, 14, 143-177.

Biehl, A.L. (1993), "Converting Image into Equity," in *Brand Equity and Advertising: Advertising's Role in Building Strong Brands*, eds. D. Aaker and A.L. Biehl, Hillsdale, NJ: Lawrence Erlbaum, 67-82.

Biehal, G. and D. Chakravarti (1983), "Information Accessibility as a Moderator of Consumer Choice," *Journal of Consumer Research*, 10 (June), 1-14.

Bindra, D. (1976), *A Theory of Intelligent Behavior*, New York: Wiley.

Bodenhausen, G.V. (1993), "Emotion, Arousal, and Stereotypic judgments: A Heuristic Model of Affect and Stereotyping," in *Affect, Cognition, and Stereotyping: Interactive Processes in Group Perception*, eds. D.M. Mackie and D.L. Hamilton, San Diego, CA: Academic Press, 13-37.

Bodenhausen, G.V. and R.S. Wyer, Jr. (1985), "Effects of Stereotypes on Decision Making and Information-Processing Strategies," *Journal of Personality and Social Psychology*, 48 (2), 267-282.

Bogart, L. (1967), *Strategy in Advertising*, New York: Harcourt, Brace & World.

Bolen, W.H. (1984), *Advertising*, 2nd Edition, New York: Wiley.

Bond, R.N., J. Welkowitz, H. Goldschmidt, and S. Wattenberg (1987), "Vocal Frequency and Person Perception: Effects of Perceptual Salience and Nonverbal Sensitivity," *Journal of Psycholinguistic Research*, 16 (4), 335-350.

Boote, A.S. (1981), "Market Segmentation by Personal Values and Salient Product Attributes," *Journal of Advertising Research*, 21 (February), 29-35.

Borgida, E. and N. Brekke (1981), "The Base Rate Fallacy in Attribution and Prediction," in *New Directions in Attribution Research*, Vol. 3, eds. J.H. Harvey, W. Ickes, and R.F. Kidd, Hillsdale, NJ: Lawrence Erlbaum.

Borgida, E. and B. Campbell (1982), "Belief Relevance and Attitude-Behavior Consistency: The Moderating Role of Personal Experience," *Journal of Personality and Social Psychology*, 42, 239-247.

Borgida, E. and B. Howard-Pitney (1983), "Personal Involvement and the Robustness of Perceptual Salience Effects," *Journal of Personality and Social Psychology*, 45 (3), 560-570.

Bovee, C.L. and W.F. Arens (1995), *Contemporary Advertising*, 5th Edition, Homewood, IL: Irwin.

Bower, G.H., J.B. Black, and T.S. Turner (1979), "Scripts in Memory for Text," *Cognitive Psychology*, 11, 177-220.

Boulding, K. (1956), *The Image*, Ann Arbor, MI: University of Michigan Press.

Braig, B.M. (1999), "Interdisciplinary Insights into Incongruity: Cognition, Language, and Art," (Special Session Summary), in *Advances in Consumer Research*, eds. E.J. Arnould and L.M. Scott, Provo, UT: Association for Consumer Research, 156-157.

Brandt, H. (1942), "An Evaluation of the Attensity of Isolation by Means of Ocular Photography," *American Journal of Psychology*, 55, 230-239.

Bransford, J.D. and M.K. Johnson (1972), "Contextual Prerequisites for Understanding: Some Investigations of Comprehension and Recall," *Journal of Verbal Learning and Verbal Behavior*, 11, 717-726.

Braun, K.A. (1999), "Postexperience Advertising Effects on Consumer Memory," *Journal of Consumer Research*, 25 (March), 319-334.

Brennen, G.A. and R. Brennen (1982), "Memory and Markets, or Why Are Your Paying $2.99 for a Widget?," *Journal of Business*, 55 (1), 147-158.

Bretherton, I., S. McNew, and M. Beeghly-Smith (1981), "Early Person Knowledge as Expressed in Gestural and Verbal Communication: When Do Infants Acquire a 'Theory of Mind'?," in *Infant Social Cognition: Empirical and Theoretical Considerations*, eds. M. Lamb and L. Sherrod, Hillsdale, NJ: Lawrence Erlbaum.

Brewer, M.B. (1988), "A Dual Process Model of Impression Formation," *Advances in Social Cognition*, 1, 1-36.

Brewer, W.F. (1974), "There Is No Convincing Evidence for Operator or Classical Conditioning in Adult Humans," in *Cognition and the Symbolic Processes*, eds. W.B. Weimer and D.S. Palermo, Hillsdale, NJ: Lawrence Erlbaum, 1-42.

Brewer, W.F. and G.V. Nakamura (1984), "The Nature and Functions of Schemas," in *Handbook of Social Cognition*, Vol. 1, eds. R.S. Wyer and T.K. Srull, Hillsdale, NJ: Lawrence Erlbaum, 119-160.

Briggs, R. and N. Hollis (1997), "Advertising on the Web: Is There Response before Click-through?," *Journal of Advertising Research*, 37 (2), 33-45.

Brisoux, J.E. and E.J. Chéron (1990), "Brand Categorization and Product Involvement," in *Advances in Consumer Research*, Vol. 17, eds. M.E. Goldberg et al., Provo, UT: Association for Consumer Research, 101-109.

Britt, S.H. (1978), *Psychological Principles of Marketing and Consumer Behavior*, London: Lexington Books.

Britt, S.H., S.C. Adams, and A.S. Miller (1972), "How Many Advertising Exposure per Day?," *Journal of Advertising Research*, 12 (1), 3-9.

Broadbent, D.E. (1958), *Perception and Communication*, Oxford, UK: Pergamon Press.

Brosius, H.B. (1989), "Influence of Information Features and New Content on Learning from Television News," *Journal of Broadcasting and Electronic Media*, 33, 1-14.

Brown, C.L. and G.S. Carpenter (2000), "Why Is the Trivial Important? A Reasons-Based Account for the Effects of Trivial Attributes on Choice," *Journal of Consumer Research*, 26 (March), 372-385.

Brown, C.L. and A. Chernev (1997), "Decision Biases in Evaluating Ambiguous Information," (Special Session Summary), in *Advances in Consumer Research*, eds. M. Brucks and D.J. MacInnis, Provo, UT: Association for Consumer Research, 173-174.

Brown, T.J. (1992), "Schemata in Consumer Research: A Connectionist Approach," in *Advances in Consumer Research*, Vol. 19, eds. J.F. Sherry, Jr. and B. Sternthal, Provo, UT: Association for Consumer Research, 787-794.

Bruce, V. and P.R. Green (1990), *Visual Perception: Physiology, Psychology, and Ecology*, Hove, UK: Lawrence Erlbaum.

Brucks, M. (1985), "The Effects of Product Class Knowledge on Information Search Behavior," *Journal of Consumer Research*, 12 (June), 1-15.

Bruner, J.S. (1957), "On Perceptual Readiness," *Psychological Review*, 64, 123-152.

Bruner, J.S. and L. Postman (1949), "On the Perception of Incongruity," *Journal of Personality*, 18, 206-223. [Reprinted as "The Perception of Incongruity," in *Visual Perception* (1970), ed. M.D. Vernon, London: Penguin Books, 319-326.]

Brunswick, E. (1952), *The Conceptual Framework of Psychology*, Chicago, IL: University of Chicago Press.

Buchholz, L.M. and R.E. Smith (1991), "The Role of Consumer Involvement in Determining Cognitive Response to Broadcast Advertising," *Journal of Advertising*, 20 (1), 4-17.

Burke, M.C. and J. Edell (1989), "The Impact of Feelings on Ad-Based Affect and Cognition," *Journal of Marketing Research*, 26 (February), 69-83.

Burke, R.R. and W.S. DeSarbo (1986), "Computer-Assisted Print Ad Evaluation," in *Advances in Consumer Research*, Vol. 13, ed. R.J. Lutz, Provo, UT: Association for Consumer Research, 93-95.

Burke, R.R. and T.K. Srull (1988), "Competitive Interference and Consumer Memory for Advertising," *Journal of Consumer Research*, 15 (June), 55-68.

Burnkrant, R.E. and H.R. Unnava (1987), "Effects of Variation in Message Execution on the Learning of Repeated Brand Information," in *Advances in Consumer Research*, Vol. 14, eds. M. Wallendorf and P. Anderson, Provo, UT: Association for Consumer Research, 173-176.

Burton, S.t and E. Blair (1988), "Response Frame Effects in Most Important Attribute Data," *Applied Marketing Research*, 28 (Spring), 32-38.

Cabanac, M. (1971), "Physiological Role of Pleasure," *Science*, 1973, 1103-1107.

Caccavale, J.G., T.C. Wanty III, and J.A. Edell (1982), "Subliminal Implants in Advertisements: An Experiment," in *Advances in Consumer Research*, Vol. 9, ed. A.A. Mitchell, Ann Arbor, MI: Association for Consumer Research, 418-423.

Calder, B.J. (1978), "Cognitive Response, Imagery, and Scripts: What Is the Cognitive Basis of Attitude?," in *Advances in Consumer Research*, Vol. 5, ed. H.K. Hunt, Ann Arbor, MI: Association for Consumer Research, 630-634.

Calder, B.J. and B. Sternthal (1980), "Television Commercial Wearout: An Information Processing View," *Journal of Marketing Research*, 27 (May), 173-186.

Calkins, M.W. (1894), "Associations," *Psychological Review*, 1, 476-483.

Calkins, M.W. (1896), "An Essay Analytic and Experimental," *Psychological Review Monograph Supplement*, No. 2.

Cantor, N. and W. Mischel (1977), "Traits as Prototypes: Effects in Recognition Memory," *Journal of Personality and Social Psychology*, 35 (1), 38-48.

Caprara, G.V. and C. Barbaranelli (1996), "La Danza degli Aggettivi,", *Micro & Macro Marketing*, 5, 7-21.

Caprara, G.V. and C. Barbaranelli (2000), *Capi di Governo, Telefonini, Bagni Schiuma: Determinanti Personali dei Comportamenti di Voto e di Acquisto*, Milano, Italy: Cortina Editore.

Caprara, G.V., C. Barbaranelli, and G. Guido (1998a), "Empirical Investigations of Determinants of Purchase Intention According to the Theory of Planned Behavior," *Ricerche di Psicologia*, 22 (3), 147-168.

Caprara, G.V., C. Barbaranelli, and G. Guido (1998b), "Personality as Metaphor: Extension of the Psycholexical Hypothesis and the Five Factor Model to Brand and Product Personality Description," in *European Advances in Consumer Research*, Vol. 3, eds. B. Englis e A. Olafsson, Provo, UT: Association for Consumer Research, 61-69.

Caprara, G.V., C. Barbaranelli, and G. Guido (forthcoming/a), "Brand Personality: How to Make the Metaphor Fit," *Journal of Consumer Psychology*.

Caprara, G.V., C. Barbaranelli, and G. Guido (forthcoming/b), "The *Prospect Model*: How to Analize and Forecast the Influence of Brand and Product Personality on Determinants of Purchase Intention", *Testing Psicometria Metodologia*.

Caprara, G.V., C. Barbaranelli, and P. Zimbardo (1997), "Politicians Uniquely Simple Personalities", *Nature*, 335, 493.

Caprara, G.V. and M. Perugini (1994), "Personality Described by Adjectives: The Generalizability of the Big Five to the Italian Lexical Context," *European Journal of Personality*, 8, 357-369.

Carpenter, G.S., R. Glazer, and K. Nakamoto (1994), "Meaningful Brands From Meaningless Differentiation: The Dependence on Irrelevant Attributes," *Journal of Marketing Research*, 31 (August), 339-350.

Carpenter, G.S. and K. Nakamoto (1989), "Consumer Preference Formation and Pioneering Advantage," *Journal of Marketing Research*, 26 (August), 285-298.

Caron, A.J. and R.F. Caron (1981), "Processing of Relational Information as an Index of Infant Risk," in *Preterm Birth and Psychological Development*, eds. S. Friedman and M. Sigman, New York: Academic Press, 219-240.

Caron, A.J., R.F. Caron, and P. Glass (1983), "Responsiveness to Relational Information as a Measure of Cognitive Functioning in Nonsuspect Infants," in *Infants Born at Risk: Physiological, Perceptual, and Cognitive Processes*, eds. T. Field and A. Sostek, New York: Grune & Stratton.

Cattell, R.B. (1945), "The Description of Personality: Principles and Findings in a Factor Analysis," *American Journal of Psychology*, 58, 69-90.

Cavanagh, J.P. (1972), "Relation between the Immediate Memory Span and the Memory Search Rate," *Psychological Review*, 79 (6), 525-530.

Celsi, R.L. and J.C. Olson (1988), "The Role of Involvement in Attention and Comprehension Processes," *Journal of Consumer Research*, 15 (September), 210-224.

Chaiken, S. (1987), "The Heuristic Model of Persuasion," in *Social Influence: The Ontario Symposium*, Vol. 5, eds. M.P. Zanna, J.M. Olson, and C.P. Herman, Hillsdale, NJ: Lawrence Elrbaum, 3-39.

Chaiken, S. and A.H. Eagly (1976), "Communication Modality as a Determinant of Message Persuasiveness and Message Comprehensibility," *Journal of Personality and Social Psychology*, 34 (4), 605-614.

Chaiken, S. and A.H. Eagly (1983), "Communication Modality as a Determinant of Persuasion: The Role of Communicator Salience," *Journal of Personality and Social Psychology*, 45 (2), 241-256.

Chaiken, S., A. Liberman, and A.H. Eagly (1989), "Heuristic and Systematic Information Processing Within and Beyond the Persuasion Context," in *Unintended Thought*, eds. J.S. Uleman and J.A. Bargh, New York: Guilford Press, 212-252.

Chakravarti, D. and J.G. Lynch, Jr. (1983), "A Framework for Exploring Context Effects on Consumer Judgment and Choice," in *Advances in Consumer Research*, Vol. 10, eds. R.P. Bagozzi and A.M. Tybout, Ann Arbor, MI: Association for Consumer Research, 289-297.

Chandler, M.J. (1977), "Social Cognition: A Selective Review of Current Research," in *Knowledge and Development*, eds. W. Overton and J. Gallagher, New York: Plenum Press.

Chang, T.M. (1986), "Semantic Memory: Facts and Models," *Psychological Bulletin*, 99, 199-220.

Chattopadhyay, A. and K. Basu (1990), "Humor in Advertising: The Moderating Role of Prior Brand Evaluation," *Journal of Marketing Research*, 27 (November), 466-476.

Chevalier, M. (1975), "Increase in Sales Due to In-Store Displays," *Journal of Marketing Research*, 12 (November), 426-431.

Childers, T.L. and M.J. Houston (1983), "Imagery Paradigms for Consumer Research: Alternative Perspectives from Cognitive Psychology," in *Advances in Consumer Research*, Vol. 10, eds. R.P. Bagozzi and A.M. Tybout, Ann Arbor, MI: Association for Consumer Research, 59-64.

Childers, T.L. and M.J. Houston (1984), "Conditions for a Picture-Superiority Effect on Consumer Memory," *Journal of Consumer Research*, 11 (September), 643-654.

Childers, T.L. and J. Jass (1995), "Effects of Spot Color on the Attentional Processing and Memory of Print Ads," Unpublished manuscript, University of Minnesota.

Choi, Incheol, R.E. Nisbett, and E.E. Smith (1997), "Culture, Category Salience, and Inductive Reasoning," *Cognition*, 65, 15-32.

Christenfeld, N. (1995), "Choices from Identical Options," *Psychological Science*, 6, 50-55.

Chung, S.-W. and K. Szymanski (1997), "Effects of Brand Name Exposure on Brand Choices: An Implicit Memory Perspective," in *Advances in Consumer Research*, eds. M. Brucks and D.J. MacInnis, Provo, UT: Association for Consumer Research, 288-294.

Churchill, G.A., Jr. (1979), "A Paradigm for Developing Better Measures of Marketing Constructs," *Journal of Marketing Research*, 16 (February), 64-73.

Cimbalo, R.S., C. McQuestion, and D.M. Witting (1997), "Short Term Memory Isolation: Null, Facilitative, and Debilitating Effects and Their Preconditions," *Journal of General Psychology*, 103, 171-178.

Clark, T. (1990), "International Marketing and National Character: A Review and Proposal for an Integrative Theory," *Journal of Marketing*, 54 (October), 66-79.

Cline, T.W. and J.J. Kellaris (1999), "The Joint Impact of Humor and Arguments Strength in a Print Advertising Context: A Case for Weaker Arguments," *Psychology and Marketing*, 16 (1), 69-86.

Cohen, C.E. (1977), "Cognitive Basis of Stereotyping," Paper Presented at the American Psychological Association Annual Meeting, San Francisco, September.

Cohen, J.B. (1982), "The Role of Affect in Categorization: Toward a Reconsideration of the Concept of Attitude," in *Advances in Consumer Research*, Vol. 9, ed. A.A. Mitchell, Ann Arbor, MI: Association for Consumer Research, 94-100.

Cohen, J.B. and K. Basu (1987), "Alternative Models of Categorization: Toward a Contigent Processing Framework," *Journal of Consumer Research*, 13 (March), 455-472.

Cohen, J.B. and D. Chakravarti (1990), "Consumer Psychology," *Annual Review of Psychology*, 41, 243-288.

Cohen, K. (1981), "The Development of Strategies of Visual Search," in *Eye Movements: Cognition and Visual Perception*, eds. D. Fisher, R. Monty, and J. Senders, Hillsdale, NJ: Lawrence Erlbaum.

Collins, A.M. and E.F. Loftus (1975), "A Spreading-Activation Theory of Semantic Processing," *Psychological Review*, 82 (6), 407-428.

Collins, A.M. and M.R. Quillian (1969), "Retrieval Time from Semantic Memory," *Journal of Verbal Learning and Verbal Behavior*, 8, 240-247.

Colman, A.M. (1997), "Salience and Focusing in Pure Coordination Games," *Journal of Economic Methodology*, 4 (1), 61-81.

Colombo, J., M. O'Brien, D.W. Mitchell, and F.D. Horowitz (1986), "Stimulus Salience and Relational Task Performance," *Infant Behavior and Development*, 9 (3), 377-380.

Consumer Psychology: Critical Perspectives (forthcoming), London: Routledge.

Cooper, L.G. (2000), "Strategic Marketing Planning for Radically New Products," *Journal of Marketing*, 64 (January), 1-16.

Coren, S. and L.M. Ward (1989), *Sensation & Perception*, Orlando, FL: Harcourt Brace Jovanovich.

Cornish, P. (1987), "Advertising That Gets Talked About," *Advertising Age*, (November 2), 64.

Costley, C.L. and M. Brucks (1992), "Selective Recall and Information Use in Consumer Preferences," *Journal of Consumer Research*, 18 (March), 464-474.

Coulter, R.H. and G. Zaltman (1994), "Using the Zaltman Metaphor Elicitation Technique to Understand Brand Images," in *Advances in Consumer Research*, Vol. 21, eds. C.T. Allen and D. Roedder-John, Provo, UT: Association for Consumer Research, 501-507.

Coupey, E. and K. Jung (1996), "Forming and Updating of Product Category Perceptions: The Influence of Goals and Discrepancy," *Psychology and Marketing*, 13 (7), 695-713.

Cowley, E. (1999), "Primacy Effects: When First Learned Is Better Recalled," in *European Advances in Consumer Research*, eds. B. Dubois et al., Provo, UT: Association for Consumer Research, 155-160.

Craig, C.S., B. Sternthal, and C. Leavitt (1976), "Advertising Wearout: An Experimental Analysis," *Journal of Marketing Research*, 13 (November), 365-372.

Craik, F.I.M. and R.S. Lockhart (1972), "Levels of Processing: A Framework for Memory Research," *Journal of Verbal Learning and Verbal Behavior*, 11, 671-676.

Crane, E. (1972), *Marketing Communications*, 2nd Edition, New York: Wiley.

Crocker, J. (1981), "Judgments of Covariation of Social Perceivers," *Psychological Bulletin*, 90 (2), 272-292.

Crocker, J. and K.M. McGraw (1984), "What's Good for the Goose Is Not Good for the Gander: Solo Status as an Obstacle to Occupational Achievement for Males and Females," *American Behavioral Scientist*, 27 (3), 357-369.

Crowder, R.G. (1976), *Principles of Learning and Memory*, Hillsdale, NJ: Lawrence Erlbaum.

Csikzentmihalyi, M. (1990), *Flow: The Psychology of Optimal Experience*, New York: Harper-Perennial.

Cupchik, G.C. and H. Leventhal (1974), "Consistency between Expressive Behavior and the Evaluation of Humourous Stimuli: The Role of Sex and Self Observation," *Journal of Personality and Social Psychology*, 30 (3), 429-442.

Curhan, R.C. (1973), "Shelf Space Allocation and Profit Maximization in Mass Retailing," *Journal of Marketing*, 37, 54-60.

Curlo, E. and D. Elrman (1999), "Danger and Excitement: An Example of Paired Opposites in Advertising," in *Advances in Consumer Research*, eds. E.J. Arnold and L.M. Scott, Provo, UT: Association for Consumer Research, 300-305.

Currim, I.S., C.B. Weinberg, and D.R. Wittink (1981), "Design of Subscription Programs for a Performing Art Series," *Journal of Consumer Research*, 8 (June), 67-75.

Damon, W. (1981), "Exploring Children's Social COgnition on Two Fronts," in *Social Cognitive Development: Frontiers and Possible Futures*, eds. J. Flavell and L. Ross, Cambridge, UK: Cambridge University Press.

Davis, L.L. (1990), "Social Salience: What We Notice First about a Person," *Perceptual and Motor Skills*, 71 (1), 334.

Dawar, N. (1992), "The Epistemological Role of Metaphor in Consumer Research," Unpublished manuscript, INSEAD (Fontainebleau), France.

Debevec, K. and E. Iyer (1986), "The Influence of Spokespersons in Altering a Product's Gender Image: Implications for Advertising Effectiveness," *Journal of Advertising*, 15 (4), 12-19.

Debren, E.K., S.T. Fiske, and R. Hastie (1979), "The Independence of Evaluative and Item Information Impression and Recall Order Effects in Behavior-Based Impression Formation," *Journal of Personality and Social Psychology*, 37 (October), 1758-1768.

DeCharms, R. (1968), *Personal Causation: The Internal Affective Determinants of Behavior*, New York: Academic Press.

Deci, E.L. (1975), *Intrinsic Motivation*, New York: Plenum Press.

De Heer, J. and T.B.C. Poiesz (1998), "Dynamic Characteristics of Motivation, Ability and Opportunity to Process Commercial Information," in *Advances in Consumer Research*, eds. J.W. Alba and J.W. Hutchinson, Provo, UT: Association for Consumer Research, 532-537.

Deighton, J. (1996), "The Future of Interactive Marketing," *Harvard Business Review*, 74 (6), 151-162.

Dember, W.N. (1960), *The Psychology of Perception*, New York: Holt, Rinehart and Winston.

Dholakia, N., N. Mundorf, and R.R. Dholakia (1991), "Acceptance of New Information and Communication Services: A Strategic Framework," Working Paper, RITIM, University of Rhode Island, Kingston, http://ritim.cba.uri.edu/wp/wp91-02.html.

Diamond, D.S. (1968), "A Quantitative Approach to Magazine Advertisement Format Selection," *Journal of Marketing Research*, 5 (November), 376-386.

Dick, A., D. Chakravarti, and G. Biehal (1990), "Memory-Based Inferences During Consumer Choice," *Journal of Consumer Research*, 17 (June), 82-93.

Digman, J.M. (1990), "Personality Structure: Emergence of the Five Factors Model," *Annual Review of Psychology*, 41, 417- 440.

Digman, J. M. (1997). "Higher-order Factors of the Big Five," *Journal of Personality and Social Psychology*, 73, 1246-1256.

Dix, T. and S. Herzberger (1983), "The Role of Logic and Salience in the Development of Causal Attribution," *Child Development*, 54 (4), 960-967.

Dobni, D. and G.M. Zinkhan (1990), "In Search of Brand Image: A Foundation Analysis," in *Advances in Consumer Research*, Vol. 17, eds. M.E. Goldberg et al., Provo, UT: Association for Consumer Research, 110-119.

Donovan, R.J. and G. Jalleh (1999), "Positively versus Negatively Framed Product Attributes: The Influence of Involvement," *Psychology and Marketing*, 16 (7), 613-630.

Dooley, R.P. and L.E. Harkins (1970), "Functional and Attention-Getting Effects of Color on Graphic Communications," *Perceptual and Motor Skills*, 31, 851-854.

Douglas, T., G.A. Field, and L.X. Tarpey (1967), *Human Behavior in Marketing*, Columbus, OH: Merrill Books.

Dover, P.A. (1982), "Inferential Belief Formation: An Overlooked Concept in Information Processing Research," in *Advances in Consumer Research*, Vol. 9, ed. A.A. Mitchell, Ann Arbor, MI: Association for Consumer Research, 187-189.

Dubois, B. (2000), *Understanding the Consumer*, London: Prentice-Hall.

Du Preez, J.P., A. Diamantopoulos, B.B. Schlegelmilch (1994), "Product Standardization and Attribute Saliency: A Three-Country Empirical Comparison," *Journal of International Marketing*, 2 (1), 7-28.

Durgee, J.F. (1988), "Commentary: Understanding Brand Personality," *Journal of Consumer Marketing*, 5 (Summer), 21-25.

Duval, S. (1976), "Conformity on a Visual Task as a Function of Personal Novelty on Attitudinal Dimensions and Being Reminded of the Object Status of Self," *Journal of Experimental Social Psychology*, 12, 87-98.

Duval, S. and V. Hensley (1977), "Extensions of Objective Self-Awareness Theory: The Focus of Attention-Causal Attribution Hypothesis," in *New Directions in Attribution Research*, Vol. 1, eds. J. H. Harvey, W.J. Ickes, and R.F. Kidd, Hillsdale, NJ: Lawrence Erlbaum.

Duval, S. and R.A. Wicklund (1972), *A Theory of Objective Self-Awareness*, New York: Academic Press.

Duval, S. and R.A. Wicklund (1973), "Effects of Objective Self-Awareness on Attribution of Causality," *Journal of Experimental Social Psychology*, 9, 17-31.

Eagly, A.H. and S. Chaiken (1993), *The Psychology of Attitudes*, San Diego, CA: Harcourt Brace Janovich.

Eastman, S.T. (1998), "The Impact of Strutural Salience within On-air Promotion," *Journal of Broadcasting and Electronic Media*, Winter, 42 (1), 50-80.

Ebbinghaus, H. (1885), *Memory*, New York: Dover.

Eco, U. (1979), *The Role of the Reader: Explorations in the Semiotics of Text*, Bloomington, IN: Indiana University Press.

Edell, J.A. and K.L. Keller (1989), "The Information Processing of Coordinated Media Campaigns," *Journal of Marketing Research*, 26 (May), 149-163.

Edell, J.A. and R. Staelin (1983), "The Information Processing of Pictures in Print Advertisements," *Journal of Consumer Research*, 10 (June), 45-61.

Ehrenberg, A., N. Barnard, and J. Scriven (1997), "Differentiation or Salience," *Journal of Advertising Research*, (November/December), 7-14.

Ehrenberg, A., J. Scriven, and N. Barnard (1997), "Advertising and Price," *Journal of Advertising Research*, (May/June), 27-35.

Einhorn, H.J. and R.M. Hogarth (1985), "Ambiguity and Uncertainty in Probabilistic Inference," *Psychological Bulletin*, 92, 433-461.

Einhorn, H.J. and R.M. Hogarth (1987), "Decision Making under Ambiguity," in *Rational Choice: The Constrast between Economics and Psychology*, eds. R.M. Hogarth and M.W. Reder, Chicago, IL: University of Chicago Press, 41-66.

Eisen, S.V. and L.Z. McArthur (1979), "Evaluating and Sentencing a Defendant as a Function of His Salience and the Perceiver's Set," *Personality and Social Psychology Bulletin*, 5 (1), 48-52.

Eiser, J.R. and W. Stroebe (1972), *Categorization and Social Judgment*, London: Academic Press.

Elio, R. and J.R. Anderson (1984), "The Effects of Information Order and Learning Mode on Schema Abstraction," *Memory and Cognition*, 12, 20-30.

Elliott, M.T. and P.S. Speck (1998), "Consumer Perceptions of Advertising Clutter and Its Impact across Various Media," *Journal of Advertising Research*, 38 (January/February), 29-41.

Endicott, C. (1997), "A Red-Letter Year: Phenomenal 13.8% in 96 Sets New Benchmark," *Advertising Age*, (May 5), 42.

Endler, N.S. and A.J. Rosenstein (1997), "Evolution of the Personality Construct in Marketing and Its Applicability to Contemporary Personality Research," *Journal of Consumer Psychology*, 6 (1), 55-66.

Engel, J.F., R.D. Blackwell, and P.W. Miniard (1997), *Consumer Behavior*, 8th Edition, Orlando, FL: The Dryden Press.

Erber, R. and S.T. Fiske (1984), "Outcome Dependency and Attention to Inconsistent Information," *Journal of Personality and Social Psychology*, 47 (4), 709-726.

Eysenck, M.W. (1979), "Depth, Elaboration, and Distinctiveness," in *Levels of Processing in Human Memory*, eds. L.S. Cermak and F.I.M. Craik, Hillsdale, NJ: Lawrence Erlbaum, 89-118.

Eysenck, M.W. and M.C. Eysenck (1980), "Effects of Processing Depth, Distinctiveness, and Word Frequency on Retention," *British Journal of Psychology*, 71, 263-274.

Eysenck, M.W. and M.T. Keane (1990), *Cognitive Psychology*, London: Lawrence Erlbaum.

Farb, P. (1978), *Humankind*, Boston, MA: Houghton Mifflin.

Farquhar, P.H. and P.M. Herr (1993), "The Dual Structure of Brand Associations," in *Brand Equity and Advertising: Advertising's Role in Building Strong Brands*, eds. D. Aaker and A.L. Biehl, Hillsdale, NJ: Lawrence Erlbaum, 263-277.

Fazio, R.H. (1981), "On the Self-Perception Explanation of the Overjustification Effect: The Role of the Salience of Initial Attitude," *Journal of Experimental Social Psychology*, 17 (4), 417-426.

Fazio, R.H. (1986), "How Do Attitudes Guide Behavior?," in *The Handbook of Motivation and Cognition: Foundations of Social Behavior*, eds. R.M. Sorrentino and E.T. Higgins, New York: Guilford, 204-243.

Fazio, R.H. (1989), "On the Power and Function of Attitudes: The Role of Attitude Accessibility," in *Attitude Structure and Function*, eds. A.R. Pratkanis, S.J. Breckler, and A.G. Greenwald, Hillsdale, NJ: Lawrence Erlbaum.

Fazio, R.H. (1990a), "Multiple Processes by Which Attitudes Guide Behavior: The MODE Model as an Integrative Framework," in *Advances in Experimental Social Psychology*, Vol. 23, ed. M.P. Zanna, San Diego, CA: Academic Press, 75-109.

Fazio, R.H. (1990b), "Testing Thirteen Attitude Scales for Agreement and Brand Discrimination," *Journal of Marketing*, 43 (Fall), 20-32.

Fazio, R.H., J. Chen, E.C. McDonel, and S.J. Sherman (1982), "Attitude Accessibility, Attitude-Behavior Consistency, and the Strength of the Object-Evaluation Association," *Journal of Experimental Social Psychology*, 18, 339-357.

Fazio, R.H., P.M. Herr, and M.C. Powell (1992), "On the Development and Strength of Category-Brand Association in Memory: The Case of Mystery Ads," *Journal of Consumer Psychology*, 1, 1-13.

Fazio, R.H., M.C. Powell, and Herr, P.M. (1983), "Toward a Process Model of the Attitude-Behavior Relation: Accessing One's Attitude upon Mere Observation of the Attitude Object," *Journal of Personality and Social Psychology*, 44, 723-735.

Fazio, R.H., M.C. Powell, and C.J. Williams (1989), "The Role of Attitude Accessibility in the Attitude-to-Behavior Process," *Journal of Consumer Research*, 16 (December), 280-288.

Fazio, R.H., D.M. Sanbonmatsu, D.M. Powell, and F.R. Kardes (1986), "On the Automatic Activation of Attitudes," *Journal of Personality and Social Psychology*, 50, 229-238.

Fazio, R.H. and C.J. Williams (1986), "Attitude Accessibility as a Moderator of the Attitude-Perception and Attitude-Behavior Relations: An Investigation of the 1984 Presidential Election," *Journal of Personality and Social Psychology*, 51, 505-514.

Fazio, R.H. and M.P. Zanna (1978), "Attitudinal Qualities Relating to the Strength of the Attitude-Behavior Relationship," *Journal of Experimental Social Psychology*, 14 (4), 398-408.

Feigenbaum, E.A. and Simon, H.A. (1962), "A Theory of the Serial Position Effect," *British Journal of Psychology*, 53 (3), 307-320.

Feldman, J.M. (1988), "Objects in Categories and Objects as Categories," *Advances in Social Cognition*, 1, 53-64.

Feldman, J.M. and J.G. Lynch, Jr. (1988), "Self-Generated Validity and Other Effects of Measurements on Belief, Attitude, Intention, and Behavior," *Journal of Applied Psychology*, 73 (3), 421-435.

Fink, G.R., J.C. Marshall, P.W. Halligan, R.J. Dolan (1999), "Hemispheric Asymmetries in Global/Local Processing Are Modulated by Perceptual Salience," *Neuropsychologia*, 37, 31-40.

Finn, A. (1988), "Print Ad Recognition Readership Scores: An Information Processing Perspective," *Journal of Consumer Research*, 25 (May), 168-177.

Fischhoffs, B. (1982), "Debiasing," in *Judgement under Uncertainty: Heuristics and Biases*, eds. D. Kahneman, P. Slovic, and A. Tversky, Cambridge, UK: Cambridge University Press.

Fishbein, M. (1963), "An Investigation of the Relationships between Beliefs about an Object and the Attitude toward the Object," *Human Relations*, 16, 233-240.

Fishbein, M. (1967), "A Consideration of Beliefs and Their Role in Attitude Measurement," in *Readings in Attitude Theory and Measurement*, ed. M. Fishbein, New York: Wiley, 257-266.

Fishbein, M. and I. Ajzen (1975), *Belief, Attitude, Intention, and Behavior*, Reading, MA: Addison-Wesley.

Fiske, S.T. (1980), "Attention and Weight in Person Perception: The Impact of Negative and Extreme Behavior," *Journal of Personality and Social Psychology*, 38 (6), 889-906.

Fiske, S.T. (1982), "Schema-triggered Affect: Applications to Social Perception," in *Affect and Cognition: The 17th Annual Carnegie Symposium*, eds. M.S. Clark and S.T. Fiske, Hillsdale, NJ: Lawrence Erlbaum, 55-78.

Fiske, S.T., D.A. Kenny, and S.E. Taylor (1982), "Structural Models for the Mediation of Salience Effects on Attribution," *Journal of Experimental Social Psychology*, 18 (2), 105-127.

Fiske, S.T. and M.A. Pavelchak (1984), "Category-Based versus Piecemeal-Based Affective Responses: Developments in Schematic-Triggered Affect," in *The Handbook of Motivation and Cognition: Foundations of Social Behavior*, eds. R.M. Sorrentino and E.T. Higgins, New York: Guilford Press, 167-203.

Fiske, S.T. and S.E. Taylor (1984), *Social Cognition*, New York: Random House.

Fiske, S.T. and S.E. Taylor (1991), *Social Cognition*, 2nd Edition, New York: McGraw-Hill.

Fiske, S.T., S.E. Taylor, N.L. Etcoff, and J.K. Laufer (1979), "Imagine, Empathy, and Causal Attribution," *Journal of Experimental Social Psychology*, 15, 356-377.

Fitzgerald Bone, P. and P. Scholder Ellen (1990), "The Effect of Imagery Processing and Imagery Content on Behavioral Intentions," in *Advances in Consumer Research*, Vol. 17, eds. M.E. Goldberg et al., Provo, UT: Association for Consumer Research, 449-454.

Folkes, V.S. (1988), "Recent Attribution Research in Consumer Behavior: A Review and New Directions," *Journal of Consumer Research*, 14 (March), 548-565.

Ford, G.T. and R.A. Smith (1987), "Inferential Beliefs in Consumer Evaluations: An Assessment of Alternative Processing Strategies," *Journal of Consumer Research*, 14, 363-371.

Forehand, M.R. and K.L. Keller (1996), "Initial Retrieval Difficulty and Subsequent Recall in an Advertising Setting," *Journal of Consumer Psychology*, 5 (4), 299-323.

Forgas, J.P. (1981), "Epilogue: Everyday Understanding and Social Cognition," in *Social Cognition: Perspectives on Everyday Understanding*, ed. J.P. Forgas, New York: Academic Press.

Forgas, J.P. (1998), "On Being Happy and Mistaken: Mood Effects on the Fundamental Attribution Error," *Journal of Personality and Social Psychology*, 75, 318-331.

Forster, K.I. and S.M. Chambers (1973), "Lexical Access and Naming Time," *Journal of Verbal Learning and Verbal Behavior*, 12 (December), 627-635.

Foss, D.J. (1982), "A Discourse on Semantic Priming," *Cognitive Psychology*, 14, 590-607.

Fournier, S. (1995), "Understanding Consumer-Brand Relationships," Harvard Business School Working Paper 96-018.

Fournier, S. (1998), "Consumers and Their Brands; Developing Relationship Theory in Consumer Research," *Journal of Consumer Research*, 24 (March), 343-373.

Fox, R.J., D.M. Krugman, J.E. Fletcher, and P.M. Fisher (1998), "Adolescents' Attention to Beer and Cigarette Print Ads and Associated Product Warnings," *Journal of Advertising*, 27 (3), 57-67.

Foxall, G.R. (1990), *Consumer Psychology in Behavioral Perspective*, London: Routledge.

Foxall, G.R., S. Brown, and R.E. Goldsmith (1998), *Consumer Psychology for Marketing*, London: Intl Thomson Business Press.

Frable, D.E., T. Blackstone, and C. Scherbaum (1990), "Marginal and Mindful: Deviants in Social Interactions," *Journal of Personality and Social Psychology*, 59, 140-149.

Friedman, A. (1979), "Framing Pictures: The Role of Knowledge in Automatized Encoding and Memory for Gist," *Journal of Experimental Psychology: General*, 108, 316-355.

Friedman, A. and L. Liebelt (1981), "On the Time Course of Viewing Pictures with a View towards Remembering," in *Eye Movements: Cognition and Visual Perception*, eds. D. Fisher, R. Monty, and J. Senders, Hillsdale, NJ: Lawrence Erlbaum, 137-155.

Friedstad, M. and E. Thorson (1993), "Remembering Ads: The Effects of Encoding Strategies, Retrieval Cues, and Emotional Responses," *Journal of Consumer Psychology*, 2 (1), 1-23.

Gardner, M.P. (1981), *An Information Processing Approach to Examining Advertising Effects*, Unpublished doctoral dissertation, Graduate School of Industrial Administration, Carnegie-Mellon University, Pittsburgh, PA.

Gardner, M.P. (1982), "Attribute Determinance: A Function of Past Memory and External Factors," in *Advances in Consumer Research*, Vol. 9, ed. A.A. Mitchell, Ann Arbor, MI: Association for Consumer Research, 177-182.

Gardner, M.P. (1983), "Advertising Effects on Attributes Recalled and Criteria Used for Brand Evaluations," *Journal of Consumer Research*, 10 (December), 310-318.

Geistfeld, L.V., G.B. Sproles and S.B. Bradenhop (1977), "The Concept and Measurement of a Hierarchy of Product Characteristics," in *Advances in Consumer Research*, Vol. 4, ed. W.D. Perreault, Atlanta: Association for Consumer Research.

Gelman, R. and E. Spelke (1981), "The Development of Thoughts about Animate and Inanimate Objects: Implications for Research and Social Cognition," in *Social Cognitive Development: Frontiers and Possible Futures*, Cambridge, UK: Cambridge University Press.

Georgescu-Roegen, N. (1958), "The Nature of Expectations and Uncertainty," in *Expectations Uncertainty, and Business Behavior*, ed. M.J. Bowman, New York: Social Science Research Council, 11-29.

Ghorpade, S. (1986), "Agenda Setting: A Test of Advertising's Neglected Function," *Journal of Advertising Research*, 26 (August/September), 23-27.

Gibbs, L.L. (1977), *The Effect of Salience and Acquiescence on Socially Desirable Responses to Questionnaire Items*, Unpublished thesis, University of Florida at Gainesville.

Gibson, E.J. (1969), *Principles of Perceptual Learning and Development*, New York: Appleton-Century-Crofts.

Gibson, J.J. (1959), "Perception as a Function of Stimulation," in *Psychology: A Study of a Science*, ed. S. Koch, New York: McGraw Hill, 456-501.

Gibson, J.J. (1966), *The Senses Considered as Perceptual Systems*, Boston, MA: Houghton Mifflin.

Gibson, L.D. (1996), "What Can One TV Exposure Do?," *Journal of Advertising Research*, 36 (March/April), 9-18.

Gilbert, D.T. and P.S. Malone (1995), "The Correspondence Bias," *Psychological Bulletin*, 117, 21-38.

Giora, R. (1999), "On the Priority of Salient Meanings: Studies of Literal and Figurative Language," *Journal of Pragmatics*, 31, 919-929.

Glass, A.L. and K.J. Holyoak (1986), *Cognition*, New York: Random House.

Glass, A.L., K.J. Holyoak, and J. L. Santa (1979), *Cognition*, Reading, MA: Addison-Wesley.

Glassman, M. and W.J. Pieper (1980), "Processing Advertising Information: Deception, Salience, and Inferential Belief Formation," *Journal of Advertising*, (Winter), 3-10.

Glick, J. (1978), "Cognition and Social Cognition: An Introduction," in *The Development of Social Understanding*, eds. J. Glick and K. Clarke-Stewart, New York: Gardner Press.

Goldberg, L.R. (1992), "The Development of the Markers of the Big-Five Factor Structure," *Psychological Assessment*, 4, 26-42.

Goldberg, L.R. (1993), "The Structure of Phenotypic Personality Traits," *American Psychologist*, 48 (1), 26-34.

Goldberg, M.E. and G.J. Gorn (1987), "Happy and Sad TV Programs: How They Affect Reactions to Commercials," *Journal of Consumer Research*, 14 (3), 387-403.

Goldberg, M.E. and J. Hartwick (1990), "The Effects of Advertising Reputation and Extremity of Advertising Claim on Advertising Effectiveness," *Journal of Consumer Research*, 17 (September), 172-179.

Goldstein, J.H., J.M. Suls, and S. Anthony (1972), "Enjoyment of Specific Types of Humor Content: Motivation or Salience?," in *The Psychology of Humor*, eds. J.H. Goldstein and P.E. McGhee, New York: Academic Press, 159-171.

Golinkoff, R.M. and C.G. Harding (1980), *The Development of Causality: The Distinction between Animates and Inanimates*, Paper presented at the International Conference on Infant Studies, April, New Haven.

Goodstein, R.C. (1993), "Category-based Applications in Advertising: Motivating More Extensive Ad Processing," *Journal of Consumer Research*, 20, 87-99.

Goodwin, S.A. (1980), "Impacts of Stimulus Variables on Exploratory Behavior," in *Advances in Consumer Research*, Vol. 7, ed. J.C. Olson, Ann Arbor, MI: Association for Consumer Research, 264-269.

Gorn, G.J., W.J. Jacobs, and M.J. Mana (1986), "Observations on Awareness and Conditioning," in *Advances in Consumer Research*, Vol. 13, ed. R.J. Lutz, Provo, UT: Association for Consumer Research, 415-416.

Gould, S.J. (1996), "Gender Identity and Gender Salience: A Dual Path, Person-Situation Approach to Gender Effects in Consumer Research," in *Advances in Consumer Research*, Vol. 23, eds. K.P. Corfman and J.G. Lynch, Provo, UT: Association for Consumer Research, 478-483.

Graeff, T.R. (1996), "Image Congruence Effects on Product Evaluations: The Role of Self-Monitoring and Public/Provate Consumption," *Psychology and Marketing*, 13 (5), 481-499.

Graeff, T.R. (1997), "Consumption Situations and the Effects of Brand Image on Consumers' Brand Evaluations," *Psychology and Marketing*, 14 (1), 49-70.

Grainger, J., J.K. O'Regan, A.M. Jacobs, and J. Segui (1992), "Neighborhood Frequency Effects and Letter Visibility in Visual Word Recognition," *Perception and Psychophisics*, 51 (1), 49-56.

Grant, S. and J. Quiggin (1998), "The Meeting Place Problem: Salience and Search," *Journal of Economic Behavior and Organization*, 33, 271-283.

Green, D.W., E.J. Hammond, and S. Supramaniam (1983), "Letters and Shapes: Developmental Changes in Search Strategies," *British Journal of Psychology*, 74, 11-16.

Green, R.T. (1956), "Surprise as a Factor in the Von Restorff Effect," *Journal of Experimental Psychology*, 52 (5344.

Green, R.T. (1958a), "The Attention-Getting Value of Structural Change," *British Journal of Psychology*, 49, 311-314.

Green, R.T. (1958b), "Surprise, Isolation, and Structural Change as Factors Affecting Recall of a Temporal Series," *British Journal of Psychology*, 49, 21-30.

Greenwald, A.G. and C. Leavitt (1984), "Audience Involvement in Advertising: Four Levels," *Journal of Consumer Research*, 11 (June), 581-592.

Greer, D., R. Potts, J. Wright, and A.C. Houston (1982), "The Effects of Television Commercial Form and Commercial Placement on Children's Social Behavior and Attention," *Child Development*, 53 (3), 611-619.

Gregory, R. (1973), "The Confounded Eye," in *Illusion in Nature and Art*, eds. R.L. Gregory and E. H. Gombrich, London: Duckworth.

Guido, G. (1991), "Implementing a Pan European Marketing Strategy", *Long Range Planning*, 24 (5), 23-33. [Reprinted as "Marketing Mix Strategies in the Europe of Post-1992", in *Euromarketing: Effective Strategies for International Trade and Export* (1994), eds. E. Kaynak e P.N. Ghauri, New York: International Business Press, 139-161.]

Guido, G. (1992), "What U.S. Marketers Should Consider In Planning a Pan-European Approach," *Journal of Consumer Marketing*, 9 (2), 29-33.

Guido, G. (1993), "Brand Awareness in Print Advertisements: An Incongruity-Salience Hypothesis," Research Papers in Management Studies, No. 22 (June), University of Cambridge, England.

Guido, G. (1995), "Lavater's Physiognomy: A Taxonomy for Endorsers in Print Advertisements", in *European Advances in Consumer Research*, Vol. 2, ed. F. Hansen, Provo, UT: Association for Consumer Research, 118-131.

Guido, G. (1996a), "A Review and Critique of Memory-based Definitions of Salience," Unpublished manuscript, University of Cambridge, England.

Guido, G. (1996b), "The Effects of Salience on Choice: An Annotated Bibliography," Unpublished manuscript, University of Cambridge, England.

Guido, G. (1997), "Increasing Memory for Advertising Messages According to the Theory of In-Salience," in *Proceedings of Three AMA Special Conferences on New and Evolving Paradigms: The Emerging Future of Marketing*, ed. T. Meenagham, Dublin, Ireland: American Marketing Association, June, 727-744.

Guido, G. (1998), "The Dichotic Theory of Salience: A Framework for Assessing Attention and Memory," in *European Advances in Consumer Research*, Vol. 3, eds. B. Englis e A. Olafsson, Provo, UT: Association for Consumer Research, 114-119.

Guido, G. (1999), *Aspetti Metodologici e Operativi del Processo di Ricerca di Marketing*, Padova, Italy: CEDAM.

Guido, G. (2000), *Economia e Gestione delle Imprese: Principi, Schemi, Modelli*, Milano, Italy: Franco Angeli Editore.

Guido, M.G. (1999), *The Acting Reader: Schema/Text Interaction in the Dramatic Discourse in Poetry*, New York: Legas.

Gunter, B. (1987), *Poor Reception: Misunderstanding and Forgetting Broadcast News*, Hillsdale, NJ: Lawrence Erlbaum.

Ha, Y.-W. and S.J. Hoch (1989), "Ambiguity, Processing Strategy, and Advertising-Evidence Interactions," *Journal of Consumer Research*, 16 (December), 354-360.

Haber, R.N. and M. Hershenson (1980), *The Psychology of Visual Perception*, 2nd Edition, New York: Holt, Rinehart and Winston.

Hagen, J.W. and K.P. Wilson (1982), "Some Selected Thoughts on Attention," *Merrill-Palmer Quarterly*, 28 (4), 529-532.

Haley, R.I. (1968), "Benefit Segmentation: A Decision-Oriented Research Tool," *Journal of Marketing*, 32, 30-35.

Haley, R.I. (1971), "Beyond Benefit Segmentation," *Journal of Advertising Research*, 11, 3-8.

Haley, R.I. (1983), "A New Approach to Image Analysis through Multidimensional Scaling," *Journal of Travel Research*, 16, 3-7.

Haley, R.I. and P.B. Case (1979), "Testing Thirteen Attitude Scales for Agreement and Brand Discrimination," *Journal of Marketing*, 43 (Fall), 20-32.

Haley, R.I. and A.L. Baldinger (1991), "The ARF Copy Research Validity Project," *Journal of Advertising Research*, 31 (April/May), 11-32.

Hamilton, D.L. (1979), "A Cognitive-Attributional Analysis of Stereotyping," in *Advances in Experimental Social Psychology*, Vol. 12, ed. L. Berkowitz, New York: Academic Press.

Hansen, F. (1972), *Consumer Choice Behavior: A Cognitive Theory*, New York: Free Press.

Hanssens, D.M. and B.A. Weitz (1980), "The Effectiveness of Industrial Print Advertisements across Product Categories," *Journal of Marketing Research*, 17 (August), 294-306.

Hartley, E.L. (1946), *Problems in Prejudice*, New York: Kings Crown Press.

Hasher, L., D. Goldstein, and T. Toppino (1977), "Frequency and the Conference of Referential Validity," *Jornal of Verbal Learning and Verbal Behavior*, 16 (February), 107-112.

Hastie, R. (1980), "Memory for Behavioral Information that Confirms or Contradicts a Personality Impression," in *Person Memory: The Cognitive Basis of Social Perception*, eds. R. Hastie et al., Hillsdale, NJ: Lawrence Erlbaum, 141-172.

Hastie, R. (1981), "Schematic Principles in Human Memory," in *Social Cognition: The Ontario Symposium*, Vol. 1, eds. E.T. Higgins, C.P. Herman, and M.P. Zanna, Hillsdale, NJ: Lawrence Erlbaum, 39-88.

Hastie, R. and P.A. Kumar (1979), "Person Memory: Personality Traits as Organizing Principles in Memory for Behaviors," *Journal of Personality and Social Psychology*, 37, 25-38.

Hastie, R., T. Ostrom, E. Ebbesen, R. Wyer, D. Hamilton, and D. Carlston (1980), *Person Memory: The Cognitive Basis of Social Perception*, (eds.), Hillsdale: Lawrence Erlbaum.

Hastie, R., B. Park, and R. Weber (1984), "Social Memory," in *Handbook of Social Cognition*, Vol. 2, eds. R.S. Wyer and T.K. Srull, Hillsdale, NJ: Lawrence Erlbaum, 151-202.

Haugtvedt, C.R., R.E. Petty, and J.T. Cacioppo (1992), "Need for Cognition and Advertising: Understanding the Role of Personality Variables in Consumer Behavior," *Journal of Consumer Psychology*, 1, 239-260.

Hawkins, D.L., R. Best, and K.A. Coney (1992), *Consumer Behavior: Implications for Marketing Strategy*, 5th Edition, Homewood, IL: Irwin.

Hawkins, S.A. and S.J. Hoch (1992), "Low-Involvement Learning: Memory without Evaluation," *Journal of Consumer Research*, 19 (September), 212-225.

Head, H. (1920), *Studies in Neurology*, London: Frowde.

Hebb, D.O. (1966), *A Textbook of Psychology*, Philadelphia, MA: Saunders.

Heckler, S.E. and T.L. Childers (1992), "The Role of Expectancy and Relevancy in Memory for Verbal and Visual Information: What Is Incongruency?," *Journal of Consumer Research*, 18 (March), 475-492.

Heider, F. (1944), "Social Perception and Phenomenal Causality," *Psychological Review*, 51, 358-374.

Heider, F. (1958), *The Psychology of Interpersonal Relations*, New York: John Wiley.

Heilman, M.E. (1980), "The Impact of Situational Factors on Personnel Decisions Concerning Women: Varying the Sex Composition of the Applicant Pool," *Organizational Behavior and Human Performance*, 26, 386-395.

Helson, H. (1959), "Adaptation Level Theory," in *Psychology: A Study of a Science: 1, Sensory Perception and Physiological Formulations*, New York: McGraw-Hill.

Helson, H. (1964), "Current Trends and Issues in Adaptation-Level Theory," *American Psychologist*, Vol. 19, 26-38.

Hendon, D.W. and E.L. Williams (1985), "Winning the Battle for Your Customer," *Journal of Consumer Marketing*, 2 (Fall), 65-75.

Hendrick, C.C. (1972), "The Effects of Salience of Stimulus Inconsistency on Impression Formation," *Journal of Personality and Social Psychology*, 22, 219-222.

Herr, P.M. (1989), "Priming Price: Prior Knowledge and Context Effects," *Journal of Consumer Research*, 16 (June), 67-75.

Herr, P.M., F.R. Kardes, and J. Kim (1991), "Effects of Word-of-Mouth and Product-Attribute Information on Persuasion: An Accessibility-Diagnosticity Perspective," *Journal of Consumer Research*, 17 (March), 454-462.

Hesslow, G. (1988), "The Problem of Causal Selection," in *Contemporary Science and Natural Explanation: Commonsense Perception of Causality*, ed. D.J. Hilton, Brighton, England: The Harvester Press.

Higgins, E.T. and J.A. Bargh (1987), "Social Cognition and Social Perception," *Annual Review of Psychology*, 38, 369-425.

Higgins, E.T. and G.A. King (1981), "Accessibility of Social Constructs: Information-Processing Consequences of Individual and Contextual Variability," in *Personality, Cognition, and Social Interaction*, eds. N. Cantor and J.F. Kihlstrom, Hillsdale, NJ: Lawrence Erlbaum, 69-121.

Higgins, E.T., G.A. King, and G.H. Mavin (1982), "Individual Construct Accessibility and Subjective Impressions and Recall," *Journal of Personality and Social Psychology*, 43 (1), 35-47.

Higgins, E.T., N.A. Kuiper, and J.M. Olson (1981), "Social Cognition: A Need to Get Personal," in *Social Cognition: The Ontario Symposium*, Vol. 1, eds. E.T. Higgins, C.P. Herman, and M.P. Zanna, Hillsdale, NJ: Lawrence Erlbaum, 395-420.

Higgins, E.T., W. S. Rholes, and C. F. Jones (1977), "Category Accessibility and Impression Formation," *Journal of Experimental Social Psychology*, 13, 141-153.

Hilton, D.J. and B.R. Slugoski (1986), "Knowledge-based Causal Attribution: The Abnormal Conditions Focus Model," *Psychological Review*, 93, 75-88.

Hilton, D.J., R.H. Smith, and M.D. Alicke (1988), "Knowledge-based Information Acquisition: Norms and the Functions of Consensus Information," *Journal of Personality and Social Psychology*, 55, 530-540.

Hintzman, D.L. (1974), "Theoretical Implications of the Spacing Effect," in *Theories in Cognitive Psychology: The Loyola Symposium*, ed. R.L. Solso, Potomac, MD: Lawrence Erlbaum, 77-99.

Hintzman, D.L. (1990), "Human Learning and Memory: Connections and Dissociations," *Annual Review of Psychology*, 41,109-139.

Hirsch, F. (1976), *Social Limits to Growth*, Cambridge, MA: Harvard University Press.

Hirschman, E.C. (1980), "Innovativeness, Novelty Seeking and Consumer Creativity," *Journal of Consumer Research*, 7 (December).

Hitchon, J. (1991), "Effects of Metaphorical vs. Literal Headlines on Advertsing Persuasion," in *Advances in Consumer Research*, Vol. 18, eds. R.H. Holman and M. Solomon, Provo, UT: Association for Consumer Research, 221-233.

Hoch, S.J. (1984), "Availability and Interference in Predictive Judgment," *Journal of Experimental Psychology: Learning, Memory, and Cognition*, 10 (4), 649-662.

Hoffman, D.D. and M. Singh (1997), "Salience of Visual Parts," *Cognition*, 63, 29-78.

Hoffman, D.L. and R. Batra (1991), "Viewer Response to Programs: Dimensionality and Concurrent Behavior," *Journal of Advertising Research*, (August/September), 46-56.

Hoffman, M.L. (1981), "Perspectives on the Difference between Understanding People and Understanding Things: The Role of Affect," in *Social Cognitive Development*, eds. J. Flavell and L. Ross, Cambridge, UK: Cambridge University Press.

Holbrook, M.B. (1978), "Beyond Attitude Structure," *Journal of Marketing Research*, 15 (November), 546-556.

Holbrook, M.B. and D.R. Lehmann (1980), "Form versus Content in Predicting Starch Scores," *Journal of Advertising Research*, 20 (August), 53-62.

Holbrook, M.B. and W.L. Moore (1981), "Feature Interactions in Consumer Judgments of Verbal versus Pictorial Presentations," *Journal of Consumer Research*, 8 (June), 103-113.

Holbrook, M.B. and J. O'Shaughnessy (1984), "The Role of Emotion in Advertising," *Psychology and Marketing*, 1 (Summer), 45-64.

Holden, S.J.S. (1993), "Understanding Brand Awareness: Let Me Give You a C(l)ue!," in *Advances in Consumer Research*, Vol. 20, eds. L. McAlister and M.L. Rothschild, Provo, UT: Association for Consumer Research, 383-388.

Holden, S.J.S. and R.J. Lutz (1992), "Ask Not What the Brand Can Evoke: Ask What Can Evoke the Brand," in *Advances in Consumer Research*, Vol. 19, eds. J.F. Sherry, Jr. and B. Sternthal, Provo, UT: Association for Consumer Research, 101-107.

Holden, S.J.S. and M. Vanhuele (1999), "Know the Name, Forget the Exposure: Brand Familiarity versus Memory of Exposure Context," *Psychology and Marketing*, 16 (6), 479-496.

Hollander, S.W. and J. Jacoby (1973), "Recall of Crazy, Mixed-Up TV Commercials," *Journal of Advertising Research*, 13 (June), 39-42.

Homer, P.M. and L.R. Kahle (1986), "A Social Adaptation Explanation of the Effects of Surrealism on Advertising," *Journal of Advertising*, 15 (2), 50-54,60.

Homer, P.M. and S.-G. Yoon (1992), "Message Framing and the Interrelationships among Ad-Based Feelings, Affect, and Cognition," *Journal of Advertising*, 21 (March), 19-32.

Hong, S.-T.i and R.S. Wyer, Jr. (1989), "Effects of Country-of-Origin and Product-Attribute Information on Product Evaluation: An Information Processing Perspective," *Journal of Consumer Research*, 16 (September), 175-187.

Hornik, J. (1980), "Quantitative Analysis of Visual Perception of Print Advertisement," *Journal of Advertising Research*, 20 (December), 41-48.

Houston, D.A. and R.H. Fazio (1989), "Biased Processing as a Function of Attitude-Accessibility: Making Objective Judgments Subjectively," *Social Cognition*, 7, 51-66.

Houston, M.J., T.L. Childers, and S.E. Heckler (1987), "Picture-Word Consistency and the Elaborative Processing of Advertisement," *Journal of Marketing Research*, 24 (November), 359-369.

Hovland, C.I., O.J. Harvey, and M. Sherif (1957), "Assimilation and Constrast Effects in Reaction to Communication and Attitude Change," *Journal of Abnormal and Social Psychology*, 55 (September), 244-252.

Howard, J.A. and J.N. Sheth (1969), *The Theory of Buyer Behavior*, New York: Wiley.

Hoyer, W.D. and S.P. Brown (1990), "Effects of Brand Awareness on Choice for a Common, Repeat-Purchase Product," *Journal of Consumer Research*, 17 (September), 141-148.

Huber, J., J.W. Payne, and C. Puto (1982), "Adding Asymmetrically Dominated Alternatives. Violations of Regularity and the Similarity Hypothesis," *Journal of Consumer Research*, 9 (June), 90-98.

Humphreys, G.W. and V. Bruce (1989), *Visual Cognition*, London: Lawrence Erlbaum.

Hung, K. (2000), "Narrative Music in Congruent and Incongruent TV Advertising," *Journal of Advertising*, 24 (1), 25-34.

Hutchinson, J.W. (1983), "Expertise and the Structure of Free Recall," in *Advances in Consumer Research*, Vol. 10, eds. R.P. Bagozzi and A.M. Tybout, Ann Arbor, MI: Association for Consumer Research, 585-589.

Isen, A.M. and A.H. Hastorf (1982), "Some Perspectives on Cognitive Social Psychology," in *Cognitive Social Psychology*, eds. A.H. Hastorf and A.M. Isen, New York: Elsevier.

Iyengar, S. and D.R. Kinder (1987), *News That Matters: Television and American Opinion*, Chicago, IL: University of Chicago Press.

Iyer, E.S. (1988), "The Influence of Verbal Content and Relative Newness on the Effectiveness of Comparative Advertising," *Journal of Advertising*, 17 (3), 15-21.

Jaccard, J., D. Brinberg, and L.J. Ackerman (1986), "Assessing Attitude Importance: A Comparison of Six Methods," *Journal of Consumer Research*, 12 (4), 463-468.

Jacoby, J., G.V. Johar, and M. Morrin (1998), "Consumer Psychology: A Quadrennium," *Annual Review of Psychology*, 49, 319-344.

Jain, S.P. and D. Maheswaran (2000), "Motivated Reasoning: A Depth-of-Processing Perspective," *Journal of Consumer Research*, 26 (March), 358-371.

Jakobovits, L.A. (1968), "Effects of Mere Exposure," *Journal of Personality and Social Psychology Supplement*, 9 (June), 30-32.

James, W. (1890), *Principles of Psychology*, New York: Holt.

Janiszewski, C. (1988), "Preconscious Processing Effects: The Independence of Attitude Formation and Conscious Thought," *Journal of Consumer Research*, 15 (September), 199-209.

Janiszewski, C. (1990), "The Influence of Print Advertisement Organization on Affect Toward a Brand Name," *Journal of Consumer Research*, 17 (June), 53-65.

Janiszewski, C. and B. Bickart (1994), "Managing Attention," in *Advances in Consumer Research*, Vol. 21, eds. C.T. Allen and D. Roedder-John, Provo, UT: Association for Consumer Research, 329.

Janiszewski, C. and T. Meyvis (2000), "Determinants of Processing Fluency in Judgments Biased by Prior Exposure," Working Paper, University of Florida at Gainesville, August.

Jarvenpaa, S.L. (1990), "Graphic Displays in Decision Making: The Visual Salience Effect," *Journal of Behavioral Decision Making*, 3 (4), 247-262.

Jeffrey, W.E. (1982), "Selective Attention: Response Inhibition or Stimulus Differentiation?," *Merril-Palmer Quarterly*, 28, 523-528.

Jenkins, W.O. and L. Postman (1948), "Isolation and Spread of Effect in Serial Learning," *American Journal of Psychology*, 61, 214-221.

Johnson, E.J. and J.E. Russo (1984), "Product Familiarity and Learning New Information," *Journal of Consumer Research*, 11 (June), 542-550.

Johnson, J.D. (1990), "Effects of Communicative Factors on Partecipation in Innovations," *Journal of Business Communication*, (Winter), 7-22.

Johnson, M.D. and J.M. Katrichis (1988), "The Existence and Perception of Redundancy in Consumer Information Environments," *Journal of Consumer Policy*, (2), 131-157.

Johnson, W.A., K.J. Hawley, S.H. Plewe, J.M.G. Elliott, and M.J. De Witt (1990), "Attention Capture by Novel Stimuli," *Journal of Experimental Psychology: General*, 119 (4), 397-411.

Jolibert, A. and G. Baumgartner (1997), "Values, Motivations, and Personal Goals: Revisited," *Psychology and Marketing*, 14 (7), 675-688.

Jones, E.E. and K.E. Davis (1965), "From Acts to Dispositions. The Attribution Process in Person Perception," in *Advances in Experimental Social Psychology*, Vol. 2, ed. L. Berkowitz, New York: Academic Press, 220-266.

Jones, E.E. and G.R. Goethals (1972), "Order Effects in Impression Formation: Attribution Context and the Nature of the Entity," in *Attribution: Perceiving the Causes of Behavior*, eds. E.E. Jones et al., Morristown, NJ: General Learning Press, 27-46.

Jones, E.E. and D. McGillis (1976), "Correspondent Inferences and the Attribution Cube: A Comparative Reappraisal," in *New Directions in Attribution Research*, Vol. 1, eds. J.H. Harvey, W.J. Ickes, and R.F. Kidd, Hillsdale, NJ: Lawrence Erlbaum, 389-420.

Jones, E.E. and R.E. Nisbett (1972), "Divergent Perceptions of the Causes of Behavior," in *Attribution: Perceiveing the Causes of Behavior*, eds. E.E. Jones et al., Morristown, NJ: General Learning Press.

Joseph, W.B. (1982), "The Credibility of Physically Attractive Communications: A Review," *Journal of Advertising*, 11 (3), 15-24.

Just, M. and P.A. Carpenter (1976), "Eye Fixations and Cognitive Processes," *Cognitive Psychology*, 8, 441-480.

Kahle, L.R. (1984), *Attitudes and Social Adaptation: A Person-Situation Interaction Approach*, Oxford, UK: Pergamon Press.

Kahle, L.R., S.E. Beatty, and P. Kennedy (1987), "Comment on Classical Conditioning Human Consumers," in *Advances in Consumer Research*, Vol. 14, eds. M. Wallendorf and P.F. Anderson, Provo, UT: Association for Consumer Research.

Kahle, L.R. and P.M. Homer (1985), "Physical Attractiveness of the Celebrity Endorser: A Social Adaptation Perspective," *Journal of Consumer Research*, 11 (March), 954-961.

Kahle, L.R. and S.G. Timmer (1983), "A Theory and Method for Studying Values," in *Social Values and Social Change: Adaptation to Life in America*, ed. L.R. Kahle, New York: Praeger.

Kahneman, D. (1973), *Attention and Effort*, Englewood Cliffs, NJ: Prentice-Hall.

Kahneman, D. and A. Tversky (1973), "On the Psychology of Prediction," *Psychological Review*, 80, 237-251.

Kahneman, D. and A. Tversky (1979), "Prospect Theory: An Analysis of Decision under Risk," *Econometrica*, 47, 263-291.

Kahneman, D. and A. Tversky (1982a), "The Simulation Heuristic," in *Judgment under Uncertainty: Heuristics and Biases*, eds. D. Kahneman, P. Slovic, and A. Tversky, New York: Cambridge University Press, 201-209.

Kahneman, D. and A. Tversky (1982b), "Variants of Uncertainty," *Cognition*, 11, 143-157.

Kamins, M.A. (1990), "An Investigation into the 'Match-Up' Hypothesis in Celebrity Advertising: When Beauty May Be Only Skin Deep," *Journal of Advertising*, 19 (1), 4-13.

Kamins, M.A., L.J. Marks, and D. Skinner (1991), "Television Commercial Evaluation in the Context of Program Induced Mood: Congruency versus Consistency Effects," *Journal of Advertising*, 20 (2), 1-14.

Kanouse, D.E. (1972), "Language, Labeling, and Attribution," in *Attribution: Perceiving the Causes of Behavior*, eds. E.E. Jones et al., Morristown, NJ: General Learning Press.

Kanouse, D.E. (1984), "Explaining Negativity Biases in Evaluation and Choice Behavior," in *Advances in Consumer Research*, Vol. 11, ed. T. Kinnear, Ann Arbor, MI: Association for Consumer Research, 703-708.

Kaplan, K.J. and M. Fishbein (1969), "The Source of Beliefs, Their Saliency, and Prediction of Attitude," *Journal of Social Psychology*, 78, 63-74.

Kardes, F.R. (1986), "Effects of Initial Product Judgments on Subsequent Memory-Based Judgments," *Journal of Consumer Research*, 13 (June), 1-11.

Kardes, F.R. (1994), "Consumer Judgment and Decision Process," in *Handbook of Social Cognition*, eds. R.S. Wyer and T.K. Srull, 2nd Edition, Hillsdale, NJ: Lawrence Erlbaum, 323-417.

Karrh, J.A. (1993), "Salience Effects of Brand Placements within Motion Pictures," Unpublished thesis, University of Florida at Gainesville.

Katona, G. (1975), *Psychological Economics*, New York: Elsevier.

Kellaris, J.J. and S. Powell Mantel (1996), "Shaping Time Perceptions with Background Music: The Effect of Congruity and Arousal on Estimates of Ad Durations," *Psychology and Marketing*, 13 (5), 501-515.

Keller, K.L. (1987), "Memory Factors in Advertising: The Effect of Advertising Retrieval Cues on Brand Evaluations," *Journal of Consumer Research*, 14 (December), 316-333.

Keller, K.L. (1991a), "Cue Compatibility and Framing in Advertising," *Journal of Marketing Research*, 28 (February), 42-57.

Keller, K.L. (1991b), "Memory and Evaluation Effects in Competitive Advertising Environments," *Journal of Consumer Research*, 17 (March), 463-476.

Keller, K.L., S.E. Heckler, and M.J. Houston (1998), "The Effects of Brand name Suggestiveness on Advertising Recall," *Journal of Marketing*, 62 (January), 48-57.

Kelley, C.A. (1989), "A Study of Selected Issues in Vividness Research: The Role of Attention and Elaboration Enhancing Cues," in *Advances in Consumer Research*, Vol. 16, ed. T.K. Srull, Provo, UT: Association for Consumer Research, 574-580.

Kelley, H.H. (1972), "Attribution in Social Interaction," in *Attribution: Perceiving the Causes of Behavior*, eds. E.E. Jones et al., Morristown, NJ: General Learning Press, 1-26.

Kelley, H.H. (1973), "The Processes of Causal Attribution," *American Psychologist*, 28 (February), 107-113.

Kelly, G.A. (1955), *The Psychology of Personality Constructs*, New York: Norton.

Key, W.B. (1972), *Subliminal Seduction: Ad Media's Manipulation of a Not So Innocent America*, Englewood Cliffs, NJ: Prentice-Hall.

Kilbourne, W.E. (1984), "An Exploratory Study of Sex Roles in Advertising and Women's Perceptions of Managerial Attributes in Women," in *Advances in Consumer Research*, Vol. 11, ed. T. Kinnear, Provo, UT: Association for Consumer Research, 84-87.

Kim, J., F.R. Kardes, and P.M. Herr (1991), "Consumer Expertise and the Vividness Effect: Implications for Judgment and Inference," in *Advances in Consumer Research*, Vol. 18, eds. R.H. Holman and M.R. Solomon, Provo, UT: Association for Consumer Research, 90-93.

Kintsch, W. (1970), "Models for Free Recall and Recognition," in *Models of Human Memory*, ed. D.A. Norman, New York: Academic Press, 331-373.

Kirk, R.E. (1982), *Experimental Design*, 2nd Edition, Belmont, CA: Brooks/Cole Publishing Company

Kirmani, A. and B. Shiv (1998), "Effects of Source Congruity on Brand Attitudes and Beliefs: The Moderating Role of Issue-Relevant Elaboration," *Journal of Consumer Psychology*, 7 (1), 25-47.

Kirmani, A. and P. Wright (1989), "Memory and Cuing Effects on Decision Framing," in *Advances in Consumer Research*, Vol. 16, ed. T.K. Srull, Provo, UT: Association for Consumer Research, 173-175.

Kirsner, S. (1997), "Jack's Hearing a Word from Sponsors: Sold," *Wired News*, (September 29), http://www.wired.com/news/news/business/story/7223.html.

Kisielius, J. and B. Sternthal (1984), "Detecting and Explaining Vividness Effects in Attitudinal Judgements," *Journal of Consumer Research*, 21 (February), 54-64.

Kisielius, J. and B. Sternthal (1986), "Examining the Vividness Controversy: An Availability-Valence Interpretation," *Journal of Consumer Research*, 12 (March), 418-431.

Kitchin, R. and S. Freundschuh (2000), *Cognitive Mapping: Past, Present and Future*, (eds.), London: Routledge.

Klayman, J. and Y.-W. Ha (1987), "Confirmation, Disconfirmation and Information in Hypothesis Testing," *Psychological Review*, 94 (2), 221-228.

Klein, J.G. and B. Shiv (1996), "Under Siege: How Consumers Respond and Marketers React to Negative Information," (Special Session Summary), in *Advances in Consumer Research*, Vol. 23, eds. K.P. Corfman and J.G. Lynch, Provo, UT: Association for Consumer Research, 456.

Klein, N.M. and S.W. Bither (1987), "An Investigation of Utility-Directed Cutoff Selection," *Journal of Consumer Research*, 14 (September), 240-256.

Kleine, R.E. III, S. Schultz Kleine, and J.B. Kernan (1993), "Mundane Consumption and the Self: A Social-Identity Perspective," *Journal of Consumer Psychology*, 2 (3), 209-235.

Koffka, K. (1935), *Principles of Gestalt Psychology*, New York: Harcourt Brace Jovanovich.

Kohan, X. (1968), "A Physiological Measure of Commercial Effectiveness," *Journal of Advertising Research*, 8 (December), 46-48.

Kollat, D.T, R. Blackwell, and J.F. Engel (1970), *Research in Consumer Behavior*, New York: Holt, Rinehart, and Winston.

Kopytoff, I. (1986), "The Cultural Biography of Things: Commodization as Process," in *The Social Life of Things: Commodities in Cultural Perspective*, ed. J. Appadurai, Cambridge, UK: Cambridge University Press, 64-95.

Koten, J. (1984), "To Grab Viewers' Attention, TV Ads Aim for the Eardrum," *The Wall Street Journal*, 33, January 26.

Krech, D. and R.S. Crutchfield (1948), *Theory and Problems of Social Psychology*, New York: McGraw-Hill Book Co.

Krishna, A., I.S. Currim, and R.W. Shoemaker (1991), "Consumer Perception of Promotional Activity," *Journal of Marketing*, 55 (April), 4-16.

Krishnan, S.H. and C.V. Trappey (1999), "Nonconscious Memory Processes in Marketing: A Historical Perspective and Future Directions," *Psychology and Marketing*, 16 (6), 451-457.

Kruglanski, A.W. (1989), *Lay Epistemics and Human Knowledge: Cognitive and Motivational Bases*, New York: Plenum.

Krugman, H.E. (1965), "The Impact of Television Advertising: Learning without Involvement," *Public Opinion Quarterly*, 29 (Fall), 349-356.

Krugman, H.E. (1966/67), "The Measurement of Advertising Involvement," *Public Opinion Quarterly*, 30 (4), 583-596.

Krugman, H.E. (1988), "Point of View: Limits of Attention to Advertising," *Journal of Advertising Research*, 28 (October/November), 47-50.

Kuhlman, T.L. (1985), "A Study of Salience and Motivational Theories of Humor," *Journal of Personality and Social Psychology*, 49 (1), 281-286.

Kumar, A. (2000), "Interference Effects of Contextual Cues in Advertisements on Memory for Ad Content," *Journal of Consumer Psychology*, 9 (3), 155-166.

Lane, D.M. and D.A. Pearson (1982), "The Development of Selective Attention," *Merrill-Palmer Quarterly*, 28 (3), 317-337.

Lane, D.M. and D.A. Pearson (1983), "Can Stimulus Differentiation and Salience Explain Developmental Changes in Attention? A Reply to Hagen and Wilson, Jeffrey, and Odom," *Merril-Palmer Quarterly*, 29 (2), 227-233.

Lane, V.R. (2000), "The Impact of Ad Repetition and Ad Content on Consumer Perceptions of Incongruent Extensions," *Journal of Marketing*, 64 (April), 80-91.

Lang, A. (1988), "Involuntary Attention and Physiologica Arousal Evoked by Formal Features and Mild Emotion in Television Commercials," Paper presented to the International Communication Association, New Orleans, LA, May.

Lang, A. and P. Lanfear (1990), "The Information Processing of Televised Political Advertising: Using Theory to Maximize Recall," in *Advances in Consumer Research*,

Vol. 17, eds. M.E. Goldberg et al., Provo, UT: Association for Consumer Research, 149-158.

Lang, A. and E. Thorson (1989), "The Effects of Television Videographics and Lecture Familiarity on Adult Cardiac Orienting Responses and Memory," Paper presented to the Information Systems Division of the International Communication Association, San Francisco, CA.

Langer, E.G., S. Fiske, S.T. Fiske, and B. Chanowitz (1976), "Stigma, Staring and Discomfort: A Novel Stimulus Hypothesis," *Journal of Experimental Social Psychology*, 12, 452-463.

Langer, E.J. and R.P. Abelson (1974), "A Patient by Any Other Name...: Clinician Group Difference in Labeling Bias," *Journal of Consulting and Clinical Psychology*, 42, 4-9.

LaTour, M.S., R.E. Pitts, and D.C. Snook-Luther (1990), "Female Nudity, Arousal, and Ad Response: An Experimental Investigation," *Journal of Advertising*, 19 (4), 51-62.

Laurent, G., J.-N. Kapferer, and F. Roussel (1995), "The Underlying Structure of Brand Awareness Scores," *Marketing Science*, 14 (3), G170-G180.

Lavidge, R.J. and G.A. Steiner (1961), "A Model for Predictive Measurements of Advertising Effectiveness," *Journal of Marketing*, 25 (4), 59-62.

Leach, M.P. and A.H. Liu (1998), "The Use of Culturally Relevant Stimuli in International Advertising," *Psychology and Marketing*, 15 (6), 523-546.

Lee, S. and J.H. Barnes, Jr. (1989/1990), "Using Color Preferences in Magazine Advertising," *Journal of Advertising Research*, (December/January), 25-30.

Lee, Y.H. and C. Mason (1999), "Responses to Information Incongruency in Advertising: The Role of Expectancy, Relevancy, and Humor," *Journal of Consumer Research*, 26 (September), 156-169.

Lehmann, D. (1994), "Characteristics of 'Really' New Products," in *And Now for Something Completely Different: 'Really' New Products*, eds. M. Adams and J. LaCugna, Working Paper Report No. 94-124, Cambridge, MA: Marketing Science Institute, 1-20.

Leigh, J.H. (1984), "Recall and Recognition Performance for Umbrella Print Advertisements," *Journal of Advertising*, 13 (4), 5-18,30.

Leigh, J.H. (1992), "Modality Congruence, Multiple Resource Theory and Intermedia Broadcast Comparisons: An Elaboration," *Journal of Advertising*, 21 (2), 55-62.

Levin, I.P. and G.J. Gaeth (1988), "How Consumers Are Affected by the Framing of Attribute Information Before and After Consuming the Product," *Journal of Consumer Research*, 15 (December), 374-378.

Levine, J.M., L.B. Resnick, and E.T. Higgins (1993), "Social Foundations of Cognition," *Annual Review of Psychology*, 44, 585-612.

Lichtenstein, M. and T.K. Srull (1985), "Conceptual and Methodological Issues in Examining the Relationship between Consumer Memory and Judgments," in *Psychological Processes and Advertising Effects: Theory Research and Applications*, eds. L.F. Alwitt and A.A. Mitchell, Hillsdale, NJ: Lawrence Erlbaum.

Lichtenstein, M. and T.K. Srull (1987), "Processing Objectives as a Determinant of the Relationship between Recall and Judgment," *Journal of Experimental Social Psychology*, 23, 93-118.

Lingle, J.H., M.W. Altom, and D.L. Medin (1984), "Of Cabbages and Kings: Assessing the Expendibility of Natural Object Concept Model to Social Things," in *Handbook of Social Cognition*, Vol. 1, eds. R.S. Wyer and T.K. Srull, Hillsdale, NJ: Lawrence Erlbaum, 71-117.

Linquist, J.D. (1974), "Meaning of Image: A Survey of Empirical and Hypothetical Evidence," *Journal of Retailing*, 50, 29-38.

Lockhart, R.S., F.I.M. Craik, and L.L. Jacoby (1976), "Depth of Processing, Recognition and Recall: Some Aspects of a General Memory System," in *Recall and Recognition*, ed. J. Brown, London: Wiley, 75-102.

Loewenstein, G. (1994), "The Psychology of Curiosity: A Review and Reinterpretation," *Psychology Bulletin*, 116 (1), 75-98.

Loken, B. and R. Hoverstad (1985), "Relationships between Information Recall and Subsequent Attitudes: Some Exploratory Findings," *Journal of Consumer Research*, 12 (September), 155-168.

Loken, B. and J. Ward (1990), "Alternative Approaches to Understanding the Determinants of Typicality," *Journal of Consumer Research*, 17 (September), 111-126.

Loundon, D.L. and A.J. Della Bitta (1993), *Consumer Behavior*, 4th Edition, New York: McGraw-Hill.

Lowrey, T.M. (1998), "The Effects of Syntactic Complexity on Advertising Persuasivess," *Journal of Consumer Psychology*, 7 (2), 187-206.

Lucas, D.B. (1942), *The Controlled Recognition Method for Checking Magazine Readership*, New York: Crowell-Collier.

Lumpkin, J.R. and W.R. Darden (1982), "Relating Television Preference Viewing to Shopping Orientation, Life Styles, and Demographics: The Examination of Perceptual and Preference Dimensions of Television Programming," *Journal of Advertising*, 11 (4), 56-67.

Lutz, K.A. and R.J. Lutz (1977), "Effects of Interactive Imagery on Learning: Application to Advertising," *Journal of Applied Psychology*, 62 (4), 493-498.

Lutz, R.J. (1979), "How Difficult Is It to Change Consumer Decision Structure?," in *Analytic Approaches to Product and Marketing Planning*, ed. A.D. Shocker, Cambridge, MA: Marketing Science Institute, 317-334.

Lutz, R.J. (1985), "Affective and Cognitive Antecedents of Attitude toward the Ad: A Conceptual Framework," in *Psychological Processes and Advertising Effects*, eds. L.F. Alwitt and A.A. Mitchell, Hillsdale, NJ: Lawrence Erlbaum, 45-63.

Lutz, R.J. (1991), "The Role of Attitude Theory in Marketing," in *Perspectives in Consumer Behavior*, eds. H.H. Kassarjian and T.S. Robertson, Englewood Cliffs, NJ: Prentice-Hall, 317-339.

Lutz, R.J. and P. Kakkar (1976), "Situational Influence in Interpersonal Persuasion," in *Advances in Consumer Research*, Vol. 3, ed. B.B. Anderson, Cincinnati: Association for Consumer Research, 370-378.

Lynch, J.G., Jr., H. Marmostein, and M.F. Weigold (1988), "Choices from Sets Including Remembered Brands: Use of Recalled Attributes and Prior Overall Evaluations," *Journal of Consumer Research*, 15 (September), 169-184.

Lynch, J.G. and D. Schuler (1994), "The Match-up Effect of Spokesperson and Product Congruency: A Schema Theory Interpretation," *Psychology and Marketing*, 11, 417-445.

Lynch, J.G., Jr. and T.K. Srull (1982), "Memory and Attentional Factors in Consumer Choice: Concepts and Research Methods," *Journal of Consumer Research*, 9 (June), 18-37.

MacEachren, A.M. and T.A. Mistrick (1992), "The Role of Brightness Differences in Figure-Ground: Is Darker Figure?," *Cartographic Journal*, 29 (December), 91-100.

MacInnis, D.J. and B.J. Jaworski (1989), "Information Processing from Advertisements: Toward an Integrative Framework," *Journal of Marketing*, 53 (October), 1-23.

MacInnis, D.J., C. Moorman, and B.J. Jaworski (1991), "Enhancing and Measuring Consumers' Motivation, Opportunity, and Ability to Process Brand Information from Ads," *Journal of Marketing*, 55 (October), 32-53.

MacInnis, D.J. and L.L. Price (1987), "The Role of Imagery in Information Processing: Review and Extension," *Journal of Consumer Research*, 13 (March), 473-491.

MacInnis, D.J. and L.L. Price (1990), "An Explanatory Study of the Effects of Imagery Processing and Consumer Experience on Expectations and Satisfaction," in *Advances in Consumer Research*, Vol. 17, eds. M.E. Goldberg et al., Provo, UT: Association for Consumer Research, 41-47.

MacKenzie, S.B. (1986), "The Role of Attention in Mediating the Effect of Advertising on Attribute Importance," *Journal of Consumer Research*, 13 (September), 174-195.

Mackworth, N.H. and A.J. Morandi (1967), "The Gaze Selects Informative Details within Pictures," *Perception and Psychophysics*, 2 (11), 547-552.

MacLeod, R.B. (1951), "The Place of Phenomenological Analysis in Social Psychological Theory," in *Social Psychology at the Cross-roads*, eds. J.H. Rohrer and M. Sherif, New York: Harper.

Maddi, S.R. (1968), "Meaning, Novelty, and Affect: Comments on Zajonc's Paper," *Journal of Personality and Social Psychology Supplement*, 9 (June), 28-29.

Mahatoo, W.H. (1985), *The Dynamics of Consumer Behavior*, New York: Wiley.

Maheswaran, D. and J. Meyers-Levy (1990), "The Influence of Message Framing and Issue Involvement," *Journal of Marketing Research*, 27 (August), 361-367.

Malaviya, P., J. Kisielius, and B. Sternthal (1996), "The Effect of Type of Elaboration on Advertisement Processing and Judgment," *Journal of Marketing Research*, 33 (November), 410-421.

Malaviya, P. and J. Meyers-Levy (1998), "Understanding Consumers' Response to Incongruent Product Information: New Research and Insights," (Special Session Summary), in *Advances in Consumer Research*, eds. J.W. Alba and J.W. Hutchinson, Provo, UT: Association for Consumer Research, 115.

Malaviya, P., J. Meyers-Levy, and B. Sternthal (1999), "Ad Repetition in a Cluttered Environment: The Influence of Type of Processing," *Psychology and Marketing*, 16 (2), 99-118.

Malaviya, P. and B. Sternthal (1997), "The Persuasive Impact of Message Spacing," *Journal of Consumer Psychology*, 6 (3), 233-255.

Mandler, G. (1967), "Organization and Memory," from *The Psychology of Learning and Motivation*, 1, 309-354. [Reprinted in *Human Memory: Basic Processes* (1977), ed. G. Bower, New York: Academic Press.]

Mandler, G. (1979), "Categorical and Schematic Organization in Memory," in *Memory Organization and Structure*, ed. C.R. Puff, New York: Academic Press, 259-299.

Mandler, G. (1980), "Recognizing: The Judgment of Previous Occurrence," *Psychological Review*, 87 (3), 252-271.

Mandler, G. (1982), "The Structure of Value: Accounting for Taste," in *Affect and Cognition: The 17th Annual Carnegie Symposium*, eds. M.S. Clark and S.T. Fiske, Hillsdale, NJ: Lawrence Erlbaum, 3-36.

Manfredo, M.J. (1989), "A Test of Assumptions Inherent in Attribute-Specific Advertising," *Journal of Travel Research*, (Winter), 8-13.

Marcel, A.J. (1983), "Conscious and Unconscious Perception: An Approach to the Relations between Phenomenal Experience and Perceptual Processes," *Cognitive Psychology*, 15, 238-300.

Markin, R.J., Jr. (1974), *Consumer Behavior: A Cognitive Orientation*, New York: Macmillan.

Marks, L.J. (1985), "Measuring the Content and Structure of Consumer Product Knowledge," Unpublished Ph.D. dissertation, Pennsylvania State University.

Marks, L.J. and M.A. Kamins (1988), "The Use of Product Sampling and Advertising: Effects of Sequence of Exposure and Degree of Advertising Claim Exaggeration on Consumers' Belief Strength, Belief Confidence, and Attitudes," *Journal of Marketing Research*, 25 (August), 266-281.

Markus, H. (1977), "Self-Schema and Processing Information about Self," *Journal of Personality and Social Psychology*, 35 (2), 63-78.

Marra, J. (1990), *Connective Thinking: Techniques for Generating Advertising Ideas*, Englewood Cliffs, NJ: Prentice-Hall.

Martineau, P. (1958), "The Personality of the Retail Store," *Harvard Business Review*, 36 (January-February), 47-55.

McArthur, L.Z. (1980), "Illusory Causations and Illusory Correlations: Two Epistemological Accounts," *Personality and Social Psychology Bulletin*, 6 (4), 507-519.

McArthur, L.Z. (1981), "What Grabs You? The Role of Attention in Impression Formation and Causal Attribution," in *Social Cognition: The Ontario Symposium*, Vol. 1, eds. E.T. Higgins, C.P. Herman, and M.P. Zanna, Hillsdale, NJ: Lawrence Erlbaum, 201-246.

McArthur, L.Z. and E. Ginsberg (1981), "Causal Attribution to Salient Stimuli: An Investigation of Visual Fixation Mediators," *Personality and Social Psychology Bulletin*, 7 (4), 547-553.

McArthur, L.Z. and D.L. Post (1977), "Figural Emphasis and Person Perception," *Journal of Experimental Social Psychology*, 13, 520-535.

McArthur, L.Z. and L.K. Solomon (1978), "Perceptions of Aggressive Encounter as a Function of the Victim's Salience and the Perceiver's Arousal," *Journal of Personality and Social Psychology*, 36 (11), 1278-1290.

McCort, D.J. and N.K. Malhotra (1993), "Culture and Consumer Behavior: Toward an Understanding of Cross-Cultural Consumer Behavior in International Marketing," *Journal of International Consumer Marketing*, 6 (2), 91-127.

McCracken, G. (1986), "Culture and Consumption: A Theoretical Account of the Structure and Movement of the Cultural Meaning of Consumer Goods," *Journal of Consumer Research*, 13 (June), 71-84.

McCrae, R.R., and O.P. John (1992), "An Introduction to Five Factor Model and its Applications," *Journal of Personality*, 60, 175-215.

McDaniel, S.R. (1999), "An Investigation of Match-up Effects in Sport Sponsorship Advertising: The Implications of Consumer Advertising Schemas," *Psychology and Marketing*, 16 (2), 163-184.

McGill, A.L. and P. Anand (1989), "The Effect of Vivid Attributes on the Evaluation of Alternatives: The Role of Differential Attention and Cognitive Elaboration," *Journal of Consumer Research*, 16 (September), 188-196.

McGuire, W.J. (1968), "Résumé and Response from the Consistency Theory Viewpoint," in *Theories of Cognitive Consistency*, eds. R.P. Abelson et al., 259.

McKinnon, G.F., J.P. Kelly, and E.D. Robinson (1981), "Sales Effects of Point-of-Purchase In-Store Signaling," *Journal of Retailing*, 57 (Summer), 49-63.

McKoon, G. and R. Ratcliff (1979), "Priming in Episodic and Semantic Memory," *Journal of Verbal Learning and Verbal Behavior*, 18, 463-480.

McKoon, G. and R. Ratcliff (1986), "Automatic Activation of Episodic Information in a Semantic Memory Task," *Journal of Experimental Psychology: Learning, Memory and Cognition*, 12 (January), 108-115.

McQuarrie, E.F. (1989), "Advertising Resonance: A Semiological Perspective," in *Interpretive Consumer Research*, ed. E.C. Hirschman, Provo, UT: Association for Consumer Research, 97-114.

McQuarrie, E.F. (1990), "How Does an Advertisement Mean - Cue, Claim, Metaphor, Resonance? Discussant's Comments," in *Advances in Consumer Research*, Vol. 17, eds. M.E. Goldberg et al., Provo, UT: Association for Consumer Research, 658-661.

McQuarrie, E.F. and D.G. Mick (1992), "On Resonance: A Critical Pluralist Inquiry into Advertising Rhetoric," *Journal of Consumer Research*, 19 (September), 180-197.

McQuarrie, E.F. and D.G. Mick (1996), "Figures of Rhetoric in Advertising Language," *Journal of Consumer Research*, 22 (December), 424-438.

McQuarrie, E.F. and D.G. Mick (1999), "Visual Rhetoric in Advertising: Text-Interpretive, Experimental, and Reader-Response Analyses," *Journal of Consumer Research*, 26 (June), 37-54.

McSweeney, F.K. and C. Bierley (1984), "Recent Developments in Classical Conditioning," *Journal of Consumer Research*, 11 (September), 619-631.

Menon, G. and M. Wanke (1998), "Accessibility Revisited: Whena dn How It Is Diagnostic for Consumer Judgments," in *Advances in Consumer Research*, eds. J.W. Alba and J.W. Hutchinson, Provo, UT: Association for Consumer Research, 264-265.

Menon, S. and D.p Soman (1999), "Managing Consumer Motivation and Learning: Harnessing the Power of Curiosity for Effective Advertising Strategies," Working Paper Report No. 99-100, Cambridge, MA: Marketing Science Institute.

Merzenich, M.M. and R.C. DeCharms (1996), "Neural Representations, Experience, and Change," in *The Mind-Brand Continuum*, eds. R. Llinas and P.S. Churchland, Cambridge, MA: MIT Press, 61-82.

Messick, D.M. and D.M. Mackie (1989), "Intergroup Relations," in *Annual Review of Psychology*, Vol. 40, eds. M.R. Rosenzweig and L.W. Porter, Palo Alto, CA: Annual Reviews.

Metcalfe, J. (1993), "Novelty Monitoring, Metacognition, and Control in a Composite Holographic Associative Recall Model: Implications for Korsakoff Amnesia," *Psychological Review*, 100 (1), 3-22.

Metha, J., C. Starmer, and R. Sugden (1997), "The Nature of Salience: An Experimental Investigation of Pure Coordination Games," *American Economic Review*, 84 (3), 658-673.

Meyer, R.J. (1981), "A Model of Multiattribute Judgments under Attribute Uncertainty and Informational Contrast," *Journal of Marketing Research*, 18, 428-441.

Meyerowitz, B.E. and S. Chaiken (1987), "The Effect of Message Framing on Breast Self-Examination Attitudes, Intentions, and Behavior," *Journal of Personality and Social Psychology*, 52, 500-510.

Meyers-Levy, J. (1988a), "Factors Affecting the Use of Conceptually Driven and Data Driven Processing," in *Advances in Consumer Research*, Vol. 15, ed. M.J. Houston, Provo, UT: Association for Consumer Research, 169-173.

Meyers-Levy, J. (1988b), "The Influence of Sex Roles on Judgment," *Journal of Consumer Research*, 14 (March), 522-530.

Meyers-Levy, J. (1989a), "Investigating Dimensions of Brand Names that Influence the Perceived Familiarity of Brands," in *Advances in Consumer Research*, Vol. 16, ed. T.K. Srull, Provo, UT: Association for Consumer Research, 258-263.

Meyers-Levy, J. (1989b), "Priming Effects on Product Judgments: A Hemispheric Interpretation," *Journal of Consumer Research*, 16 (June), 76-86.

Meyers-Levy, J. (1989c), "The Influence of a Brand Name's Association Set Size and Word Frequency on Brand Memory," *Journal of Consumer Research*, 16 (September), 197-206.

Meyers-Levy, J. (1991), "Elaborating on Elaboration: The Distinction between Relational and Item-specific Elaboration," *Journal of Consumer Research*, 18 (December), 358-367.

Meyers-Levy, J. and D. Maheswaran (1990), "Message Framing Effects on Product Judgments," in *Advances in Consumer Research*, Vol. 17, eds. M.E. Goldberg et al., Provo, UT: Association for Consumer Research, 461-466.

Meyers-Levy, J. and P. Malaviya (1999), "Consumer Processing of Persuasive Advertisements: An Integrative Framework of Persuasion Theories," *Journal of Marketing*, 63 (Special Issue), 45-60.

Meyers-Levy, J. and L.A. Peracchio (1992), "Getting an Angle in Advertising: The Effect of Camera Angle on Product Evaluations," *Journal of Marketing Research*, 29 (November), 454-461.

Meyers-Levy, J. and A.M. Tybout (1989), "Schema Congruity as a Basis for Product Evaluations," *Journal of Consumer Research*, 16 (June), 39-54.

Meyers-Levy, J. and A.M. Tybout (1997), "Context Effects at Encoding and Judgment in Consumption Settings: The Role of Cognitive Resources," *Journal of Consumer Research*, 24 (June), 1-14.

Mick, D.G. (1986), "Consumer Research and Semiotics: Exploring the Morphology of Signs, Symbols, and Significance," *Journal of Consumer Research*, 13 (September), 196-213.

Mick, D.G. (1988), "Schema-Theoretics and Semiotics: Toward More Holistic, Programmatic Research on Marketing Communication," *Semiotica*, 70, 1-26.

Millar, M.G. and A. Tesser (1986), "Thought-Induced Attitude Change: The Effect of Schema Structure and Commitment," *Journal of Personality and Social Psychology*, 51, 259-269.

Millar, M.G. and A. Tesser (1990), "Attitudes and Behavior: The Cognitive-Affective Mismatch Hypothesis," in *Advances in Consumer Research*, Vol. 17, eds. M.E. Goldberg et al., Provo, UT: Association for Consumer Research, 86-89.

Miller, G.A. (1956), "The Magical Number Seven, Plus or Minus Two: Some Limits to Our Capacity for Processing Information," *Psychological Review*, 63 (2), 81-97.

Miller, K.E. and J.L. Ginter (1979), "An Investigation of Situational Variation in Brand Choice Behavior," *Journal of Marketing Research*, 16 (February), 111-123.

Miller, S. and L. Berry (1998), "Brand Salience versus Brand Image: Two Theories of Advertising Effectiveness," *Journal of Advertising Research*, (September/October), 77-82.

Miniard, P.W., S. Bhatla, K.R. Lord, P.R. Dickson, and H.R. Unnava (1991), "Picture-based Persuasion Processes and the Moderating Role of Involvement," *Journal of Consumer Research*, 18 (June), 92-107.

Miniard, P.W., H.R. Unnava, and S. Bhatla (1989), "Inhibiting Brand Name Recall: A Test of Salience Hypothesis," in *Advances in Consumer Research*, Vol. 16, ed. T.K. Srull, Provo, UT: Association for Consumer Research, 264-270.

Misra, S. and S.E. Beatty (1990), "Celebrity Spokeperson and Brand Congruence," *Journal of Business Research*, 21, 159-173.

Mitchell, A.A. (1982), "Models of Memory: Implications for Measuring Knowledge Structures," in *Advances in Consumer Research*, Vol. 9, ed. A.A. Mitchell, Ann Arbor, MI: Association for Consumer Research, 45-51.

Mitchell, A.A. (1983), "The Effects of Visual and Emotional Advertising: An Information-Processing Approach," in *Advertising and Consumer Psychology*, eds. L. Percy and A.G. Woodside, Lexington, MA: Lexington Books, 197-217.

Mitchell, A.A. and J.C. Olson (1981), "Are Product Attribute Beliefs the Only Mediator of Advertising Effects on Brand Attitude?," *Journal of Marketing Research*, 18 (August), 318-332.

Mittal, B. (1988), "Achieving Higher Seat Beal Usage: The Role of Habit in Bridging the Attitude-Behavior Gap," *Journal of Applied Social Psychology*, 18, 993-1016.

Mittelstaedt, R.A., S. Grossbart, W. Curtis, and S. Devere (1976), "Optimal Stimulation Level and the Adoption Decision Process," *Journal of Consumer Research*, 3 (September), 84-94.

Mizerski, R.W. (1982), "An Attribution Explanation of the Disproportionate Influence of Unfavorable Information," *Journal of Consumer Research*, 9 (December), 301-309.

Moran, W.T. (1990), "Brand Presence and the Perceptual Frame," *Journal of Advertising Research*, 30 (October/November), 9-16.

Morgan, S.E. and T. Reichert (1999), "The Message is in the Metaphor: Assessing the Comprehension of Metaphors in Advertisements," *Journal of Advertising*, 28 (4), 1-12.

Motes, W.H., C.B. Hilton, and J.S. Fielden (1992), "Language, Sentence, and Structural Variations in Print Advertising," *Journal of Advertising Research*, (September/October), 63-77.

Mowen, J.C. (1983), "Attribution, Self-Perception, Salience, and Weird Interactions," in *Advances in Consumer Research*, Vol. 10, eds. R.P. Bagozzi and A.M. Tybout, Ann Arbor, MI: Association for Consumer Research, 56-58.

Mowen, J.C. (1993), *Consumer Behavior*, 3rd Edition, New York: Macmillan.

Murdock, B.B. and P.O. Dufty (1972), "Strength Theory and Recognition Memory," *Journal of Experimental Psychology*, 94 (2), 284-290.

Murry, J.P., J.L. Lastovicka, and S. Singh (1992), "Feeling and Liking Responses to Television Programs: An Examination of Two Explanations for Media-Context Effects," *Journal of Consumer Research*, 18 (4), 441-451.

Myers, J.H. and M.I. Alpert (1968), "Determinant Buying Attitudes: Meaning and Measurement," *Journal of Marketing*, 32 (October), 13-20.

Myers, J.H. and M.I. Alpert (1977), "Semantic Confusion in Attitude Research: Salience vs. Importance vs. Determinance," in *Advances in Consumer Research*, Vol. 4, ed. W.D. Perrault, Jr., Atlanta, GA: Association for Consumer Research, 106-110.

Narayana, C.L. and R.J. Markin (1975), "Consumer Behaviour and Product Performance: An Alternative Conceptualisation," *Journal of Marketing*, 39.

Natchez, P.B. and I.C. Bupp (1986), "Candidates, Issues, and Voters," *Public Policy*, 17, 409-437.

Nazir, T., D. Heller, and C. Sussmann (1992), "Letter Visibility and Word Recognition: The Optimal Viewing Position in Printed Words," *Perception and Psychophysics*, 52 (3), 315-328.

Nedungadi, P. (1990), "Recall and Consumer Consideration Sets: Influencing Choice without Altering Brand Evaluations," *Journal of Consumer Research*, 17 (December), 263-276.

Nedungadi, P. and J.W. Hutchinson (1985), "The Prototypicality of Brands: Relationships with Brand Awareness, Preference and Usage, in *Advances in Consumer Research*, Vol. 12, eds. E.C. Hirschman and M.B. Holbrook, Provo, UT: Association for Consumer Research, 498-503.

Neely, J.H. (1977), "Semantic Priming and Retrieval from Lexical Memory: Roles of Inhibitionless Spreading Activation and Limited Capacity Attention," *Journal of Experimental Social Psychology: General*, 106, 226-254.

Neisser, U. (1967), *Cognitive Psychology*, New York: Appleton.

Neisser, U. (1976), *Cognition and Reality: Principles and Implications of Cognitive Psychology*, San Francisco, CA: Freeman.

Nesdale, A.R., S. Dharmalingam, and G.K. Kerr (1987), "Effect of Subgroup Ratio on Stereotyping," *European Journal of Social Psychology*, 17, 353-356.

Neuberg, S.L. and S.T. Fiske (1987), "Motivational Influences on Impression Formation: Outcome Dependency, Accuracy-Driven Attention, and Individuating Processes," *Journal of Personality and Social Psychology*, 53 (3), 431-444.

Nevid, J.S. (1981), "Effects of Brand Labeling on Ratings of Product Quality," *Perceptual and Motor Skills*, 53 (2), 407-410.

Newcomb, T.M. (1972), "Expectations as a Social Psychological Concept," in *Human Behavior in Economic Affairs*, eds. B. Strumpel, J.N. Morgan, and E. Zahn, Amsterdam: Elsevier, 109-118.

Niemi, R.G. and L.M. Bartels (1985), "New Measures of Issue Salience: An Evaluation," *Journal of Politics*, 47 (4), 1212-1220.

Nisbett, R.E. and E. Borgida (1975), "Attribution and the Psychology of Prediction," *Journal of Personality and Social Psychology*, 32 (5), 932-943.

Nisbett, R.E., E. Borgida, R. Crandall, and H. Reed (1976), "Popular Induction: Information Is Not Necessarily Informative," in *Cognition and Social Behavior*, eds. J.S. Carroll and J.W. Payne, Hillsdale, NJ: Lawrence Erlbaum.

Nisbett, R. and L. Ross (1980), *Human Inference: Strategic and Shortcomings of Social Judgment*, Englewood Cliffs, NJ: Prentice-Hall.

Norman, D.A. (1969), *Memory and Attention*, 1st Edition, New York: Wiley.

Norman, D.A. (1976), *Memory and Attention*, 2nd Edition, New York: Wiley.

Nowlis, S.M. and I. Simonson (1997), "Attribute-Task Compatibility as a Determinant of Consumer Preference Reversals," *Journal of Marketing Research*, 34 (May), 205-218.

Oakes, P.J. and J.C. Turner (1986), "Authors' Rejoinder to Jahoda and Tetlock," *British Journal of Social Psychology*, 25, 257-258.

Obermiller, C. (1985), "Varieties of Mere Exposure: The Effects of Processing Style and Repetition of Affective Responses," *Journal of Consumer Research*, 12 (June), 17-30.

Obermiller, C. (1995), "The Baby Is Sick/The Baby Is Well: A Test of Environmental Communication Appeals," *Journal of Advertising*, 24 (Summer), 55-70.

O'Brien, E.J. and J.L. Myers (1985), "When Comprehension Difficulty Improves Memory for Text," *Journal of Experimental Psychology: Learning, Memory, and Cognition*, 11 (1), 12-21.

Odom, R.D. (1982), "Lane and Pearson's Inattention to Relevant Information: A Need for the Theoretical Specification of Task Information in Developmental Research," *Merrill-Palmer Quarterly*, 28 (3), 339-345.

Ogilvy, D. (1983), *Ogilvy on Advertising*, New York: Crown.

Oliver, R.L. (1980), "A Cognitive Model of the Antecedents and Consequences of Satisfaction Decisions," *Journal of Marketing Research*, 17, 460-469.

Oliver, R.L. (1981), "Effects of Satisfaction and Its Antecedents on Consumer Preference and Intention," in *Advances in Consumer Research*, Vol. 8, ed. K.B. Monroe, Ann Arbor, MI: Association for Consumer Research, 88-93.

Oliver, R.L. (1993), "Cognitive, Affective, and Attribute Bases of the Satisfaction Response," *Journal of Consumer Research*, 20 (December), 418-430.

Oliver, R.L. (1997), *Satisfaction: A Behavioral Perspective on the Consumer*, New York: Irwin/McGraw-Hill.

Oliver, R.L. and R.R. Burke (1999), "Expectation Processes in Satisfaction Formation: A Field Study," *Journal of Service Research*, 1 (February), 196-214.

Oliver, R.L. and W. DeSarbo (1988), "Response Determinants in Satisfaction Judgments," *Journal of Consumer Research*, 14 (March), 495-507.

Oliver, R.L. and R.S. Winer (1987), "A Framework for the Formation and Structure of Consumer Expectations: Review and Propositions," *Journal of Economic Psychology*, 8 (December), 469-499.

Olney, T.J., M.B. Holbrook, and R. Batra (1991), "Consumer Responses to Advertising: The Effects of Ad Content, Emotions, and Attitude toward the Ad on Viewing Time," *Journal of Consumer Research*, 17 (March), 440-453.

Olshavsky, R.W. and D.H. Granbois (1979), "Consumer Decision Making - Fact or Fiction?," *Journal of Consumer Research*, 6 (September), 93-100.

Olsen, G.D. (1997), "The Impact of Interstimulus Interval and Background Silence on Recall," *Journal of Consumer Research*, 23 (March), 295-303.

Olson, J.M. and M.P. Zanna (1993), "Attitudes and Attitude Change," *Annual Review of Psychology*, 44, 117-154.

Olson, J.C. and P. Dover (1979), "Disconfirmation of Consumer Expectations through Product Trial," *Journal of Applied Psychology*, 64, 179-189.

Olson, J.C. and J. Jacoby (1972), "Cue Utilization in Quality Perception Processes," in *Proceedings of the Association of Consumer Research*, ed. M. Venkatesan, 167-179.

Olson, J.C., R. Kawar, and A. Muderrisoglu (1979), "Clarifying the Confusion Regarding Salience, Importance, and Determinance Concepts in Multi-Attribute Attitude Research," in *AMA Educators' Conference Proceedings*, eds. N. Beckwith et al., Chicago, IL: American Marketing Association, 286-290.

Olson, J.C. and A. Muderrisoglu (1979), "The Stability of Responses Obtained by Free Elicitation: Implications for Measuring Attribute Salience and Memory Structure," in *Advanced in Consumer Research*, 269-275.

Olson, J.C. and K. Sentis (1986), *Advertising and Consumer Psychology*, London: Praeger.

Onkvisit, S. and J. Shaw (1987), "Self-Concept and Image Congruence: Some Research and Managerial Implications," *Journal of Consumer Marketing*, 4 (1), 13-23.

Ortony, A., R.J. Vondruska, M.A. Foss, and L.E. Jones (1985), "Salience, Similes, and the Asymmetry of Similarity," Technical Report No. 332, Center of the Study of Reading, University of Illinois at Urbana Champaign, March.

O'Shaughnessy, J. (1992), *Explaining Buyer Behavior*, New York: Oxford University Press.

O'Shaughnessy N. and G. Guido (1996), "La 'Reversal Theory': Implicazioni per la Pubblicità ed il Marketing Aziendale," *Rivista Italiana di Ragioneria ed Economia Aziendale*, 95 (Maggio/Giugno), 238-248.

Ostrom, T.M. (1984), "The Sovereignty of Social Cognition," in *Handbook of Social Cognition*, Vol. 1, eds. R.S. Wyer and T.K. Srull, Hillsdale, NJ: Lawrence Erlbaum, 1-36.

Ostrom, T.M., J.H. Lingle, J.B. Pryor, and N. Geva (1980), "Cognitive Organization of Person Impressions," in *Person Memory: The Cognitive Basis of Social Perception*, eds. R. Hastie et al., Hillsdale, NJ: Lawrence Erlbaum.

Ozanne, J.L., M. Brucks, and D. Grewal (1992), "A Study of Information Search Behavior during the Categorization of New Products," *Journal of Consumer Research*, 18 (March), 452-463.

Page, M.M. (1973), "On Detecting Demand Awareness by Postexperimental Questionnaire," *Journal of Social Psychology*, 91 (December), 305-322.

Paivio, A. (1971), *Imagery and Verbal Processes*, New York: Academic Press.

Paivio, A. (1986), *Mental Representations: A Dual Coding Approach*, Oxford, UK: Oxford University Press.

Palmer, S.E. (1975), "Visual Perception and World Knowledge: Notes on a Model of Sensory-Cognitive Interaction," in *Explorations in Cognition*, eds. D.A. Norman and D.E. Rumelhart, San Francisco, CA: Freeman, 297-307.

Parducci, A. (1968), "The Relativism of Absolute Judgments," *Scientific American*, 219, 84-90.

Park, L. (2000), "The Mediating Effects of Mood on the FAE: Reasons Why We Make the Fundamental Attribution Error," *Electronic Journal of Undergraduate Research*, http://www.ejur.or/issue01/fundamental/index.shtml.

Park, C.W. and V.P. Lessig (1981), "Familiarity and Its Impact on Consumer Decision Biases and Heuristics," *Journal of Consumer Research*, 8 (September), 223-230.

Park, J. W. and M. Hastak (1994), "Memory-based Product Judgments: Effects of Involvement at Encoding and Retrieval," *Journal of Consumer Research*, 21 (December), 534-547.

Peak, H. (1958), Psychological Structure and Person Perception," in *Person Perception and Interpersonal Behavior*, eds. R. Tagiuri and L. Petrullo, Stanford, CA: Stanford University Press.

Pechmann, C. and S. Ratneshwar (1992), "Consumer Covariation Judgments: Theory or Data Driven," *Journal of Consumer Research*, 19 (December), 373-387.

Pechmann, C. and S. Ratneshwar (1994), "The Effects of Antismoking and Cigarette Advertising on Young Adolescents' Perceptions of Peers Who Smoke," *Journal of Consumer Research*, 21 (September), 236-251.

Pechmann, C. and D.W. Stewart (1991), "How Direct Comparative Ads and Market Share Affect Brand Choice," *Journal of Advertising Research*, (December), 47-55.

Peltier, J.W. (1989), "The Effects of Schema-congruent and Schema-incongruent Character Usage in Advertisements on Processing and Memory," Unpublished Ph.D. dissertation, University of Wisconsin - Madison.

Peltier, J.W. and J.A. Schibrowsky (1994), "Need for Cognition, Advertisement Viewing Time and Memory for Advertising Stimuli," in *Advances in Consumer Research*, Vol. 21, eds. C.T. Allen and D. Roedder-John, Provo, UT: Association for Consumer Research, 244-250.

Percy, L. and J.R. Rossiter (1992), "Advertising Stimulus Effects: A Review," *Journal of Current Issues and Research in Advertising*, 14 (Spring), 75-90.

Peter, J.P. (1981), "Construct Validity: A Review of Basic Issues and Marketing Practices," *Journal of Marketing Research*, 28 (May), 133-145.

Peter, J.P. and J.C. Olson (1998), *Consumer Behavior and Marketing Strategy*, 5rd Edition, Homewood, IL: Irwin.

Peterman, M.L. (1997), "The Effects of Concrete and Abstract Consumer Goals on Information Processing," *Psychology and Marketing*, 14 (6), 561-583.

Petty, R.E. and J.T. Cacioppo (1981), "Issue Involvement as Moderator of the Effects on Attitude of Advertising Content and Context," in *Advances in Consumer Research*, Vol. 8, ed. K.B. Monroe, Ann Arbor, MI: Association for Consumer Research, 20-24.

Petty, R.E. and J.T. Cacioppo (1984), "Source Factors and the Elaboration Likelihood Model of Persuasion," in *Advances in Consumer Research*, Vol. 11, ed. T. Kinnear, Provo, UT: Association for Consumer Research, 668-672.

Petty, R.E. and J.T. Cacioppo (1986), *Communication and Persuasion: Central and Peripheral Routes to Attitude Change*, New York: Springer-Verlag.

Petty, R.E., D.T. Wegener, and L.R. Fabrigar (1997), "Attitudes and Attitude Change," *Annual Review of Psychology*, 48, 609-647.

Pham, M.T. (1997), "*Really*-Low Involvement Consumer Learning," (Special Session Summary), in *Advances in Consumer Research*, eds. M. Brucks and D.J. MacInnis, Provo, UT: Association for Consumer Research, 121-122.

Piaget, J. (1926), *The Language of Thought of the Child*, London: Routledge and Kegan Paul.

Piaget, J. (1952), *The Origin of Intelligence in Children*, New York: Norton.

Piaget, J. (1954), *The Construction of Reality in the Child*, New York: Basic Books.

Pieters, R.G.M. and T.H.A. Bijmolt (1997), "Consumer Memory for Television Advertising: A Field Study of Duration, Serial Position, and Competition Effects," *Journal of Consumer Research*, 23 (March), 362-372.

Pieters, R.G.M., E. Rosbergen, and M. Wedel (1999), "Visual Attention to Repeated Print Advertising: A Test of Scanpath Theory," *Journal of Marketing Research*, 26 (November), 424-438.

Pieters, R.G.M., L. Warlop, and M. Hartog (1997), "The Effect of Time Pressure and Task Motivation on Visual Attention to Brands," in *Advances in Consumer Research*, eds. M. Brucks and D. J. MacInnis, Provo, UT: Association for Consumer Research, 281-287.

Plummer, J.T. (1984/1985), "How Personality Makes a Difference," *Journal of Advertising Research*, 24 (December/January), 27-32.

Poiesz, T.B.C. (1989), "The Image Concept: Its Place in Consumer Psychology," *Journal of Economic Psychology*, 10, 457-472.

Poiesz, T.B.C. and H.S.J. Robben (1996), "Advertising Effects under Different Combinations of Motivation, Capacity, and Opportunity," in *Advances in Consumer Research*, Vol. 23, eds. K.P. Corfman and J.G. Lynch, Provo, UT: Association for Consumer Research, 231-236.

Pollay, R.W. and S. Mainprize (1984), "Headlining of Visual in Print Advertising: A Typology of Tactical Techniques," in *Proceedings of the 1984 Convention of the American Academy of Advertising*, ed. D.R. Glover, Denver, CO: American Academy of Advertising, 24-28.

Pool, I. (1983), "Tracking the Information Flow," *Science*, 221, 609-613.

Popper, E.T. and K.B. Murray (1989), "Format Effects on an In-Ad Disclosure," in *Advances in Consumer Research*, Vol. 16, ed. T.K. Srull, Provo, UT: Association for Consumer Research, 221-230.

Potocky, M. and S. Murgatroyd (1993), "What Is Reversal Theory," in *Advances in Reversal Theory*, eds. J.H. Kerr, S. Murgatroyd, and M.J. Apter, Amsterdam: Swets & Zeitlinger, 13-26.

Posner, M.I. (1969), "Abstraction and the Process of Recognition," in *The Psychology of Learning and Motivation*, Vol. 3, eds. G.H. Bower and J.T. Spence, New York: Academic Press.

Posner, M.I. (1978), *Chronometric Explorations of the Mind*, Hillsdale, NJ: Lawrence Erlbaum.

Posner, M.I. and S.W. Keele (1970), "Retention of Abstract Ideas," *Journal of Experimental Psychology*, 83, 304-308.

Posner, M.I. and C.R.R. Snyder (1975), "Attention and Cognitive Control," in *Information Processing and Cognition*, ed. R.L. Solso, Hillsdale, NJ: Lawrence Erlbaum.

Posner, M.I. and R.E. Warren (1972), "Traces, Concepts and Conscious Constructions," in *Coding Processes in Human Memory*, eds. A.W. Melton and E. Martin, Washington, D. C.: V.H. Winston & Sons.

Powell, M.C. and R.H. Fazio (1984), "Attitude Accessibility as a Function of Repeated Attitudinal Expression," *Personality and Social Psychology Bulletin*, 10, 139-148.

Pracejus, J.W. (1995), "Is More Exposure Always Better? Effects of Incidental Exposure to a Brand Name on Subsequent Processing of Advertising," in *Advances in Consumer Research*, eds. F.R. Kardes and M. Sujan, Provo, UT: Association for Consumer Research, 319-322.

Pracejus, J.W. (1999), "Fit, Similarity and Congruity: An Exploration of Overlap in 'Alikeness' Constructs," (Special Session Summary), in *European Advances in Consumer Research*, eds. B. Dubois et al., Provo, UT: Association for Consumer Research, 238-239.

Prakash, V. (1992), "Sex Roles and Advertising Preferences," *Journal of Advertising Research*, (May/June), 43-52.

Prelec, D., B. Wernerfelt, and F. Zettelmeyer (1997), "The Role of Inference in Context Effects: Inferring What You Want from What Is Available," *Journal of Consumer Research*, 24 (June), 118-125.

Preston, I.L. and E. Thorson (1984), "The Expanded Association Model: Keeping the Hierarchy Concept Alive," *Journal of Advertising Research*, 24 (1), 59-65.

Price, L.J. (1993), "The Indirect Effects of Negative Information on Attitude Change," INSEAD Working Paper No. 93/43/MKT, Fontainebleau, France.

Pryor, J.B. and M. Kriss (1983), "The Cognitive Dynamics of Salience in the Attribution Process," *Journal of Personality and Social Psychology*, 35 (1), 49-55.

Pullack, J. (1997), "Anthropomorphic Cigs Star in Ads for Benson & Hedges," *Advertising Age*, April 14.

Pyszcynski, T. and J. Greenberg (1981), "Role of Discorfirmed Expectations in the Instigation of Attributional Processing," *Journal of Personality and Social Psychology*, 40, 31-38.

Raaijmakers, J.G.W. and R.M. Shiffrin (1981), "Search of Associative Memory," *Psychological Review*, 88 (March), 93-134.

Rabbitt, P. (1984), "The Control of Attention in Visual Search," in *Varieties of Attention*, eds. R. Parasuraman and D.R. Davies, Orlando, FL: Academic Press, 273-291.

Raden, D. (1985), "Strength-Related Attitude Dimensions," *Social Psychology Quarterly*, 48, 312-330.

Raju, P.S. (1980), "Optimum Stimulation Level: Its Relationship to Personality, Demographics, and Explanatory Behavior," *Journal of Consumer Research*, 7 (December), 272-282.

Raju, P.S. and M. Venkatesan (1980), "Exploratory Behavior in the Consumer Context: A State of the Art Review," in *Advances in Consumer Research*, Vol. 7, ed. J.C. Olson, Ann Arbor, MI: Association for Consumer Research, 258-263.

Rao, A.R. and K.B. Monroe (1988), "The Moderating Effect of Prior Knowledge on Cue Utilization in Product Evaluations," *Journal of Consumer Research*, 15 (September), 253-254.

Ratneshwar, S., D.G. Mick, and G. Reitinger (1990), "Selective Attention in Consumer Information Processing: The Role of Chronically Accessible Attributes," in *Advances in*

Consumer Research, Vol. 17, eds. M.E. Goldberg et al., Provo, UT: Association for Consumer Research, 547- 553.

Ratneshwar, S., C. Pechmann, and A.D. Shocker (1996), "Goal-Derived Categories and the Antecedents of Across-Category Consideration," *Journal of Consumer Research*, 23 (December), 240-250.

Ratneshwar, S.L. Warlop, D.G. Mick, and G. Seeger (1997), "Benefit Salience and Consumers' Selective Attention to Product Features," *International Journal of Research in Marketing*, 14, 245-259.

Reardon, R. and D.J. Moore (1996), "The Greater Memorability of Self-Generated versus Externally Presented Product Information," *Psychology and Marketing*, 13 (3), 305-320.

Reber, A.S. (1985), *Dictionary of Psychology*, London: Penguin Books.

Reder, L.M. and J.R. Anderson (1980), "A Partial Resolution of the Paradox of Interference: The Role of Integrating Knowledge," *Cognitive Psychology*, 12, 447-472.

Reed, S.K. (1972), "Pattern Recognition and Categorization," *Cognitive Psychology*, 3, 382-407.

Reeves, B., E. Thorson, M. Rothschild, D. McDonald, J. Hirsch, and R. Goldstein (1985), "Attention to Television: Intrastimulus Effects of Movement and Scene Changes on Alpha Variation over Time," *International Journal of Neuroscience*, 25, 241-245.

Regan, D. and J. Totten (1975), "Empathy and Attribution: Turning Observers into Actors," *Journal of Personality and Social Psychology*, 32 (5), 850-856.

Reingen, P.H. and W.O. Bearden (1983), "Salience of Behavior and the Effects of Labeling," in *Advances in Consumer Research*, Vol. 10, eds. R.P. Bagozzi and A.M. Tybout, Ann Arbor, MI: Association for Consumer Research, 51-55.

Restall, C. and W. Gordon (1993), "Brands - The Missing Link; Understanding the Emotional Relationship," *Marketing and Research Today*, 21 (2), 59-68.

Restle, F. (1961), *The Psychology of Judgment and Choice*, New York: Wiley.

Rethans, A.J., J.L. Swasy, and L.J. Marks (1986), "Effects of Television Commercial Repetition, Receiver Knowledge, and Commercial Length: A Test of the Two-Factor Model," *Journal of Marketing Research*, 23 (February), 50-61.

Reyes, R.M., W.C. Thompson, and G. Bower (1980), "Judgmental Biases Resulting from Differing Availabilities of Arguments," *Journal of Personality and Social Psychology*, 39, 2-12.

Reynolds, T.J. and J. Gutman (1984), "Advertising Is Image Management," *Journal of Advertising Research*, 24, 27-37.

Rice, C. (1993), *Consumer Behaviour: Behavioural Aspects of Marketing*, Oxford, U.K.: Butterworth-Heinemann Ltd.

Richins, M. and P.H. Bloch (1986), "After the New Wears Off: The Temporal Context of Product Involvement," *Journal of Consumer Research*, 13 (September), 280-285.

Robertson, T.S., J. Zielinski, and S. Ward (1984), *Consumer Behavior*, Glenview, IL: Scott, Foresman and Company.

Robinson, J. and L.Z. McArthur (1982), "Impact of Salient Vocal Qualities on Causal Attribution for a Speaker Behavior," *Journal of Personality and Social Psychology*, 43 (2), 236-247.

Roediger, H.L., III and J.H. Neely (1982), "Retrieval Blocks in Episodic and Semantic Memory," *Canadian Journal of Psychology*, 36 (2), 213-242.

Rogers, E.M. (1986), *Communication Technology: The New Media in Society*, New York: Free Press.

Rosbergen, E., R. Pieters, and M. Wedel (1997), "Visual Attention to Advertising: A Segment-Level Analysis," *Journal of Consumer Research*, 24 (December), 305-314.

Rosch, E. (1975), "Cognitive Reference Points," Cognitive Psychology, 7, 532-547.

Rosch, E. (1978), "Principles of Categorization," in *Cognition and Categorization*, eds. E. Rosch and B.B. Lloyd, Hillsdale, NJ: Lawrence Erlbaum, 27-48.

Rosch, E. and C.B. Mervis (1975), "Family Resemblances: Studies in the Internal Structure of Categories," *Cognitive Psychology*, 7, 573-605.

Rosemberg, M.J. (1956), "Cognitive Structure and Attitudinal Affect," *Journal of Abnormal and Social Psychology*, 53, 367-372.

Rosemberg, M.J. (1960), "An Analysis of Affective-Cognitive Consistency," in *Attitude Organization and Change*, eds. C.I. Hovland and M.J. Rosemberg, New Haven, CN: Yale University Press, 15-54.

Rosenzweig, M.R. (1966), "Environmental Complexity, Cerebral Change, and Behavior," *American Psychologist*, 21, 321-332.

Ross, M. (1975), "Salience of Reward and Intrinsic Motivation," *Journal of Personality and Social Psychology*, 32, 245-254.

Ross, M. and R.F. Shulman (1973), "Increasing the Salience of Initial Attitudes: Dissonance versus Self-Perception Theory," *Journal of Personality and Social Psychology*, 28, 138-144.

Rossiter, J.R. and L. Percy (1987), *Advertising and Promotion Management*, New York: McGraw Hill.

Rothschild, M.L. and E. Thorson (1983), "Electroencephalographic Activity as a Response to Complex Stimuli: A Review of Relevant Psychophysiology and Advertising LIterature," in *Advertising and Consumer Psychology*, eds. L. Percy and A.G. Woodside, Lexington, MA: Lexington Books, 239-251.

Rubin, E. (1921), *Visuell Wahrgenommene Figuren*, Copehagen, Denmark: Glydendalske. [Reprinted as "Figure and Ground," in *Readings in Perception* (1958), eds. D.C. Beardslee and M. Wertheimer, Princeton, NJ: D. van Nostrand, 194-204.]

Rumelhart, D.E. (1984), "Schemata and the Cognitive System," in *Handbook of Social Cognition*, Vol. 1, eds. R.S. Wyer and T.K. Srull, Hillsdale, NJ: Lawrence Erlbaum, 161-188.

Rumelhart, D.E. and A. Ortony (1977), "The Representation of Knowledge in Memory," in *Schooling and the Acquisition of Knowledge*, eds. R.C. Anderson, R.J. Spiro, and W.E. Montague, Hillsdale, NJ: Lawrence Erlbaum, 99-136.

Rundus, D. (1973), "Negative Effects of Using List Items as Recall Cues," *Journal of Verbal Learning and Verbal Behavior*, 12 (February), 43-50.

Ruscher, J.B. and S.T. Fiske (1990), "Interpersonal Competition Can Cause Indivituating Processes," *Journal of Personality and Social Psychology*, 58 (5), 832-842.

Ruth, W.J., H.S. Mosatch, and A. Kramer (1989), "Freudian Sexual Symbolism: Theoretical Considerations and an Empirical Test in Advertising," *Psychological Reports*, 60 (June), 1131-1139.

Ryan, M.J. and M.J. Etzel (1976), "The Nature of Salient Outcomes and Referents in the Extended Model," in *Advances in Consumer Research*, Vol. 3, ed. B.B. Anderson, Cincinnati, OH: Association for Consumer Research, 485-490.

Sampson, P. and P. Harris (1970), "A User's Guide to Fishbein," *Journal of the Market Research Society*, 12 (July), 145-189.

Sandage, C.H., V. Fryburger, and K. Rotzoll (1979), *Advertising Theory and Practice*, 10th Edition, Homewood, IL: Richard D. Irwin.

Sarbin, T.R. and V.L. Allen (1968), "Role Theory," in *Handbook of Social Psychology*, Vol. 1, 2nd Edition, eds. G. Lindzey and E. Aronson, Reading, MA: Addison-Wesley, 488-567.

Saul, E.V. and C.E. Osgood (1950), "Perceptual Organization of Materials as a Factor Influencing Ease of Learning and Degree of Retention," *Journal of Experimental Psychology*, 40, 372-379.

Sawyer, A.G. (1973), "The Effects of Repetition of Refutational and Supporting Advertising Appeals," *Journal of Marketing Research*, 10 (February), 23-33.

Schaefer, W. (1989), "Aided Recall and Recognition in Belson's Studies in Readership," *Marketing and Research Today*, 17 (1), 41-52.

Schank, R.C. and R.P. Abelson (1977), *Scripts, Plans Goals and Understanding: An Inquiry into Human Knowledge Structures*, Hillsdale, NJ: Lawrence Erlbaum.

Schellinck, D.A. (1983), "Cue Choice as a Function of Time Pressure and Perceived Risk," in *Advances in Consumer Research*, Vol. 10, eds. R.P. Bagozzi and A.M. Tybout, Ann Arbor, MI: Association for Consumer Research, 470-475.

Schelling, T.C. (1960), *The Strategy of Conflict*, Cambridge, MA: Harvard University Press.

Schiffman, L.G. and L.L. Kanuk (1991), *Consumer Behavior*, 4th Edition, Englewood Cliffs, NJ: Prentice-Hall.

Schindler, R.M. (1988), "Effect of Odd Pricing on Choice of Items from a Menu," in *Advances in Consumer Research*, Vol. 15, ed. M.J. Houston, Provo, UT: Association for Consumer Research, 348-353.

Schindler, R.M. and M. Berbaum (1983), "The Influence of Salience on Choice," in *Advances in Consumer Research*, Vol. 10, eds. R.P. Bagozzi and A.M. Tybout, Ann Arbor, MI: Association for Consumer Research, 416-418.

Schindler, R.M., M. Berbaum, and D.R. Weinzimer (1986), "How an Attention-Getting Device Can Affect Quick Choice among Similar Alternatives," in *Advances in Consumer Research*, Vol. 13, ed. R.J. Lutz, Provo, UT: Association for Consumer Research, 505-509.

Schleuder, J. (1990), "Effects of Commercial Complexity, the Candidate, and Issue vs. Image Strategies in Political Ads," in *Advances in Consumer Research*, Vol. 17, eds. M. E. Goldberg et al., Provo, UT: Association for Consumer Research, 159-168.

Schleuder, J. and S. Gaiser (1989), "How Complexity Interacts with Content Features of Televised Political Messages to Affect Cognitive Processing," Unpublished manuscript, University of Texas, College of Communication Cognitive Research Laboratory.

Schleuder, J., M. McCombs, W. Wanta (1991), "Inside the Agenda-Setting Process: How Political Advertising and TV News Prime Viewers to Think about Issues and Candidates," in *Television and Political Advertising*, eds. F. Biocca et al., Hillsdale, NJ: Lawrence Erlbaum, 265-309.

Schleuder, J., E. Thorson, and B. Reeves (1987), "Effects of Complexity and Scene Reordering on Attention to Television Messages," Paper presented to the Mass Communication Division of the International Communication Association, New Orleans.

Schleuder, J., E. Thorson, and B. Reeves (1988), "Effects of Time Compression and Complexity on Attention to Television Commercials," Paper presented to the Mass Communication Division of the International Communication Association, New Orleans.

Schmitt, B.H. (1999), *Experiential Marketing: How to Get Customers to Sense, Feel, Think, Act, and Relate to Your Company and Brands*, New York: Free Press.

Schmitt, B.H., F. LeClerc, and L. Dubé-Riox (1988), "Sex Typing and Consumer Behavior: A Test of Gender Schema Theory," *Journal of Consumer Research*, 15 (June), 122-128.

Schmitt, B.H., N.T. Tavassoli, and R.T. Millard (1993), "Memory for Print Ads: Understanding Relations among Brand Name, Copy, and Picture," *Journal of Consumer Psychology*, 2 (1), 55-81.

Schneider, D.J. (1991), "Social Cognition," *Annual Review of Psychology*, 42, 527-561.

Schneider, D.J. and B.L. Blankmeyer (1983), "Prototypes Salience and Implicit Personality Theories," *Journal of Personality and Social Psychology*, 44 (4), 712-722.

Schneider, D.J., A.H. Hastorf, and P.C. Ellsworth (1979), *Person Perception*, 2nd Edition, Reading, MA: Addison-Wesley.

Scholten, M. and M. Faia-Correia (1994), "Footnotes to Fishbein: The Contrast Model of Stimulus Evaluation," *Analise Psicologica*, 12 (1), 79-92.

Schuman, H. and M.P. Johnson (1976), "Attitudes and Behavior," *Annual Review of Sociology*, 2, 161-207.

Schumann, D.W. (1986), "The Impact of Television Program on Processing of Commercials," in *Proceedings of the Division of Consumer Psychology*, ed. J. Saegert, Washington, DC: American Psychological Association.

Schumann, D.W., R. Petty and D.S. Clemons (1990), "Predicting the Effectiveness of Different Strategies of Advertising Variation: A Test of the Repetition-Variation Hypotheses," *Journal of Consumer Research*, 17 (September), 192-202.

Schumann, D.W. and E. Thorson (1990), "The Influence of Viewing Context on Commercial Effectiveness: An Intensity-Affect Response Model," *Journal of Current Issues and Research in Advertising*, 12 (1), 1-24.

Schwarz, N. and H. Bless (1991), "Happy and Mindless, But Sad and Smart? The Impact of Affective States on Analytic Reasoning," in *Emotion and Social Judgments*, ed. J. Forgas, Oxford, UK: Pergamon, 55-71.

Schwarz, N. and F. Strack (1981), "Manipulating Salience: Causal Assessment in Natural Settings," *Personality and Social Psychology Bulletin*, 6 (December), 554-558.

Sears, D.O., L.A. Peplau, and S.E. Taylor (1991), *Social Psychology*, 7th Edition, Englewood Cliffs, NJ: Prentice-Hall.

Sen, S. (1999), "The Effects of Brand Name Suggestiveness and Decision Goal on the Development of Brand Knowledge," *Journal of Consumer Psychology*, 8 (4), 431-455.

Severn, J.a, G.E. Belch, and M.A. Belch (1990), "The Effects of Sexual and Non-Sexual Advertising Appeals and Information Level on Cognitive Processing and Communication Effectiveness," *Journal of Advertising*, 19 (1), 14-22.

Shackle, G.L.S. (1952), *Expectation in Economics*, 2nd Edition, Cambridge, UK: Cambridge University Press.

Shank, M.D. and J.T. Walker (1989), "Figure-Ground Organization in Real and Subjective Contours: A New Ambiguous Figure, Some Novel Measures of Ambiguity, and Apparent Distance across Regions of Figure and Ground," *Perception and Psychophysics*, 46 (2), 127-138.

Shapiro, S. (1999), "When an Ad's Influence Is beyond Our Conscious Control: Perceptual and Conceptual Fluency Effects Caused by Incidental Ad Exposure," *Journal of Consumer Research*, 26 (June), 16-36.

Shapiro, S., D.J. MacInnis, and S.E. Heckler (1997), "The Effects of Incidental Ad Exposure on the Formation of Consideration Set," *Journal of Consumer Research*, 24 (June), 94-104.

Shavitt, S. (1989), "Products, Personalities and Situations in Attitude Functions: Implications for Consumer Behavior," in *Advances in Consumer Research*, Vol. 16, ed. T.K. Srull, Provo, UT: Association for Consumer Research, 300-305.

Shavitt, S. and R.H. Fazio (1990), "Effects of Attribute Salience on the Consistency of Product Evaluations and Purchase Predictions," in *Advances in Consumer Research*, Vol. 17, eds. M.E. Goldberg et al., Provo, UT: Association for Consumer Research, 91-97.

Shavitt, S. and R.H. Fazio (1991), "Effects of Attribute Salience on the Consistency between Attitudes and Behavior Predictions," *Personality and Social Psychology Bulletin*, 17 (5), 507-516.

Shepard, R.N. (1990), *Mind Sights*, New York: W. H. Freeman and Co.

Sherif, M. and H. Cantril (1945), "The Psychology of Attitudes: I," *Psychological Review*, 52, 295-319.

Sherif, M. and H. Cantril (1946), "The Psychology of Attitudes: II," *Psychological Review*, 53, 1-24.

Sherman, S.J. and E. Corty (1984), "Cognitive Heuristics," in *Handbook of Social Cognition*, Vol. 1, eds. R.S. Wyer and T.K. Srull, Hillsdale, NJ: Lawrence Erlbaum, 189-286.

Sherman, S.J., K.S. Zehner, J. Johnson, and E.R. Hirt (1983), "Social Explanation: The Role of Timing, Set, and Recall on Subjective Likelihood Estimates," *Journal of Personality and Social Psychology*, 44, 1127-1143.

Shields, M.M. (1978), "The Child as Psychologist: Construing the Social World," in *Action, Gesture and Symbol*, ed. A. Lock, New York: Academic Press.

Shimp, T.A. (1981), "Attitude Toward the Ad as a Mediator of Consumer Choice Behavior," *Journal of Advertising*, 10, 9-15.

Shimp, T.A., E.W. Stuart, and R.W. Engle (1991), "A Program of Classical Conditioning Experiments Testing Variations in the Conditioned Stimulus and Context," *Journal of Consumer Research*, 18, 1-12.

Shiv, B., J.A. Edell, and J.W. Payne (1997), "Factors Affecting the Impact of Negatively and Positively Framed Ad Messages," *Journal of Consumer Research*, 24 (December), 285-294.

Shomer, R.W. and R. Centers (1970), "Differences in Attitudinal Responses under Conditions of Implicitly Manipulated Group Salience," *Journal of Personality and Social Psychology*, 12 (2), 122-132.

Siegel, P.S. (1943), "Structure Effects within a Memory Series," *Journal of Experimental Psychology*, 33, 311-316.

Simon, H.A. (1976), "Discussion: Cognition and Social Behavior," in *Cognition and Social Behavior*, eds. J. Carroll and J. Payne, Hillsdale, NJ: Lawrence Erlbaum.

Simonson, I., J. Huber, and J. Payne (1988), "The Relationship Between Prior Brand Knowledge and Information Acquisition Order," *Journal of Consumer Behavior*, 14 (March), 566-578.

Simonson, I. and S.M. Nowlis (2000), "The Role of Explanations and Need for Uniqueness in Consumer Decision Making: Unconventional Choices Based on Reasons," *Journal of Consumer Research*, 27 (June), 49-68.

Simonson, I. and A. Tversky (1992), "Choice in Context: Tradeoff Contrast and Extremeness Aversion," *Journal of Marketing Research*, 29 (August), 281-295.

Singh, S.N. and M.L. Rothschild (1983), "Recognition as a Measure of Learning from Television Commercials," *Journal of Marketing Research*, 20 (August), 235-248.

Singh, S.N., M.L. Rothschild, and G.A. Churchill, Jr. (1988), "Recognition versus Recall as Measures of Television Commercial Forgetting," *Journal of Marketing Research*, 25 (February), 72-80.

Sirgy, M.J. (1987), "A Social Cognition Model if Consumer Problem Recognition," *Journal of the Academy of Marketing Science*, 15 (Winter), 53-60.

Sirgy, M.J. (1983), *Social Cognition and Consumer Behavior*, New York: Praeger.

Sirgy, M.J. and J.S. Johar (1999), "Toward an Integrated Model of Self-Congruity and Functional Congruity," in *European Advances in Consumer Research*, eds. B. Dubois et al., Provo, UT: Association for Consumer Research, 252-256.

Skowronski, J.J. and D.E. Carlston (1987), "Social Judgment and Social Memory: The Role of Cue Diagnosticity in Negativity, Positivity, and Extremity Biases," *Journal of Personality and Social Psychology*, 52 (4), 689-699.

Skowronski, J.J. and D.E. Carlston (1989), "Negativity and Extremity Biases in Impression Formation: A Review of Explanations," *Psychological Bulletin*, 105 (1), 131-142.

Slamecka, N.J. (1968), "An Examination of Trace Storage in Free Recall," *Journal of Experimental Psychology*, 76, 504-513.

Slamecka, N.J. (1969), "Testing for Associative Storage in Multitrial Free Recall," *Journal of Experimental Psychology*, 81, 557-560.

Slemrod, J., C. Christian, R. London, J.A. Parker (1997), "April 15 Syndrome," *Economic Inquiry*, 35 (October), 695-709.

Smith, E.E., E.J. Shoben, and L.J. Rips (1974), "Structure and Process in Semantic Memory: A Featural Model for Semantic Decisions," *Psychological Review*, 81, 214-241.

Smith E.R. and F.D. Miller (1979), "Salience and the Cognitive Mediation of Attribution," *Journal of Personality and Social Psychology*, 37, 2240-2252.

Smith, K.H. (1973), "Effect of Exception on Verbal Reconstructive Memory," *Journal of Experimental Psychology*, 97, 119-139.

Snedecor, G.W. and W.G. Cochran (1967), *Statistical Methods*, Ames, IO: Iowa State University Press.

Snyder, C.R. and H.L. Fromkin (1979), *Uniqueness: The Human Pursuit of Difference*, New York: Plenum Press.

Soelberg, P.O. (1967), "Unprogrammed Decision Making," *Industrial Management Review*, 89, 155-181.

Sokolov, E.N. (1969), "The Modeling Properties of the Nervous System," in *A Handbook of Contemporary Soviet Psychology*, eds. M. Cole and I. Malzman, New York: Basic Books, 671-704.

Sokolov, E.N. (1975), "The Neuronal Mechanisms of the Orienting Reflex," in *Neuronal Mechanism of the Orienting Reflex*, eds. E.N. Sokolov & O.S. Vinogradova, New York: Wiley, 217-238.

Solomon, M.R., C. Surprenant, J.A. Czepiel, and E.G. Gutman (1985), "A Role Theory Perspective on Dyadic Interactions: The Service Encounter," *Journal of Marketing*, 49 (Winter), 99-111.

Spangler, E., M.A. Gordon, and R.M. Pipkin (1978), "Token Women: An Empirical Test of the Kanter Hypothesis," *American Journal of Sociology*, 84 (1), 160-170.

Sparkman, N., Jr. and L.M. Austin (1980), "The Effects on Sales of Color in Newspaper Advertisements," *Journal of Advertising*, 10 (Fourth Quarter).

Speck, P.S. (1991), "The Humorous Message Taxonomy: A Framework for the Study of Humorous Ads," *Journal of Current Issues and Research in Advertising*, 13, 1-44.

Speck, P.S., D.W. Schumann, and C. Thompson (1988), "Celebrity Endorsements - Scripts, Schemas and Roles: Theoretical Framework and Preliminary Tests," in *Advances in Consumer Research*, Vol. 15, ed. M.J. Houston, Provo, UT: Association for Consumer Research, 69-76.

Sperber, D. and D. Wilson (1986), *Relevance: Communication and Cognition*, Oxford, UK: Blackwell.

Srull, T.K. (1980), "Person Memory: The Role of Processing Strategy, Expectancy, and Level Incongruity in the Processing of Interindividual and Intraindividual Behavior Variability," Unpublished Ph.D. dissertation, University of Illinois.

Srull, T.K. (1981), "Person Memory: Some Tests of Associative Storage and Retrieval Models," *Journal of Experimental Psychology: Human Learning and Memory*, 7 (6), 440-463.

Srull, T.K. (1983), "The Role of Prior Knowledge in the Acquisition, Retention, and Use of New Information," in *Advances in Consumer Research*, Vol. 10, eds. R.P. Bagozzi and A.M. Tybout, Ann Arbor, MI: Association for Consumer Research, 572-576.

Srull, T.K. and R.S. Wyer, Jr. (1980), "Category Accessibility and Social Perpcetion: Some Implications for the Study of Person Memory and Interpersonal Judgments," *Journal of Personality and Social Psychology*, 38, 841-856.

Stafford, E.R., B.A. Walker, and V.J. Blasko (1996), "Headline-Visual Consistency in Print Advertisements: Effects on Processing and Evaluation," in *Advances in Consumer Research*, Vol. 23, eds. K.P. Corfman and J.G. Lynch, Provo, UT: Association for Consumer Research, 56-62.

Stafford, T.F. (2000), "Alert or Oblivious? Factors Underlying Consumer Responses to Marketing Stimuli," *Psychology and Marketing*, 17 (9), 745-760.

Stanaland, A.J.S. (2000), "A Theoretical Model of Incongruity between Sexy Pictures and Advertised Products," in *Advertising Research: The Internet, Consumer Behavior, and Strategy*, ed. G. Zinkhan, Chicago, IL: American Marketing Association.

Stangor, C. and D. McMillan (1992), "Memory for Expectancy-Congruent and Expectancy-Incongruent Information, A Review of the Social and Social Developmental Literatures," *Psychological Bulletin*, 111, 42-61.

Stangor, C. and D.N. Ruble (1989), "Strength of Expectancies and Memory for Social Information: What We Remember Depends on How Much We Know," *Journal of Experimental Social Psychology*, 25, 18-35.

Stapel, D.A., W. Koomen, and A.S. Velthuijsen (1998), "Assimilation or Contrast?: Comparison Relevance, Distinctness, and the Impact of Accessible Information on Consumer Judgments," *Journal of Consumer Psychology*, 7 (1), 1-24.

Stapel, J. (1998), "Recall and Recognition: A Very Close Relationship," *Journal of Advertising Research*, 38 (July/August), 41-45.

Stayman, D.M., D.L. Alden, and K.H. Smith (1992), "Some Effects of Schematic Processing on Consumer Expectations and Disconfirmation Judgments," *Journal of Consumer Research*, 19 (September), 240-255.

Stern, B.B. (1988), "Figurative Language in Services Advertising: The Nature and Uses of Imagery," in *Advances in Consumer Research*, Vol. 15, ed. M.J. Houston, Provo, UT: Association for Consumer Research, 185-190.

Stern, B.B. (1989), "Literary Criticism and Consumer Research: Overview and Illustrative Analysis," *Journal of Consumer Research*, 16 (December), 322-334.

Stern, B.B. (1990), "*Other-Speak*: Classical Allegory and Contemporary Advertising," *Journal of Advertising*, 19 (3), 14-26.

Sternthal, B. and C.S. Craig (1974), "Fear Appeals: Revisited and Revised," *Journal of Consumer Research*, 1 (December), 22-34.

Sternthal, B. and C.S. Craig (1982), *Consumer Behavior: An Information Processing Perspective*, Englewood Cliffs, NJ: Prentice-Hall.

Stevens, J.P. (1990), *Intermediate Statistics: A Modern Approach*, Hillsdale, NJ: Lawrence Erlbaum.

Stoltman, J.J. (1990), "Advertising Effectiveness: The Role of Advertising Schemas," Paper presented at the Winter Meeting of the American Marketing Association.

Storms, M.D. (1973), "Videotape and the Attribution Process: Reversing Actors' and Observers' Point of View," *Journal of Personality and Social Psychology*, 27 (2), 165-175.

Stryker, S. and A. Statham (1985), "Symbolic Interaction and Role Theory," in *Handbook of Social Psychology*, Vol. 1, 2nd Edition, eds. G. Lindzey and E. Aronson, Reading, MA: Addison-Wesley, 311-378.

Sujan, M. (1985), "Consumer Knowledge: Effects on Evaluation Strategies Mediating Consumer Judgments," *Journal of Consumer Research*, 12 (June), 31-46.

Sujan, M. and J.R. Bettman (1989), "The Effects of Brand Positioning Strategies on Consumers' Brand and Category Perceptions: Some Insights from Schema Research," *Journal of Marketing Research*, 26 (November), 454-467.

Sujan, M., J.R. Bettman, and H. Sujan (1986), "Effects of Consumer Expectations on Information Processing in Selling Encounters," *Journal of Marketing Research*, 23 (November), 346-352.

Sutherland, M. and J. Galloway (1981), "Role of Advertising: Persuasion or Agenda Setting?," *Journal of Advertising Research*, 21 (October), 25-29.

Swan, J.E. and W.S. Martin (1981), "Testing Comparison Level and Predictive Expectation Models of Satisfaction," in *Advances in Consumer Research*, Vol. 8, ed. K.B. Monroe, Ann Arbor, MI: Association for Consumer Research, 77-82.

Tagiuri, R. (1958), "Introduction," in *Person Perception and Interpersonal Behavior*, eds. R. Tagiuri and L. Petrullo, Stanford, CA: Stanford University Press.

Tagiuri, R. (1969), "Person Perception," in *Handbook of Social Psychology*, Vol. 3, eds. G. Lindzey and E. Aronson, Reading, MA: Addison-Wesley.

Taylor, S.E. (1975), "On Inferring One's Own Attitudes from One's Behavior: Some Delimiting Conditions," *Journal of Personality and Social Psychology*, 31 (1), 126-131.

Taylor, S.E. (1981), "The Interface of Cognitive and Social Psychology," in *Cognition, Social Behavior, and the Environment*, ed. J.H. Harvey, Hillsdale, NJ: Lawrence Erlbaum, 189-211.

Taylor, S.E. (1991), "Asymmetrical Effects of Positive and Negative Events: The Mobilization-Minimization Hypothesis," *Psychological Bulletin*, 105 (1), 131-142.

Taylor, S.E. and J. Crocker (1981), "Schematic Bases of Social Information Processing," in *Social Cognition: The Ontario Symposium*, Vol. 1, eds. E.T. Higgins, C.P. Herman, and M.P. Zanna, Hillsdale, NJ: Lawrence Erlbaum, 89-134.

Taylor, S.E., J. Crocker, S.T. Fiske, and J.D. Winkler (1979), "The Generalizability of Salience Effects," *Journal of Personality and Social Psychology*, 37, 357-368.

Taylor, S.E. and S.T. Fiske (1975), "Point of View and Perceptions of Causality," *Journal of Personality and Social Psychology*, 32 (3), 439-445.

Taylor, S.E. and S.T. Fiske (1978), "Salience, Attention, and Attribution: Top of the Head Phenomena," in *Advances in Experimental Social Psychology*, Vol. 2, ed. L. Berkowitz, New York: Academic Press, 249-288.

Taylor, S.E. and S.T. Fiske (1981), "Getting Inside the Head: Methodologies for Process Analysis," in *Directions in Attribution Research*, Vol. 3, eds. J.H. Harvey, W.J. Ickes, and R.F. Kidd, Hillsdale, NJ: Lawrence Erlbaum, 459-524.

Taylor, S.E., S.T. Fiske, M. Close, C. Anderson, and A. Ruderman (1977), "Solo Status as a Psychological Variable: The Power of Being Distinctive," Unpublished manuscript, Harvard University.

Taylor, S.E. and E.J. Langer (1977), "Pregnancy: A Social Stigma?," *Sex Roles*, 3 (1), 27-35.

Taylor, S.E. and S.C. Thompson (1982), "Stalking the Elusive 'Vividness' Effect," *Psychological Review*, 89 (2), 155-181.

Tellis, G.J., R.K. Chandy, and P. Thaivanich (2000), "Which Ad Works, When, Where, and How Often? Modeling the Effects of Direct Television Advertising," *Journal of Marketing Research*, 37 (February), 32-46.

Tesser, A. (1978), "Self-generated Attitude Change," in *Advances in Experimental Social Psychology*, Vol. 11, ed. L. Berkowitz, New York: Academic Press, 289-338.

Thorndyke, P. (1977), "Cognitive Structures in Comprehension and Memory of Narrative Discourse," *Cognitive Psychology*, 9 (1), 77-110.

Thorson, E. and A. Lang (1988), "The Effects of Videographic Complexity on Memory for Televised Information," Paper Presented to the International Communication Association, New Orleans, LA, May.

Thorson, E., B. Reeves, and J. Schleuder (1985), "Message Complexity and Attention to Television," *Communication Research*, 12, 427-454.

Thorson, E., B. Reeves, and J. Schleuder (1987), "Attention to Local and Global Complexity in Television Messages," in *Communication Yearbook 10*, ed. M. McLaughlin, Beverly Hills, CA: Sage.

Thorson, E. and X. Zhao (1988), "Attention Overtime: Behavior in a Natural Viewing Environment," Paper presented to the American Academy of Advertising, Chicago, IL.

Titchener, E.B. (1908), *Lectures on the Elementary Psychology of Feeling and Attention*, New York: Macmillan, 171-206. [Reprinted as "Attention as Sensory Clearness," in *Attention: An Enduring Problem in Psychology* (1966), ed. P. Bakan, Princeton, NJ: D. Van Nostrand Co.]

Tolman, E.C. (1932), *Purposive Behavior in Animals and Men*, New York: Appleton-Century-Crofts.

Tom, G., T. Bennett, W. Lew, and J. Selmants (1987), "Cueing the Consumer: The Role of Salient Cues in Consumer Perception," *Journal of Consumer Marketing*, 4 (Spring), 23-27.

Tom, G. and A. Eves (1999), "The Use of Rhetorical Devices in Advertising," *Journal of Advertsing Research*, 39 (July/August), 39-43.

Trawick, I.F. and J.E. Swan (1980), "Inferred and Perceived Disconfirmation in Consumer Satisfaction," in *Marketing for the 80's*, eds. R.P. Bagozzi et al., Chicago, IL: American Marketing Association, 97-100.

Tse, D.K. and G.J. Gorn (1993), "An Experiment on the Salience of Country-of-Origin in the Era of Global Brands," *Journal of International Marketing*, 1 (1), 57-76.

Tulving, E. and Z. Pearlstone (1966), "Availability versus Accessibility of Information in Memory for Words," *Journal of Verbal Learning and Verbal Behavior*, 5 (August), 381-391.

Tulving, E. and D. Schacter (1990), "Priming and Human Memory Systems," *Science*, 247, 301-306.

Tversky, A. (1977), "Features of Similarity," *Psychological Review*, 84, 327-350.

Tversky, A. and D. Kahneman (1973), "Availabity: A Heuristic for Judging Frequency and Probability," *Cognitive Psychology*, 5, 207-232.

Tversky, A. and D. Kahneman (1974), "Judgment under Uncertainty: Heuristics and Biases," *Science*, 185 (4157), 1124-1131.

Tversky, A. and D. Kahneman (1981), "The Framing of Decisions and the Psychology of Choice," *Science*, 211 (January), 453-458.

Tversky, A., S. Sattath, and P. Slovic (1988), "Contingent Weighting in Judgment and Choice," *Psychological Review*, 95 (July), 371-384.

Tybout, A.M. and N. Artz (1994), "Consumer Psychology," *Annual Review of Psychology*, 45, 131-169.

Tybout, A.M. and R.R. Yalch (1980), "The Effect Experience: A Matter of Salience?," *Journal of Consumer Research*, 6 (March), 406-413.

Ulhaque, E. and K.D. Bahn (1992), "A Spreading Activation Model of Consumers' Asymmetric Similarity Judgment," in *Advances in Consumer Research*, Vol. 19, eds. J.F. Sherry, Jr. and B. Sternthal, Provo, UT: Association for Consumer Research, 782-786.

Unnava, H.R., S. Agarwal, and C.P. Haugtvedt (1996), "Interactive Effects of Presentation Modality and Message-Generated Imagery on Recall of Advertising Information," *Journal of Consumer Research*, 23 (June), 81-88.

Unnava, H.R. and R.E. Burnkrant (1991a), "An Imagery-Processing View of the Role of Pictures in Print Advertisements," *Journal of Marketing Research*, 28 (May), 226-231.

Unnava, H.R. and R.E. Burnkrant (1991b), "Effects of Repeating Varied Ad Executions on Brand Names Memory," *Journal of Marketing Research*, 28 (November), 406-416.

Vakratsas, D. and T. Ambler (1999), "How Advertising Works: What Do We Really Know?," *Journal of Marketing*, 63 (January), 26-43.

Van Raaij, W.F. (1987), "Causal Attributions in Economic Behavior," in *Economic Psychology: Intersections in Theory and Application*, eds. A.J. MacFadyen and H.W. MacFadyen, Amsterdam, The Netherlands: North-Holland, 353-379.

Van Raaij, W.F. (1991), "The Formation and Use of Expectations in Consumer Decision Making," in *Handbook of Consumer Behavior*, eds. T.S. Robertson and H.H. Kassarjian, Englewood Cliffs, NJ: Prentice-Hall, 401-418.

Van Schie, E.C.M. and J. Van der Pligt (1995), "Influencing Risk Preference in Decision Making: The Effects of Framing and Salience," *Organizational Behavior and Human Decision Processes*, 63 (3), 264-276.

Vernon, M.D. (1962), *The Psychology of Perception*, Baltimore, MD: Penguin Books.

Von Heusinger, K. (1997), "Salience and Definiteness," *Prague Bulletin of Mathematical Linguistics*, 67, 5-23.

Von Restorff, H. (1933), "Uber die Virkung von Bereichsbildungen im Spurenfeld," *Psychologie Forschung*, 18, 299-342.

Vroom, V.H. (1964), *Work and Motivation*, New York: Wiley.

Walker, D. and M.F. Von Goten (1989), "Explaining Related Recall Outcomes: New Answers from a Better Model," *Journal of Advertising Research*, 29 (June/July), 11-21.

Walker, E.L. (1964), "Psychological Complexity as a Basis for a Theory of Motivation and Choice," in *Nebraska Symposium on Motivation*, ed. D. Levine, Lincoln, NE: Nebraska University Press.

Wallace, W.P. (1965), "Review of the Historical, Empirical, and Theoretical Status of the Von Restorff Phenomenon," *Psychological Bulletin*, 63 (6), 410-424.

Wallendorf, M. and E.J. Arnould (1988), "'My Favorite Things': A Cross-Cultural Inquiry into Object Attachment, Possessiveness, and Social Linkage," *Journal of Consumer Research*, 14 (March), 531-547.

Varaldo, R. and G. Guido (1997), "Il Consumatore come Prodotto: 'Customer Satisfaction' Come Qualità del Cliente," *Micro & Macro Marketing*, 6 (Aprile), 9-40.

Ward, J. and W. Gaidis (1990), "Metaphor in Promotional Communication: A Review of Research on Metaphor Comprehension and Quality, in *Advances in Consumer Research*, Vol. 17, eds. M.E. Goldberg et al., Provo, UT: Association for Consumer Research, 636-642.

Ward, J. and B. Loken (1988), "The Generality of Typicality Effects on Preference and Comparison: An Explanatory Test," in *Advances in Consumer Research*, Vol. 15, ed. M.J. Houston, Provo, UT: Association for Consumer Research, 55-61.

Ward, J. and P.H. Reingen (1990), "Sociocognitive Analysis of Group Decision Making among Consumers," *Journal of Consumer Research*, 17 (December), 245-262.

Warmer, J.S. and R.E. McCray (1969), "Influence of Word Frequency and Length on the Apparent Duration of Tachistoscopic Presentations," *Journal of Experimental Psychology*, 79 (January), 56-58.

Warren, R.E. (1972), "Stimulus Encoding and Memory," *Journal of Experimental Psychology*, 94, 90-100.

Warrington, P. and S. Shim (2000), "An Empirical Investigation of the Relationship between Product Involvement and Brand Commitment," *Psychology and Marketing*, 17 (9), 761-782.

Warshaw, P.R. (1980), "Predicting Purchase and Other Behaviors from General and Contextually Specific Intentions," *Journal of Marketing Research*, 27 (February), 26-33.

Watkins, M.J. (1975), "Inhibition in Recall with Extralist 'Cues'," *Journal of Verbal Learning and Verbal Behavior*, 14, 294-303.

Webster, R.A. (1997), "The Properties of One: Single Distinctive Stimuli and Their Effects," *Journal of General Psychology*, 124, 319-338.

Webb, P. and M. Ray (1979), "Effects of TV Clutter," *Journal of Advertising Research*, 19 (1), 7-12.

Weilbacher, W.M. (1984), *Advertising*, 2nd Edition, New York: Macmillan.

Weinberger, M.G., C.T. Allen, and W.R. Dillon (1981), "Negative Information Perspectives and Research Directions," in *Advances in Consumer Research*, ed. K. Monroe, Ann Arbor, MI: Association for Consumer Research, 398-404.

Weisstein, N. and C.S. Harris (1974), "Visual Detection of Line Segments: An Object Superiority Effect," *Science*, 186, 752-755.

Weitz, B.A. (1981), "Effectiveness in Sales Interactions: A Contigency Framework," *Journal of Marketing*, 45 (Winter), 85-103.

Wells, W., J. Burnett, and S. Moriarty (1992), *Advertising: Principles and Practice*, 2nd Edition, Englewood Cliffs, NJ: Prentice-Hall.

White, R. (1999), "What Can Advertising Really Do for Brands?," *International Journal of Advertising*, 18 (1), 3-17.

Whitfield, T.W.A. (1981), "Salient Features of Color Space," *Perception and Psychophisics*, 29 (2), 87-90.

Wickelgren, W.A. (1981), "Human Learning and Memory," *Annual Review of Psychology*, 32, 21-52.

Wicker, A.W. (1969), "Attitudes versus Action: The Relationship of Verbal and Overt Behavioral Responses to Attitude Objects," *Journal of Social Issues*, 25, 41-78.

Wicklund, R.A. (1975), "Objective Self-Awareness," in *Advances in Experimental Social Psychology*, Vol. 8, ed. L. Berkowitz, New York: Academic Press.

Widgery, R. and J. McGaugh (1993), "Vehicle Message Appeals and the New Generation Woman," *Journal of Advertising Research*, 33 (September/October), 36-42.

Wiggins, J.S., and A.L. Pincus (1992), "Personality: Structure and Measurement," *Annual Review of Psychology*, 43, 473-504.

Wilder, D.A. (1986), "Social Categorization: Implications for Creation and Reduction of Intergroup Bias," in *Advances in Experimental Social Psychology*, Vol. 19, ed. L. Berkowitz, New York: Academic Press, 291-355.

Wilkie, W.L. (1990), *Consumer Behavior*, 2nd Edition, New York: John Wiley and Sons.

Wilkie, W.L. (1994), *Consumer Behavior*, 3rd Edition, New York: John Wiley and Sons.

Wilkie, W.L. and E.A. Pessemier (1973), "Issues in Marketing's Use of Multi-Attribute Attitude Models," *Journal of Marketing Research*, 10 (November), 428-441.

Wilkie, W.L. and R.P. Weinreich (1972), "Effects of the Number and Type of Attributes Included in an Attitude Model: More Is Not Better," Proceedings of the Third Annual Conference of the Association for Consumer Research, 325-340.

Williams, K.C. (1986), *Behavioral Aspects of Marketing*, London: Heinemann.

Williams, K.J., T.P. Cafferty, and A.S. DeNisi (1990), "The Effect of Performance Appraisal Salience on Recall and Ratings," *Organizational Behavior and Human Decision Processes*, 46, 217-239.

Wolman, C. and H. Frank (1975), "The Solo Woman in a Professional Peer Group," *American Journal of Orthopsychiatry*, 45 (1), 164-171.

Woods, W.A. (1981), *Consumer Behavior: Adapting and Experiencing*, New York: North Holland.

Woodworth, R.S. and H. Schlosberg (1954), *Experimental Psychology*, New York: Holt.

Wright, P. (1974), "The Harassed Decision Maker: Time Pressures, Distractions, and the Use of Evidence," *Journal of Applied Psychology*, 59 (October), 555-561.

Wright, P. (1981), "Cognitive Responses to Mass Media Advocacy," in *Cognitive Responses in Persuasion*, eds. R.E. Petty, T.M. Ostrom, and T.C. Brock, Hillsdale, NJ: Lawrence Erlbaum, 263-282.

Wright, P. and F. Barbour (1975), "The Relevance of Decision Process Models in Structuring Persuasive Messages," *Communication Research*, 2 (July), 246-259.

Wright, P. and P.D. Rip (1980), "Product Class Advertising Effects on First Time Buyers' Decision Strategies," *Journal of Consumer Research*, 7 (September), 176-188.

Wyckham, R.G. (1985), "Implied Superiority Claims: Parity Parading as Superiority," in *Recherches sur la Communication/Promotion*, Proceedings of the 12th International Research Seminar in Marketing, La Londe les Maures, France, 360-387.

Wyer, R.S. (1974), "Changes in Meaning and Halo Effects in Personality Impression Formation," *Journal of Personality and Social Psychology*, 29, 829-835.

Wyer, R.S., G.V. Bodenhausen, and T.K. Srull (1984), "The Cognitive Representation of Person and Groups and its Effect on Recall and Recognition Memory," *Journal of Experimental Social Psychology*, 20, 445-469.

Wyer, R.S. and D.E. Carlston (1979), *Social Cognition, Inference, and Attribution*, Hillsdale, NJ: Lawrence Erlbaum.

Wyer, R.S. and T.K. Srull (1980), "The Processing of Social Stimulus Information: A Conceptual Integration," in *Person Memory: The Cognitive Basis of Social Perception*, eds. R. Hastie et al., Hillsdale, NJ: Lawrence Erlbaum, 227-300.

Wyer, R.S. and T.K. Srull (1986), "Human Cognition in Its Social Context," *Psychological Review*, 93 (3), 322-359.

Yarbus, A.L. (1967), *Eye Movements and Vision*, New York: Plenum.

Yi, Y. (1990), "The Effects of Contextual Priming in Print Advertisements," *Journal of Consumer Research*, 17 (September), 215-222.

Yi, Y. and K.C. Gray (1996), "Revisiting Attribute Diagnosticity in the Context of Product Typicality," 13 (6), 605-632.

Zadny, J. and H.B. Gerard (1974), "Attributed Intentions and Informational Selectivity," *Journal of Experimental Social Psychology*, 10, 34-52.

Zaichkowsky, J.L. (1985), "Measuring the Involvement Construct," *Journal of Consumer Research*, 12 (December), 341-352.

Zaichkowsky, J.L. (1986), "The Emotional Aspect of Product Involvement," in *Advances in Consumer Research*, Vol. 13, ed. R.J. Lutz, Provo, UT: Association for Consumer Research, 32-35.

Zaichkowsky, J.L. (1994), "The Personal Involvement Inventory: Reduction, Revision, and Application to Advertising," *Journal of Advertising*, 23, 59-70.

Zajonc, R.B. (1954), "Structure of the Cognitive Field," Unpublished Doctoral Dissertation, University of Michigan.

Zajonc, R.B. (1968), "Attitudinal Effects of Mere Exposure," *Journal of Personality and Social Psychology Supplement*, 9 (June), 1-27.

Zajonc, R.B. (1980), "Feeling and Thinking: Preferences Need No Inference," *American Psychologist*, 35 (February), 151-171.

Zaltman, G. and M. Wallendorf (1983), *Consumer Behavior: Basic Findings and Management Implications*, New York: Wiley.

Ziamou, P. and J. Gregan-Paxton (1999), "Learning of New Products: Moving Ahead by Holding Back," (Special Session Summary), in *Advances in Consumer Research*, eds. E.J. Arnold and L.M. Scott, Provo, UT: Association for Consumer Research, 365-367.

Zielske, H.A. (1959), "The Remembering and Forgetting of Advertising," *Journal of Marketing*, 23 (January), 239-243.

Zielske, H.A. and W.A. Henry (1980), "Remembering and Forgetting Television Ads," *Journal of Advertising Research*, 20 (April), 7-13.

Zinkhan, G.M. (1986), "Three Consumer Behavior Studies and Their Implications for Marketing Communications," in *Advances in Consumer Research*, Vol. 13, ed. R.J. Lutz, Provo, UT: Association for Consumer Research, 502-504.

Zinkhan, G.M., W.B. Locander, and J.H. Leigh (1986), "Dimensional Relationships and Aided Recall and Recognition," *Journal of Advertising*, 15 (1), 38-46.

Zuckerman, M., R.W. Mann, and F.J. Bernieri (1982), "Determinants of Consensus Estimates: Attribution, Salience, and Representativeness," *Journal of Personality and Social Psychology*, 42 (5), 839-852.

Index